THE GREATEST TENNIS MATCHES OF ALL TIME

THE GREATEST TENNIS MATCHES OF ALL TIME

BY STEVE FLINK

NEW CHAPTER PRESS

The Greatest Tennis Matches of All time is published by New Chapter Press (www.NewChapterMedia.com) and distributed by the Independent Publishers Group (www.IPGBook.com). Randy Walker is the Publisher/Managing Partner for New Chapter Press. Follow this book on FACEBOOK at *"The Greatest Tennis Matches of All Time"* fan page.

The cover and interior was designed by Kirsten Navin.

The front cover photos are courtesy of Getty Images.

The back flap photo of Steve Flink is courtesy of Ed Goldman.

Photos of Suzanne Lenglen, Helen Wills, Bill Tilden, Henri Cochet, Helen Wills Moody and Helen Jacobs, Fred Perry, Ellsworth Vines, Don Budge and Baron Gottfried von Cramm, Jack Kramer, Don Budge, Maureen Connolly and Doris Hart, Pancho Gonzales, Lew Hoad, Tony Trabert, Margaret Smith, Maria Bueno, Rod Laver, Tony Roche, Charlie Pasarell and Pancho Gonzales, Margaret Smith Court, Billie Jean King, Stan Smith and Ilie Nastase, Evonne Goolagong, Jimmy Connors and Arthur Ashe, John McEnroe and Bjorn Borg, Martina Navratilova, Chris Evert, Monica Seles and Steffi Graf, Boris Becker and Pete Sampras, Martina Hingis, Andre Agassi, Jennifer Capriati, Justin Henin, Serena Williams, Maria Sharapova, Roger Federer, Rafael Nadal, Andy Roddick and Novak Djokovic are courtesy of Getty Images.

Photos of Rod Laver and Ken Rosewall from the 1972 WCT Finals in Dallas are courtesy of the Dallas Morning News.

Photos of Jimmy Connors and Bjorn Borg from the 1976 US Open and of Mats Wilander and John McEnroe from Davis Cup in 1982 are courtesy of the Associated Press.

ISBN – 978-0942257939

Printed in the United States.

To my father, Stanley Flink, an invaluable ally, mentor and friend who inspired me to write about tennis for a living.

FOREWORD

When you look back at the big moments in the history of tennis—at least as I see them—time seems to stand still. When you read this book, time will stand still for you. You will return to special moments in the lives of great players, to times and matches that defined these champions. You will have the chance to relive wonderful points, remarkable shot-making and moments that mattered. Some of you will rekindle old memories, while others will learn about great matches you haven't heard of.

In these pages there are a lot of familiar names. Many of them played so long ago, however, that they have become remote figures. In this book, the history-making players will come to life. You will discover not only their styles of play but also gain insight into their personalities and characters. They will no longer be one-dimensional people.

For me, it is a great compliment to be included in this big picture of tennis. Tennis is such a wonderful sport, with so many colorful characters, that to be recognized for some of my matches gives me a nice feeling. My rivalry with Martina Navratilova was very special for both of us and, I hope, for the public. Any of us who have played in some of the best matches of all time have tried to add something to the history of the game and to bring it where it is today—an exciting international sport.

Steve Flink is the right person to take on the task of selecting the best matches of all time. He knows the game of tennis as well as anybody. He is a good journalist, but he also has a tennis player's mind. Steve knew my results and matches better than I did. All through my career in the 1970s and 1980s, it caused much laughter between us when I would be asked a question about my record at a press conference. I would always look over to Steve and he would have the answers. In many cases, I would inaccurately recall an important detail about a match and Steve would have to interrupt me to set the record straight.

I have always admired Steve's style of writing for its fairness and accuracy. We have seen big matches in our lives the same way. He has never written an article about the U.S. Open, or other major tournaments, that failed to capture the essence of a match. We have always been on the same page about tennis.

His fairness is a real strength in his reporting. It seems to me that many writers do not describe what really happens on the court. Steve characteristically gets deep inside the matches and reports them as well as anyone in the field. I think the readers of the book will agree with me.

Chris Evert
Boca Raton, Florida
February, 2012

INTRODUCTION

Although tennis was invented in 1874 by an Englishman, Major Clopton Wingfield, it was not until the following century that the game proliferated and developed a worldwide following. While tennis had many admirable male and female champions in the formative stages, the first towering figures and fascinating match-ups among top players emerged in the 1920's. That was a particularly dynamic decade for tennis and the sports world at large. Tennis, as a viable spectator sport, made strong advances behind such powerful players as Bill Tilden, Suzanne Lenglen, Helen Wills and the renowned French " Four Musketeers"—Rene Lacoste, Henri Cochet, Jean Borotra and Jacques Brugnon.

At the end of 1999, I felt compelled to write a book called "*The Greatest Tennis Matches of the Twentieth Century.*" The first full century of international tennis competition was winding down, so I took on the considerable challenge of selecting the 30 best matches played during that span. Tennis had expanded dramatically from a sport observed almost exclusively by the wealthy, to a much wider and more diversified cast of participants and fans around the world. Major changes in the game had occurred in the latter stages of the twentieth century. "Open Tennis" emerged in 1968 and, for the first time, amateurs and professionals were allowed to compete against each other. Two years later, the tiebreaker was introduced officially at major tournaments, shortening matches and heightening the drama for the spectators.

In that book focusing on the twentieth century, I tried to tell a larger story about the game and its evolution. But now, more than twelve years have passed and the sport has flourished and changed in many ways. When my original book was published, Roger Federer had just finished his first year as a professional player and was far from his zenith. Rafael Nadal was 13 and Novak Djokovic was one year younger. Serena Williams had only just secured her first major and, at 12, Maria Sharapova was nothing more than a champion in the making. Prodigious competitors like Justine Henin and Andy Roddick had not yet surfaced in the upper levels of the game.

I realized over the last year how many top flight players have recently come to the forefront of tennis and how many compelling matches have been played across the last decade or so. Hence, the time has come for the release of this new book, *The Greatest Tennis Matches of All Time*. I have added six crucial new matches for inclusion in this book, including an epic contested earlier this year at the Australian Open between Djokovic and Nadal. Moreover, I have added a new section in this book called "The Best Strokes of All Time," ranking the top five men and women in a wide range of categories. I have included an all-time top ten list of the best male and female players, a ranking of the 30 top matches and an honorable mention list of matches. I hope all of these sections will add to your enjoyment in reading this book.

The early part of the 21st Century has been exhilarating for passionate observers of the sport. This book brings a new era more sharply into focus and celebrates standouts like Nadal, Federer and Williams, players who have enriched the sport so significantly during the formative stages of a new century.

The contests included in this book stand alone as pieces of a mosaic, but when they are placed in sequence they illustrate how the game has evolved, and signal the champions who have made the most substantial contributions to that process. By visiting, or perhaps for some readers revisiting, these great moments involving legendary players, we gain a better view of how certain matches shaped tennis history and why the personalities at their center left us with such enduring memories.

This journey takes us from Bill Tilden to Novak Djokovic and Suzanne Lenglen to Serena Williams. Looking in some depth at the most celebrated confrontations, we are reminded of the individual men and women who were pitted against each other in a struggle that tested not only their skills, but their stamina—and, at the end of the day, their imaginations.

In the early days of tennis, the field of competition was limited and the leading players focused their attention on only a few rivals. In fact, defending champions at Wimbledon were given the luxury of an automatic ticket to the final round, which left them waiting for the winner of an "All-Comers" event to find out who they would face in the championship match. That system lasted from 1877 to 1922. Ever since, the title holders have had to endure the arduous progression of six and eventually seven matches to reach their ultimate destination. Over the same span, the array of promising young players clearly multiplied in both the men's and women's tournaments.

Some of the matches I have selected for this book are picked from landmark occasions. Others are less obvious, but nonetheless meaningful to the growth and distinction of tennis competition at the highest level. Most of the matches included are from the major championships—the Grand Slam events. Three are Davis Cup encounters in deference to that incomparable international team competition. A few were lifted from less glamorous settings, because they transcended the occasion and brought luster to a particular era. For example, consider the many years leading up to "Open Tennis" in 1968. From the 1930's until that pivotal year, the pros were relegated to near obscurity in the media. They could not play at Wimbledon or Forest Hills or other major championships. But, with few exceptions, they were playing the best tennis in the world. With that fact in mind, I picked three professional matches—one each from the 1930's, 1940's and 1950's—in an attempt to do justice to tennis luminaries like Vines, Perry, Kramer, Budge, Hoad and Gonzales.

The battles waged by these stalwart competitors had to be represented in this collection; their contribution to tennis history was as substantial as that of Bjorn Borg, Pete Sampras, Chris Evert, Martina Navratilova, Nadal, Federer and other modern figures. In any case, all of the selections in this book are showdowns between distinctive, accomplished players, duels which captured the admiration of the public and flourished in the recollections of those who reported on them.

Let me elaborate briefly on the criteria for the matches I have chosen as the top 30 of all time. There were a number of important considerations. In my mind, most of the meetings had to be finals, because so much was riding on the outcomes. Furthermore, it was important to do justice to all of the eras of tennis, to the dominant players who have emerged in every decade since the 1920's. Therefore, included in this book are at least two matches from each of those decades. Some readers may question including so many matches from the 1970's right up until this year. Why is the book weighted so heavily on the modern era? The answer is that tennis competition at the highest level has grown profoundly across history, with a cavalcade of players emerging decade after decade to capture the public imagination. Included in this segment of the book are Billie Jean King, Jimmy Connors, Bjorn Borg, John McEnroe, Monica Seles, Steffi Graf, Pete Sampras, Andre Agassi, Serena Williams, Roger Federer, Rafael Nadal, Jennifer Capriati and Novak Djokovic. And there are two Martina Navratilova-Chrissie Evert contests—taken from the most memorable and enduring rivalry of all time—included in the book. This is not to suggest that the modern champions have been any more compelling than those who preceded them at the top. Rather, it is my judgment that the public has been treated to more widely anticipated matches from the seventies on than ever before.

Another factor must be mentioned. In my top 30 list, the women and men do not receive equal treatment. There are slightly more men's matches included. Why? It is my view that the women have irrefutably contributed every bit as much to the game's history as the men. Over the years, however, female champions have traditionally lasted longer at the top than their male counterparts and that distinction somewhat narrowed the selection process. I decided that no more than two matches should be chosen for the top 30 section from the career of any one player. I did not want the book to be too heavily slanted toward a particular champion of either gender. Drawing the line at two matches was a sensible solution.

I have been an avid follower of the game since I was 12, when my father took me out to Wimbledon for the first time. Since that memorable introduction in 1965, I have had the good fortune to be present for 44 of the last 47 editions of the world's premier tournament. I have been an observer/reporter at 34 French Opens and I have missed only one United States [Open] Championship since 1965. All in all, I have seen an extraordinary amount of top notch tennis across the years. I have made my living writing about tennis since 1974.

Nevertheless, many of the greatest matches ever played took place before I was born. As a historian, I was able to draw on a vast library of material on these matches, relying on books and newspaper accounts about these legendary battles. I interviewed many of the players to get their recollections. In the case of modern matches, I looked at tapes of some contests and drew on my own experiences of watching these performances in person.

Tennis equipment has changed radically over the course of time. While the dimensions of the court have remained unaltered since the game's inception—78 feet long and 27 feet wide for singles and nine feet wider for doubles—racket technology has advanced dramatically. With few exceptions, wood rackets were used by all competitors—recreational and tournament class—until the 1960's. At that time, many highly-rated competitors began switching to steel and aluminum rackets which gave them added power, arguably without the loss of control. In the mid to late 1960's, Billie Jean King, Butch Buchholz and Clark Graebner were among the top players who made the move to steel and Pancho Gonzales traded in his old and trusted wood model for aluminum. Jimmy Connors followed on the heels of those players with his Wilson T2000, a trademark for nearly his entire career.

Over time, graphite frames were added to the marketplace. By the early 1980's, wood was nearly extinct in the upper levels of tennis. John McEnroe went to graphite in 1983, as did Chrissie Evert the following year. As for Connors, he stuck with his T2000 long after it was readily available in the marketplace. Once, in the mid-1980's, he made a public plea to fans watching on television during the U.S. Open. He was running out of rackets. Would someone be kind enough to send him any spare T2000's they might have in their homes? A number of fans obliged, enabling Connors to stick with an antiquated frame to which he was wedded from his youth.

Pete Sampras started playing with a graphite racket as a junior and stuck with it to the very end of his career in 2002. Wilson at one time took that racket off the shelves, but decided to re-release it because Sampras and other top players kept it so visible on the public stage. Sampras earned a well-deserved reputation as a complete player who placed a premium on power—not only on serve, but off the ground. And yet, toward the end of his 15 year career on the ATP World Tour, Sampras sensed he was falling behind the times in technology because so many larger racket frames were being wielded brilliantly by younger competitors. In his final year on the tour, he said, "The racket I am playing with now against these guys with the newer technology makes it very tough for me."

As Sampras moved through his late thirties and on into his forties, he did take advantage of newer rackets as he competed in exhibitions and senior events. But the biggest change in the way the game was played from 2003 and beyond was with the vastly improved synthetic strings. Players began to feel that no matter how hard they swung, they could still keep the ball in the court. Moreover, the implementation of severe topspin became more accessible to all players with the new strings.

Another significant change in the quality of tennis over the decades has been measured by athleticism. Today's breed of player is better conditioned than ever before, faster off the mark, more prepared to play a strenuous point to the hilt for hours at a time. Their level of physicality can often be staggering. They cover the court with astounding alacrity. The baseline rallies in today's game of tennis are much more punishing than ever before. The sport is so physically taxing that it can often seem as if tennis is a contact sport. These players are phenomenal athletes.

And yet, it can still be persuasively argued that if Bill Tilden, Don Budge or Jack Kramer were given modern equipment and today's diets and training techniques, they would have remained at the head of the class. The same can be said for Suzanne Lenglen, Helen Wills and Maureen Connolly.

Remembering the players who stirred our emotions with their talents provides the narrative of this book. To be sure, this is not a definitive scholarly history of the game—an enterprise which has been taken up by a number of distinguished writers over the years. The view here is more narrowly focused in scope, but made ambitious by the very nature of the material. Closely examining epochal matches illustrates changes in style and strategy and invariably finds the real drama in the clash of personality and character.

All of the matches included here are between two individuals who have pursued the same lofty goals, but have come to the court with different psychological and athletic resources. The essential excitement of tennis has always been one-on-one, mano a mano. They are out there on their own, isolated in a space surrounded by spectators, cameras and capricious weather. The pressure speaks in an inner voice and is fueled by sometimes supportive and occasionally hostile audiences. The best players have been able to summon their finest tennis when it has mattered the most, to perform magnificently in the face of intensely contested exchanges, to rise above and beyond themselves on the big points.

This book is, finally, not merely a compilation of the outstanding matches ever contested. I have set out to make it much more than that by examining not only the matches but the atmospherics, the preparation and the publicity surrounding these events. My purpose has been to provide a reflective picture of how tennis evolved among those inspired players who uniquely gave the game color and suspense. Great tennis requires an almost ineffable excellence on court. It emerges from both the observable and the mysterious. Progression from one tournament to another—along with training and equipment—are visible details, easily chronicled. The mystery is in the mind and heart of a player who determines that he or she will simply not be defeated. Finding the words to reveal some of that chemistry is the aspiration of the pages which follow.

Steve Flink
Katonah, New York
February, 2012

CONTENTS

• CHAPTER ONE •

Suzanne Lenglen *vs.* Helen Wills

CANNES, FRANCE, FINAL, FEBRUARY 16, 1926

A mythic Frenchwoman plays a young American in what was to be their only meeting.
It would never be forgotten.

PROLOGUE

No tennis match played between two women across the storied history of the game has been more eagerly anticipated than the extraordinary meeting between Helen Wills of California against the Frenchwoman, Suzanne Lenglen, at Cannes on February 16, 1926. They were the two leading players of their era, and they also would be recognized by the cognoscenti as the best in the first half of the century. When they clashed for the only time in their distinguished careers that morning in Cannes, Lenglen was fast approaching twenty-seven and had suffered only a single defeat in the decade. She was a tightly-strung woman, entirely conscious of her fame and popularity, ruled by her deep emotions, as theatrical and graceful as any tennis player has ever been. As the renowned dress designer and historian Ted Tinling observed, "Suzanne was treated like Cleopatra in those days."

Wills was hardly less celebrated, but decidedly more understated as a personality. She was twenty and still a student at the University of California when she took a semester off to travel to France for appearances in a series of tournaments leading up dramatically to a showdown with Lenglen. Wills had already secured three consecutive U.S. Championships at Forest Hills (1923-25) and had established herself unequivocally as the lone authentic threat to Lenglen's enduring supremacy. While Lenglen was known to display her emotions vividly and unrestrainedly, Wills was stoic and stern, unwilling to reveal much about her feelings. She was classified by sportswriters

1

as "Little Miss Poker Face."

The two protagonists were brought up on opposite sides of the ocean by parents with contrasting plans and priorities. Lenglen's father Charles was a wealthy pharmacist who drove his daughter forcefully in the direction of technical and tactical excellence. From the outset, he demanded that Suzanne demonstrate unerring accuracy with her ground strokes. She was admonished that hitting any stroke into the net was an unforgivable mistake, an automatic loss of a point, a self-inflicted wound. Charles Lenglen insisted it was much less a risk to hit within inches of the baseline because you might get the benefit of a good call on a shot that was possibly out.

Charles Lenglen was a perfectionist, placing handkerchiefs at specific locations just inside the baseline and sidelines, testing Suzanne's patience and precision, making her strive for difficult targets. She was unmistakably groomed for success, trained to be a champion by a parent who believed unabashedly that she should settle for nothing less than the best. She responded favorably to his large goals and made them her own.

Wills was guided by parents who were pleased by the prospect of her playing tennis, but she developed an interest in the competitive game largely on her own. Her father, Dr. Clarence Wills, practiced medicine in Berkeley, California. The family lived modestly and did not want to stand in the way of her immense talent once she blossomed on the court as a teenager. But they did not anticipate her worldwide fame and prestige in that arena, not by a longshot. Helen Wills recalled in 1986, when she was eighty, that it was a considerable struggle to get her parents' consent to make the journey to France for the Lenglen confrontation sixty years earlier. "My father didn't see much point in it," she reflected. "And my mother did not want me to go. I don't know why they thought it was the end of the world to leave college for a term and go to the south of France. I almost cried I wanted to go so much. I begged and begged until my parents gave in, and looking back all that fuss doesn't make any sense at all."

Those strong sentiments were released six decades after the shining occasion, when perhaps some of the luster had been lost. But when Wills left California in January 1926 on a one week journey

Suzanne Lenglen

by boat to face a formidable world-class adversary for the first time, she knew she was on a mission, and recognized the need to follow her instincts and widen the range of her tennis aspirations. Neither Wills nor Lenglen could possibly predict how long their imminent contest would live in the public imagination, nor could they know that this would be a solitary experience, a one-time battle for supremacy that would not be repeated.

As the reigning queen of international tennis, Lenglen was prepared for her collision with Wills, and determined to stage this crucial event in her own country, on the slow red clay courts that she preferred. It was no accident that Wills was required to confront Lenglen in France rather than in the United States, or in a neutral place. Wills was forced to endure the long week of travel and then gradually adjust to her foreign surroundings while practicing for the Cannes tournament. Lenglen was right where she wanted to be, in her home land, on her favorite slow courts, bolstered by the notion of appearing in front of an audience who would bathe her in the warm fountain of sustained applause.

The dramatic buildup in the several weeks preceding Cannes was palpable. Here was Lenglen, a ferocious yet fragile competitor, a woman with a strong need to control her environment, to set the agenda in every sense. She had appeared only once at the U.S. Championships, coming to Forest Hills in 1921, leaving the courts in tears and turmoil after losing the first set of her match with Molla Mallory, defaulting the match as a severe cold weakened her stamina. Lenglen was so shattered by that experience that she never returned to Forest Hills despite the undeniable significance of that championship.

Wills, meanwhile, had played the vast majority of her tournaments in the United States, competing at Wimbledon only once, in 1924. She had yet to make her mark at that fabled place where Lenglen had succeeded so handsomely over the years. The stylish Frenchwoman moved about the court like a ballerina, and had been victorious on the Wimbledon grass courts during six of the previous seven years.

Both women had performed brilliantly on different continents, but their paths had not yet crossed anywhere in the world. Now, in the winter of 1926, at a time when the game of tennis was clearly on

Helen Wills

the ascendancy, the imperious Lenglen and the quietly imposing Wills had made an appointment to share a court at last. Neither woman would experience anything quite like this confrontation again.

THE MATCH

The stage was set at the Carlton Club tournament on the well-kept red clay courts in Cannes. The players were ready. But, as if by design, raising the level of the drama surrounding the proceedings to nearly impossible heights, nature intervened. After Lenglen and Wills easily recorded semifinal victories to reach the final without the loss of a set, rain fell steadily for two days and postponed the alluring matchup. By then, the battle and its significance had reached almost mythical proportions in the worldwide press, and with the football season finished and baseball not yet underway, America attached immense curiosity and passion to the match. It was a story that virtually wrote itself in the sports sections of newspapers all across the United States.

The small club in Cannes could only accommodate about one-thousand spectators, but others looked down from trees surrounding the facility and still more crowded near the fence behind the court to get at least a partial view of the play. With a scarcity of tickets available for afficionados, an Englishwoman bought up a bundle of them and sold them for as much as $50 apiece—an exorbitant sum in those days.

Ultimately, the weather cleared and the sun was shining as Lenglen and Wills walked on the court at 11 a.m. on a Saturday morning in February of 1926, for their historic showdown. The officials for this important contest were chosen carefully with the full consent of both participants, and the linesmen included Lord Charles Hope and Cyril Tolley, a revered golf champion from Great Britain. Commander George Hillyard—a distinguished veteran who had called many Wimbledon finals—was given the great honor of presiding as umpire. The presence of these Englishmen gave the occasion an air of essential integrity, providing at the very least the appearance of impartiality in the decision making.

Briefly, at the outset, Wills gave Lenglen cause for consternation.

The American broke serve for a 2-1 lead by exploiting her superior strength and power off the ground, but then Lenglen retaliated, displaying better ball control than her adversary. With a concentrated run of superb backcourt craft, Lenglen moved to a 4-2 lead. Wills stood her ground stubbornly and took the seventh game to close the gap. At that critical stage Lenglen asserted herself, conceding only two more points in the next two games to seal the set, 6-3. But playing this remarkable brand of tennis against such an accomplished rival was already taking its toll on Lenglen, who sipped brandy at the changeovers to calm her nerves.

In the second set, the pattern of play shifted in this engrossing spectacle. Wills began to rule the rallies with her potent strokes off both wings, forcing her foe into mistakes and coming up with the winner when she had the opening. The American grew visibly more confident and became much bolder in the process as she built a 3-1 lead, but then temporized and lost her edge. With Wills drifting dangerously into caution, Lenglen reestablished her authority and drew level at 3-3, seemingly within striking distance of victory. But the strain was increasingly evident in her demeanor and she walked to her chair at the side of the court to take sips of brandy after psychologically strenuous points, no longer waiting for the changeovers.

Wills was well aware that she was still very much in the match, and recognized that a third set could prove fatal for her fragile foe. The American moved ahead 4-3, then held her penetrating and skillfully placed serve again to reach 5-4. Lenglen was in an agitated state during this stretch, admonishing a boisterous audience to keep quiet, advertising her instability with her actions. But remarkably Lenglen lifted her game once more to take a 6-5, 40-15, double-match-point lead. Not afraid to lose and still believing she could prevail, the imperturbable Wills walloped a forehand crosscourt for an apparent winner. Both players heard an emphatic cry of "Out!" from the corner of the court. They assumed the ball had gone beyond the line and believed their battle was over.

An exhilarated Lenglen threw a ball in the air in celebration as she came forward to shake Wills's hand, feeling certain she had completed her mission. To her considerable chagrin, she had not. Linesman Hope came forward, pushing his way through the flocking fans, urgently trying to get the attention of Commander Hillyard. When he finally reached the chair umpire, Hope explained that he had not made that call on the sideline, that in fact it had been an overly excited spectator who had screamed "Out." Hope confirmed that Wills's scorching shot had been just inside the sideline for a winner.

Hillyard clarified the situation for the players and bewildered fans, and after a brief uproar, play resumed with a shaken Lenglen now at 40-30, still at match point. Wills was neither euphoric nor distracted by her second chance to succeed; she simply got on with her task, calm and resolute. She produced a crackling forehand that Lenglen could not return, and moments later was back in business at 6-6.

Lenglen's legion of supporters, and indeed the champion herself, were apprehensive as a revived Wills served. The American sensed the possibility of bringing about a third set. In a long and extraordinarily hard-fought game, Wills had a point for 7-6. She seemed to have gained the upper hand. She believed she was heading toward a sparkling triumph.

But Lenglen was not willing to let go. She fought valiantly to hold Wills back, and broke serve for 7-6. With that burst of effective shotmaking, Lenglen successfully negotiated a second chance to serve for the match. She thoughtfully probed the Wills arsenal, breaking down the American's backhand, arriving at 40-30 and a third match point. Then a first-serve fault. Lenglen paused before hitting her second serve, then tossed. It was a double fault.

Had she squandered too many pivotal chances? Was the game's greatest match player losing her renowned ability to play her best under pressure? She answered those questions without hesitation, moving back to match point for the fourth time, then opening up the court with a deep forehand crosscourt, following with a clean winner into a wide open space.

That last perfect placement gave Lenglen a 6-3, 8-6 triumph—in precisely one hour. This time Lenglen knew her victory was official as she ran up to the net to greet Wills. The Frenchwoman seemed to float on the sounds of an ovation, surrounded by friends and admirers, clutching flowers like a ballerina. Wills—so gallant and poised in defeat, able to detach herself and witness the wild jubilation around Lenglen with fascination rather than frustration—picked up her belongings a few minutes later and departed, almost unnoticed by the swarming Lenglen fans. Wills understood this was France, where Lenglen was larger than life. The American was not feeling sorry for herself, and she unreluctantly admired the persistence and artistry her opponent had exhibited.

"It had to be the most dramatic match I've ever seen," said Tinling, who was fifteen when he witnessed this clash, and subsequently saw more great matches (before his death in 1990) than any other authority. "There will never be anything quite like it again with the whole tra-la-la of the buildup. Suzanne and Helen was the first big show business match in the history of tennis, a sort of precursor for Billie Jean King and Bobby Riggs in 1973. If there was one match I could go back and see again, Lenglen-Wills would be it."

EPILOGUE

The consensus among the experts of the time was that Lenglen and Wills would renew their rivalry frequently, and perhaps rekindle some of the magic evident in their Cannes showdown. But the two superb performers never faced each other again. Wills remained in Europe that winter and spring of 1926, and it seemed inevitable that she would confront Lenglen in the final of the French Championships in June. That would have been another tense encounter on red clay, but this time the stakes would have been even higher with a major championship on the line. As fortune would have it, in the middle of the tournament Wills was stricken with severe stomach pain and sent to the hospital, where she had an emergency appendectomy.

That setback kept Wills out of action for the rest of the major tournaments that season, and removed her from the circuit altogether. Lenglen, meanwhile, went through a crisis of her own. After winning that French Championship easily, with Wills not in her path, she went to Wimbledon in search of a seventh singles title. She was scheduled for an early-round match with Queen Mary in attendance, but a major misunderstanding occurred and Lenglen did not turn up at the scheduled hour. When she was informed later that afternoon that she had kept the queen waiting, a disconsolate Lenglen could not bear the pain of her mistake, and fainted. She pulled out of the tournament, humiliated by what had happened, unable to get over the embarrassment. That summer, Lenglen signed a contract to play on the first professional tennis tour in the United States, winning all thirty-eight of her head-to-head contests with Mary K. Browne of the United States. But with Wills remaining an amateur and still competing for the great traditional prizes, it was no longer possible for the two superstars to meet each other in official competition.

Wills arrived at the peak of her powers in the years ahead. Between 1927 and 1938, she won eight Wimbledon singles titles—a record until Martina Navratilova broke it in 1990—and collected fifty match victories in a row. That mark has never been equaled in men's or women's play on the fabled lawns of the All England Club.

Returning to Paris with high aspirations, Wills took the French Championships four times from 1928 to 1932 and secured four more of her U.S. Championships at Forest Hills to lift her total to seven. She triumphed in that tournament in 1927, 1928, 1929, and 1931. Wills concluded her career with nineteen Grand Slam singles titles, a record surpassed only by Margaret Court and Steffi Graf. Wills was beaten a mere three times across the years in twenty-two major events, a standard of excellence no other player has ever achieved.

As Wills's tennis career ended in the late-1930s, an ailing Lenglen passed away. Having struggled with her health for much of the decade, the charismatic woman from France died on July 4, 1938, of pernicious anemia. She was thirty-nine. The tragic departure of Lenglen occurred within days of Wills's final championship run at Wimbledon. But while Wills had thrived on the court into her early thirties, she was sorting through some problems in her personal life.

On her trip to the French Riviera to confront Lenglen, she had met an American stock broker named Freddie Moody and they soon became inseparable. They were married in 1929, but the union ended in divorce eight years later. In 1939, two years after her breakup with Moody, Helen was married for the second time, to film writer Aidan

Roark. They were divorced in the early 1970s.

For twenty-five years thereafter, Helen Wills Moody Roark led a reclusive life in California, although her interest in tennis never waned. She was unfailingly gracious in her remarks about champions like Chris Evert and Martina Navratilova. In January 1998, at the age of ninety-two, she passed away.

The death of Wills seemed to stir the embers of debate, among those experts who had observed her career, as to where she stood when measured against Lenglen on the historical tennis ladder. Many have speculated on what might have transpired had they been able to play more matches against each other. The experts have concluded that Wills would surely have surpassed Lenglen within a year of their Cannes encounter, and would have controlled their rivalry in the late 1920s and beyond. Wills was then beginning to reach her absolute prime, while Lenglen was arguably declining.

And yet, many knowledgeable tennis reporters take the firm position that Lenglen at her peak, in the early to mid-1920s, would have been too cunning and capable even for Wills, and would have dominated during that stretch.

Lenglen's record on paper is far less impressive than that of Wills. She had to settle for eight official major championships, eleven fewer than Wills. But that is a somewhat misleading fact because Lenglen in her time of true triumph was every bit as invincible as Wills became, perhaps even more so.

For tennis historians, the Cannes duel achieved an incandescence beyond any other women's match of that time. Both ladies came away from that contest having gained respect for each other, and having learned something substantial about themselves. Even after the decades passed and a cavalcade of champions succeeded them, Wills remembered her meeting with Lenglen in very lucid terms, and had no regrets that they did not test each other again.

As Wills recalled in 1986, "Suzanne was a great player and had more generalship on the court than I did. She had the game down to a pattern in her mind which was the best according to her ability. I had more power and endurance. But I was not disappointed not to play her again. I remember we all went out to dinner that night after the tennis match, everybody all dressed up in dinner clothes, and I didn't feel sad. I was very young for my age then and I just thought I would win the next time I played Lenglen."

CHAPTER TWO

Bill Tilden *vs.* Henri Cochet

WIMBLEDON, SEMIFINAL, JUNE 30, 1927

No player had more theatrical flair and tactical acuity than Tilden. Cochet was a gifted shotmaker and a tireless competitor. The two champions staged a classic confrontation.

PROLOGUE

Only one year after the much heralded clash between Helen Wills and Suzanne Lenglen at Cannes—a battle between a legendary French-woman and a young American of immense promise—Henri Cochet of France and "Big Bill" Tilden of the United States collided in the semi-finals at Wimbledon in 1927. As one of the famed "Four Musketeers" from the celebrated Davis Cup team (Rene Lacoste, Jean Borotra, and Jacques Brugnon were the others) Cochet was a player of remarkable originality and imagination, a competitor of rising fortunes. But in Tilden he was confronting the master of his craft, and the man who had sweepingly dominated tennis all through that decade. Cochet came from a very modest background, but because his father was the secretary of a tennis club in Lyon, young Henri had the opportunity to learn tennis. He had natural gifts, practiced little, and was largely self-taught.

Tilden, on the other hand, enjoyed his childhood in a very com-fortable family. He lived a short walk away from the Germantown Cricket Club in Philadelphia, and was considered to be a "mother's boy." His mother kept him out of school until he was fifteen, insisting that he be tutored at home, where he also spent hours listening to his mother play the piano. Tilden once said if he was asked to give up tennis or music, it would be tennis. Nonetheless, he began playing tennis at the age of five. In 1915, during his last year at the University of Pennsylvania, both his father and brother died. Tilden had not been good enough to make the varsity tennis team at Penn. But he would coach the team at the Germantown Academy. Almost inevitably, this led him into competitive tennis at a much higher level.

So towering a figure in his field was Tilden that he became the champion of his country no fewer than six consecutive times between 1920 and 1925. At age twenty-six, he had been beaten by his countryman, "Little Bill" Johnston, in the 1919 Forest Hills final. Having suffered that setback, he realized that it was a single stroke in his repertoire that was holding him back. It was time to strengthen his backhand, rather than continue muddling through with his barely adequate defensively designed shot off that side. So he spent the winter of 1920 attending to that task, remodeling his stroke, learning to drive through the ball aggressively. Tilden turned his backhand into a versatile and effective weapon more closely aligned with his classic forehand. His glaring weakness was gone, and his game was decidedly enhanced by the new component, lifting him to another level.

Tilden established himself not only as a supreme ground stroker with nearly impeccable mechanics, but a superb server who could deliver the "cannonball" with regular success, and volley with conviction when he made his infrequent visits to the net. And yet, beyond the wide range of his technical capabilities, Tilden was the first great tactician the game had known. He had an astonishing and intuitive sense of how to play points, what would bother his opponents most, and when he would need to alter his patterns and shift his strategic focus. He relished opportunities to exploit the vulnerabilities of his rivals, picking them apart with sharp and purposeful execution. He was a maestro on the tennis court, a showman, but above all a keen student of the game. As he wrote perceptively in *Match Play and the Spin of the Ball*, "I may sound unsporting when I say that the primary object of tennis is to break up your opponent's game, but it is my honest belief that no man is defeated until his game is crushed, or at least weakened. Nothing so upsets mental and physical poise as to be continually led into error."

Cochet was just coming into his own as he approached this meeting with the world champion. The previous year at Forest Hills, he had ended Tilden's bid for a seventh straight championship with an

Bill Tilden

Henri Cochet

impressive victory in the quarterfinals. Earlier in 1926, he had won his own French Championships for the first time on the red clay courts at Roland Garros in Paris. With his fellow "Four Musketeers," he would play a pivotal role in leading France to victory in the Davis Cup for six consecutive years—1927 to 1932. In many ways, he was the ideal opponent for Tilden. He mixed his ground strokes adroitly by varying not only the pace but the length of his shots. His serve lacked Tilden's power and punch but he could place it precisely, and he was deceptive. He could conclude points with uncommon skill on the volley, and no one before his arrival had exhibited such consistent control and effectiveness on the half volley. His flair and flexibility on that shot were striking, and his handling of low balls by making quick, aggressive pickups was something that separated him from the rest of the opposition in that era. He was the best half-volleyer of his time.

Both competitors knew this would be a match of lasting consequences, but neither could have been prepared for the full extent of the drama they would produce in this duel.

THE MATCH

Despite being the dominant player of the decade, Tilden was placed at No. 2 behind Lacoste in this groundbreaking year of seeded players on the grass courts at Wimbledon. The primary reason he was not given the top spot was that he had not been back to the All England Club since winning in 1920 and 1921. In any case, Cochet was seeded fourth. Tilden had moved into the penultimate round with few obstacles and the loss of only one set—to Brugnon in the quarterfinals. In that same round, Cochet had conceded the first two sets to Tilden's capable doubles partner Frank Hunter, but the Frenchman struck back boldly to win in five sets.

With Tilden playing the more confident brand of tennis, the American was the firm favorite to win as they faced each other on a cloudy afternoon. At the outset, Tilden performed with both power and panache. He served thunderbolts that even the quick-handed Cochet could not return. He found the corners with his heavy ground strokes, and dictated the pace for nearly three sets. Tilden took a commanding 6-2, 6-4, 5-1 lead and was on the verge of an unmistakable rout.

As Englishman Stanley Doust wrote in the *Daily Mirror*, "How could anyone have lived against such wonderful lawn tennis as Tilden played? Was there anyone who could beat him?" Cochet had the answers to those questions. From 1-5, 15-15 in the third set, seemingly caught in a hopeless corner, Cochet proceeded to collect seventeen points in a row on his way to a six-game sweep for the set. It was a combination of Cochet's courage and determination and an uncharacteristic lapse from Tilden that altered the complexion of the match, but the American's mastery was over. Despite some resistance from Tilden, Cochet closed out the set. He was maneuvering Tilden in a manner few had thought possible. Cochet took the fourth set after Tilden recovered from 4-2 down to reach 4-4. Then a resurgent Tilden rediscovered his early match form to break for a 3-2, fifth-set lead.

It seemed that Tilden would regain the initiative and run out the match, but that was not the case. Cochet channeled his energy and emotions into one last four-game burst, and Tilden collapsed down the stretch. At 3-2, he served a pair of double faults and at 3-4 he served two more. An electrifying reversal of fortunes was over, much to the dismay of the proud American who bowed 2-6, 4-6, 7-5, 6-4, 6-3. "Seldom has there been such enthusiasm at a lawn tennis victory," wrote Doust. "Enthusiasm not because Tilden was beaten but because of Cochet's marvelous recovery from what looked like certain defeat to a glorious victory."

Revered American journalist Al Laney of the *New York Herald Tribune* wrote revealingly about it in his book *Covering the Court*. He conceded, "I could not explain what happened to Tilden then, and I can not now. I think now the explanation might be found in a remark Tilden addressed to me immediately after the match, or as quickly as I could reach the dressing room. 'Maybe you were right' he said, and he said it with what I thought was scorn, but in a voice that carried a certain hatred, too. He was referring to the statement that he had now passed his best years and could no longer call on his matchless stamina."

EPILOGUE

Not content with one of the most riveting comebacks in the history of big-time tennis, Cochet managed in the final to produce another masterpiece of turnaround. Once again, he trailed two sets to love, this time against the stubborn Borotra. Borotra had won Wimbledon twice—including the year before—and could not have come closer to retaining his title against a coolly defiant Cochet. In this pendulum-swinging battle of the Frenchmen, Borotra—less talented but every bit as resilient a competitor—sealed the first two sets with relative ease, but then lost the next two as Cochet sank his teeth more deeply into the contest.

The fifth set, however, became a forum for Borotra to return almost effortlessly to the top of his game. He moved swiftly to a 5-2 lead and had a match point on Cochet's serve in the eighth game. When Cochet gamely saved himself and held serve, the odds still seemed heavily stacked against him with Borotra serving for the championship at 5-3. Here Borotra had five more match points, but his tenacious adversary was not about to surrender. Taking full advantage of an errant volley from Borotra on the last of the match points, Cochet proceeded to finish off this clash with elan, winning 4-6, 4-6, 6-3, 6-4, 7-5. By virtue of this stunning feat, Cochet achieved a unique record among Wimbledon champions by completing his mission with three straight victories from two-sets-to-love down.

In the ensuing years, Cochet distinguished himself with steady conviction. He won three more French Championships (1928, 1930 and 1932) to lift his total to four. He won Wimbledon again for the second time in 1929, and was the winner of the United States Championships at Forest Hills in 1928, garnering that championship with another hard-fought, five-set triumph in the final over Frank Hunter. To be sure, his extraordinary exploits at Wimbledon in 1927 set the stage for a very productive period in the years ahead. Overcoming Tilden despite the darkest of circumstances, and then toppling Borotra with similar grit, had propelled Cochet to a stature he had never found before. Meanwhile, he contributed mightily to the enduring success of the "Four Musketeers."

Altogether, Cochet, Lacoste, Borotra, and Brugnon amassed fifty-three major titles in singles and doubles. It was irrefutably the golden age of French men's tennis and there would be nothing quite like it again through the rest of the twentieth century.

And what of Tilden? In many ways, he never fully recovered from the bewildering defeat suffered against Cochet. He was clearly not finished as a major force, ruling at Wimbledon for the third and last time in 1930, after a seventh and last U.S. Championships title at Forest Hills the previous season. But the towering man from Philadelphia—at 6'2" he was unusually tall for his time—was never quite the same player after the devastating failure to vanquish Cochet. Tilden won ten major championships—seven U.S. and three Wimbledon titles—but took only two of those crowns after his 1927 surrender.

In retrospect, there was a certain logic to his diminished fortunes. He was thirty-four when he fell to Cochet. He had lost his capacity for playing the big points with automatic precision. He no longer controlled the agenda of critical matches with the force of his will and the skill of his shot selection. Tilden had moved irrevocably past his prime, and yet he remained a top-notch competitor for many years to come.

He turned professional in 1931 at thirty-eight, and played until he was nearly fifty. But while his court sense remained unimpeachable, his footspeed was dwindling, and his serve was a much lesser weapon. In his pro tour match series with a first-rate Ellsworth Vines, Tilden came out on the wrong end of a 47-26 record. Seven years later, in 1941, he was obliterated 51-7 in his meetings with another prodigious countryman, Don Budge. By then, he was forty-eight and fading steadily, but he was still a magnificent player.

Sadly, his personal life was shaded by his stepping beyond the boundaries of the law. Forced to conceal his homosexuality—a sports celebrity's reputation could be ruined by such a revelation in his day—Tilden was sent to prison in 1947 and again in 1949 on morals charges. His arrests were kept relatively quiet by the newspapers, but he had to live with the consequences of his actions.

Meanwhile, Tilden had lost most of his money on ill-advised theater ventures. A man who cherished drama on the tennis court—he was fond of digging deficits for himself in matches so that he could climb out of those predicaments and win in heroic fashion—Tilden invested in plays unwisely, and performed on stage in roles he could not master. None of these ventures worked, but Tilden remained convinced he could be an accomplished actor nevertheless.

His genuine love of tennis was evident until the end of his life. He would show up to play casual doubles matches on friends' private courts in California, dressed in ragged clothing, speaking in his familiar high-pitched voice, instructing his admiring partners what to do. He remained largely a reclusive figure, poignantly trying to recover his high standards. And then on June 5, 1953, at sixty, he died of a heart attack in Los Angeles. He had packed his suitcase and was planning to compete in the U.S. Pro Championships at Cleveland.

He left behind an enviable record. As of 2011, only five men had secured more Grand Slam singles championships. They are: Roger Federer with sixteen, Pete Sampras with fourteen, Roy Emerson with twelve, followed by Rod Laver and Bjorn Borg with eleven each. In 2011, Rafael Nadal recorded his tenth major singles tournament triumph at Roland Garros. But it must be recorded that Tilden's rate of success was equally impressive. He never played the Australian Championships, and failed to win the French Championships in three attempts, but triumphed regularly at Wimbledon and Forest Hills, where he was beaten only ten times in twenty combined appearances. From 1920 through 1926, he led the Americans to victory in the Davis Cup. And he celebrated six consecutive years as the top-ranked player in tennis, a feat not replicated until Sampras did it in 1998.

Tilden was a central figure in the evolution of his sport, and until he lost to Cochet there was no better big-match player. Many writers, players, and historians placed Tilden at the top of the list of players who appeared in the first half of the twentieth century. For seven years—from 1920-26—he was virtually unstoppable. He understood the game on a sophisticated level, breaking it down systematically in his orderly mind, calculating the right strategic approach to take away his opponents' strengths and exploit his own.

It must be said that Tilden did not attack as persistently as future champions automatically would. A strong case can be made that it was not necessary in his day to conclude many points with decisive volleys or unanswerable smashes. The design of his court craft was a product of his era, of how the game was played at that time, and of his personal preference for plotting longer points which did much more to reveal his virtuosity and supreme talent for playing chess on the tennis court.

This much is certain: Tilden in the 1920's was as masterful a player as the men's game had yet witnessed.

CHAPTER THREE

Helen Wills Moody *vs.* Helen Jacobs
WIMBLEDON, FINAL, JULY 6, 1935

These two very talented backcourt players met many times, but this clash was their epiphany.

PROLOGUE

Nearly thirty years old, Helen Wills Moody was slightly past her prime as she pursued a seventh Wimbledon championship in 1935. Her best seasons followed her once-in-a-lifetime battle with Suzanne Lenglen in 1926. After her loss to Lenglen, she was not beaten again until 1933. In that span, Mrs. Moody had taken four French Championships, four United States Championships, and six Wimbledon singles titles. She was as dominant during that stretch as Lenglen had been in the first half of the twenties.

The unbeaten streak achieved by Wills Moody was broken by the perseverance of her countrywoman Helen Hull Jacobs, who was born in Globe, Arizona, in 1908. The family moved to San Francisco just before World War I, and later occupied a home in Berkeley, California, where Helen Wills had lived. Like Wills, Jacobs learned to play at the Berkeley Tennis Club. She attended the University of California. In 1933, she became the first woman to wear shorts at Wimbledon. She was always a favorite of tennis fans because of her friendly, cheerful manner.

Jacobs, three years younger than her rival, was defending her title at Forest Hills in 1933. She took on her old nemesis in the final. They waged a tough battle in the opening set before Jacobs prevailed, 8-6. Moody answered by taking the second set, 6-3. Jacobs established a 3-0 lead in the third and final set. She seemed likely to move from there to the title, exploiting her comfortable lead.

At that point, Mrs. Moody walked up to the net and conceded defeat. She claimed her back was causing her too much pain to continue. She withdrew to the locker room in her customary long coat, and chose to remain silent on the subject of her default. Four years later, in her autobiography titled, *Fifteen Thirty*, Helen Wills Moody explained why she had left the scene and denied Jacobs a legitimate, full-scale triumph.

Her back had been bothering her for weeks, long before Forest Hills had begun. Her husband, Freddie Moody, advised her not to participate in the National Championships. She believed she might never have the chance to play at Forest Hills again. A few weeks before the tournament, the pain was excruciating, running down her back, into her leg, and even into the toes of her right foot. At times, her right leg felt numb.

Two weeks prior to the Nationals, Mrs. Moody was forced to withdraw from the Wightman Cup (U.S. vs. Great Britain) team competition after being examined by doctors who cited symptoms of instability in her vertebra. She took it easy for a few days, then resumed light practice. In her mind, she had to ignore the injury, or else she would be revealing weakness and apprehension.

Wills Moody reached the final of Forest Hills more on reputation than execution. After her semifinal victory, it rained heavily for an entire week, delaying the final. In that time off, she isolated herself in her room near the courts, but did not do anything physically strenuous. Her body stiffened. When the rain finally ceased, she faced Jacobs, who had consulted with Suzanne Lenglen earlier in the year about how to play Wills Moody. Lenglen urged Jacobs to hit short crosscourt shots to draw her opponent forward.

Wills Moody described that 1933 final with Jacobs in her book. She wrote, "I was trying to meet the competition of the match and at the same time was carrying on another fight within myself—one that was between my brain, which was commanding, and my muscles, which were bound in an iron-clad spasm trying to protect the injured nerves of my back. When I could not break through their grip, I was unable to bend or run, and when I could the pain was blinding.... I knew it was the end when the stadium began to swirl in the air, and I saw

Helen Wills Moody and Helen Jacobs

Miss Jacobs and the court on a slant. If I had fainted on the court, it would have been thought a more conclusive finish to the match in the eyes of many of the onlookers, for then they would have been convinced that I could not continue. However, my choice was instinctive rather than premeditated. Had I been able to think clearly I might have chosen to remain. It was unfortunate that Miss Jacobs could not have had a complete victory, as it would have been had I been able to remain a little longer on the court. But being naturally selfish, I thought only of myself. I could understand her feeling of disappointment, but the match would have ended this way no matter against whom I had been playing."

Mrs. Moody went into the hospital and stayed there for a month. She had a weight placed on her leg, pulling on it to build strength. She feared she would not play the game of tennis again. The following January, she took osteopathic treatments, and that made a substantial difference. She was clearly on the mend, but playing Wimbledon in 1934 was out of the question. She was asked to write about the event by London's *Daily Mail*, and enjoyed the detached experience.

By the spring of 1935, Wills Moody was ready to make another run at Wimbledon, prepared to pursue a seventh title on the grass courts at the All England Club. During her absence, Jacobs had flourished. At Forest Hills in 1934, she took the championship for the third consecutive year, defeating the rising Sarah Palfrey Fabyan in the final.

Jacobs, however, had never won Wimbledon. To round out her record and place herself irrevocably among the great players of her era, she needed that title. The two Helens had a great deal in common. Both had trained in their formative years at the Berkeley Tennis Club in California, and they shared the experience of attending the University of California.

Despite the common threads that ran through their lives; there were fundamental differences. Jacobs's game contrasted sharply with that of Wills Moody. Jacobs was comfortable anywhere on the court, volleying with confidence and aggression, smashing capably. She had a prodigious doubles record, where she put her attacking skills to good use.

Her singles game did have some holes in it. She had to find ways to disrupt Wills Moody, who was more powerful and precise off the ground. Wills Moody hit through the ball unfailingly and found the corners with regularity, forcing her opponents into defensive positions all the while. Jacobs relied heavily on underspin off both sides, and did not break her adversaries down as easily from the backcourt as Wills Moody could. And yet, Mrs. Moody was often heavy footed and vulnerable against short angles and drop shots. Jacobs was a better athlete, quicker at covering the whole court.

THE MATCH

Jacobs had a distinct advantage over Wills Moody as they advanced through the women's draw at Wimbledon in 1935. She had been competing steadily and knew essentially what to expect from herself. Wills Moody had been out of action since her abrupt departure against Jacobs two years earlier at Forest Hills. In that time, Wills Moody had slowly re-acclimated to the rigors of playing competitive tennis, pursuing points which had once been automatic but no longer were. Mrs. Moody played a couple of minor tournaments in preparation for Wimbledon, but even that plan had its pitfalls as the constant rain in England cut deeply into her schedule and left her considerably short of where she wanted to be in her tuneup.

Having been away from the game for so long, Wills Moody was seeded fourth at Wimbledon, one place behind Jacobs. The English-woman Dorothy Round was seeded first and Germany's Hilde Sperling—who had won her first of three straight French Championships that year—was the No. 2 seed.

Round bowed in the quarterfinals and Sperling was routed by Jacobs 6-3, 6-0 in the semifinals. Wills Moody had a frightening round of sixteen meeting with Slecna Cepkova. The Czechoslovakian had Mrs. Moody in disarray for a set-and-a-half. The American trailed by a set and was 4-1 down in the second. She recovered her poise and her will just in time to salvage a three-set victory. That was the only set she conceded on her way to the final. Miss Jacobs did not lose any sets in her half of the draw. The two Americans had set up a widely anticipated final, their first since 1933 at Forest Hills.

As Al Laney wrote in the *New York Herald Tribune*, "Receiving the first service, Miss Jacobs brought into play the chop stroke she has made her own and Mrs. Moody swung into the ball and hit for the corner. There was the story of the match given in its very first exchange. For thirty games to follow Mrs. Moody attacked and Miss Jacobs defended and each player did her part superlatively well."

Mrs. Moody's hard hitting boosted her to an early lead against an opponent who had been beaten in all three of her previous appearances in the Wimbledon final. Moody took a 3-0 lead in the first set before Jacobs found her range. Jacobs struggled back to 3-3 and had Moody at 0-40 in the crucial seventh game.

Mrs. Moody had drifted into a difficult patch at that stage, losing eleven points in a row. Had she lost her serve again to trail 3-4, she conceivably would have surrendered the set. Instead, with her confidence restored, Moody held on for 4-3, broke in the following game, and served out the set, 6-3.

Jacobs was well aware that Moody was not in top tournament shape. She began directing her ground strokes closer to the sidelines, making her opponent move as much as possible, trying to tire her rival in the process. By the middle of the second set, that pattern was succeeding. From 3-3 in the second set, Jacobs collected three games in a row to draw level at one set all.

With the capacity Centre Court crowd murmuring, Moody held up her hand and asked for quiet as she started serving the opening game of the third set. It was apparent then that she was weary. After a pair of hard fought games, Jacobs broke for 2-1 as Moody's serve seemed devoid of all pace. Although Mrs. Moody managed to break back for 2-2, she lost her serve again in the following game. At 3-2, Jacobs slipped to 15-40, saved the first break point, and then reached deuce with a solid smash. After a series of deuces, Jacobs held on for 4-2.

Serving in the seventh game, Moody rebounded from 15-40 to deuce, only to miss an easy overhead from short range, well wide of the sideline. Jacobs got the insurance break for 5-2, and served for the match in the eighth game. She reached 30-30, two points from the triumph, but Moody was not obliging. She broke for 3-5. In the ninth game, Mrs. Moody served to save the match. Both players were bearing down frantically. One long point after another was played. Neither woman wanted to take any unnecessary chances with so much riding on the outcome of this game. A resolute Jacobs arrived at match point. She had the gumption to go into the net. Moody lifted a lob into the air. Jacobs was poised to smash it out of the reach of her adversary. If she could connect solidly, the match would belong to her.

An instant before contact, a burst of wind blew the ball slightly away from a baffled Jacobs. She sent her overhead tentatively into the net. Mrs. Moody had saved a match point, and she held her serve for 4-5. Jacobs still had another chance to close out the account, another opportunity to win it on her serve. At 5-4, she served for the match a second time.

Once more, Jacobs progressed to 30-30, two points from the triumph. Moody added velocity to her shots and played them into safe spaces, several feet from the sidelines. She broke back gamely for 5-5, then held for 6-5. With Jacobs serving to save the match in the twelfth game, the two competitors endured a three-deuce game. Moody reached match point. They had one of their longest rallies of the day. Jacobs got the short ball she wanted, approached the net, then had a volley well within her range with the court open ahead of her. She overplayed it. The shot landed long. Mrs. Moody was the victor, 6-3, 3-6, 7-5, coming through for the seventh time at Wimbledon, denying Jacobs the chance to secure a first crown.

Mrs. Moody offered an intriguing analysis of her turnaround in *Fifteen Thirty*. She wrote of her recovery from match point down, "I knew naturally that the set point had been saved, but there was no way to tell that the match had been rescued. During the last couple of games, my 'wind' had returned—why, I don't know. It may have been 'second wind' or it may have been a quieting down of the breathing process induced because of the demands of what seemed to me to be an emergency."

Both Wallis Myers and Al Laney had their notions of why Helen Wills Moody had persevered. Myers wrote in the *Daily Telegraph*, "Courage, as Stevenson has said, respects courage, and both these girls, inspired by the intensity of the other's, revealed more of it on Saturday than I have ever seen on a lawn tennis court. Yet valor, like the other virtues, has its limitations; it was the technique of Mrs. Moody which finally triumphed. In fluent footwork, Miss Jacobs was the superior; without this supreme asset she never could have made those wonderful redemptions in the corner that startled both the crowd and her opponent. But Miss Jacobs, with all her great agility and her unbreakable heart, had not the 'happiness of style' that belonged to her adversary."

Laney wrote in the *Herald Tribune*, "No women's match in the longest memory at Wimbledon ever has been fought with such grimness or presented so many tense situations. It is not likely that Miss Jacobs ever played so well before or that she will ever come so close again and fail. She staked all of her unyielding defense against Mrs. Moody's unremitting attack and, although she defended wonderfully well for an hour and a half—so well, in fact, that she saw her greatest ambition about to be realized—her defenses finally crumbled under pressure of an attack that never let up from the first point to the last."

EPILOGUE

When Moody did not return to Wimbledon in 1936, the gallant Jacobs took her chance at last to win the world's most prestigious tennis tournament. Late in 1935, Jacobs was offered $50,000 by a promoter to play a professional tour series against Moody. Determined to make her breakthrough at Wimbledon, she turned the lucrative offer down. She was well rewarded for her decision.

In the 1936 Centre Court final, Jacobs had her fifth opportunity to win a Wimbledon championship match. She met Hilde Sperling and led by a set and 3-1. Sperling bounced back, took the second set, and fought hard all through the third, but Jacobs triumphed, 6-2, 4-6, 7-5.

Jacobs made it to the final of the U.S. Championships in 1936 for the fifth year in a row, took the first set from the gifted Alice Marble, but bowed in three sets. Top seeded in defense of her Wimbledon title in 1937, Jacobs was beaten in the quarterfinals by Dorothy Round. Mrs. Moody had secluded herself again in her married life in California. When she wrote her autobiography in 1937, she seemed to have put her tennis career behind her, looking forward to other endeavors away from the arena.

But in 1938, she could not resist one more journey back to Wimbledon. She had not lost a match there since 1924, had amassed seven singles titles since, and seemed incapable of playing anything but her best tennis in that preeminent setting. Mrs. Moody and Jacobs met each other in the final for the fourth time. They were engaged in a typically spirited showdown when Jacobs aggravated an ankle she had injured in her quarterfinal. Jacobs was serving at 4-4, 40-30 when she landed painfully on the sore ankle. Thereafter, she could put up only token resistance as Moody glided to a 6-4, 6-0 victory for a record-breaking eighth singles title.

Mrs. Moody was approaching thirty-three. She realized her resources were dwindling, and quit competitive tennis. Jacobs remained a formidable force for a few more years, reaching two more Forest Hills finals, losing both to the blossoming Alice Marble in 1939 and 1940. She left the game with five major singles championships in her possession, fourteen fewer than the major trophies won by Moody. Jacobs, who passed away in 1997 at 88, was overshadowed by Moody on one side of her career and Marble on the other. But there was no doubt about her standing as one of the finest players of her era.

CHAPTER FOUR

Fred Perry *vs.* Ellsworth Vines

PRO TOUR SERIES OPENING, NEW YORK, JANUARY 7, 1937

A dashing Englishman and his explosive American rival played a magnificent pro tour against each other. This was the first battle of a scintillating series.

PROLOGUE

The 1920s was a crucial decade in the evolution of tennis as a sport worthy of widespread international attention. The impact of Bill Tilden, the "Four Musketeers," Suzanne Lenglen and Helen Wills gave tennis an immeasurable boost. It was a time of unparalleled glamour and growth for tennis, a period of passionate interest among fans everywhere in the world.

The decade that followed was almost as remarkable in its cavalcade of champions. Late in the 1930s, the Americans, Don Budge and Alice Marble, achieved eminent successes. Their personalities and performances were alluring to all close followers of the game. Two other men made their mark during that period and established themselves as great stars of their era: The versatile Californian, Ellsworth Vines, and the dashing Englishman, Fred Perry. Vines played semi-professional baseball when he was fifteen and center for the USC varsity basketball team in his sophomore year. But it was tennis that engaged his deepest commitment.

Perry was born in Stockport, England, a textile town not far from Liverpool. His father Sam worked as a spinner in the mills but became a union president at twenty-one and a Justice of the Peace before he was thirty. The Perry family moved to London after World War I, where Fred attended the County School, winning honors in cricket and soccer. He also became a champion ping-pong player, winning the world championship at Budapest—the first non-Hungarian to do so. He started to play tournament tennis at the age of fifteen and at twenty he qualified for the 1929 Wimbledon.

The American and the Englishman showcased their talents appealingly. Vines came to the forefront first. He provided a bright series of matches in 1931 and 1932. In the former season, still a few weeks shy of his twentieth birthday, Vines and Perry clashed for the first time in a match of meaning. Vines—the No. 1 seed among U.S. players— took on Perry, the top-seeded foreign participant, in the semifinals of the U.S. Nationals at Forest Hills. Perry led two sets to love before Vines brushed him aside in five sets. Vines then won the tournament—his first major—over fellow American George Lott (who became one of the all-time great doubles players) in four sets. In 1932, Vines captured both Wimbledon and Forest Hills.

A very slender 6'2," he weighed about 140 pounds. Vines, nevertheless, was a power player of remarkable strength. His big first serve was a "cannonball" opponents did not relish trying to return. He could crack the forehand with demonic speed and depth. He set the pace in most of his matches with the sheer velocity of his strokes. As the esteemed critic Lance Tingay of the *Daily Telegraph* wrote in *200 Years at Wimbledon*, "It is to be doubted if ever a player hit the ball harder than did Vines in his last three rounds at Wimbledon in 1932." At that 1932 Wimbledon, he defeated the gifted Australian Jack Crawford in the semifinals after Crawford had accounted for Perry in the previous round. Vines then handled Englishman Bunny Austin with ease in a straight-set final. He staked his claim as the best amateur player in the world when he safely defended his turf at Forest Hills. Seeded first again among Americans, he made a gallant recovery from two-sets-to-love down in the semifinals and ousted countryman Cliff Sutter. In the final, he beat top foreign seed Henri Cochet 6-4, 6-4, 6-4.

After taking those three major tournaments in 1931-32, Vines was in a position to turn professional. He elected to remain in the amateur game for 1933, but was not up to the same standards. At Wimbledon, he did manage to play inspired tennis for the fortnight. He confronted Crawford in the final. The Australian reversed the result of their 1932 semifinal meeting, prevailing 4-6, 11-9, 6-2, 2-6, 6-4. Perhaps somewhat shaken by that loss in one of the most heralded Wimbledon finals,

Fred Perry

Vines fell again at Forest Hills, bowing in a straight-set, round-of-sixteen match against a scrappy and diminutive compatriot named Bitsy Grant.

Furthermore, Vines lost a major battle with Perry in the U.S.-Great Britain Interzone final of Davis Cup at Paris. Vines led two sets to one before dropping the fourth set 7-5. In the fifth, serving at 6-7, Vines collapsed after hitting a serve. He had twisted an ankle severely earlier, but would not surrender because he did not want to be called a quitter. He fought on despite the pain until that fourteenth game, when he fell on his way to the net. The match was abruptly over. Vines left the court only half conscious.

Despite his failure to hold on to his coveted crowns, Vines had not seriously diminished the reputation he had built for years and he turned professional after the 1933 season.

Meanwhile, Perry was just coming into his own. The Englishman had not emerged from a privileged background. When Perry decided to try lawn tennis, he was given an ultimatum by his father that he had to make his mark within a year. His father took him out of school and gave him that brief time frame to demonstrate his potential.

Perry met the paternal standard. Before he became twenty-two he was good enough to represent his nation on the Davis Cup team. In 1933, when he was twenty-four, he captured his first major championship at Forest Hills, winning the U.S. Nationals over Crawford, recouping from two-sets-to-one down to take the final in five sets. He would win that tournament two more times.

Perry was progressing rapidly. From 1934-36, he was the best player in the world of amateur tennis. Perry secured the Australian Championship title in 1934 and won the French Championships a year later. He won three consecutive Wimbledon singles titles in that stretch. In the first of those finals, he took apart Crawford in straight sets. In the 1935 and 1936 finals, he routed Germany's Gottfried von Cramm in straight sets. But oddly, Perry was not greeted with enthusiasm by the crowd at Wimbledon.

In *Fred Perry, An Autobiography*, he explained why he believed he was given short shrift by the fans. "I've always been regarded as an upstart who didn't really belong in such exalted company," he wrote. "I was

Ellsworth Vines

someone who didn't have the right credentials for this noble game. But I don't think the frostiness of the Wimbledon crowds towards my first victory in 1934 was simply a question of snobbery or resentment. There was more to it than that. You see, they had never really seen an Englishman of this era who didn't like to lose. I freely admit I wasn't a good loser: I didn't go out there to lose and it hurt me very much if I did. I was confident and I was arrogant, because in one-to-one confrontations like boxing and tennis you have to be."

Perry learned to compete wherever he went, relying on his own convictions to carry him through. His third and last triumph at Forest Hills raised his number of major championship victories to eight. In the process, he demonstrated beyond doubt that he was at his best under intense pressure. After overcoming Crawford in that five-set final of 1933, and holding back the American Wilmer Allison 8-6 in the fifth set of the 1934 final, Perry stopped Don Budge 2-6, 6-2, 8-6, 1-6, 10-8 for the 1936 U.S. Nationals title.

The triumph over Budge transcended pride. Perry knew he would be turning professional after the tournament but the offer would be larger if he beat Budge. He led two sets to one and was prepared to start serving the first game of the fourth set when the umpire announced a ten-minute intermission. Perry remembered that the match had already been stopped once and he did not want to take another break. Incensed, believing—probably erroneously—that the American officials were trying to give an advantage to a tiring Budge, Perry was disconcerted throughout the fourth set.

At 5-3 in the fifth, Budge served for the match (with new balls) but double faulted that critical game away. Perry collected three games in a row and served for the match himself at 6-5. Budge drove four blazing winners past Perry to break back for 6-6. The Englishman went on to another break for 9-8 and served out the match. He was ready to leave his amateur days behind him and he signed a large contract to become a professional. Perry would be touring in 1937 with his old rival from the United States, Ellsworth Vines. Vines had been playing professional tennis since the start of the 1934 season. In his rookie year, Vines bested Bill Tilden 47-26 in their seventy-three-match series. He celebrated his twenty-third birthday late in that season. Tilden was forty-one. The younger man was too potent and agile for the aging champion. The following year, Vines won the most matches on a tour with Tilden, Lester Stoefen, Bruce Barnes, and other players. Vines was the winner over Tilden and other rivals again in 1936. He was familiar with the debilitating lifestyle of professional tennis.

So a rivalry which had begun much earlier in the decade was ready to resume in a grueling series of battles fought across the United States. Two of the game's authentic champions—men who had played the game in the best-known settings from Roland Garros to Wimbledon to Forest Hills—were competing again under very different circumstances.

Appropriately, the first Perry-Vines match on their 1937 tour took place in the noisy arena of Madison Square Garden in New York City.

THE MATCH

On a cold evening in January 1937, Vines welcomed Perry to pro tennis before a record crowd of 17,630. The highest priced tickets sold for $9.90 as the fans paid more than $58,000 at the gate, an unsurpassed figure at the time. The American audience was eager to witness the Englishman's transition after he had left behind an enviable record in the amateur game. Since both men would be in direct combat all through a long season, it was an important opportunity to gain a psychological edge with a victory in New York.

The first set was pivotal. With Vines serving his customary cannonballs and blasting away forcefully off the forehand, little separated the two players at the outset. They both wanted to get on the board in the opening set of this best-of-five-set confrontation. Perry was showing his innate capacity to take the ball on the rise, whipping his continental forehand into the corners, neutralizing Vines's power as often as possible.

Vines kept firing away with his powerful shots. They were on level ground until 5-5. Perry proceeded to raise his game a small yet significant notch to take the last two games for the set. He attacked Vines's second serve, moved easily around the court, and played the big points with assurance.

Vines gathered his game admirably in the second set, getting an early break, serving better than he would at any other stage of the match. He was clearly a confident man, going for his shots more freely, picking on Perry's backhand with persistence. Vines collected that 6-3 set without much difficulty and at one set all he looked capable of finishing the job.

Perry was not buying that perception. He was fitter and fresher. The British player found the range off his forehand again, seldom allowed Vines to break down his backhand and was sound and thoughtful in the forecourt. He took the third set 6-3 with some superb returning at the end and effective attacking on serve. Perry had a two-sets-to-one lead. He liked his chances.

At the start of the fourth, Vines tried desperately to even the match. He held serve commandingly and made Perry work harder on his own delivery. Vines played perhaps his highest quality tennis of the match.

It was not enough. Perry was too competitive a player to allow Vines back into the match. Stubbornly, Perry pushed on with his all-court tactics, keeping Vines at bay, maintaining his momentum. With two confident service games at the end, Perry closed it out in style, defeating Vines 7-5, 3-6, 6-3, 6-4.

Allison Danzig wrote in *The New York Times*, "Perry concentrated throughout on Vines's backhand and it was the vulnerability of the American there that hastened his downfall. Once the weakness was exposed, Perry attacked it incessantly and in the fourth set Vines' backhand crumpled. The victor played a beautiful match in which attack and defense were skillfully blended. He could stay back and trade drives with Vines in magnificent rallies, waiting for an error or the winning opening, or he could go to the net and put away his volley with all the dispatch of Vines. Perry's handling of Vines's service, too, was a vital factor. He not only got the ball in play but scored outright winners with deftly shaded passing shots straight down or across court from the backhand. Those returns had Vines shaking his head in discouragement."

Perry had struck the first telling blow, but there was much in store for both players in their 1937 campaign.

EPILOGUE

In the end, Perry and Vines played a total of sixty-one times that season. Perry had taken a 3-0 lead when he backed up his New York triumph with wins in Cleveland and Chicago. Vines then went into the hospital with nervous exhaustion. Tilden took his place for a while. When the Californian returned, he gained the upper hand and came out on top 32-29. The matches were played mostly in the United States, but they expanded their series into England and Canada to give it international credibility.

As Perry observed in his autobiography, "I quickly discovered the professional life was far different from the one I had been used to. Now I was pitched into a fast and furious way of living. In the winter we travelled everywhere by train and when the weather got better we went by car for greater convenience. There were usually four or five hundred miles between stops, which made the travelling hectic and complicated."

The stress on both players was considerable. They would play a singles match at approximately 7:30 in the evening. In the big cities like New York, Los Angeles, Boston, and San Francisco, they would play best-of-five sets while they settled for best-of-three in smaller settings. They would follow with a doubles match, then race for the train that would take them to the next destination.

The players frequently had no time to shower before they departed, and they had no time to eat or find the refreshments they needed. They would arrive in the next town the following morning, go straight to their hotel, and meet with reporters who would ask the same questions over and over again. They would go back to their rooms to get some sleep, waking at 4 p.m. in time to have a meal. By 6 p.m., they were off to rival radio stations to give their tour crucial publicity. And so it went.

They played on every conceivable kind of surface and setting, indoors and out, on slow and fast courts. Sometimes when they competed in school gymnasiums, the baseline had to be moved in a few inches. Perry remembered standing with his back against the gymnasium wall and pushing off as he maneuvered to make his return of serve. Once, they even appeared in New York's majestic Yankee

Stadium, with a court marked out between first and second bases.

After their 1937 tour was over, Vines and Perry pooled their resources and bought into the Beverly Hills Tennis Club with the money they had made from their series. It was an exclusive club then with only 125 members and six courts, along with a modest clubhouse. Perry and Vines altered the layout, added a swimming pool, and modernized it in many ways.

In that time, as business partners, they socialized with people like Errol Flynn, David Niven, Charlie Chaplin and the Marx Brothers. After they had finished with their alterations and were ready to operate, Perry and Vines played a doubles exhibition. Perry and Chaplin faced Vines and Groucho Marx. Chaplin walked on court carrying an enormous number of rackets and a large suitcase. When he opened the suitcase, Groucho Marx emerged. The crowd erupted in uproarious laughter.

Perry and Vines remained business partners in this enterprise until the 1950s and were friends for life. They also took ownership of the professional tennis tour in 1938. Vines was then following his passion for golf and taking time to qualify for events in that sport. Nevertheless, Vines beat Perry 48-35 in a 1938 series. In 1939, Budge—the new pro—stopped Vines 21-18 and handled Perry 18-11. As late as 1942, when he was thirty-three, Perry competed in professional tennis against a variety of opponents. Vines had withdrawn by then.

Perry passed away in 1995 at eighty-five. Eleven years earlier, Wimbledon had accorded him their highest honor, erecting a Fred Perry statue just inside the grounds of the All England Club. He was deeply touched by the gesture, posing proudly for pictures with friends in front of the statue, accepting the accolade with grace and humility. Vines died at eighty-two in 1994. They were two of the game's trailblazers. They were among the best ever to play the game, and their time on the road together provided a bright and memorable chapter in professional tennis history.

CHAPTER FIVE

Don Budge *vs.*
Baron Gottfried von Cramm
DAVIS CUP, WIMBLEDON, JULY 20, 1937

Perhaps the best of all Davis Cup matches pitted a German nobleman against America's most Promethean shotmaker.

PROLOGUE

When the United States took on the Germans in the Interzone Final of 1937, the Davis Cup was a team competition of mounting prestige all around the world. But the Americans were particularly determined to win that year because they had not triumphed since Bill Tilden's teams had won every year from 1920-26. Now, eleven years later, John Donald Budge considered the return of the Cup as his mission. Budge was twenty-two, nearing his absolute prime, and playing tennis with such uninhibited confidence that only a scant few could stay with him when he was anywhere near the top of his game.

Budge had grown up in Oakland, California, and was a superb athlete who played all the popular team sports, including baseball and basketball. His father had been a professional soccer star in Scotland, but moved to California because of respiratory illnesses. Don preferred baseball as a boy, and paid little attention to tennis until he was thirteen. His brother, Lloyd, was playing on the tennis team at the University of California at that time and persuaded him to take tennis seriously. Red-haired and fleet of foot, Budge developed a complete game that was built around his magnificent backhand, the best the game had yet seen. Trained by renowned teaching pro Tom Stow, Budge struck his backhand so forcefully that he made the stroke his most formidable weapon. He came over the ball with a shade of top-spin, producing a sweeping follow through, spreading apprehension

Don Budge and Baron Gottfried von Cramm

Tinling was aware that someone was on the telephone asking to talk with Cramm, but the Englishman did not want to hold up the proceedings. He admonished the German to hurry. "Come on, you can't keep Queen Mary waiting." The Baron followed his own instincts and told Tinling he had better take the call. "It might be an emergency," said the German.

While Tinling and Budge stood within hearing distance of Cramm's telephone conversation, they did not have a clue who was at the other end. When Cramm concluded the brief conversation and gathered his belongings, he told Tinling and Budge in an understated manner. "It was Hitler." Baron von Cramm, who was known to have no sympathy for the Nazis, said. "He wanted to wish me luck." That was as much information as Cramm wanted to volunteer. But half a century later, Budge speculated, "Hitler was apparently telling Cramm that they had had enough of the Americans winning everything in the Olympics over there. They were hoping—and Hitler was hoping—that Cramm could beat me and bring the Cup back to Germany."

And so the battle began. The American broke the German to establish a 5-4 first set lead and served for the set in the tenth game. Budge connected with four consecutive first serves, directing each one of them deep into the box, figuring he could force Cramm into either weak responses or errors. The Baron was in no mood to follow that script. He produced four straight dazzling return winners. Having performed that significant feat, Cramm carried on and seized the first set 8-6 with another service break in the fourteenth game.

The pattern of the second set was very similar. Budge went up a break again but could not hold the lead. Later, serving at 5-6, Budge bolted to a 40-0 lead, but that game slipped inexplicably from his grasp. The set went to the German, 7-5, and the American was in a deep deficit, down two sets to love. But rather than dwell on his losing predicament, Budge was fueled by an inner anger he refused to reveal to the Centre Court audience, or to his concentrated opponent. Finding the range off his backhand, serving with more authority, cutting down considerably on his errors, Budge took the third set 6-4, earning a much appreciated ten-minute rest period in the locker room. After that reprieve, it was apparent that the man from the United

States was on his way to a comeback, while the self-assured ease of his opponent seemed to erode.

The German had served with more penetration and precision than Budge over the first two sets, but no longer. Budge broke at love in the first game of the fourth, broke once more to reach 3-0, and glided through the set 6-2 to reach a fifth set. He would recall later, "Cramm always said that anytime he got anyone into a fifth set, he felt he had a 3-to-1 advantage over them because of his physical condition, and because he had won so many five set matches without any losses."

Balancing that set of facts was this: Budge was gaining confidence as he began the fifth set. The ten-minute break after the third had given him time to rest and reassess his plans. But Cramm was also ready at the start of that final set, and with his piercing service returns doing the damage again, he took a commanding 4-1 lead. At court-side, Tilden was delighted with Cramm's progress, and was confident that the German had the momentum and the shot-making to close out the contest in style. Tilden— ever the showman—turned around from his seat and flashed a victory sign at Henner Henkel, who was seated just a few rows behind Lukas, Benny and Sullivan. Incensed by what he considered Tilden's inexcusably poor taste, Sullivan had to be restrained by Benny and Lukas from going after Tilden and throwing a punch. Through it all, Tilden smiled smugly, seemingly delighted to arouse the wrath of Sullivan and others. But Budge knew he was not beaten.

"I held my serve for 2-4," he said decades later, "and then when Cramm was serving in the seventh game I said to myself, 'I'm getting a little of the worst of it from the baseline so if he misses his first serve, I'm going to take the second serve and go into the net behind my return.' I played inside the baseline to receive his serve so I had a good head start. Fortunately for me, he missed his four first serves by inches and I was able to take his second serve and make good, deep approach shots to set up winning volleys. So I broke his serve and now it was 3-4 and I was serving."

Budge had correctly sensed the right game plan. While it was true that he needed some luck as Cramm missed that succession of first serves by the slimmest of margins, Budge had shrewdly calculated that Cramm's high-kicking second serve was vulnerable. The kicker bothered many players with weak backhands, but here Budge had the opportunity to exploit fully his aggressive shot off that side. He took all the returns on the rise—negating the effectiveness of the kick serve—and was on his way back into the match.

Budge held for 4-4, and then twice served to save the match at 4-5 and 5-6. Had he wavered in the least in either of those games, Cramm would surely have had him. But Budge was typically assertive when it counted. At 6-6, he broke Cramm to take a 7-6 lead. In the following game, it was Cramm who made a last, heroic stand. He saved four match points, but Budge came through on the fifth with an astonishing winner. The American raced to his right for a wide forehand on the dead run, cognizant that Cramm was in a strong position at the net. The instant before he made contact with the ball, Budge realized he would be unable to stop himself from toppling to the turf. As he looked up after falling on the grass court, he could not judge where his shot had landed. He was informed by the wild reaction from the crowd. Budge got up, and scrambled to the net to greet a sportsman of the highest standards. "Don," said Cramm, "this was absolutely the finest match I have ever played in my life. I'm very happy that I could have played it against you, whom I like so much." Budge had triumphed, 6-8, 5-7, 6-4, 6-2, 8-6.

That both men played brilliantly is validated by the statistics: Cramm made 105 placements and only sixty-five errors, while Budge had 115 placements and only fifty-five errors. Budge served nineteen aces, Cramm seventeen.

When the long and exhausting confrontation was over, Budge had carried the United States into the Challenge Round to face and eventually defeat the British. Budge was greeted in the locker room by Jack Benny. "He thanked me for the tickets," Budge remembers, "but he did it in a very lukewarm way. He said, 'Thanks a lot Don, I appreciate your getting me the tickets today. It was a nice win.'"

Budge was disconcerted by Benny's indifference. But three months later—when Budge was playing the Pacific Southwest Championships in Los Angeles—Benny approached Budge effusively, congratulating him again for the great Davis Cup triumph over Cramm. Budge was delighted by Benny's belated reaction, but also baffled.

"Jack, you weren't this enthusiastic right after you saw the match. How come you are so much more animated now?" Budge had asked. "He told me that my match with Cramm was the first he had ever seen and that since then he had seen a lot of tennis matches which were terrible by comparison."

Budge placed that victory in a category of its own among his most cherished moments. "It was the best and most important match that I ever played," Budge said when he was in his seventies. "Coming right after I had beaten Gottfried at Wimbledon in the final of the tournament in straight sets, we were trying as hard as we could to win the Davis Cup, which the U.S. had not done for a period of eleven years. So it was not only a personal thing but also a matter of helping my country win the Davis Cup which meant so much to me."

Asked in 1987 if he might have suffered some long-term psychological damage if he had not managed to overcome Gottfried von Cramm in their monumental battle, Budge replied, "I don't think so. I still think I would have won the Grand Slam the next year, but who knows? Maybe I wouldn't have. I just don't think the loss of one match—even one as important as this—would have hurt me that much. If you took one point away and gave it to Cramm, he would have been the winner. So one point one way or the other isn't going to kill you. Once a match is over, it shouldn't cloud the rest of your career."

EPILOGUE

The following year, Budge became the first tennis player ever to sweep the four major championships and record a "Grand Slam"—a description used by Allison Danzig, the distinguished tennis analyst.

At the end of 1937, former U.S. champion, (and Tilden rival) "Little Bill" Johnston had invited Budge to lunch in California, hoping to persuade him to turn professional while his earning power was substantial. He had received offers in the range of $50,000 to play pro tennis, and that was an exorbitant sum in those days. Johnston feared that Budge might seriously injure himself and lose financial security by remaining an amateur for the 1938 season.

"It was damned nice of Billy to give me his advice," said Budge in 1998. "But I told him I was going to take a chance and try to become the first to win the four major championships in one year. No one had ever done that so I felt I would be worth more to any promoter if I achieved a Grand Slam."

Budge was rewarded in many ways for his bold thinking. From the outset, his all-consuming quest for a Grand Slam fell neatly into place. Cramm, the player who would surely have been his worthiest adversary, was detained by the Nazis in Germany, and beset by personal problems. Perry and Ellsworth Vines were playing one-night stands on the pro tour, and were ineligible for the four major championships. No one else had the talent or the temerity to test Budge comprehensively. The determined American had good reason to expect success.

Budge did have one serious problem—his health. In 1998 on the sixtieth anniversary of his golden season, he said, "That year my health was at its worst. I lost my voice in the finals of the Australian. Then I had diarrhea during the whole French Championships in Paris and had to have sandwiches brought to the court for me during my matches. At Wimbledon, I lost my voice again. So not long before the U.S. Nationals at Forest Hills, I went to a dentist in New York and he discovered that I had an abscessed tooth which had been bugging my whole system. He gave me a shot of penicillin and yanked the tooth and at Forest Hills I was stronger again."

The record shows that Budge was so much better than his peers in amateur tennis that even his struggle to stay well did not hinder him significantly. In the opening Grand Slam event at the Australian Championships, he lost only one set in the entire tournament, dropping the opening set to the Australian Adrian Quist but winning easily from there in four. At the French Championships, he had his only five-set Grand Slam match of the year, but he produced his best to take the final set 6-1 against Franjo Kukuljevic of Yugoslavia. He conceded no more sets in winning that tournament.

On the grass at Wimbledon, back at the same hallowed site where he had won the tournament the year before and where he had overcome Baron von Cramm in their classic encounter, Budge did not drop a set. He then completed his cycle through the majors by winning Forest Hills again at the cost of only a single set—to his doubles partner Gene Mako. Budge had too much versatility and firepower for his friend and he stopped Mako, 6-3, 6-8, 6-2, 6-1.

Reflecting on his 1938 sweep of the majors six decades later, Budge was relieved and appreciative that he had managed his mission so smoothly despite feeling below par for most of the season. "I was lucky as hell to get through that year doing that well, not knowing I needed to get the poison tooth out of my body. It is amazing as I look back because the only final that lasted over an hour was the one with Mako at Forest Hills. I beat John Bromwich in a 57-minute Australian final, defeated Roderich Menzel in 58 minutes in the French final, and although rain delayed my Wimbledon final with Bunny Austin, the playing time was still under an hour. Gene Mako knew my game and was playing very well at the time, so that final was a tougher test for me."

In the fall of 1938, about a month after his Forest Hills triumph gave him the Grand Slam, Budge did turn professional, signing for approximately twice what he had originally been offered a year earlier. He had nothing left to interest him in amateur tennis and had won the last six major championships in a row, dating back to Wimbledon in 1937. In those two years, he had suffered only three defeats.

Budge maintained his momentum when he started his professional career and toppled the best players in admirable fashion. From 1939 through 1942, he was the best in the business, defeating Vines 21-18 in their 1939 series and handling Perry, 18-11, in their battles contested the same year. In 1941, he crushed an aging Tilden fifty-one matches to seven, and in 1942 he won fifty-four of seventy-two matches in a round-robin tour against the likes of Bobby Riggs, Frank Kovacs, and Fred Perry. Budge was on top of the world. "I was the amateur champion for two years and then the pro champion for many years after that," Budge said near the end of his life. "There was no one who could beat me. Just think of how many more Wimbledons I could have won?" Immodest perhaps, but true.

As for Cramm, he survived his difficulties at home and continued competing on a high level for a long while. He had lost the 1937 U.S. Championship final to Budge two months after their historic Davis

Cup duel. Then he reached the final of the Australian Championships in doubles with Henkel early in 1938, but his political problems escalated. Refusing to show sympathy for the Nazi cause, he was sent to prison by the Gestapo that year. After World War II, however, he resumed competition and took the last two of his six German Championship titles in 1948 and 1949. By then, he had turned forty.

Cramm represented Germany in Davis Cup competition as late as 1953 when he was forty-four. He remained formidable in singles and doubles, but was devoting the bulk of his time to being a businessman. He became president of a tennis club in Berlin and earned a good reputation in that role. Not until Boris Becker arrived in the upper echelons of the game as a robust teenager in the 1980s, was there a player of Baron von Cramm's caliber in Germany. He had won fifty-eight of sixty-eight singles matches for Germany in the Davis Cup, had taken two Grand Slam singles titles, won the French and U.S. doubles championships, and reached three consecutive Wimbledon singles finals. He had lived a long and productive life in and around tennis. When he was killed in a 1976 car crash, he was sixty-seven.

CHAPTER SIX

Jack Kramer *vs.* Don Budge

U.S. PRO CHAMPIONSHIPS, FOREST HILLS, JUNE 19, 1948

A remarkable contest between the dominant player of the 1930s, and the leading competitor of the 1940s. The quality of world tennis had been lifted by both men in different times.

PROLOGUE

As a boy growing up in Las Vegas, Nevada, long before he moved with his family to California during his high school years, Jack Kramer was the quintessential all-American kid. He played baseball, football, and basketball. His father was a senior engineer for the Union Pacific Railroad. As a seven-year-old, Jack had seven mitts, a catcher's mask, and a wide collection of bats and balls. He did not turn to tennis until he was thirteen. He had broken his nose and separated his ribs in accidents suffered on the football field. Kramer's mother decided she would not stand by any longer while Jack came home bruised and battered from contact sports. She purchased a secondhand tennis racket and gave it to her embarrassed son who pleaded with her not to let his friends know what she had done. He had the same mistaken notion that many other young Americans harbored at that time—that tennis was simply a game for sissies. He did not want to be humiliated by his buddies.

But in the fall of 1934, when he was thirteen, Kramer's family moved to San Bernardino, California, and in that community devoted himself enthusiastically to junior tournaments, and won the National Boys' 15 Championships in 1936. Two years later in 1938, he captured the National Interscholastic Championships. He was on his way to the top tier of tennis, and he knew it.

By 1943, Kramer was polished enough as a player to reach the final of the U.S. National Championships at Forest Hills. Kramer lost to

Lieutenant Joe Hunt. Kramer had joined the Coast Guard, but by the beginning of 1946 had been discharged and he returned with overwhelming zest and ambition to amateur tennis. From the early stages of 1946 through the 1947 season, he was nearly invincible. The only match of consequence he lost in that stretch was to the Czechoslovakian left-hander Jaroslav Drobny in the round of sixteen at Wimbledon in 1946, bowing 2-6, 17-15, 6-3, 3-6, 6-3. Blisters contributed to his defeat, but he made no complaints.

Later that year, Kramer was triumphant at Forest Hills, halting countryman Tom Brown in a straight-set final to take the U.S. Championship. The following year, he seized the two most prestigious championships, making the summer of 1947 particularly meaningful. At Wimbledon, he swept through seven matches and lost only thirty-seven games, routing Brown 6-1, 6-3, 6-2 in the final.

Coming home to defend his title at Forest Hills, he confronted another American, Frank Parker, in a hard-fought final. Kramer was down two sets to love, but he played his way out of near defeat and prevailed in five sets.

That triumph coupled with his Wimbledon victory was crucial for Kramer. It set the stage for him to turn professional. As he said in 1997 on the fiftieth anniversary of his triumph on Centre Court, "I guess I was the first one to win Wimbledon playing in shorts. I enjoyed visiting with the king and queen, and it was a wonderful afternoon for me when I won Wimbledon. I am sorry I never had another chance to have that exhilarating feeling of standing up in the Royal Box in the post-match ceremony. They later moved it down to the Centre Court itself. But it was quite a thrill for me and it was the most important stepping stone towards the professional career I had in mind for myself."

Having said that, Kramer realized that his value to the pro promoters would be that much larger with Forest Hills added to the package. In 1946-47, Kramer had been beaten only three times, but a fourth defeat in an event of the magnitude of Forest Hills would have tarnished his prestige as a world champion moving confidently into the professional arena. Although Kramer did drop his debut pro tour match against Bobby Riggs at New York's Madison Square Garden on

Jack Kramer

December 26, 1947 in front of more than fifteen thousand fans, he was not to be denied often in those days.

In his overall tour of one-night showdowns against the crafty Riggs, Kramer came out on top 69-20 during 1947-48. He would dominate the pro game for the next five years against other formidable foes. In the middle of this period, he had his only significant career confrontation against the durable Don Budge. Budge had lost much of his sting by then after a shoulder injury robbed him of essential power on his overhead and serve, but as a proud and disciplined competitor he was determined to keep his high ranking while making some hard-earned money as a professional.

He was thirty-three and Kramer was approaching twenty-seven when they clashed at the U.S. Pro Championships at Forest Hills in the summer of 1948. In 1946 and 1947, while Kramer was wrapping up his amateur career so successfully, Budge was struggling. The Budge who had overwhelmed all of his chief rivals in pro tennis from 1939 to 1942 was gone, and his opponents knew what had happened to his shoulder during the war. Riggs was especially adept at exploiting a wounded adversary, and the guileful American stopped Budge in twenty-three of forty-four matches contested in 1946-47. He lobbed Budge ceaselessly, knowing Don could not hit the overheads effectively.

When he joined Kramer, Riggs, and other professionals on the lawns of Forest Hills in 1948, Budge was anxious to return to the top of his game. The U.S. Pro Championships was the tournament that mattered more than any other to the leading professional players, and a "dream match" developed between the best player of the 1930s and the greatest competitor of the 1940s.

THE MATCH
Budge and Kramer ended up on the same side of the draw. Kramer nearly missed his appointment with his revered rival, surviving despite a less-than-top-of-the-line performance against Welby Van Horn. Kramer astutely explained the importance of his battle with Budge in his 1979 book, *The Game, My 40 Years in Tennis* (with Frank DeFord). After clarifying that winning the U.S. Pro was Budge's one and only chance to get back on top after his losing tour against Riggs, Kramer

Don Budge

wrote of his meeting with his fellow American, "It was a great match. Although Don and I are only a few years apart, we never played in the amateurs, and the bond-drive exhibitions we played during the war (when they let amateurs and pros share the same court) were only that—exhibitions. We played later several times, but this match in June of 1948 was really the only time we met under tournament conditions with something on the line. All that was lacking was that only one of us, me, was in his prime."

As Kramer recalled, he was sending his best shot right to Budge's strong side. Kramer's inside-out forehand—hit with biting sidespin and allowing him to take control in the forecourt—was a shot he would not give up, even if it meant going up against a stroke as lethal and overpowering as Budge's backhand. Kramer was the man who had galvanized the game with his style of play. He introduced what was known as the "Big Game," wasting no opportunities to conclude points with telling volleys, rushing the net religiously behind his serve, approaching behind his return whenever possible, avoiding long rallies if he had the chance to force his way in. No one had ever built such a commanding and all-out aggressive approach to match play before.

But Budge presented Kramer with problems. He virtually took away Jack's serve-and-volley game because his returns were so penetrating, and made Kramer wait for the appropriate mid-court ball before coming in. Kramer found himself squandering opportunities after taking the opening set. He wanted a two-sets-to-love lead and pressed hard to achieve it, but Budge was counterattacking magnificently on an oppressively humid afternoon. Budge sealed the long second set 10-8 by finding the narrow openings to drive the ball past Kramer, and when he pinned his opponent to the baseline Budge had the advantage in prolonged points.

Budge's successful bid to take the long second set inevitably carried him straight through the third and now the underdog led two sets to one. Twice, Budge broke Kramer to establish fourth-set leads, but Kramer replied promptly each time to get back on level terms. Kramer managed a remarkable forehand crosscourt placement at full stretch on the run when Budge led 2-1, deuce. Later, Budge served for a 5-3 lead. If he could hold in that vital game and do it once more after that, Budge would gain a win of major dimensions.

Kramer knew he had no alternative but to take risks that might raise his game, and he did. In the next three games, he won twelve of seventeen points to finish off the set. From then on, Kramer was in control, collecting twenty-four of twenty-five points in the fifth set as Budge faded in the heat. Both men recognized the consequences of their confrontation. Kramer's pride and match playing prowess had prevented Budge from making one last push to the top. Budge had shown his gutsiness for three sets and nearly came through in four, but he did not have the stamina to take it in five. Budge had come agonizingly close to a victory that might have given him another year or two of big-time matches, but he was beaten by a better player in the end—6-4, 8-10, 3-6, 6-4, 6-0.

Kramer would defeat Riggs in a four-set final the next day to claim the U.S. Pro title, and from there he would tour in 1949 and 1950 with a brilliant but still budding Pancho Gonzales. Kramer controlled their match series, 96-27. Considering the era, Kramer made good money for his efforts, taking in $85,000 against Riggs and $72,000 against Gonzales.

In a 1950-51 series, Kramer bested a sprightly Pancho Segura, 64-28, despite Segura's searing two-handed forehand drives and returns. Kramer believed Segura's two-hander was one of the best-ever shots in the history of tennis. In 1953, his final complete year as a professional player, Kramer overcame the Australian Frank Sedgman, 54-41. But Budge was no longer a prime-time player. He played on into the fifties but his skills had been sorely diminished and his legs could not carry him around the court with the alacrity they once provided.

EPILOGUE

Following his distinguished playing years, Kramer took on a wide range of roles in the game. For the next ten years, he was the pro-moter of the pro tour, signing all the leading amateur players to con-tracts, lining up locations for the matches, and finding a forum for this small legion of the game's greatest players. Kramer carried on in this capacity until the early 1960s, hoping that "Open Tennis" would arrive soon and allow all of the best players, "amateur and professional," to compete on the same courts. Among those who signed contracts with Kramer were the Australian "Whiz Kids," Lew Hoad and Ken Rosewall, and the American star Tony Trabert.

Talking about his time as a professional player and promoter, Kramer once said, "I felt insistent that we should always try to follow the more successful way that golf was promoting itself, adding players to their game, getting courses built, and so forth. So I think the idea of me playing the tour with Riggs and Segura and Gonzales and Sedgman and then becoming the promoter, where I tried to get the best amateur player of each year to play in the pros, sold the game tremendously well, especially in America."

After "Open Tennis" was initiated in 1968, Kramer remained an indispensable figure. He came up with the concept for an international "Grand Prix" of tournaments culminating with The Masters for the top eight players in 1970. That structure for men's tennis remains in place to this day. In 1972, Kramer was named the first executive director for the Association of Tennis Professionals (ATP), the men's players association. The following year, Kramer and his players stood firmly behind Yugoslav player Nikki Pilic, who had been suspended from Wimbledon by the International Tennis Federation.

Renowned players like Rod Laver, John Newcombe, Stan Smith, and Arthur Ashe boycotted the biggest tournament of them all in protest over Pilic's suspension, which they felt was unjustified. The players were treated harshly by large segments of the British press, but no one was hit harder than Kramer, who was criticized vitriolically. A man of firm convictions and unshakable integrity, Kramer would say more than a decade later, "I was proud of what we did with the boycott. I think it showed something about my character and competitiveness."

Meanwhile, Kramer, who died in 2009 at eighty-eight, was the game's keenest analyst on television from the 1950s into the 1970s. He covered fourteen Wimbledons in that period for the BBC, and all but two U.S. Championships between 1952 and 1973 for the three major U.S. networks. After his stint as executive director of the ATP, Kramer served ably on the Men's Tennis Council. He was a first-rate tournament director in his hometown of Los Angeles, and a vital voice of reason behind the scenes. Looking at the major figures in the world of tennis across the twentieth century, no one was as multifaceted as Kramer. No one accomplished as much in so many roles. If there was a "Man of the Century" in tennis, it was surely Jack Kramer.

Budge also remained a fine ambassador for the game. After stretching his career as long and as far as it would go, and reaching his last U.S. Pro final in 1953 against Gonzales at the age of thirty-eight, Budge would be seen at all the major championships, observing the emerging champions, sharing his knowledge of the game, and enjoying the surroundings. As he grew older and became more removed from younger generations of players, very few knew much about his vast accomplishments. Hardly anyone sought his counsel. But John McEnroe did in the early 1980s when he was losing consistently to Ivan Lendl, and Budge was delighted to pass along his views.

"John is the only modern player who ever asked me to talk about anything that was wrong in their game," Budge said in 1998. "I was happy to point out to him what I had noticed, which was that he was giving Lendl too many angles to pass him. I told him to approach the net down the middle and cut those angles off. He began beating Lendl regularly after that."

For his part, Budge learned some vital lessons early in his career that he carried with him unfailingly for the rest of his life. Recalling his early matches with Fred Perry, Budge said, "I didn't know what the game was about until I first played Fred Perry. He dominated the play and I wondered why, until I realized he was taking the ball early on the rise and rushing me off the court. That was when I realized I had to change my game. Once I started taking the ball early and hitting harder, the game became easy for me because I could jump on everyone."

In 1998, the International Tennis Federation honored Budge on the sixtieth anniversary of his Grand Slam. Remembering Budge's triumphs over the years, Kramer spoke about how highly he regarded Budge as a player. Asked then where he placed Budge on the historical ladder, Kramer responded, "Don was totally equipped with the best all-around game that we have ever had. I still believe that. I don't know what these young players today would be doing against Don, but if they came in against him Don would knock the ball at their feet or pass them. And he would come in himself on good ground strokes. I still believe he is the best player I ever competed against or saw."

Budge, who passed away in 2000 at eighty-four, admired Kramer every bit as much. He said, "The players who competed against Kramer would pick him over anyone because he was someone who only volleyed once. In other words, you had to pass him the first time because you didn't get too many shots at him when he was up at the net. He would put that first volley away almost every time. I don't know how I would have done if I had come up against Jack in 1938 when I was going for the Grand Slam. I would have had a hard time against him."

Recalling his compelling 1948 match with Kramer at Forest Hills, Budge confessed, "When you are involved in a match like that you don't always know how good it was, but everyone said it was a great match. I had those two service breaks in the fourth set, but I couldn't put it across. I think I controlled play a little better than Jack did in that match, but he still beat me. He was a great player."

Asked if there is anything he would have done differently in his tennis career, Budge ruminated, "I don't have many regrets, but I wish I could have played when the game went open. We wouldn't have needed the pro tours with one-night matches to make our money. We could have made it by winning tournaments where the prizes amounted to a lot more than playing one-nighters, and people would have been paying a lot more attention to what we were doing."

Most authorities rank Budge and Kramer among the top-ten players of all time. Budge has the more glamorous record because he is one of only two men ever to win the Grand Slam, but Kramer, at his best, was surely the better man. Only on clay could Budge have contained Kramer, but it seems safe to say that Kramer would have had the edge on all of the faster surfaces with his ability to set the tempo and apply pressure relentlessly.

In any event, their Forest Hills battle belongs in a treasure chest as one of the rare gems in tennis history. It was a match that received little recognition because professional tennis was played in such obscurity in those days, but the longer view of history will keep it sharply in focus as long as tennis remains in our field of vision.

CHAPTER SEVEN

Maureen Connolly *vs.* Doris Hart

WIMBLEDON, FINAL, JULY 4, 1953

No one could challenge the daunting "Little Mo" more convincingly than the well-prepared Doris Hart. This was their most compelling confrontation.

PROLOGUE

During the 1920s and 1930s, Suzanne Lenglen and Helen Wills Moody dominated the world of women's tennis in regal fashion. They seldom lost matches, and their contrasting personalities attracted fervent supporters. Other players of great talent emerged in the late 1930s and through the 1940s. The Californian, Alice Marble—winner of four United States singles championships and one at Wimbledon—was the first pure serve-and-volleyer among the women. Pauline Betz and Sarah Palfrey Cooke had days of triumph in the 1940s.

As the curtain opened on the 1950s, another Californian came onstage. Maureen Connolly was relatively short (5'4") and somewhat stocky. Her father, who became a lieutenant commander in the U.S. Navy, was an accomplished athlete. He divorced his wife when Maureen was four years old, and she did not see him again until her adult years. Maureen was raised by her aunt and her mother. She learned how to play the piano and went to a ballet class when she was five years old. At the age of nine, she was one of two fine young tennis players competing in her hometown of San Diego, and was so transfixed by the game that she resolved to make it her major extracurricular interest. Connolly built her game entirely around flat, clean, piercing ground strokes. She drove through the ball in exemplary fashion, getting extraordinary depth on her shots, dictating matches with her sound execution and superior concentration. The fate of her clashes with the opposition was almost always in her hands. She hit very hard, missed very infrequently, and made her rivals work for every point.

Connolly was propelled into top-flight tennis by Eleanor "Teach" Tennant, the same exacting woman who had guided the career of Alice Marble in the late 1930s. Tennant pushed Connolly incessantly. They met when Connolly was twelve and she shaped her student's game for a productive period until they parted ways in 1952 when Maureen was nearly eighteen.

In her autobiography *Forehand Drive*, Connolly wrote revealingly about her strong-minded instructor. "Tennis, to Teach, was never a game, it was a battle, and no field marshal mapped strategy more carefully. She scouted every formidable opponent I faced and spotted strength and weakness with absolute accuracy. She was the field officer, I the troops, and we went into action with deadly purpose and total concentration. If Teach knew the enemy, she also knew me, and how close she might drive me to the breaking point in practice before easing the pressure.... Her confidence was a living, glowing thing, without limits, and she had the magic power of being able to transfer it. Lose was not a word in her tennis vocabulary. Teach believed everything in my life should be sublimated to tennis."

That all-embracing dictum was highly successful. At sixteen, Connolly became the youngest ever to win the championship of her country. Not until 1979 when Tracy Austin won the U.S. Open was that record broken. Connolly triumphed at Forest Hills in 1951, defeating Doris Hart and Shirley Fry, who were seeded first and second in the event.

She made her first journey to Wimbledon in 1952. She had sadly parted with Tennant, who wanted her to withdraw from the tournament because of an injured shoulder. Two points from defeat in the fourth round against Susan Partridge, Connolly came through 6-3, 5-7, 7-5. She took the title with wins over Fry and Louise Brough, another accomplished American. Then at Forest Hills, Connolly defended her title with repeat victories over Fry and Hart. There were high expectations for "Little Mo" in 1953. Appearing in the Australian Championships for the first time, she ousted her doubles partner Julie Sampson 6-3, 6-2 on the grass in the final. At the French Championships in

Paris, she accounted for Hart 6-2, 6-4 in the final, thus avenging a loss to the same player weeks before at the Italian Championships. She was at the halfway point in her bid for a Grand Slam, a player of growing stature.

As she set her sights on Wimbledon, she had the wise Australian coach Harry Hopman helping her develop strategy. She was not happy with the caliber of her tennis on the way to the final, but it was good enough to get her there. Connolly conceded only eight games in ten sets contested over five matches. She dismissed the third-seeded Fry 6-1, 6-1 in the semifinals, but attributed that score to Fry's poor play rather than her own inspiration.

Waiting for the top-seeded Connolly in the title match was Doris Hart, the No. 2 seed and a player of the highest caliber. Hart had a misleadingly frail appearance. As a child, she had suffered from a knee infection that threatened to leave her crippled when she was not yet two years old. A false rumor later circulated that she had battled polio. Because of an error in diagnosis, her infection spread until it was feared she might have gangrene. One specialist recommended that she have her leg amputated. Her father consulted the family doctor, who rejected amputation and performed a minor operation on the Hart kitchen table to drain off the infected fluids. Her ailment actually was osteomyelitis, which prevented her from walking properly until she was three. Doctors believed she would always walk with a limp and the family moved from St. Louis to Florida so that she could swim every day in salt water, which seemed to help. At ten, following her older brother Bud, she took up the game of tennis.

In her twenties, Hart progressed rapidly. She took the Australian singles title in 1949, won Wimbledon in 1951 with a 6-1, 6-0 rout of Fry in the final, and captured the French Championships in 1950 and 1952. In 1951, she was the top-ranked player in the world with Connolly residing one place behind her. She was a formidable all-court competitor who excelled on all surfaces, and a top-notch doubles player who would secure twenty-nine of her thirty-five major championships alongside a range of talented partners in women's and mixed competition.

If anyone was going to deny Connolly the Wimbledon singles title

Maureen Connolly and Doris Hart

of 1953, it was Doris Hart. She had the experience and the guile to get the job done. She was not apprehensive about playing her illustrious compatriot. She welcomed the challenge.

THE MATCH

At 11:45 on the morning of her final-round match with Hart, Connolly went to Queen's Club to practice. She worked out on an indoor varnished wood court which made the grass seem slow by comparison. Hopman lined up the Australian Davis Cupper Mervyn Rose to practice with "Little Mo."

Both Hopman and Rose stood at the net and punched volleys, sending Connolly from side to side to work on her ground strokes. Connolly then moved up to the net while they fired from the baseline. After that, all three players practiced volleys at close range.

The entire session lasted only half an hour, but Connolly had herself primed for the big occasion. She sat in a hot bathtub for five minutes for relaxation, then went out to Wimbledon. At 1:30—half an hour before the final—she hit for fifteen minutes with another Australian Davis Cupper named Ken Rosewall.

Connolly returned to the locker room and waited in the wings with Hart to be summoned to Centre Court. The players made their much applauded entrance, then started a battle each would call her best. The tennis was wonderful from the outset as both players were bold without making careless mistakes. The two Americans held their serves for the first seven games of the match, giving little away, making the most of their openings.

Serving at 3-4, Hart suffered a wounding double fault and that brief lapse was critical. Connolly gained the break for a 5-3 lead. But the Californian delivered two double faults of her own in the ninth game to allow Hart back into the set. Hart held on for 5-5. With the two women locked in a grinding backcourt battle, they held even. But Hart had to serve to save the set at 5-6. She did so ably.

Connolly was backing up her useful, but not extraordinary, serve with a barrage of forehand and backhand drives. She kept Hart at bay with her power and accuracy. Hart served again at 6-7, slipped to 0-40, then saved two set points. At 30-40, she could not contain Connolly who seized the set behind a cluster of beautifully struck backhands.

Hart served at 1-2, 40-0 in the second set but lost the game. Connolly was once again in command with a 3-1 lead. Hart rallied to 3-3 with a concentrated run. They stayed on serve to 4-4. The ninth game was the hardest fought of the match. It reached deuce six times. Hart gallantly pursued the favorite in closely contested baseline exchanges. She rarely approached the net, knowing Connolly could produce extraordinary passing shots off both wings.

At last, after eighteen points and a series of wonderful rallies, Connolly held for 5-4 and was four points away from a second Wimbledon and third consecutive Grand Slam title. Hart was serving to save the match. She played as if she were ahead, moving to 5-5 after a solid game. Connolly forged ahead on serve again to 6-5. This time, Hart could not win a point. She had thrown everything she had at Connolly, including her chop forehand, an array of disguised drop shots, and flat, penetrating drives. In the end, it was to no avail. With Connolly adding velocity to her shots and bearing down visibly on every point, she broke at love to complete an exhausting 8-6, 7-5 triumph.

"I can't stop shaking," Connolly told Alan Hoby of the (London) *Sunday Express*. "That's the toughest match I've ever had and I'm still all keyed up. I certainly never played better."

Hart felt essentially the same way. She told Hoby, "I went out to attack Maureen. I concetrated on hitting the ball down the middle and waiting for the opening. It was the best I've ever played against Little Mo.... But it wasn't enough."

The British press concurred with the players about the match. As J.L. Manning wrote in the *Sunday Dispatch*, "There will never be perfection in sport, but I was near to seeing it yesterday at Wimbledon. For an hour Maureen Connolly and Doris Hart showed hardly an error of judgment, a slackening of concentration or a weakening of effort in a never-to-be-forgotten lawn tennis match. At the end of this magnificent demonstration of what two determined girls can achieve in sport, Little Mo had won. And she had won the hard way. The 26 games were loaded with 187 points, each fought for with ice-cold skill and with unrelieved application of the game's best arts. All those points, but just four surrendered on service faults. What a lesson for our girls!"

Connolly herself would rate her match with Hart at the top of her personal list of best performances. In *Forehand Drive*, she recalled that Hart told her as they came off the court, "Maureen, this is the first time in my life I have lost a match and still felt as though I had won it." Connolly confessed, "For me, it was a tremendous win. I had played the finest tennis of my life, my game soared, and to have won against such a great adversary, at the very height of her game.... it's a thrill beyond description."

EPILOGUE

Only one major tournament stood between Connolly and a Grand Slam. No woman had ever swept the "Big Four" in a single year. The only tennis player who had realized that feat was Don Budge fifteen years earlier. Connolly came to New York for Forest Hills feeling she could handle any opponent after her testing time at Wimbledon.

The Californian was in convincing form all through the tournament. There was no glimmer of apprehension. She was on the edge of an astounding accomplishment, and was playing with a sense of serenity. Connolly knew she was the best player in women's tennis, and was eager to confirm her talent at a place where she had thrived.

In the quarterfinals of Forest Hills, she took on the fast-rising African-American Althea Gibson, a powerful, attacking player who would win both Wimbledon and Forest Hills in 1957 and 1958. Gibson was called frequently for foot faults, but did not correct the flaw in her technique. The crowd began booing as the match was disrupted by repeated infractions. Connolly won 6-2, 6-3 feeling relieved that the fiasco was over, and baffled by Gibson's continuous foot faulting.

In the semifinals, she repeated her Wimbledon win over Shirley Fry, winning with an identical 6-1, 6-1 score. All that was left to complete her mission was a final-round encounter with Hart. Connolly wrote in *Forehand Drive*, "It was not the same Doris who opposed me at Wimbledon for most of the match. In the second set I had her 5-2.

Then she had a bold and glorious stand, and a crowd of 12,000 roared encouragement to her as she came up and I led by a scant game, 5-4. The crowd was tense now; the pressure was on as I served. I made it 15-0 when Doris netted a shot. I reached 30-0 on a service ace. Then, on a placement, I made it 40-0. In our next rally, I smashed a forehand cross-court for an outright placement, taking the game, set, and match, 6-2, 6-4. That slashing drive was to be my Forest Hills swan song."

Having secured her Grand Slam, Connolly seemed invincible in the next Grand Slam events. She won the French Championships for the second time in 1954 with relative ease, then won her third-straight Wimbledon with a 6-2, 7-5 triumph over Louise Brough of the United States, erasing a 5-2 deficit to take five consecutive games for the title. She had collected six major championships in a row, and had secured the last nine Grand Slam events she had entered, dating back to the 1951 Forest Hills tournament.

Back home in San Diego after winning the U.S. Clay Court Championships, Connolly went horseback riding with two friends. They came around a blind curve and saw a cement-mixer truck heading in their direction. The sight of that truck made the horses uneasy. Connolly and her friends shouted at the truck driver, hoping he would slow down or stop. The driver didn't seem to notice them. He stayed in the middle of the road. The horse in front of Connolly reared and the truck driver could not stop in time. Maureen felt the harsh pain in her right leg as she fell off her horse. Her right leg buckled when she tried to get up. It had been "slashed to the bone."

As Connolly sat on the side of the road, she was assisted by a trained nurse who happened to be passing by. An ambulance was called. She soon found out at the hospital that calf muscles had been severed, and the fibula bone broken. She was not yet twenty years old, but her tennis career was over.

Not long after, Little Mo married and later had two daughters. She came to terms with her tragedy and conducted tennis clinics whenever possible, working informally with aspiring players. She wrote an entertaining, sharp-edged column for *Tennis Magazine* in the 1960s, and did some television commentary and newspaper reporting at Wimbledon in the 1950s and 1960s. In 1969, at thirty-four, Connolly passed away, a victim of cancer.

Doris Hart, in those years after Little Mo's accident, played a number of fine winning matches. She had lost four finals at Forest Hills, two to Margaret Osborne duPont in 1949 and 1950, and two to Connolly in 1952 and 1953. Later in that summer of 1954, she took her U.S. Championship at last in one of the tightest finals ever—6-8, 6-1, 8-6 over Louise Brough. Hart saved three match points in the final set.

In 1955, she won Forest Hills again, less arduously, defeating Pat Ward 6-4, 6-2 in the final. By then she was thirty, and decided to ease out of tennis competition, taking an enviable record with her.

In the last analysis, Connolly would have surely collected at least half a dozen more major titles. She might well have won another Grand Slam. As British writer Duncan Macaulay wrote in a piece published in *The Fireside Book of Tennis*, "Had Connolly been able to compete for another five or six years, her total of major championships could well have been quite unparalleled. As it was, she deserves to be ranked among the very greatest women's singles players ever to have lived. And her character and temperament remained durable and unruffled in all circumstances."

CHAPTER EIGHT

Lew Hoad *vs.* Tony Trabert

DAVIS CUP CHALLENGE ROUND, MELBOURNE, DECEMBER 30, 1953

On a damp and demanding day "Down Under," the Australian and the American produced a performance of skill and sparkle with both men stretched to their limits.

PROLOGUE

The 1950s were the "Golden Age" of Davis Cup competition. The international men's team competition had grown in stature since its inception at the turn of the century. The pride of playing for country rather than self was an inspiring endeavor for the leading players of that era. Later, after Open Tennis emerged in 1968, the major tournaments took on an unprecedented significance. With the professional calendar more crowded than ever before, Davis Cup gradually was forced to compete for the priorities of the top players.

In 1953, that was not the case. At the time, the rivalry between the United States and Australia was flourishing. The two countries met in the "Challenge Round" (the finals) of the Davis Cup for the tenth consecutive time since 1938, including a six-year gap in 1940-45 when World War II forced a postponement of the competition. The Americans and Australians delighted in representing their nations during this highly-charged period. They looked to produce great performances in a conflict unlike any other in their game. They hoped and believed they could contribute something larger than the sum of their own achievements.

As the United States and Australia assembled in Melbourne for the 1953 Challenge Round, the Americans came to the Kooyong stadium knowing they had their work cut out for them. Captain Billy Talbert, one of the game's great ambassadors who was a member of the victorious U.S. Davis Cup teams of 1948 and 1949, brought two men who would try to carry their country to triumph. One was Wimbledon champion Vic Seixas, a native of Philadelphia, and a diligent competitor who would win the U.S. Championships the following year. The other was Tony Trabert, who had grown up in Cincinnati. A few months earlier, Trabert had secured his first major singles title at Forest Hills, taking the U.S. Championship with a straight-set victory over Seixas in the final. Trabert, the son of an engineer, had played basketball at the University of Cincinnati, and also won the U.S. Intercollegiate tennis singles title while there in 1951. A year earlier, at the French Championships of 1950, he had taken his first major prize, claiming the doubles crown with one of the all-time-great doubles players, Billy Talbert, now the non-playing U.S. captain.

Trabert had spent the first half of 1953 finishing an obligation to the armed services. When Trabert joined Seixas for the Challenge Round a few days after Christmas, he was twenty-three. A good athlete and determined competitor, Trabert was maturing observably as a tennis player. His sound, attacking game was just what his nation needed on the grass courts at Kooyong.

Trabert had a well-rounded strategy featuring an extraordinary backhand. Off that side, the rugged, muscular Trabert could release flat, forcing drives, or he could come over the ball to produce slight top-spin. His forehand was not as flamboyant, but it was stable and aggressive. He was a first-rate volleyer off both sides, his smash was formidable, and his serve was an underrated strength. Trabert had the tools to compete against anyone, and the versatility to shine on all surfaces.

The Australian captain was the renowned Harry Hopman, a former player who had as his team anchors the "Whiz Kids," Ken Rosewall and Lew Hoad. Rosewall had won two Grand Slam events that season, the Australian and French Championships. Hoad, barely nineteen, had won three Grand Slam doubles championships in 1953 alongside Rosewall, but had not hit his stride yet in singles.

Even so, Hoad was already a frontline player. Blonde and burly, Hoad was one of the most explosive shotmakers of his time. Hoad's father was an Australian tramwayman. Lew quit school early to pursue his tennis career. He could fire winners off both flanks with no hesitation, hitting his ground strokes with immense power, serving

Lew Hoad

with authority, volleying with remarkable assurance. He could hit the ball with blinding speed, but he could hurt his chances with rash mistakes, errors born of impatience and lack of restraint. Be that as it may, Hoad was a player of pure and raw talent who could strike fear into anyone when he was on his game.

As the best-of-five-match battle between the two nations commenced, Trabert and Hoad each gave their teams reason to cheer. Hoad routed Seixas in straight sets to put Australia out in front, then Trabert answered with a 6-3, 6-4, 6-4 win over Rosewall. In the doubles, Hoad and Rex Hartwig were decisively defeated by Trabert and Seixas. The U.S. held a 2-1 lead heading into the last afternoon. The pivotal contest would see Hoad facing Trabert.

THE MATCH

On a damp day with rain falling lightly on the grass courts at Kooyong, Trabert and Hoad walked on court deeply aware of the magnitude of the moment. If Trabert prevailed, he would clinch the world team championship for his country. The Americans had suffered three consecutive defeats against the men from Down Under from 1950-52. They wanted to regain possession of the coveted Davis Cup, and Trabert was in a position to make that happen.

The first set was fought indefatigably by both players. It lasted twenty-four games. Through the first twenty-three, there was not a single service break. Both men were playing grass court tennis of a very high quality, backing up their big serves with solidly struck first volleys. They were returning serve adeptly, but the conditions were slick and negotiating a service break was no simple task.

Trabert, however, was frequently on the verge of sealing the set. Hoad was living precariously, facing break point no fewer than eleven times in a cluster of different service games. Trabert was making more effective returns, forcing Hoad into binds, then narrowly missing his mark. With Trabert serving at 11-12, 30-40, Hoad made a low, chipped return. Trabert had to lift his volley as he approached the net. Hoad had followed his return in and Trabert was required to make a choice. He moved to his backhand side. Hoad cut off his volley and made a volley of his own past Trabert into the open court. Hoad had the set, 13-11. The capacity crowd of 17,500 at Kooyong applauded loudly.

In *The Story of the Davis Cup*, Alan Trengove wrote appealingly, "The crowd's thunderous applause was echoed by groups clustered around radio sets throughout the continent. Outside the stadium, in Glenferrie Road, a tram conductor clambered onto the top of a stationary tram, making sure he avoided the electrified pole. He saw the scoreboard and shouted the news to the passengers."

The grass court was increasingly greasy as the soft rain fell intermittently. In a 1999 interview, Trabert recalled that he told captain Talbert he wanted to wear spikes when he was behind 2-3 in the second set. Trabert said, "You would run up to the net, put the brakes on, and slide ten or twelve feet. I told Talbert I was going to put on the spikes. Talbert spoke to the referee, Cliff Sproule, who talked to Hopman. Hopman said, 'My boy's okay.' "

Trabert was at a loss to explain why, but Hoad—despite the slippery court—did not want to switch from his tennis shoes to spikes. Trabert reluctantly kept his tennis shoes on as he served at 2-3. He remembers, "When I served that game, I came in twice and just fell making routine moves trying to go right or left. He broke me and held for 5-2. When we changed ends of the court that time, I put on spikes without asking anybody. I wanted to see who was going to take them off of me. By that time I was down a set and a break."

The shift to spikes gave Trabert the firmer footing he sorely needed. Although Hoad served out the second set at 5-3 despite a 15-40 deficit—building a two-sets-to-love lead in the process—the American was encouraged by his improved mobility. Trabert moved swiftly to a 4-1 third-set lead. At the changeover after the fifth game, Hoad finally made the switch to spikes himself.

Even so, he lost his serve again, and with it the set, 6-2. The players took a brief intermission and returned to the locker room. When they resumed the match, Trabert was still confident. As Alan Trengove reported, "Hoad was unable to slide into his shots and his form had become patchy.... Trabert now was repeatedly going to the net behind his sliced returns that kept low on the wet turf, and Hoad made errors trying to pass him." Trabert sustained his fast-paced tactics. He took

Tony Trabert

the fourth set 6-3. As they moved into the fifth, the rain was falling and the balls were heavier. Trabert was at a distinct disadvantage as he served the entire set from behind, but Tony Trabert was holding his delivery with ease. On his way to 5-5, he lost a mere eight points in five service games.

Hoad had slipped and tumbled onto the damp grass as he chased a Trabert volley. He was stretched out on the court, not moving for a few long moments. Then, as Trengove recounts, "Hopman jumped up, grabbing the towel from his lap. As Lew looked up, Hopman threw the towel over his player's head and said, 'Come on, Muscle-bound, you can't lie there forever.' "

Hoad grinned, got up, and held. Both players tenaciously protected their service games. Trabert served to save the match at 4-5 and completed the task. Hoad, undismayed, forged ahead 6-5.

In the twelfth game, Trabert served again to save the contest. Hoad opened with a perfect placement off the return, struck with great power past a charging Trabert. The Australian then used his court sense again to force the American into an errant volley for 0-30. Trabert hit a hard first serve, which missed its mark. He then went for the wide second serve in the deuce court, attempting to avoid the Australian's lethal backhand wing. The serve was out.

The double fault put Trabert at 0-40, but neither he nor Hoad heard the call. They played the point out with Hoad finally hitting an apparent winner. Trengove reported that few in the crowd had heard the linesman cry "fault," and they thought Hoad had won the point with a placement. Trabert, realizing he had double-faulted and was now triple match point down, believed the crowd had cheered his double fault in a breech of traditional tennis civility.

As Trabert said forty-six years later, the incident still alive in his memory, "I thought it was unfair for them to clap my double fault. They say in retrospect that Lew hit a forehand down the line that would have been a winner and that is why they were clapping. That is all history and hindsight."

Either way, Trabert was understandably distressed at the time, placing his hands on his hips for a long moment, looking up disapprovingly at the crowd. At triple match point, his percentage first serve was directed deep to Hoad's backhand. The Australian returned the serve with a sharply angled crosscourt winner. Trabert was beaten by a superb final stroke, broken at love. Hoad triumphed 13-11, 6-3, 2-6, 3-6, 7-5.

Said Trabert many years later, "That match stands out for me as I look back at my career, even though it was a losing cause on my part. It was Davis Cup and we could have won the Cup if I had won my match. It was a special match for its importance, its competitiveness and the length of it."

It was left to Seixas to salvage victory for the United States. With the two countries locked at two matches apiece, the American confronted Rosewall the next day. Seixas battled gamely, after losing the opening set, to take the second. His comeback did not last. Rosewall was too consistent, ruling in four sets, keeping the Davis Cup in the capable hands of the Australians.

EPILOGUE

In 1954, Trabert and Seixas returned to a spacious stadium seating 25,578 in White City (Sydney). This time, the Americans toppled Hoad and Rosewall to take back the Cup. When Trabert and Hoad clashed again, the Australian served for a two-sets-to-one lead at 7-6 in the third. Trabert saved a set point in the fourteenth game, and went on to win the set 12-10. He took the match in four sets. Hoad would tell Trabert years later, "You should have won in 1953 in Melbourne and I should have won the next year in White City."

Trabert mused, "Winning the cup in 1954 was the biggest thrill I ever had in tennis because I was representing my country. Instead of the umpire saying, 'Game Trabert;' he says, 'Game, United States.' And you suddenly realize that you are representing at that stage 185 million people. You are halfway around the world with a chance to do something for your country. In those days, the Davis Cup was huge."

Trabert celebrated what he calls his "banner year" in 1955. After losing to Rosewall in the semifinals of the Australian Championships in the first Grand Slam event of the season, he swept the last three major tournaments at Roland Garros, Wimbledon, and Forest Hills, where he vanquished both Hoad and Rosewall in straight sets. Beaten only five times in twenty-three tournaments that year, he closed out his amateur career in style.

Trabert turned professional in December 1955, lost his series with Pancho Gonzales seventy-four matches to twenty-seven, and played on productively into the early sixties. He became U.S. Davis Cup captain from 1976-80, with two of his teams taking the title. Beginning in the early 1970s and continuing through the 1990s, Trabert was a superb analyst for CBS television at the U.S. Open and elsewhere.

Hoad had his best amateur season after Trabert's departure for the pro ranks. In 1956, he beat Rosewall in a four-set Australian Championship final, came through at Roland Garros to claim the French title, then ousted his doubles partner Rosewall again in the Wimbledon final. Hoad was closing in on a Grand Slam, ready to become the first man since Budge in 1938 to sweep the four major titles in a single year.

The dynamic Australian with the high velocity game came within one match of his goal, only to lose to a flawless Rosewall in four sets at Forest Hills. Following that superb season—reminiscent in many ways of Trabert's 1955—Hoad turned professional, barnstorming with Gonzales.

Looking back upon his battles with Hoad, Trabert would say generously of his adversary, "If Lew Hoad played his best and I played my best, he would beat me because he was more talented and more gifted than I was. But I had the ability to stay at a pretty high level. That is how I won three of my five Grand Slam singles titles without losing a set. I could get up for a tournament and stay there. So if I caught Lew when he was down a little bit and he was not quite at his best, I could beat him. But when he was playing as well as he could play, he could play as well as anybody."

Trabert—a proud, earnest, and ultimately humble man—is not comfortable placing himself in historical context. And yet, he concludes, "From the time I got out of the service in June of 1953 until the end of 1955 I won five Grand Slam singles and four Grand Slam doubles championships. That was a pretty short time to win all those Grand Slam events. I think I would certainly be somewhere in the top ten of all the American players, but that is up to other people to figure out. All I can say is my mother thought I was the best ever."

CHAPTER NINE

Pancho Gonzales *vs.* Lew Hoad

U.S. PRO CHAMPIONSHIPS, CLEVELAND, FINAL, MAY 4, 1958

This encounter pitted the power of Gonzales against the prodigal talent of Hoad in a stupendous indoor collision.

PROLOGUE

Richard "Pancho" Gonzales was perhaps the most evocative tennis champion the game has yet seen. Standing at 6'2," weighing a muscular 180 pounds, staring down rivals and officials with defiant, gleaming eyes, he strode onto a tennis court like a gladiator and stirred audiences all over the world. Of all the great male players who competed during the second half of the twentieth century, only Ken Rosewall and one time protégé Jimmy Connors remained formidable for as long as Pancho.

He was driven by powerful private engines—exploding with rage at linesmen who gave him questionable calls and showing disdain for opponents who were disturbed by his antics. Pancho was one of seven children born into a Mexican-American family, who lived on the south side of Los Angeles where tennis was surely not the game of choice. During the depression, the entire family lived in two rooms. His father was a housepainter, and his neighborhood was impoverished. As a young boy, Pancho became fascinated by the game of tennis. When he was thirteen, he started to skip school and hang around various Los Angeles tennis centers. He was almost entirely self-taught and in 1943 became the No. 1 boys player in Southern California. He controlled his matches with the coiled force of his personality, turning many of his appearances into dramatic experiences that reached beyond the boundaries of a tennis court.

Even as a junior player, Gonzales was seldom far away from the center of conflict. When he was fifteen, he told the Southern California Tennis Association that he was going to drop out of school to concentrate on his tennis. They told him that dropping out was unacceptable. Gonzales would not obey. He was suspended for a year from all official tournament competition. By his late teens, Gonzales had put most of the commotion behind him and was moving forward as a world-class player. He won back-to-back U.S. Championships at Forest Hills in 1948 and 1949, making a fiery comeback from two-sets-to-love down in the latter final against Ted Schroeder. Those twin triumphs gave Gonzales the credentials he needed as the leading amateur to graduate into professional tennis.

The transition was perilous in the early days. Jack Kramer had been competing as a pro for two years and was the better player. He played 123 matches against Gonzales in 1949 and 1950. Kramer won ninety-six of those contests. Kramer made the case in his 1979 book, *The Game*, that Gonzales had been given a false sense of security after recovering so admirably against Schroeder at Forest Hills in 1949. It made Gonzales believe he was better than he actually was.

As Kramer said, "Pancho was just in way over his head. He had no idea how to live or take care of himself. He was a hamburger-and-hot-dog type of guy and had no concept of diet in training. I had learned, for example, that if we got a couple of days off in a row I had to stop eating or I couldn't burn it up. He'd eat at the same pace and I always beat him in the next match. On the court, Pancho would gulp Coca-Cola throughout a match. I had learned from Perry and Budge to bring sweetened tea to the court.... Also, Gonzales was a pretty heavy cigarette smoker." Despite the humbling indoctrination, Gonzales worked to establish his position in pro tennis. After being crushed for two years by the match-playing prowess of Kramer, Gonzales gradually ironed out the wrinkles in his game and in his training. By 1953, he had developed winning habits. He took his first U.S. Pro Championships title that season over Don Budge after losing the previous two finals to Pancho Segura. He repeated as champion of that important event for the next four years, defeating the wily Segura in the 1955-57 finals.

Meanwhile, Gonzales was taking over the pro tour of one-night stands. He beat both Frank Sedgman and Segura in 1954, defeated Trabert 74-27 in 1955-56, and handled Rosewall 50-26 the following year. A new challenger was needed for Gonzales. With his big first serve and fluent second delivery—both were the best in his trade—he could overpower his opponents across the board. He had a first-rate overhead, a solid and forceful volley off both sides, and ground strokes that did not betray him despite their lack of sparkle.

As the 1958 season approached, it was apparent who was best equipped to tour with Gonzales. It was an Australian who was in many ways a more gifted player. He had much more punch off the ground. He could serve nearly as well. He was a dazzling shot-maker with decidedly more flair than Gonzales, and perhaps a better overhead. His name was Lew Hoad.

Hoad had joined the pro ranks in 1957 following his outstanding 1956 season. At 5'8," he was about six inches shorter than Gonzales. His series with Gonzales began late in 1957. Hoad had won his second consecutive Wimbledon singles title in July. He was supremely talented in every facet of the game, but some keen observers believed he did not have the psychology of most champions, the fierce will to win under any circumstances.

In the Hoad-Gonzales 1958 tour, they started in Brisbane, Australia. After thirteen matches, Hoad was in front 8-5. Kramer recalled years later how Gonzales competed courageously with bleeding fingers in Adelaide while Hoad coped with a painful forearm muscle in Sydney. They returned to the United States and Gonzales closed the gap to 9-7. Hoad burst into brilliant form again to take an 18-9 lead. He seemed to have the American measured.

On March 1, 1958, the two toughened competitors played on a cold, crisp evening in Palm Springs, Calif. Hoad woke up the next morning with a stiff back. Thereafter, Gonzales ruled the rivalry. But they had many rigorous duels in front of them during the late fifties, most notably in the historic final of the U.S. Pro Championships in Cleveland.

THE MATCH

Over time, the U.S. Pro Championships shifted locations and moved

Pancho Gonzales

from one arena to another. Even the official name of the event was altered. Ultimately, it would be known as the United States Professional Championships, arguably the most prestigious of all events for those who competed for money. In 1958, however, it was called The World Pro Championships and it took place at The Arena in Cleveland. Gonzales and Hoad came to town with the cream of the crop in their profession. They were joined by Tony Trabert and Pancho Segura, an aging Fred Perry, and the 1944-45 U.S. champion Frank Parker. Gonzales ousted Segura 6-4, 6-3 in his semifinal; Hoad accounted for Trabert 6-2, 13-11. The most important Gonzales-Hoad clash was on course. Throughout the spring on their tour, the American and the Australian had played an absorbing series of matches. Between March 31 and April 20, they played twenty-one times. They moved in and out of towns like Atlanta and New Haven, Philadelphia and Montreal, Princeton and Bermuda. Gonzales held only a slim 12-9 edge in that span. In Cleveland, they were to play on a fast canvas court. The conditions were suited to both contestants. They were mean fast-court players. By now, they knew each other's games inside out. The edge in this final would go to the player who executed better on the big points. Since Hoad had suffered his back injury two months earlier in Palm Springs, he began to produce some surprisingly good tennis against his glowering adversary.

With 2,700 fans watching the American and the Australian's climactic match the first weekend in May, it became clear that service breaks were difficult but essential. Hoad got the early break for 2-0 in the opening set and held throughout to prevail 6-3. Gonzales did not want to fall into a deeper deficit. He served steadily to 4-4 in the second set, but could not gain a break himself. Hoad then broke through with some blazing backhands to take a 5-4 lead. Self-assured and given the chance, Hoad held on comfortably to take the second set 6-4 for a two-sets-to-love lead.

The third set featured both men at their best. An obstinate Gonzales was willing to pursue any policy to keep himself in the match. He persisted with his firepower on serve, backed up by decisive volleying. Hoad was anxious to finish his job in straight sets, knowing that Gonzales was a warrior who would not surrender. Gonzales had the

Lew Hoad

advantage of serving first in the set, but Hoad was staying with the favorite through every sequence.

The pressure grew on the twenty-three-year-old Australian. Gonzales kept inviting him to concede the set, but Hoad refused. In a battle between the two premier servers in professional tennis, neither man was found wanting. Gonzales kept moving in front, only for Hoad to blast his way back to even territory.

From 4-5 in this pivotal set, Hoad served to save it eight times. Gonzales pressed him, but to no avail. Hoad answered his adversary emphatically every time. He was quick and confident in the forecourt, cutting off the volleys at short range, reading nearly every Gonzales passing shot, giving the American few second chances.

Gonzales remained on course. He held on for 13-12 and finally proceeded to set point on the Australian's serve. Hoad came in behind a penetrating approach. Gonzales responded meekly off the backhand. His passing shot was tentative. But the ball hit the tape, and somehow fell over. Set to Gonzales, 14-12.

Buoyant after that good fortune, Gonzales coasted through the fourth set 6-1 behind two service breaks. He gained an early fifth set break, and there was no halting him from there. The American, five days shy of his thirtieth birthday, was much fresher and fitter in the end. Hoad was hindered by a leg injury late in the contest. Those facts notwithstanding, it was a superb match that decorated the greatness of both players.

As Chuck Heaton wrote in the *Cleveland Plain Dealer*, "The three hour match—played before an estimated 2,700 fans—was the longest and perhaps most exciting in the nine years the pros have fought it out in Cleveland. The sixth straight World Pro Championship for swarthy Pancho added blonde Lew to a list of final victims which includes Don Budge, Frank Sedgman and Little Pancho Segura."

Tournament promoter Jack March wrote in *World Tennis*, "According to Don Budge, Bobby Riggs and Pancho Segura, it was the greatest match they had ever seen. It was also the single greatest display of shotmaking, with Aussie Lew Hoad making most of the shots but losing the match.... It was the first time Gonzales was up against an opponent who surpassed him in stroke equipment, condition, anticipation, speed, and court coverage. But Gonzales won this year on brains, fight, and guts."

March later reflected, "For the first time, distinct weaknesses were revealed in Gonzales' game. These weaknesses were never evident before because Gonzales had never faced a stronger, faster, and better player than himself. It is a credit to the champion that he could beat a player whose stroke equipment was superior."

Gonzales himself recognized one department of his game as instrumental in his triumph. He told Heaton, "Lew and I both play the same style of tennis that we have used on the tour. My serve worked as well as it ever has. In fact, it was even clicking for me in the sets I lost. Lew was just volleying too well for me in the early part of the match. Then he slowed down and wasn't getting to the net quite as fast. That always makes the other fellow look better."

Gonzales was asked about his shrewd lobbing and semi-lobbing to work his way back into big points. He responded, "That's a trick I learned from 'Little Sneaky' Segura. It's a change of pace that keeps the other guy running. In a long match like this, all of those steps add up."

Was Gonzales fortunate to overcome Hoad in their most celebrated meeting? Perhaps. The fact remains that his tenacity was crucial to his cause. He made his own breaks by competing so fiercely in the latter stages of the third set when he could easily have succumbed. He recognized one fundamental fact: Great matches are taken not only by the better player; they are won by those who want them the most.

EPILOGUE

Gonzales and Hoad finished their 1957-58 tour with the American the winner in fifty-one of eighty-seven matches. In 1959, they met again for the World (U.S.) Pro Championship. The gap between them had widened considerably. Gonzales was the victor 6-4, 6-2, 6-4. Two years later, Gonzales took that title for the eighth and last time with a straight-set win over Sedgman.

He remained a complicated man, wearing his grievances disdainfully, altering his moods so frequently no one could ever be certain what to expect from him. In any case, he continued as a major force in professional tennis through the sixties. He would play during his thirties in relative obscurity, testing himself against the leading competitors who turned pro after taking major championships.

Hoad struggled in many ways. After that spring of 1958, the record reveals he was never quite the same player. He competed hard and often splendidly, but his level of consistency decreased. He could not play past his pain and be the soaring competitor he had once been. That was a sadness for him, and for tennis. Hoad was not even twenty-four when he produced so many magical moments during his tour with Gonzales in 1958. Thereafter, he was permanently past his peak.

Despite his decline, he was still a strikingly good tennis player. After Rod Laver won his first Grand Slam as an amateur in 1962, he turned professional and was battered by Hoad all through the early stages of 1963. Hoad continued to surprise Gonzales in some pro events in the mid-sixties. *World Tennis* editor Gladys M. Heldman wrote of Hoad in 1964, "Lew is still the most exciting shotmaker in the world."

Historians have had a hard time deciding where Hoad belongs among the all-time great players. His time at and near the top was relatively short. And yet, most experts place him in a category alongside Ellsworth Vines. At their best, both of these big hitters could have held their own with anyone on given afternoons when they were in full form. Hoad was in that zone when he battled against Gonzales in Cleveland during their final of 1958. The Kramer analysis: "When you sum Hoad up, you have to say that he was overrated. He might have been the best, but day-to-day, week-to-week, he was the most inconsistent of all the top players. Overall, he lost to Rosewall, to Gonzales, to Segura, to Trabert.... Generally, he is held in higher esteem that he deserves.... But when Hoad felt like getting up, boy was he something."

In the sixties, Hoad's back trouble became an inescapable burden. He could no longer play the same dazzling brand of tennis. By the time Open Tennis arrived in 1968, it was entirely too late for Hoad. He did appear in the first open Wimbledon that June, and was seeded seventh, a sentimental gesture by the committee. He reached the third round but fell in five sets to the South African Bob Hewitt. When he competed there for the last time in 1970, John McPhee wrote about him lyrically in *Wimbledon: A Celebration*. "Hoad on Court 5, weathered and leonine, has come from Spain, where he lives on a tennis ranch in the plains of Andalusia. Technically, he is an old hero trying a come-back, but, win or lose, for this crowd it is enough of a comeback that Hoad is here. There is a tempestuous majesty in him."

Gonzales was able to claim a much higher mark for himself in the early history of the Open Era. He, too, was a heroic figure returning to the places that had barred him for decades while he played as a professional. But, unlike Hoad, Gonzales's body had not penalized him. He could still survive tests and produce performances that were reminiscent of his prime. The glint in his eyes, the fluid serving, were adamant.

He was still Richard "Pancho" Gonzales.

CHAPTER TEN

Maria Bueno *vs.* Margaret Smith

WIMBLEDON, FINAL, JULY 4, 1964

The graceful artist from Brazil took on the tall athlete from Australia. As always, they brought out the best in each other.

PROLOGUE

Over the first half of the 1960s, two women set the agenda and settled more big matches than any other players. They delighted galleries all over the world with their contrasting personalities yet similarly aggressive styles. They attacked each other's games unwaveringly and intelligently, and more often than not brought out the best in each other. Brazil's Maria Bueno and the Australian Margaret Smith were clearly the preeminent players of that era, taking the women's game into another realm, a slower but in many ways more captivating type of serve-and-volley tennis than that of the men. Bueno-Smith matches were not to be missed. They added value to the major championships simply by showing up.

Both players had made their mark by the time they clashed in the 1964 Wimbledon final. Smith, who grew up in New South Wales, Australia, was the daughter of a foreman at a cheese and butter processing plant. Her first tennis racket was given to her by a sympathetic neighbor. She began refining her game at a private tennis club not far from her home. When she was eight years old, she would creep under the fence of the courts to play against boys who were members of the club. She won her first tournament before she was ten.

Margaret was a natural left-hander when she began playing the game as a young girl. She was persuaded to switch the racket to her right hand by boys in her neighborhood who made fun of her. As she explained in her book, *Court on Court, A Life in Tennis* (with George

McGann), "I got so many taunts that I finally switched the racket to my right hand and played that way thereafter. I've always felt that if I had remained a left-hander I would never have experienced so many problems with my serve."

Difficult or not, Smith made the adjustment. By 1964, she had secured five consecutive Australian Championships. Earlier that year in Brisbane, she won with remarkable command of the court in a 6-3, 6-2 final-round triumph over countrywoman Lesley Turner. A month before that she had taken her second singles championship on the red clay of Roland Garros, winning the French Championships in Paris with a come-from-behind, three-set victory over Bueno. Two years earlier, she had erased a match point against her in a three-set win over Turner on the same court.

In 1962, Margaret had ruled at Forest Hills, taking the U.S. Championship title. On that occasion, Smith stopped the talented American, Darlene Hard—Bueno's accomplished doubles partner—in a hard-fought, 9-7, 6-4 final. In the 1963 Centre Court title match at Wimbledon, she was too good for an American named Billie Jean Moffitt (soon to be Billie Jean King). Smith triumphed, 6-3, 6-4.

She was well on her way to a record-breaking career. Not yet twenty-two, she had nine major singles titles in her possession. She was nearly six feet tall, and despite her large frame (the press constantly referred to her as statuesque), she covered the court swiftly. She was particularly adept at blanketing the net, making the stretch volley with regular and unprecedented success, showing her opponents how tough it was to drive the ball past her. A superb athlete, Smith could count on her strength to carry her through long afternoons of competition.

Bueno's father, Pedro, was a veterinarian who had an interest in tennis. Though demure and trim, she grew tall enough at 5'7" to make her presence known. She, too, had enjoyed multiple successes in England and elsewhere in the years leading up to a vintage 1964 Wimbledon. While Smith was more of a programmed player who won her matches through self-discipline and careful application of her skills, Bueno was at her core an artist. A fluid shotmaker who often played points spontaneously, she took great pleasure in being inventive and

Margaret Smith

bold. She was something of a ballerina on the tennis court (not unlike Suzanne Lenglen), gracefully gliding through many of her matches, making shots effortlessly. With this deceptively flowing ability, Bueno captured Wimbledon in 1959 and 1960. The following year, she was almost always in bad health and there was some talk that she might not compete again. But she returned with vigor in 1962, and was soon on her way to the top of her game.

In the 1959 Wimbledon final, Bueno had halted the No. 4 seed Darlene Hard 6-4, 6-3 to win her first major crown. She was only nineteen, and seeded sixth in that event. The Brazilian conceded sets in her second and third round matches, but did not drop another in her last four appearances as her game seemed to improve every time she stepped on court. The following year, she returned as the favorite, seeded No. 1. She lost only one set in that tournament—to the No. 4 seed Christine Truman in a 6-0, 5-7, 6-1 semifinal victory—and defeated No. 8 seed Sandra Reynolds of South Africa 8-6, 6-0 in the final.

Bueno's success was international. She had also captured two U.S. Championships at Forest Hills. In 1959, she had a close call with the American Jeanne Arth before escaping 4-6, 6-3, 7-5 in the third round. She took off confidently from there, not losing another set, defeating Hard and Truman in decisive meetings at the end. Four years later, she got her title back at Forest Hills, coming through with a pair of clutch victories to close out that first-rate tournament. In the semifinals, Bueno took on the formidable Englishwoman Ann Jones, a left-hander who knew how to use every inch of the court. Six years later, Jones would crown her career by winning Wimbledon, but in this collision she failed to make good on an early lead over an out-of-sorts Bueno. Jones won the first set and was not behind until 6-5 in the final set. Bueno prevailed 9-7 in the third. In the final, she had another top-notch match against Smith, who had beaten her the previous year in the semifinals. Bueno was dazzling in this duel, and she clipped Smith 7-5, 6-4.

On that occasion, the Brazilian was down 1-4, 0-30 in the second set, about to be pushed into a final set by the persistent Australian. Bueno simply turned up her intensity, sharpened her familiar shots, and did not lose another game. It was among the most celebrated sets of her career, and it left Smith dazed and disconsolate when it was over. Bueno loved nothing more than big match conditions, delighting in performing with her back to the wall. Bueno's record worldwide was comparable to Smith's; the difference between them was Smith's mastery of her native turf, her complete domination of the Australian Championships.

As they approached this Wimbledon Centre Court clash, their accomplishments elsewhere in the Grand Slam game were similar. Smith had won two French Championships along with one triumph at both Wimbledon and Forest Hills. Bueno had her twin triumphs at Wimbledon and Forest Hills but had not prevailed in Paris. The moment had arrived for them to collide again in a major final, and they both were ready.

THE MATCH

Appropriately, Smith was the top seed at Wimbledon in 1964, while Bueno was placed second. On her way to the final, Smith had only one match that gave her cause for consternation. In the third round, she came up against 1962 titlist Karen Susman, who was not playing regularly anymore on the circuit. Susman was still a seasoned grass court player. She gave the Australian a thorough test in the opening set, looking very impressive in the process, but Smith prevailed 11-9, 6-0. She moved on easily to the semifinals where she met Billie Jean Moffitt. The American had beaten the top-seeded Smith in the second round two years earlier, then reached the final the previous year before losing to Margaret 6-3, 6-4. This time, Smith won by the identical score.

Bueno played superlatively all through the tournament, until she faced the canny Lesley Turner, the No. 4 seed, in the semifinals. Turner's forceful, flat ground strokes were very effective on the low bouncing grass, troubling Bueno all through the first set. Bueno shrewdly made adjustments and rebounded 3-6, 6-4, 6-4. The final that all close followers of the game had wanted was on the line. Could Bueno summon the inspiration to overcome Smith with her superior, if streakier, shot-making? Would Smith gain the upper hand with her physical advantages, her reach at the net, her greater size and strength? Who would stand up better to the pressure of a Wimbledon final, an experience unlike any other in the sport?

At the outset, Smith was riddled with apprehension, suffering from serious anxiety as she often did before Centre Court matches. In the opening game, Margaret double faulted on break point, her second serve falling feebly into the net. The Australian broke back at love for 1-1, boosted visibly by a backhand half volley pass as she attacked behind her return for 0-40. The revival was brief. Flashing a superb backhand passing shot with slice down the line for break point, followed by a well-concealed backhand slice lob over Smith's head, Bueno had the break again for 2-1. The Brazilian mixed her game adroitly to hold for 3-1, but serving in the sixth game she wasted three game points and Smith drew level at 3-3.

At 4-4, Smith's emotional fragility surfaced again. At 15-40, she attempted an American twist second serve which landed in the wrong service box, ten feet wide. Bueno was not going to waste her opportunity to serve out the set. At 5-4, 40-30, she stayed back on her second serve, then worked her way in behind a backhand slice approach which clipped the sideline. Smith's running forehand passing shot was wide. Bueno had secured the set, 6-4.

Troubled by her loss of the opening set, Smith fell behind 15-40 in the first game of the second. Here she was helped by an overanxious Bueno, who missed a backhand return and a backhand passing shot. At game point, Smith found her confidence, making a classic forehand volley winner at full stretch. She broke in the next game with three soundly struck passing shots for 2-0, then served a commanding love game for 3-0 as she connected with every first serve.

Sensing the possibilities at that stage, Smith broke again for 4-0 with a backhand return winner past a charging Bueno. Soon Margaret stood at 4-0, 40-15. Bueno's piercing returns brought her back to deuce. Smith double faulted, saved the first break point, only to double fault again at break point down. Bueno held on from 30-30 for 2-4. Smith sorely needed to reassert herself in the seventh game on serve.

She fell far short of that goal. Off the mark with four out of five first serves, double faulting once more, she was broken again by a tricky chipped backhand return to her feet. At 3-4, Bueno missed seven of eight first serves, but she survived that game by producing some excellent play from the backcourt. Bueno had climbed to 4-4. Would she run out the match as Smith dwelled on her lost chances?

The ninth game stretched into nine deuces. Bueno reached break point five times. Yet Smith remained steadfast, connecting on seventeen of twenty-two first serves, and finding other ways to unsettle Bueno. On game point, the Australian stayed back after a first serve, a tactic that worked as the Brazilian drove a forehand return wide. At 5-5, Smith was obstinate on serve again, holding from 15-40, saving two break points. She had fought her way to 6-5.

Smith held at love for 7-6 with deft volleying, then held at love again for 8-7 by scampering in alertly to cover a drop shot before snapping an overhead into the clear. With Bueno serving at 7-8, Smith increased the pressure. She moved in behind her return of Bueno's

Maria Bueno

second serve to put away an emphatic forehand volley. After Bueno netted a backhand volley, Smith drove a stinging forehand passing shot down the line to force Bueno into an errant volley. Despite squandering the 4-0, 40-15 lead, Smith had reached far inside herself to seal the set.

Until the middle of the final set, Smith seemed to be the better player. She lost only two of fourteen points in three dominant service games, connecting on thirteen of fourteen first serves. She was getting better depth on her serve, closing in tighter for the first volley, forcing Bueno into more mistakes. At 1-2, Bueno was break point down. She saved it with a flourish, punching a penetrating first volley, retreating rapidly for a lob from the Australian and smashing it away. Bueno lifted herself to game point with a strong forehand volley placement off a Smith down-the-line passing shot. Bueno held on for 2-2.

Smith served an ace to hold for 3-2. Bueno was not daunted. She held at love for 3-3 with a flat backhand passing shot, then broke Smith for 4-3. Margaret had served-and-volleyed before moving back for an overhead as Bueno lifted a lob high into the air. Smith's smash lacked severity, and Bueno drove a forehand crosscourt that forced Margaret into the backcourt. Bueno came in and Smith missed a backhand pass. The net had been taken away from her. The match seemed to be slipping away as well.

Bueno moved to 5-3 at the cost of only one point. In concluding that game, she was letter perfect. The Brazilian charged into the net behind her serve, made a solid, deep volley, and knew where Margaret was going with the passing shot before Smith did. Bueno was on top of the net for a scintillating forehand volley winner. Smith served to save the match at 3-5, double-faulted to 0-30, and fell behind 15-40, double match point. Bueno lofted another effective lob, forcing Smith to play a soft overhead. Anticipating that response, Bueno moved in and played a backhand half volley approach from mid-court.

The ball floated high over the net but Smith was too stunned to react. She stood there deep in the court, frozen, realizing she had no chance to reach the ball. Bueno had hit a nearly impossible shot at match point to prevail 6-4, 7-9, 6-3. In collecting the last four games in a row, Bueno had won sixteen of nineteen points. Her streak to the finish line was reminiscent of her Forest Hills victory over Smith the year before. Bueno was the Wimbledon champion for the third time, and had never been better.

As the eloquent David Gray wrote in *The Guardian*, "Miss Bueno was scoring points with capricious ease. The Brazilian spent points as wastefully as ever, but in the crisis of the match she invariably found it possible to produce luxurious quantities of shots which were rich and imaginative, graceful and deadly. She was the more effective server, she did not miss a smash and, in the recollections of even the oldest members, no woman has hit so many beautiful and piercing forehand volleys. She stirred the Centre Court as she did in the first dazzling days of her royalty."

EPILOGUE

Later that summer, Bueno underscored her status as the best player in the world by winning Forest Hills for the second straight year. In the final, she routed the capable American Carole Graebner 6-1, 6-0. Smith—who was beaten only twice all season—was ousted in three sets by Susman in the round of sixteen. The Australian had captured the Australian and French Championships but Bueno had taken the two most important titles in tennis by coming through at the All England Club and Forest Hills. She had lost a significant meeting to Smith in Paris, but had gathered the two prizes she valued the most. It was her most productive season.

The following year, Smith was leading Bueno 5-2 in the third set of the Australian Championships final when the Brazilian had to retire with an injury. Smith went on to win Wimbledon by taking Bueno 6-4, 7-5 in a well-played final. She also took the U.S. Championships with a final-round win over Billie Jean Moffitt. Her lone Grand Slam defeat was in Paris, where she lost the final to the meticulous back-court play of Turner. Smith was nearly invincible across that season, winning fifty-eight matches in a row, and capturing eighteen tournaments during the year.

Bueno, hampered severely that year by a knee injury, underwent surgery. She was not the player she had been in 1964, but the following year she was revitalized. In the 1966 Wimbledon, Smith and Bueno were seeded first and second again. Bueno moved as expected to the final but Smith was ousted by Billie Jean Moffitt King, who had married in the autumn of 1965. King beat Bueno for the title.

The Brazilian was in peak form at Forest Hills, winning the U.S. Championship for the fourth and final time, capturing her last Grand Slam championship. In the final, she was down 0-2 in the first set against the determined Texan Nancy Richey. From that juncture, Bueno's virtuosity was too much for her doubles partner, with whom she had won at Wimbledon two months earlier. Bueno soared to a 6-3, 6-1 victory. She was not yet twenty-seven when she collected that crown with bright sequences of freewheeling shotmaking. It seemed entirely possible that Bueno would celebrate another five years in the upper echelons of the game.

In fact, she would no longer play at that level. Beginning in 1967, she was hindered by a wide assortment of injuries. The primary problem for Bueno was her arm. That year, she lost in the round of sixteen at Wimbledon to the rapidly rising American Rosie Casals. She withdrew from the U.S. National Championships at Forest Hills, where she was seeded sixth. The pain was persistent near her shoulder. Bueno was drifting out of tennis, much to the dismay of her large legion of admirers.

The following year, she did play respectably in the majors. King defeated her in the quarterfinals of the first French Open. Richey beat her in the same round at Wimbledon. At Forest Hills, she performed better than she had for a long while. At that initial U.S. Open, she was seeded fifth. In the quarterfinals, she upset the No. 4 seed Margaret Smith Court 7-5, 2-6, 6-3—their last meeting of consequence. Maintaining that form in her semifinal session with King, Bueno took the first set before bowing 3-6, 6-4, 6-2. She was ranked in the top five in the world for the year.

The pain in her arm persisted. Bueno's career was essentially over. She did make what amounted to a sentimental comeback in 1976 and 1977, when she was in her late thirties, but the majestic match playing qualities were gone. Her comeback was brief, although it must have been worth her while since fans greeted her appearances with genuine warmth. Bueno remained a powerful presence on the tennis stage, even if her skills and speed had been diminished.

Smith was another story. She continued her complete domination of the Australian Championships, extending her streak to seven consecutive titles in 1966. In 1967, Smith married Barry Court, and she pondered retirement for a while. By 1968, with Open Tennis a reality, Margaret Smith Court was not content to rest on her laurels. She turned twenty-six in the middle of that year. She had not realized all of her ambitions, and was determined to come back to the courts triumphantly, sharing the victories with her husband, who joined her on the road and provided much encouragement. Barry Court wanted his wife to enjoy her tennis, and she did.

The first year of the open game was lukewarm for Margaret. She was shy of her best as she reacquainted herself with the rigors of match play. Not present for the French Open, she was seeded second at Wimbledon behind King, appearing for the first time on the draw as Mrs. B. M. Court. In the quarterfinals, she fell surprisingly to countrywoman Judy Tegart 4-6, 8-6, 6-1. She won the U.S. Nationals over Bueno, but the Brazilian retaliated in the quarterfinals of the U.S. Open. Court took her place, however, among the top five in the world despite her lackluster showings in the two foremost tournaments.

In 1969, she had one of her greatest seasons, sweeping three of the four major championships, losing her lone "Big Four" match to the British left-hander Ann Jones in the semifinals of Wimbledon. At the age of twenty-seven, she had already captured a total of sixteen major singles titles.

There was much more in store for this woman of quiet dignity and high ambitions.

CHAPTER ELEVEN

Rod Laver *vs.* Tony Roche

AUSTRALIAN OPEN, SEMIFINAL, JANUARY 25, 1969

At the peak of his powers, Laver was confronted by a tenacious countryman. They fought ferociously through a long afternoon in debilitating heat.

PROLOGUE

Very few players in the annals of tennis have earned such universal respect and admiration as the Australian, Rod Laver. A somewhat sickly child, he grew up on his father's cattle ranch in Queensland. Left-handed and low key, he became an explosive competitor who expressed his personality through the inspiration of his inventive shotmaking. A champion capable of winning on any surface, he established himself as only the second man to win the Grand Slam (the other was Don Budge) when, in 1962, he seized the four major championships of Australia, France, Great Britain and the United States. The press and the players called him "The Rocket."

Laver was twenty-four when he completed that run. He had shown extraordinary determination when the big points of a match were being contested. Laver's pattern of play was appealingly different from most left-handers. He did not rely too heavily on his serve. His game involved mastering all the shots. He could win his share of points with cleverly directed kick and slice serves, pulling his opponents wide in both the deuce and advantage courts, then punching irretrievable volleys into open spaces. But what distinguished Laver from most of the competition was his versatility off the ground. He ushered in heavy topspin long before the arrival of Bjorn Borg, but Laver did more damage, in many ways, with both the forehand and the backhand than the Swede could deliver.

The hallmark of his fully rounded game was the passing shot.

A relatively small man at 5'8," he moved swiftly and surely, with exemplary footwork. Even when he was on the run, he could drive the ball past his opponents with astonishing force and accuracy, demoralizing them with counterattacking instincts. Furthermore, Laver would tantalize his rivals with his cleverly concealed under-spin lobs off the backhand. He probed and picked his rivals apart astutely. In short, Laver had the entire package, including an unflappable temperament.

Laver was, however, a habitual risk taker who had his share of off days. He played daringly and almost defiantly, always looking for new ways to win rather than merely avoiding a loss. He took his chances sensibly, seeming to balance his tactics between percentage and possibility. In his 1962 Grand Slam season, he moved in and out of precarious positions throughout the four majors. He started his venture smoothly at the Australian Championships, but then was forced into three exacting five-set struggles at the French Championships in Paris.

Down match point in the fourth set against countryman Marty Mulligan, Laver escaped and won 6-2 in the fifth. Another Australian (and fellow left-hander) Neale Fraser pushed The Rocket to 7-5 in the fifth set of the semifinals. In the final, he trailed two sets to love against future doubles partner Roy Emerson, but salvaged that one 3-6, 2-6, 6-3, 9-7, 6-2. At Wimbledon, Laver climbed much closer toward the top of his game and lost only one set in seven matches, crushing Mulligan 6-2, 6-2, 6-1, in the final. And then at Forest Hills, Laver surpassed himself, winning against Emerson in a four-set final.

After that historic Slam, Laver turned professional. His rookie season of 1963 was inevitably a rude awakening. He had graduated with honors from the amateur game, but the brigade of seasoned professionals—ranging from Rosewall to Gonzales—sent him back to the classroom. The level of play was higher across the board. By 1964, Laver had made the improvements, and he was unofficially the best player in the world again right up to the emergence of Open Tennis in 1968. The previous year, Laver had returned with the professionals for an all-pro event at Wimbledon, and had won it without much

Rod Laver

suspense. He had also taken the U.S. Pro Championships three of four years between 1964 and 1967.

When Laver, Rosewall, Gonzales and company were permitted at last to play the major championships, Rod was indisputably the man to beat. He lost to Rosewall in the first open tournament at Bournemouth, England, in April 1968, and fell again to his Australian com-

Tony Roche

his win over Roche. In the final, The Rocket coasted against a passive Gimeno and came away a 6-3, 6-4, 7-5 winner to capture the first of the four majors.

EPILOGUE

Four months later, Laver set his sights on Paris and the French Open. He came close to making a second-round exit when he faced his countryman Dick Crealy, a streaky player who took the first two sets of their meeting. But Laver was the beneficiary of some good luck again. After the third set, the match was delayed until the following morning. A new day provided the opportunity to put the finishing touches on a 3-6, 7-9, 6-2, 6-2, 6-4 victory.

Thereafter, Laver was unstoppable on the clay. He dropped the first sets of his quarterfinal and semifinal contests with Gimeno and Tom Okker, but never looked like he would give further ground. In the final, reversing the 1968 result, Laver took Rosewall apart 6-4, 6-3, 6-4. He would say later of that victory, "From a sustained standpoint, my game was elevated against Kenny to the biggest peak I ever reached on clay. Once in a while you might play five games where you go bang, bang, bang, and all the shots go in and you just can't miss. But then you come back to your senses. That day against Kenny, I kept it up for three sets."

Two down, two remaining. Laver was half way to winning a second Grand Slam. He was favored by a larger margin at Wimbledon than he was in Paris. But the second round was again a menacing time for the Australian maestro. He trailed Indian Davis Cupper Premjit Lall 3-6, 4-6, 3-3 before sweeping fifteen consecutive games for the match. Future titlist Stan Smith drew Laver into another five-set test in the round of sixteen, but it was his semifinal with a scintillating Arthur Ashe that everyone would remember.

Ashe was sprinkling the court with one winner after another off his dazzling backhand, employing that stroke with awesome potency, giving Laver little chance to respond. As Laver reflected afterward, "I could only hope Arthur would hit earth at some stage because he was playing unbelievably well. He was thrashing the ball past me. He almost outplayed himself."

Ultimately, Ashe did just that. He found it impossible to maintain his ferocious and relatively error-free brand of play, and Laver calmly kept on track. The ginger-haired Australian got the job done 2-6, 6-2, 9-7, 6-0 answering Ashe's soaring first set three times.

In the final, Laver was locked at one set all, but down 1-4 in the third, against the best grass court player of them all, John Newcombe. Had Newcombe managed to move on and establish a two-sets-to-one lead, he might well have won. But Laver caught him, took the third, and came away a 6-4, 5-7, 6-4, 6-4 winner.

He was closing in tight on his target now, only one major championship away from the Grand Slam. He would be back on the lawns of Forest Hills, at the U.S. Open, where he had completed the Slam seven years earlier. In the round of sixteen, Laver came upon a player who would beat him one year later on the same court, a man who possessed some of the purest strokes in modern tennis, Dennis Ralston. Ralston took a two-sets-to-one lead into the locker room for the ten-minute intermission. Laver, during the break, listened intently to some words of wisdom from his comrades Stolle and Emerson.

They told him he was tossing the ball too low on his serve, urging him to make an adjustment and raise his first serve percentage. Laver obliged, and ran away from Ralston in the last two sets, coming home with a 6-4, 4-6, 4-6, 6-2, 6-3 victory. In the quarterfinals, Emerson provided stern opposition, but after a slow start Laver gradually gained the upper hand and prevailed 4-6, 8-6, 13-11, 6-4.

Laver now took on the defending champion Ashe. His versatility was too much for the American. Laver succeeded 8-6, 6-3, 14-12, propelling himself into the final. He was only a single match away from his goal. His opponent was a rugged serve-and-volleyer who had been his most formidable rival all year long. The No. 3 seed, Tony Roche, had achieved a significant win over the still formidable Pancho Gonzales, and reached the final by ousting Newcombe, 8-6, in the fifth set. He had come this far to reach his first Grand Slam tournament final since losing to Laver at Wimbledon the year before. Roche was eager for revenge this time around.

Roche had every reason to believe in his chances. He held a winning record over The Rocket for the year, defeating the game's greatest player on no fewer than five occasions. He knew he was viewed with high regard by Laver, who was not fond of playing fellow lefthanders. Why was Roche such a difficult puzzle for Laver to solve? Newcombe had observed, "One factor was the way Tony served so well into Rod's body. The other factor was that in 1969 Tony Roche was playing bloody good tennis."

Roche took the first set narrowly as both players moved carefully on the wet grass court. They were competing on a Monday afternoon in front of a half-empty stadium at Forest Hills.

At one stage, there were six consecutive service breaks. Roche then served for the first set at 6-5. Laver struck back, only to fall away again. Roche finally took it, deservedly, 9-7.

Laver felt that the court was getting increasingly slick, so he asked tournament director Billy Talbert if he could put on spikes. He said afterward, "Billy had told me he wanted me to start the match without the spikes but he had no problem with my switching to them later if I felt I needed them."

Laver changed to the spikes at the start of the second set, and it was clear that his mobility was enhanced. He began making his customary on the run passing shots. He took the second set at the cost of only the sixth game. After the first game of the third, there was a thirty-one minute rain delay, but Laver was not going to be halted by anything or anyone, neither the elements nor his friend Roche. Laver devised a 7-9, 6-1, 6-2, 6-2 victory. His second Grand Slam was a far more impressive feat than his first because he had faced the leading players in his field rather than only the best of the amateurs as he had in 1962.

A self-deprecating Laver said in 1989, "It's not as tough fronting up a second time. I had it all going for me. I just didn't feel I had that huge amount of pressure. I figured all I could do was prepare. When you do that, you are fortunate to play your best tennis. As Tony Trabert says, it's amazing how lucky you get when you prepare. I think there is a lot of truth in that."

Newcombe, one of the game's sharpest analysts as well as an all-time great player, says of Laver's 1969 campaign, "Rocket read the battle plan perfectly that year. He knew when to change and when not to change his game plan. I really admired him for coming up with a slight but important tactical change to keep us off balance."

As Laver summed it up himself, "Winning a second Grand Slam changed my whole life. But I always get brought back to reality when I remember the matches I lost very convincingly. I don't put myself in any category that says I'm the best that ever lived. I really don't. There are so many ups and downs in a career, but it's nice to know I've been put down as one of the top players of all time."

After 1969, Laver slowly receded from his peak. He was thirty-one by the time he won Forest Hills to seal his second Slam, so a decline was expected. He continued as a major force in the sport and was a prolific tournament winner in 1970 and 1971. In fact, he had a superb run indoors during the winter and spring of 1971. By winning thirteen matches in a head-to-head competition called the Tennis Champions Classic against Newcombe, Roche, Ashe, Ralston, and company, Laver earned a total of $160,000, a record sum in those days.

Roche, meanwhile, remained a hard luck fellow. In 1970, he made it back to the final of Forest Hills, but lost to Rosewall, the same man he had halted at Wimbledon two years earlier. He had won the U.S. Pro Championships in Boston earlier that summer with a five-set win over Laver, so his failure to come through at Forest Hills was a deep disappointment.

Roche remained an enormous success in doubles alongside New-combe, with whom he won Wimbledon five times. But in singles he never did collect another Grand Slam title after taking the French Championships as an amateur in 1966. In 1969, despite several victories over Laver, he lost the two that mattered the most in Brisbane and New York. He held the distinction of being a premier rival for the great Laver when the Rocket was at his peak, but did not do himself full justice. By 1971, he started having severe problems with his elbow. He went to visit a faith healer in the Philippines and had a recovery of sorts—reaching the Wimbledon semifinals in 1975 before losing in five sets to Ashe—but this was not the Roche of 1968 to 1970.

Tony Roche will be remembered above all for his showdowns

with Laver in 1969, his distinguished final round appearance against his countryman at Forest Hills, and his extraordinary match against Rod at Brisbane.

Laver had no tougher test all year in his Grand Slam quest.

CHAPTER TWELVE

Pancho Gonzales *vs.* Charlie Pasarell

WIMBLEDON, FIRST ROUND, JUNE 24/25, 1969

The volatile Gonzales and the quietly driven Pasarell put on an heroic display of fast-court tennis in a Wimbledon classic that took two days to compete.

PROLOGUE

Puerto Rico's Charlie Pasarell was a teaching professional's perfect model of how to play the game of tennis. His strokes were taken straight out of the book. He hit the ball cleanly and precisely off both sides. His forehand was his most penetrating shot and an opponent served to that side at his own peril. He was authoritative at the net, punching his volleys sharply, moving nimbly back under lobs to employ his flawless overhead.

Pasarell was not merely a flamboyant stylist, which might have been considered a genetic quality because his father and mother were both singles champions of Puerto Rico and his brother was ranked in the American top forty. Charlie was a competitor who agonized over every point. After big matches in the major tournaments, he would frequently be heard replaying each critical shot in excruciating detail to his colleagues. He was known among the people in his profession as an uncommonly decent man.

In the middle 1960s, he was among a promising cast of gifted Americans expected to perform effectively in the big events. Pasarell was the classic fast-court competitor who played his best tennis on grass. With three of the four Grand Slam events held on that surface during his prime, he was prepared. Critics and fellow competitors were in agreement regarding Pasarell. It was a matter of marrying talent with temperament. He had the former, but seemed to lack the latter on too many occasions.

Be that as it may, Pasarell had moved to the top of the rankings in the United States as an amateur in 1967. His picture appeared on the cover of the U.S.L.T.A. yearbook the following spring. He looked convincingly like a world champion, reaching for a backhand volley with his weight moving forward, his knees bent, his arms extended. Pasarell's 1967 rise to No. 1 in his country featured two essential achievements—he defeated his close friend and revered rival Arthur Ashe to win the U.S. Indoor Championships and he toppled the defending champion Manuel Santana in the first round of Wimbledon. No one before had ever upset the title-holder in an opening round men's match in the history of the tournament.

Pasarell was as dedicated a craftsman as anyone in his field. In many ways, he probably cared too much, coming down hard on himself after losses, remembering every missed opportunity with complete clarity. Pasarell was still an amateur when Open Tennis started in the spring of 1968. He was clearly one of the "dangerous floaters" in the draw at Wimbledon that summer. In the second round on Centre Court, he took a two-sets-to-one lead over the No. 2 seed Ken Rosewall, and led 2-0 in the final set. But he was beaten 6-3 in the fifth.

As a veteran of the American Davis Cup team, Pasarell—a keen student of the game— had profited from the wisdom of some excellent coaching over the years. One of his mentors was Pancho Gonzales. Gonzales had delighted in sharing his deep knowledge of the game with the younger American players of the 1960s before the advent of the Open Era.

To most of these young men—Arthur Ashe and Cliff Richey were others in that camp—Gonzales was a hero. They had grown up watching and reading about him. They recognized in Gonzales much of what they aspired to be themselves. He embodied the ineffable characteristics of a champion. Pancho's advice on strategy and tactics was always welcomed.

When Open Tennis was introduced in the spring of 1968, Gonzales's role among his countrymen was altered. After nineteen years away from the major championships, he was permitted at last to compete again in those events. In the twilight of his career, he was rejuvenated by the chance to appear again at Roland Garros, Wimbledon and Forest Hills.

Gonzales was perhaps the greatest tennis player never to have won Wimbledon. He had last played there when he was twenty-one in 1949. Seeded second, he bowed in the fourth round. After Forest Hills later that summer, he turned professional. In the inaugural open season, he was a surprise semifinalist at the French Open. At Wimbledon, seeded eighth, he fell in an early round to the Russian Alex Metreveli, a future finalist. At the U.S. Open, Gonzales was in strikingly good form, ousting the second-seeded Tony Roche to reach the quarterfinals, then losing an elegant battle with the Dutchman Tom Okker.

As the 1969 Wimbledon approached, Gonzales and the other leading players realized that Rod Laver was the putative favorite. Gonzales wanted to make amends for his disappointing return in 1968. As for Pasarell, he hoped to give the Centre Court audience a demonstration of his grass-court skill.

When the draw for the 1969 Wimbledon was released, Pasarell found himself slated to play one of the game's legendary figures, a fellow American sixteen years his senior named Gonzales.

THE MATCH

The two Americans walked onto Centre Court at nearly 6:30 p.m. on Tuesday, June 24, 1969. They looked like a pair of movie stars taking the stage. In the *London Times*, Rex Bellamy described Pasarell deftly. "Splay-footed and broad-shouldered, he has the shambling gait of some Western heroes. He walks with a drawl, arms swinging menacingly at his sides as if itching for a challenge to a fast draw."

Shifting his attention to Gonzales, Bellamy wrote, "Gonzales is one of the few personalities in Wimbledon history who can dominate the Centre Court instead of letting it dominate him. The man smolders with character. There are dark, brooding depths in his intense concentration. He has the loose-limbed ease of the natural athlete. He has the mannerisms of the well-rehearsed actor treading a familiar stage—the fingers of his left hand flicking away the sweat and hitching his sodden shirt back to his shoulders."

As the combatants waged a service battle in the fading early evening light, it was clear that the opening set would be settled by a single break. Gonzales and Pasarell earnestly went about their business, comfortable on the fast, green surface, producing their effortless moves with graceful efficiency. They were searching for that one opportunity to break. In the forty-sixth game of a marathon set, Pasarell finally broke Gonzales to seal the first set 24-22. Sets like this one led to the adoption of the tiebreaker the following year.

Gonzales wanted the match postponed at that point because of darkness, but his request for a suspension of play was denied. Infuriated by the rejection, distressed by the loss of the long opening set, the forty-one-year-old seemed distracted in the second set. His concentration completely broken, his rhythm gone on serve, Gonzales collected only a single game. With Pasarell up two sets to love, the match was halted. Gonzales had banged his racket against the back of the umpire's chair when he left the court after two hours and eighteen minutes. He was booed by an audience largely unsympathetic to his actions. It was nearly 9 p.m. as the players departed in the darkness.

They returned on Wednesday afternoon in bright sunlight. The third set had the tone and texture of the first. Both men were unbreakable on serve and the urgency for Gonzales grew with every point. He was resuming this conflict at two sets to love down and could afford no lapses. The older American held his delivery fifteen consecutive times in that third set, but Pasarell assiduously tended his own pattern of play.

In the thirtieth game, serving to save the set for the eleventh time, Pasarell missed five straight first services. He opened that game with a double fault, then served another for 15-40. When Gonzales sent a stinging forehand passing shot down the line to force an errant backhand volley from Pasarell, he had the break, and with it the set.

The Centre Court crowd of nearly fifteen thousand showered warm applause upon Gonzales. He was still trailing two sets to one, but the bright light of the new day was giving him cause for optimism. Both players had chances to break early in the fourth. Despite three double faults, Pasarell escaped two break points to hold for 1-1. Gonzales connected with fourteen first serves in a row in the following game, but still needed to cast aside a break point himself.

Pasarell seemed certain of himself and his chances as he served at 3-4. In that critical game, however, he faltered. He missed five of six first serves. At 30-30, Gonzales struck. He dinked a backhand passing shot crosscourt, forcing Pasarell to play an ineffectual backhand volley down the line. Gonzales was in place and rolled a forehand passing shot crosscourt for a winner to reach set point. Surprised and apprehensive, Pasarell double faulted, his second serve hitting the net.

Gonzales easily served out the set, holding in the ninth game without missing a single first serve. Pancho had moved his delivery from corner to corner throughout the set, keeping Pasarell off guard. His depth, placement and variety were awesome. Along the way, he hit his target with twenty-nine of thirty-four first serves, an astonishing percentage in light of his immense power.

With the Centre Court fans applauding him generously, Gonzales had brought himself back to two sets all. He had left his early misfortunes behind him. He seemed fully capable of completing a victory.

Pasarell still had the advantage of youth. Moreover, he would be serving first in the fifth set. Pasarell made the most of it. He moved through the early games of the final set with an air of confidence, perhaps buoyed by the sight of Gonzales leaning wearily on his racket between points. In the first six games of the fifth set, neither man was close to a break point. In that stretch, Gonzales conceded only two points in three service games while Pasarell allowed his adversary only five.

At 3-3, in the seventh game, Gonzales applied pressure with a rush of energy. He reached 15-30 with his favorite tactic, following his backhand chip return into the forecourt to challenge the charging Pasarell. The veteran's return was low and effective. Pasarell volleyed up. Gonzales was perfectly positioned for a backhand volley winner. Pasarell was pushed to deuce in that game, but he held for 4-3 when another Gonzales chip-and-charge failed. Pasarell punched a forehand volley calmly past Pancho for 4-3.

At 3-4, Gonzales was debilitated. At 40-30, he produced a weak first serve and then surredered the point with an off-target backhand first volley wide down the line. Pasarell was two points away from serving for the match. But Gonzales once again summoned hidden strength, serving deep to the Pasarell backhand to elicit a mistake, then cracking an ace to reach 4-4.

Pasarell seemed unperturbed. He held for 5-4 with a safely guided inside-out smash well out of his opponent's reach. Serving in the tenth game, Gonzales was in deep trouble. On the first point, he re-treated for a smash as Pasarell lofted a fine lob off his backhand side. Gonzales mishit the overhead off the top of his frame for 0-15. Pasarell made it 0-30 when his forehand passing shot clipped the net cord and provoked an error from Gonzales. Then Pasarell played a solid, chipped backhand return and Gonzales's volley was long.

It was 4-5, 0-40 in the fifth. Gonzales was triple match point down. He moved in behind his second serve, played a percentage volley cross-court and Pasarell went once more for the lob with his back-hand. The shot was long. Gonzales added pace to his next first serve deep to the backhand to force Pasarell to return long. It was 30-40. Another first serve from Gonzales was answered by a fine backhand return from Pasarell. Gonzales bent low for the forehand volley and placed it deep down the line. Pasarell lobbed over Gonzales and the older man turned and scampered after it. If the ball had landed in-bounds, the match would have been over. It was inches out. Deuce. Gonzales served-and-volleyed, played one cautious overhead, then put the second one away emphatically. He was at game point. Pasarell re-covered to deuce, two points away from victory again. Pasarell made another testing return but Gonzales went behind him with a firm backhand volley down the line to lure his foe into another mistake. When Pasarell missed a return on the next point, Gonzales had held almost miraculously for 5-5, saving three match points in the process, earning a sustained ovation from an appreciative audience.

Pasarell may have been troubled by Gonzales's bold stand, but the twenty-five-year-old did not show it. At 5-5, 15-30, he seemed at his ri-val's mercy. Gonzales stepped around his backhand for a forehand re-verse crosscourt passing shot. The shot missed narrowly. Pasarell held for 6-5. An emboldened Pasarell went after Gonzales full force again. He stepped up his pace to coax Gonzales into a backhand volley error for 0-15. He took the net away from the older man with a well-placed lob, then closed in tight for a forehand volley winner, making it 0-30.

When Gonzales popped his forehand volley up meekly on the following point, Pasarell unhesitatingly drove a flat backhand cross-court passing shot into the clear. Gonzales stood at triple match point against him for the second time. He served deep to the backhand, placed his volley deep, and clipped his overhead confidently for a placement to make it 15-40. He served deep to the backhand again, directing his volley to Pasarell's weaker backhand wing. Pasarell went down the line with a passing shot, keeping the ball tantalizingly low. Gonzales read it early, opened his racket face, and deposited a delicate, angled forehand drop volley winner for 30-40. Swinging with deceptive speed, Gonzales then released a strong first serve to Pasarell's backhand. The return was well out. Deuce.

Gonzales advanced to game point before Pasarell responded with a superbly struck forehand passing shot crosscourt. Deuce for the second time. Pasarell made a first-rate low forehand return off a second serve. Gonzales displayed his considerable courage, executing another extraordinary forehand drop volley for a winner. At game point for the second time, Gonzales came through with a classic, serve-and-volley combination, then put away his second volley with cool efficiency. It was 6-6. The crowd gave the older American another rousing round of applause.

The younger man had endured a pair of humbling setbacks. Gonzales had twice held from triple match point down, saving six match points. Pasarell met that stern challenge with perhaps his best service game of the match. He held at love, did not miss a first serve, and finished off that game with an ace for 7-6.

The players changed ends of the court and took only twenty seconds as they toweled off and sipped their refreshments. The tiebreaker would be introduced to the Grand Slam events the following year at Forest Hills. Wimbledon would begin with the tie-break in 1971. But as Gonzales and Pasarell came down the stretch in a record-breaking encounter on Centre Court, they did not sit down as they moved from one side of the court to the other. Television had not established that imperative yet. Gonzales gathered himself for another crisis. He served at 6-7, missed an approach for 0-15, then collected four points in a row with calm authority. He was back to 7-7. His problems were not behind him. Pasarell held at the cost of only a single point for 8-7, concluding that game with an ace wide to Pancho's forehand. Gonzales glided to 40-15, was caught at deuce, then reached game point for the third time. Pasarell connected with a backhand chip return cross-court for a winner. On the next point, he ran around his backhand for a forehand passing shot.

For the seventh time in three different service games, Gonzales was down match point. On the previous six, he had missed only one first serve. This time around, he missed another first serve. Nevertheless, he came up with a second serve of remarkable depth. Pasarell could not attack it. Gonzales closed in for an aggressive first volley. Pasarell had no alternative. He went back to his trusted lob off the backhand. His touch was gone. The ball was out by a wide margin.

On the next two points, Gonzales took command at the net again. Pasarell lifted a lob long, then another. It was 8-8. Pasarell must have been dismayed, but he held easily for 9-8. Gonzales served to save the match for the fifth time at 8-9. He found the range with all five of his first serves, coming up with three service winners, making it 9-9 by drawing Pasarell wide to the forehand with the serve, setting up a forehand volley winner. He conceded only a single point in that game.

At 9-9, Pasarell seemed to buckle. He served a double fault for 0-15. Gonzales made him stretch low for a forehand volley, which he punched crosscourt. Pasarell poked the ball wide. It was 0-30. Tearing a page out of Pasarell's playbook, Gonzales lobbed crosscourt off the backhand. Pasarell was caught off guard. The shot landed safely in the corner. Now it was 0-40. Gonzales waved his arms in a brief display of animation. He then guided a backhand return down the line. Pasarell could not handle the low forehand volley.

Gonzales had broken at love and was set to serve for the match. A deep second serve provoked Pasarell into a backhand error for 15-0. Gonzales put away an overhead off a midcourt lob for 30-0. Pasarell charged in behind his return of serve but Gonzales placed a backhand volley that went behind his foe for a winner. He then held at love as Pasarell's last futile lob off the backhand landed long. Gonzales had connected on fifty-seven of sixty-nine first serves in his triumphant fifth set.

With the capacity Centre Court audience now standing to deliver a roar of acclamation, the victor stood for a moment in the sunshine, contemplating an incredible two-day turnaround. When he left the court with an understandably despondent Pasarell, Gonzales had succeeded 22-24, 1-6, 16-14, 6-3, 11-9 in a record-breaking five hours and twelve minutes. It was the longest match in Wimbledon history.

Two hours and fifty-four minutes of that monumental effort had taken place on the second day. After saving the seven match points and twice holding from 0-40, triple match point down, Gonzales had collected twelve of the last thirteen points to take the match.

"His was one of the greatest individual achievements in tennis or any other sport," wrote Bellamy in the *London Times*. "This is a man who was born to greatness and did not scorn the gift."

Lance Tingay of London's *Daily Telegraph* put Gonzales lucidly into perspective. He wrote, "Ricardo Gonzales, who has never won the singles at Wimbledon and almost certainly never will, yesterday put himself into the annals of the championships as predominately as any champion ever did. Despite its heroic standards, this was only a first round match. It is one of the tragedies of lawn tennis that Wimbledon never saw Gonzales at his peak."

On the same afternoon that Gonzales celebrated his comeback against Pasarell, Rod Laver found himself down two sets to love against the Indian Premjit Lall. Laver was destined to win his second Grand Slam. Every match he played was given close scrutiny by the cognoscenti. But even this ultimate champion seemed forgotten in the glow of Pancho's timeless triumph.

EPILOGUE

Gonzales reached the round of sixteen of that tournament without difficulty, but then he bowed to Ashe in a well-played four-set skirmish. Later in 1969, he strung together four remarkable matches in a row to win the Howard Hughes Open in Las Vegas. He knocked out John Newcombe 6-1, 6-2, ousted Rosewall, bested Stan Smith and then routed Ashe 6-0, 6-2, 6-4 in the final.

In January, 1970, as he approached forty-two, the astounding Amer-

Charlie Pasarell and Pancho Gonzales

ican defeated Laver in five-set match at New York's Madison Square Garden, a victory achieved only four months after Laver had won his Grand Slam. He stopped Laver again that spring. On his best days, he was still good enough to beat anyone in the world. At Wembley, outside London in November 1970, he stopped Smith again, saving seven match points in another display of grit under pressure. When he was three months away from his forty-fourth birthday, Gonzales became the oldest player in the Open Era to win a singles tournament. He finished the season among the top ten in his country.

Gonzales passed away in 1995 at sixty-seven. He had led a tumultuous life, marrying six times, twice to the same woman. One of his wives was Rita Agassi, the sister of Andre Agassi, with whom he had a son. To the end, he was a man of many moods and inner conflicts.

Asked in the late 1980s how the champions of his time might have fared against the leading players who followed him, Gonzales replied, "If you took the athlete of my time in the 1950s and played him in 1987 under the same circumstances, he would be much stronger, play much harder, and therefore he would play better. If you took the player of 1987 and sent him back to the middle fifties, he wouldn't play any better than the players who were around then."

No one who observed Gonzales in a major tournament would scoff at his thesis. By performing so skillfully in his early forties and upending so many leading players when he was well past his prime, Gonzales demonstrated that he was certainly among the all-time great champions in his sport. Does he belong up there in a class with Kramer, Budge, Sampras or Federer? There are always those who, perhaps nostalgically, would say yes.

Charlie Pasarell is one player who will testify that Gonzales must be considered among the most fearsome competitors ever. Pasarell, who became a prominent tournament director, is no doubt still replaying his match with Gonzales and still wishing he could find a way to alter the result.

CHAPTER THIRTEEN

Billie Jean Moffitt King *vs.*
Margaret Smith Court

WIMBLEDON, FINAL, JULY 3, 1970

*Both champions were hindered by injuries, but went gamely about their business
in the most hard fought of their many struggles with each other.*

PROLOGUE

The world of women's tennis was irrevocably changed by the arrival
of Billie Jean Moffitt in the early 1960s. Full of bounce and brio, dynamic and demonstrative, she wasted no time in establishing herself
not only as a great player, but also as a powerful personality. It was
apparent from the outset of her ascendancy that she would leave some
lasting impressions in her sport, both on and off the court.

Coming out of California, she broke into the top five in the United
States in 1960. Billie Jean had been brought up in a religious Bible-
reading, middle-class family. As a young girl, she wanted to do mis-
sionary work. Her father was a fireman, and her brother Randy became a pitcher for the San Francisco Giants. She was invited to play
tennis at a local country club by a friend who told her she had to
wear white. Her mother made a pair of white shorts and her friend
lent her a racket. When she heard about free tennis lessons at a local
park, she saved her allowance until she had $8, with which she bought
a tennis racket with violet-colored strings. She later told people that
the moment she owned her own racket, she knew what she was going
to do with her life.

She achieved worldwide prominence. Visiting Wimbledon for the
first time, she took the doubles title alongside Karen Hantze Susman
in 1961. They won it again the next year, when Susman also secured

the singles title. Billie Jean was surely a player of immense promise then, although for two years (1961-62) she had to settle for a No. 3 American ranking behind the veteran Darlene Hard and Susman.

In those years, the intensely competitive American was establishing her serve-and-volley game, refining it, learning to cope with a multitude of highly competent backcourt players who liked the targets she presented to them with her net-charging style. And yet, she precociously imposed her authority in big matches. At the 1962 Wimbledon, she encountered the top-seeded Margaret Smith in the second round. In that setting, she demonstrated how dangerous a player she would become.

Smith swept through the first set, losing only a single game. Moffitt countered to take the second, but the Australian surged to 5-2 in the third with relative ease. At 5-3, the favorite served for the match and reached 30-15, only two points away from the triumph. Moffitt was not intimidated. She broke back, took four games in a row, and created a major upset with a 1-6, 6-3, 7-5 win. The American entered the quarterfinals where Ann Jones ended her run.

In 1963, Billie Jean reached the final of Wimbledon, the first time she had appeared on her own in the title match of a major event. She toppled both Maria Bueno and Jones to get there, but Smith avenged her 1962 defeat with a 6-3, 6-4 victory. Moffitt was clearly a formidable force in singles, capable of controlling many fast court matches with her aggressive style. For the next few years, though, the achievements of Bueno, Smith, Jones, and Nancy Richey were more consistent.

It all changed for Billie Jean in 1966. She had taken on a new last name. With her huband Larry King, she would establish the groundbreaking World Team Tennis in the 1970s.

She captured her first of three consecutive Wimbledon singles titles that summer, defeating Bueno in the final. In the semifinals, she beat the top-seeded Smith 6-3, 6-3. King had moved to the zenith of her world, finishing the year as the universally acknowledged No. 1 female competitor.

Her 1967 season was even better. At Wimbledon, she won the title without the loss of a set, cutting down Jones in the final. At Forest Hills, she took the championship of her country for the first time, defeating Jones again for the title. When Open Tennis commenced in 1968, King set the pace for the third consecutive season, although her status at the top was seriously challenged. In the semifinals of the French Open, her countrywoman and chief domestic rival Nancy Richey upset her in a three-set semifinal. Richey had made a stirring comeback to eclipse King three months before at New York's Madison Square Garden in a small invitational event. On that occasion— with the two premier Americans meeting for the first time since Richey had taken their last clash at Forest Hills in 1964—Richey trailed 6-4, 5-1 but captured twelve games in a row for the victory, saving a match point along the way. King was not easily stripped of her confidence. She won Wimbledon, coming from behind to oust Jones (who served for the match) in a three-set semifinal. Then she defeated Judy Tegart in a 9-7, 7-5 final. Despite a final-round defeat at the U.S. Open against the big serving Englishwoman Virginia Wade, King held her ground at the top.

Not so in 1969. As Margaret Smith Court displayed her match-playing prowess all through the season—losing only once in the four major events—King had by her standards a lackluster campaign. At the Australian Open, she was soundly beaten by Court 6-4, 6-1 in the final. King lost in the French Open quarterfinals to another accomplished baseliner and two-time former titlist Lesley Bowrey in straight sets. She sought a fourth Wimbledon singles championship in a row, but did not find it, falling in the final against an inspired Jones. With one last opportunity to capture a major crown, King met Richey in a dramatic quarterfinal showdown on the U.S. Open Grandstand court. Richey stopped Billie Jean for the second time at Forest Hills and the third time in a Grand Slam event, winning 6-4, 8-6. Court beat Richey in the final.

After her very productive 1969 season, Court wanted to capture all four major titles in 1970. She made that her mission. Having won nineteen of twenty-four tournaments the previous year, her confidence was at an all-time high. In five matches at the Australian Open, she lost a mere twelve games, defeating Kerry Melville 6-1, 6-3 in the final.

Mrs. Court figured to have more comprehensive tests in Paris on the slow red clay that blunted her big game to some degree. In the second round, she faced future finalist Olga Morozova. Morozova was not a typical clay-court player. She was cut from almost the same cloth as Court, attacking whenever possible, seeking the chance to volley. She nearly toppled the favorite before Court came through 3-6, 8-6, 6-1. The path from there was clear. Not conceding another set the rest of the way, Court beat Germany's elegant Helga Niessen 6-2, 6-4 in the final.

Halfway to her destination, Court came to Wimbledon. She carried with her many memories of hard defeats against talented rivals, losses she believed she could have prevented. Centre Court had been a burdensome place for her to perform in across the years, making her self-conscious at crucial moments, reducing her at times to tentative, makeshift shots. She knew this would be the hardest hurdle. She also realized that her chief adversary on the lawns of the All England Club would very likely be Billie Jean.

They had confronted each other several times that season. Court had beaten King indoors at Dallas and at the U.S. Pro Indoor in Philadelphia. King stopped Court in Sydney, only to lose to Court the next time on hard courts in South Africa. In Durban, King defeated Court. They were the two finest female players in the game; avoiding each other was a virtual impossibility. The rivalry flourished because so little separated them. Adding to Court's challenge was King's affection for the Centre Court surroundings. She was absolutely enamored of the place. She would often go out to the grounds before the start of the tournament and sit in the ghostly shadows, thinking about how much history had been made in that empty arena, knowing she could play better there than anywhere else.

The stage was set for an exhilarating match. Court was halfway to her goal of the Grand Slam. King was primed for her favorite event. The fans anticipated an unforgettable contest.

THE MATCH

Neither the top-seeded Mrs. Court nor the No. 2 seed Mrs. King was unduly troubled en route to their final-round matchup. Court lost a long opening set to No. 8 seed Helga Niessen, but recouped quickly and thoroughly for a 6-8, 6-0, 6-0 quarterfinal victory. In the semi-finals, she ousted the diminutive Californian, Rosie Casals 6-4, 6-1. King, too, was pushed to three sets only once. In her quarterfinal, she trailed the towering Australian Karen Krantzcke. Thereafter, King held the upper hand in a 3-6, 6-3, 6-2 triumph. She followed with a 6-3, 7-5 success against the Frenchwoman Francoise Durr. The two best play-ers had reached the final, with Court striving to win her third Centre Court crown and King hoping to capture her fourth.

Heightening the drama surrounding this occasion was the physical uncertainty of both combatants. Court had taken four injections in the hours leading up to the match to soothe a sprained ankle. She wore a brace for further protection. King was bothered by a bad knee that had lingered for a long time. The two players were in unmistakable pain throughout their struggle and yet they did an honorable job of concealing their ailments and got on with their business at full force. As King would contend later, "I can't see where her ankle was hurting her at all. She was trying for everything. In the heat of the battle you forget about injuries like that."

King practiced what she preached, wincing only on occasion, moving surprisingly well under the circumstances. These were two seasoned professionals giving nothing away, willing to extend them-selves to their limits and seemingly beyond, knowing that the final of Wimbledon is not a time for offering excuses. That attitude was reflected by the length and scope of a tremendous opening set that witnessed King often on the edge of success. Three times—at 5-4, 7-6, and 8-7—she served for it. Court ably denied her every opportunity.

King revealed unexpected vulnerability on the last of those chances. At 8-7, she served a double fault for 15-30. She missed a low backhand first volley on the following point off a trademark stroke from the Australian—a surgically sliced backhand return. King had missed four consecutive first serves in this critical segment of the match, but she finally connected at 15-40. Court was prepared, made a solid return, then lobbed offensively over King. Billie Jean chased it down but could not get the ball back into play. It went to 8-8.

After a sequence of four straight service breaks, both women settled into solid holding patterns. Court held at love for 9-8; King responded

Margaret Smith Court

with a love game of her own for 9-9. Each was successful on three out of four first serves in those games. Both were serving with more sting and better placement now, setting up easier first volleys, taking complete command at the net. They both held to knot the score at 10-10.

The pattern continued. Missing only one first serve again, Court held at love for 11-10. Conceding only one point, King leveled at 11-11 with a magnificent backhand volley winner past a chip-and-charging

Court. Serving at 11-12, King found herself down 30-40, one point away from losing the set. She missed her first serve, but came in behind the second, punched an assertive first volley and opened up the court for a coolly controlled forehand drop volley. Defiantly, King had reached 12-12.

At this stage, Court would not have surprised veteran observers if she had fallen victim to self-doubt, after rescuing herself so persistently every time King served for the set. But the Australian was remarkably composed, almost serene. She held on safely for 13-12.

With King serving, Court moved to 0-40, triple set point after a series of commanding returns. She managed to take the set at last with a backhand crosscourt return that forced King into error. Court had won the set 14-12. The match, however, was a long way from finished. After an early exchange of service breaks at the start of the second set, the two supreme serve-and-volleyers launched another prolonged battle. Court exploited her extraordinary reach at the net and her overhead was a weapon of security. King displayed her superb volleying technique—the best of all the women—and her touch off the backhand was notable as well. Time and again, she exploited the drop shot off that side to lure Court in. King was more creative. Court had the edge as the slightly better percentage player. As King would say many times afterward, "I knew everything Margaret was going to do and could figure out almost every time whether she was going crosscourt or down the line. But that did not mean I could stop her from executing exactly what she wanted."

At 5-6 in the second set, King served for the second time to save the match. She was poised once more under humbling pressure, holding serve with one of her patented backhand drop volleys. Court made it 7-6, exploiting the primary weakness in Billie Jean's game, the forehand return in the deuce court. With King serving at 6-7, 0-30, she was precariously close to making an exit. Court's return was at the American's feet. King managed to make a deep half volley off the backhand. Court tried to come in off her next shot and had King stretching for a forehand volley. King knew she had to spank that volley or the court would be wide open for the Australian. The volley was firm and Court could not handle the pace.

Billie Jean Moffitt King

King had more danger ahead. Court reached match point with a telling backhand volley down the line. King missed her first serve but came in calmly behind a deep second delivery. Court's slice backhand return was unusually high. King's approach volley had too much on it. She held for 7-7.

Although Court marched to 40-0 in the next game, she encountered strong resistance from King. The American collected the next four points to reach break point, but Court hit a high backhand volley winner for deuce. King got to break point for the second time, only to net a routine backhand. Court proceeded to play two solid overheads in succession, holding for 8-7, preventing Billie Jean from serving for the set and altering the pace of the contest.

King—perhaps more worried about her knee—was staying back frequently on first and second serves, but skillfully orchestrating the points and maneuvering Court with precision. Court kept pressing forward, exploiting her reach at the net. She held for 9-8, with five straight first serves finding their mark. King prevailed for 9-9 after coming within two points of defeat.

Court conceded only one point on her way to a 10-9 lead. King served to save the match for the sixth time. Court went briskly to work, reaching 15-40, double match point with one of her teasing slice backhand down the line passing shots. King's response was decisive. She produced a perfect inside-out overhead winner, then released a stinging service winner to Court's backhand side.

King had saved two match points in this game, three altogether. But her woes were not over. On the next point, King played one of her backhand drop shots to force Court in, then lobbed over the Australian. King followed with another drop shot, but this time Court caught her with a scathing forehand down the line. At match point for the fourth time, Court attacked. King replied with a courageous backhand down-the-line pass, clipping the sideline.

The Centre Court audience was exhausted by the determination and ingenuity of two all-time greats. They showered applause on Billie Jean as she stood once more at deuce. Moving in swiftly for a low ball on her forehand, Court passed King with sidespin. It was match point for the fifth time. King attacked Court's backhand and covered the attempted pass. She delivered a forehand volley winner crosscourt. It was deuce for the third time.

Court must have been agonized by her missed opportunities, but she did not reveal even a trace of apprehension. She raced to her right for a forehand passing shot which grazed the net-cord, forcing King into a volleying error. Down a match point for the sixth time,

King stayed back behind her second serve. Court sensibly chipped and charged, coming in on the American's backhand side. King drove the ball crosscourt. The shot went lamely into the net. Court was a worthy 14-12, 11-9 winner after two hours and twenty-seven minutes. It was a record-breaking afternoon on a number of fronts. The Court-King clash was the longest ever women's final at Wimbledon with its forty-six games, exceeding by two the record set by Lenglen and Dorothea Lambert Chambers in 1919. Furthermore, the twenty-six-game opening set was the longest ever in any singles final contested by men or women in that event. This protracted battle, superbly fought by the two greatest female players of their era, raised the level of respect for women's tennis enduringly.

Court would confess later, "I have never had a harder match than this and I have never played better at Wimbledon than I have this year."

Lance Tingay wrote in *The Daily Telegraph*, "It is academic where there have been better finals. Perhaps there have been one or two. This, though, was among those that will be long remembered, and had the American got the decision, sporting prowess would have been just as well rewarded."

In her fifth consecutive Wimbledon singles final, King had given a great performance in defeat. The fact remained that Court had captured her third straight major singles title in the 1970 season. She had taken a 3-2 lead in her Wimbledon career series with King, gaining a 2-0 edge in finals. More importantly, Court stood only one major title away from a Grand Slam.

EPILOGUE

Court came into the U.S. Open at Forest Hills with growing confidence, while King had to step aside and skip the last of the Grand Slam events for the season. The American decided to bypass the championship of her country to have a much needed knee operation. Court thus became an overwhelming favorite. Who else could stop her on the grass courts in New York?

Court was strikingly efficient in her five matches on the way to the final. She was winning so easily that the pressure of her historic quest was vastly reduced. In the semifinal, she met Nancy Richey, her final-round victim the year before. She removed the American baseliner 6-1, 6-3.

Court was still concerned about her ankle, which raised her incentive to win all of her matches in short order. On her way to the title match, she lost a total of only thirteen games. Richey was the only player to extend Court to 6-3 in any set.

The morning of her final against Rosie Casals, Court went to a church. She wanted spiritual calming before she played the most important match of her life. Casals stayed with her until 2-2 in the first set. Then Court collected four games in a row. That 6-2 first set verdict was typical of the entire fortnight. Court was almost there. But she conceded in her book, *Court on Court, A Life in Tennis*, that she lost her concentration at that stage. "Suddenly my mind began to wander as I began anticipating victory," she wrote. "Consequently, I dropped my service, not once but three times in a row as Rosie stormed back to take the second set 6-2 and even the match. The huge crowd of 14,000, quite naturally on the side of their compatriot, cheered wildly as they sensed a major upset. But the roars for Rosie had a quieting effect on me. As we took our places for the final set, I prayed: 'Dear Lord, please help me. I can't lose now.'

Court proceeded to break Casals at love for a 2-0 final-set lead, and never looked back, progressing to a 6-2, 2-6, 6-1 victory. She had become only the second woman to win the Grand Slam. Court deserved her triumph. In an extraordinary two-year stretch, she had won seven of the eight Grand Slam singles championships. At twenty-eight, she had realized her grandest dream with her sweep of the majors.

Four months later, Court ousted a countrywoman of originality and immense talent. In the final of the Australian Open, she took her tenth title in that Grand Slam championship with a closely contested 2-6, 7-6 (0), 7-5 win over Evonne Goolagong. The two Australians clashed again in the final of Wimbledon. Goolagong, nineteen, toppled Court, 6-4, 6-1, after ousting King in the semifinal round.

Court did not return to the U.S. Open because she was expecting her first child. She came back strongly in the summer of 1972. Despite a semifinal loss to King at the U.S. Open, Court knew her game was moving in the right direction. Her 1973 season was reminiscent of 1969 as she took three of the four Grand Slam events, falling only at Wimbledon in a surprise semifinal loss to a rookie professional named Chrissie Evert. Court had beaten Evert in an engrossing French Open final, 6-7, 7-6, 6-4, after Evert served for the match at 5-3 in the second set. It was easily one of Court's top five victories during her career.

Thereafter, Court declined. She had two more children. She staged a few more comebacks in 1975 and 1977. After the latter season, when she was thirty-four, she withdrew from serious competition and returned to a more tranquil life with her family in Australia. She took with her an unparalleled record, which included twenty-four Grand Slam singles championships (eleven Australian Opens, five French Opens, five U.S. Opens and three Wimbledons) and sixty-two majors (including women's and mixed doubles). With her prodigious numbers, Court was considered by some authorities as the best female tennis player of all time.

King moved on resolutely after her 1970 loss to Court at Wimbledon. Faster and more agile after her knee operation that autumn, she had one of her greatest years in 1971, taking the U.S. Open, becoming the first woman athlete to earn more than $100,000 in a year, winning nineteen tournaments, and playing a pivotal role in the first full year of the Virginia Slims circuit for women. The women had broken out on their own the previous year when *World Tennis* publisher/editor Gladys M. Heldman signed nine leading women, led by King, to professional contracts, and convinced Joe Cullman of Philip Morris to bring Virginia Slims in as the tour sponsor.

Heldman had been the crucial leader behind the bold move to establish a separate identity for women's tennis. King had emerged as a champion on and off the court in advocating the cause. That did not distract her from gaining the No. 1 world ranking among nearly all the authorities. In 1972, King had a remarkable record, winning her first French Open, capturing Wimbledon for the fourth time, and securing a third championship of her country at Forest Hills. Never before had she won three major titles in a year; the pity was that she skipped the Australian Open at the start of that season. Had she made the journey Down Under, she might have replicated the achievement of Court and

Connolly (1953) by capturing the Grand Slam.

King's 1973 season was not as successful, but it was a productive time for her. Before she turned thirty in November, she won her fifth Wimbledon with a signature performance against Evert in the final. Two months later, she recorded her most renowned triumph when she ousted Bobby Riggs, 6-4, 6-3, 6-3, in the famed "Battle of the Sexes" at the Houston Astrodome. The match was witnessed by 30,472 spectators that evening in Texas, and an enormous television audience.

King had hoped to avoid such a confrontation, but when Court lost her match with Riggs on Mother's Day, without much resistance, 6-2, 6-1, King felt compelled to accept the challenge. The fifty-five-year-old Riggs was a master hustler who had won Wimbledon in 1939 before moving on to professional tennis nearly a decade later. Court was not prepared for Riggs, but the savvy King fully understood what was at stake.

Billie Jean King advanced the women's game profoundly with her contribution to the Virginia Slims circuit, and her triumph over Riggs. She had started the 1970s with her narrow and dramatic loss to Court, and had moved into the middle of that decade with untrammeled ambitions. By then, her riveting rivalry with Court was ending, but she would face other fierce challenges in the immediate years ahead.

CHAPTER FOURTEEN

Rod Laver *vs.* Ken Rosewall

WCT FINALS, DALLAS, MAY 14, 1972

Rosewall, at 37, and Laver, at 33, produce a sparkling nationally televised indoor show-down. Their match measurably enhanced the public interest in tennis.

PROLOGUE

His appeal to tennis purists was without bounds. He hit the ball so cleanly and efficiently that his strokes appeared to have been lifted right out of the pages of a manual. His footwork was exemplary. And at 5'7," weighing in the range of 140 pounds throughout his entire career, Ken Rosewall lasted longer than anyone else in the upper ranks of the men's game in the twentieth century. A master of understatement about himself and his successes, Rosewall let his accomplishments speak for him. They spoke with striking clarity.

Another in the remarkable line of authentic Australian champions, Rosewall came from a family of very modest means. His father bought a grocery store that had three clay tennis courts behind it. It was here that Ken learned to play tennis, using a racket with a sawed-off grip that made it easier for him to play as a small boy. From the courts behind the store, Rosewall progressed steadily over the years toward a world-class game. His style of play enabled him to reach high levels in his teens. His fundamentals were so sound and consistently reliable that he seldom gave a poor performance. Diminutive and dark haired, Rosewall came of age quickly during his days as an amateur in the 1950s. He won the Australian and French Championships in 1953 when he was only eighteen, and joined his country's esteemed Davis Cup team that same season. He took the Australian final with unexpected ease over countryman Mervyn Rose 6-0, 6-3, 6-4. In Paris, he defeated the nimble American Vic Seixas in a four-set final. Most experts placed Rosewall at No. 2 in the world among the amateurs for

1953. He was demoted to No. 3 in 1954, but in 1955 and 1956 he rose to No. 2 again. In that period, Rosewall was the model of precision and purposeful play. He reached his first Wimbledon final in 1954 before losing to the obstinate lefthander from Czechoslovakia, Jaroslav Drobny. He won his second Australian Championship in 1955 with a straight-set conquest of his fellow "Whiz Kid" Lew Hoad. And at Forest Hills in 1956, he denied Hoad a Grand Slam by ousting his doubles partner, friend, and rival in a four-set final. That string of successful ventures gave Rosewall the opportunity to sign a fourteen-month, $65,000 professional contract, which he wisely did. As Laver would discover six years later, professional tennis was of a considerably higher quality than the amateur game, and Rosewall rapidly had to come to terms with that reality.

It was in the late 1950s that he devised a new strategy. He learned to get in behind his serve on fast surfaces against the likes of Pancho Gonzales, Tony Trabert and Pancho Segura as a means of self-protection. Although he did not alter his serve in a substantial way— it remained a deep, safe, tricky slice that was hard to attack—he began backing it up with a superb first volley. Although he lost his 1957 pro series to Gonzales, he was still evolving as a competitor and developing his resources. Despite dropping fifty of seventy-six tour head-to-head meetings with Gonzales that year, Rosewall remained upbeat.

His standing in the professional game was similar to where he stood among the amateurs. He improved steadily in some of the most prestigious tournaments. He won the Roland Garros pro event in 1960 by defeating Hoad, and took Wembley indoors in England over Segura, a brilliant tactician with an incomparable two-handed forehand. In 1961, Rosewall upended Gonzales in Paris and Hoad at Wembley. He toppled Hoad at Wembley again in 1962 while overcoming Gimeno in the same event.

From 1963-67, Rosewall held his ground ably in the obscure world of professional tennis. When the professionals started sharing venues all over the world with the amateurs, Rosewall was perhaps the best prepared player at the outset. He won the first "Open" tournament in history on the clay courts at Bournemouth, England by defeating Laver in the final. At the French Open, he was victorious over Laver in the final again 6-3, 6-1, 2-6, 6-2. He had triumphed once more at Roland Garros in the world's premier clay court championship fifteen years after his initial triumph.

Rosewall would turn thirty-four late in 1968, but he played like a man much younger. Although he was seeded second at Wimbledon and third at Forest Hills, he did not reach either final-round appointment with the top-seeded Laver. Roche cut him down in the round of sixteen at Wimbledon, while Okker stopped him in the semifinals of the U.S. Open. Most experts ranked him third in the world that year behind Laver and U.S. Open titlist Arthur Ashe.

Rosewall had a lackluster 1969 season, although he did reach the French Open final again. That was his only Grand Slam confrontation with Laver. Nevertheless in 1970, Rosewall came through once more in a major championship. Seeded third, he dismissed No. 2 seed John Newcombe in straight sets, avenging his five-set loss to his fellow Australian in the Wimbledon final two months earlier. In the Forest Hills final, he surpassed Roche 2-6, 6-4, 7-6, 6-3. Fourteen years after he first won Forest Hills, Rosewall had done it again, setting a record for spanning so many years between titles.

An aging Rosewall was on the ascendancy. He won the 1971 Australian Open with an emphatic 6-1, 7-5, 6-3 triumph over Ashe in the final, taking that title eighteen years after his first triumph. At Wimbledon, he was beaten soundly by Newcombe in the semifinals, and he did not defend his U.S. Open title. But at the end of that year, having just turned thirty-seven, he conquered Laver in the first World Championship Tennis (WCT) Finals championship match at Dallas.

Rosewall won that inaugural event for the top eight participants on the circuit 6-4, 1-6, 7-6, 7-6, and Rex Bellamy of the *London Times* wrote, "This three hour match was so thrilling that the strain of watching it—never mind playing it— became almost unendurable." Rosewall was the recipient of a check for $50,000, the largest tournament cash prize awarded at that time.

Laver at thirty-three was playing superlative tennis himself at that stage, although he was no longer able to make it last for two weeks at a major. That had become apparent the year before when British left-hander Roger Taylor beat him in the round of 16 at Wimbledon, and Dennis Ralston ousted him in the same round at the U.S. Open. In 1971, he lost to Mark Cox in the round of sixteen at the Australian Open and was cut down by Tom Gorman in the quarterfinals at Wimbledon.

Despite his setbacks in the major events, Laver was still dangerous in the one-week events. He won four WCT tournaments and was the top-ranked player on that tour heading into Dallas. But while he was still regarded by his colleagues as the best, Laver was ranked third in the world for 1971 behind Newcombe and Stan Smith, the U.S. Open champion.

As the leading players shifted back indoors in the winter and spring of 1972 for the now established WCT circuit, Laver wanted to get another crack at Rosewall in Dallas, which had become one of the five top tournaments in tennis. En route to Dallas, Laver beat Rosewall in both Philadelphia (at the U.S. Pro Indoor) and Toronto. Laver won five tournaments in that run-up while Rosewall took only two. It was time to settle the supremacy issue in Dallas.

THE MATCH

Laver and Rosewall took their expected places in the final of the eight-man Dallas playoff. Laver downed Newcombe routinely in straight sets, but then needed to make a concerted effort to escape against the solid serve-and-volley game of the American Marty Riessen. Laver came from two-sets-to-love down to win in five. He conceded only three games in the last three sets. Rosewall handled the Americans Bob Lutz and Arthur Ashe with relative ease. And so the rematch was a reality, and despite his difficulty with Riessen, Laver seemed certain to win on this occasion.

Competing on a medium-speed, Supreme Court carpet, both players sparkled. Laver tried to set the agenda with persistent serve-and-volleying, but Rosewall countered with his own stamp of authority. Most importantly, both men produced passing shots of contrasting styles. Rosewall exploited his vintage slice backhand to the hilt, driving the ball past Laver through very small loopholes, making dipping chip returns to Rod's feet, lobbing with touch and disguise. Laver

Rod Laver

delivered devastating doses of his explosive topspin backhand, whipping them by Rosewall with high velocity, hiding his intentions until
the last possible instant.

At the outset, Laver was too sharp and versatile. He surged to 4-0,
then 5-1. Rosewall appeared out of luck, but not for long. In winning
the next three games, he served two love games, broke Laver once,
and almost got another break when Laver served for the set at 5-4.
Laver was twice down break point in the tenth game but he kept
pressing forward and his volleying saved him. Laver had the set 6-4
and the lead.

Rosewall was not dismayed. He was neutralizing Laver's heavier
hitting game with his accuracy, and he collected the next two sets, 6-0,
6-3. He was dismantling Laver in every department, making the per-

centages work for him, forcing Laver to go for improbable winners. When Rosewall seized the early break to move ahead 3-1 in the fourth, his control of the match seemed complete. Laver was well aware that his time to respond was limited. He raised his returning game slightly, and Rosewall wavered to some degree. Laver was back in business at 3-3. They proceeded to a tiebreak.

Once more, Rosewall established an edge. He led 2-0 in the tie-breaker before conceding the next four points. A brilliant backhand pass lifted Laver to 5-2, and he took that sequence convincingly 7-3. Laver was even at two sets all, and anxious to get on with his task in the fifth and final set.

So, too, was the indefatigable Rosewall. With his backhand flowing, his serve carrying sustained depth, and his volley crisp and compact, he built a 4-2 lead. Laver was in yet another bind, wondering how he could dig himself out. He did it with typically robust hitting off both sides, making the break back in the seventh game with a scorching backhand down the line. Laver held at love for 4-4, but then faced a match point at 30-40 in the tenth game. Methodically, he delivered an ace down the middle and held on courageously for 5-5.

Both players held to reach a climactic tiebreaker. In these latter stages of the fifth set, Laver seemed invigorated compared to the lethargic Rosewall. As Richard Evans wrote in *World Tennis*, "Watching Rosewall stand there, forlorn and boyish as ever, waiting for the ball boy to throw him the ball, one felt there was no way he could win. He was so tired he couldn't even catch the ball; when it fell out of his hand, he watched it roll away as though the effort of bending down with his racket to flip it up was beyond him. But the second he put that ball in play he was a different man."

When Laver hit a forceful return at Rosewall's feet to make it 3-1 in the tiebreak, he was ready to win the only important title of his time to elude him. But Rosewall took his next service point to close the lead to 3-2. Then Laver suffered a double fault for 3-3. As they changed ends, Laver appeared shaken by Rosewall's recovery.

Nevertheless, Laver attacked, Rosewall lobbed long, and it was 4-3 for the favorite. Laver followed with a stinging shot directed at Rosewall's midsection. Volleying off his belly button, Rosewall watched his shot go wide. It was 5-3 for Laver. He was two points away from his goal. This match was his for the taking.

Rosewall would not surrender. He came in, punched his volley crosscourt, and Laver needed one of his dazzling forehand winners on the run. He tried to hook the ball back into the court from a wide position, but he was off the mark. Rosewall now had four points to Laver's five.

Laver produced a fine serve, only to be caught helpless by a surgically struck Rosewall backhand chip return. Laver's half volley was long. Now it was 5-5. Serving to Rosewall's backhand was always a dangerous gambit, but Laver went to that side again. Rosewall sliced the return with speed and accuracy down Laver's forehand sideline. It was a clean winner. Rosewall led 6-5. Match point for the underdog.

They had been engaged in this superb encounter for more than three-and-a-half hours, and Laver's temerity had kept him in the match several times when Rosewall seemed certain to win. But this time, there was no answer. Rosewall's first serve went deep to the backhand. The return failed. Rosewall had won 4-6, 6-0, 6-3, 6-7, 7-6, and the crowd of over eight thousand in Moody Coliseum rose spontaneously to its feet, applauding both players with heartfelt admiration, feeling as much sorrow for Laver as joy for Rosewall.

WCT Executive Director Mike Davies—a professional player himself during the 1960s— said at the presentation ceremony, "Ladies and gentlemen, that is probably the greatest tennis match I have ever seen in my life." Some might have seen Davies's comment as self serving, given that he was a highly paid employee of Lamar Hunt's organization. He was, in fact, Hunt's right-hand man. All the same, the match was worthy of the comment. The standards set by the two Australians that May afternoon were awesomely high.

Five years later, looking back fondly on his triumph over Laver, Rosewall said, "It was just a flip of the coin as to who won that match. Probably my form was equal in every set while Rod's was rather up and down. That 6-0 set was just not normal against a player like Rod Laver. But it was very rewarding for me because WCT was the first world professional circuit and it really helped make tournament tennis what it is today."

Ken Rosewall

EPILOGUE

Rosewall's assessment of Laver resonated often thereafter. Laver had some productive years. He was ranked No. 8 in the world on the ATP computer for 1973, finished No. 4 for 1974, and ended 1975 at No. 10. In 1975, he took on then world champion Jimmy Connors in a special Las Vegas challenge match shown on CBS television. For two sets, Connors made the thirty-six-year-old Laver look older. The younger man was blasting Laver off the court. It appeared that Laver had made a misjudgment by playing Connors, especially in a best-of-five-set showdown.

Appearances were misleading. Laver's pride was wounded, and he was unwilling to make an embarrassing exit in a match seen by so many viewers across America. He made an exhilarating run through the third set, took it 6-3, and fought honorably through a high tension fourth set. At 4-5, Laver was serving to save the match. Five times he fought off match points before making it to 5-5. The crowd in Las Vegas applauded the dignified Australian not only for that brave stand, but for the breadth of his long and illustrious career.

From 5-5, Laver had little left in his competitive resources. Connors confidently closed it out 6-4, 6-2, 3-6, 7-5. He was irrefutably the better player on that day. However, what might have happened had both men been placed in a time warp when they were at peak efficiency? There were few knowledgeable observers who doubted that Laver would have been the master under those circumstances.

After 1974 and 1975—when Laver had some stirring struggles with a budding Bjorn Borg (including a five-set loss in Dallas in the latter year)—the Australian left-hander cut down considerably on his schedule. He made a final appearance at Wimbledon in 1977 during the centenary celebration, acquitting himself admirably in a four-set, second-round loss to the capable American Dick Stockton, the No. 9 seed, who was at his best. Laver then withdrew from the men's tour and moved on to the seniors, but not before scoring a good win over New Yorker Vitas Gerulaitis in a WCT event. Gerulaitis was ranked No. 4 in the world for that year.

Rosewall, meanwhile, used his Dallas 1972 triumph as a springboard to other substantial achievements. He was ranked sixth in the world for 1973, finishing two places above Laver on the charts. Rosewall turned thirty-nine at the end of that year. It seemed certain that he had left his days as a big time competitor behind him. How could he hold his own against much younger and presumably stronger opposition?

With his sterling showings at the two most prestigious tournaments of 1974, Rosewall answered those questions. At Wimbledon, "The Little Master" was seeded ninth, but he put together a string of feisty matches to reach the final. Rosewall removed the big-serving Roscoe Tanner—a future finalist—to set up a quarterfinal meeting with No. 1 seed Newcombe, winning that one 6-1, 1-6, 6-0, 7-5. In the semifinals, he was down two sets to love and match point in the third-set tiebreaker against the 1972 titlist Stan Smith. Rosewall revived to oust the No. 4 seed in five sets. In the final, he met the charismatic Jimmy Connors. The surge was over. He could not contain the American left-hander, bowing 6-1, 6-1, 6-4. But Rosewall had made it to his fourth Wimbledon final twenty years after his first, setting another record with that feat.

At Forest Hills, the leading players knew they had to look out for Rosewall as he took his polished game onto the grass for a last, serious chance of winning a major event. Seeded fifth, Rosewall lasted longer than anyone but Connors. He stopped the second-seeded Newcombe 6-7, 6-4, 7-6, 6-3 in the semifinals to reach a second consecutive Grand Slam tournament final. His title match with Connors was delayed until Monday afternoon by rain. The sports pages projected a significantly stronger showing from Rosewall against his American adversary this time. Yet Connors—covering the court with great speed, producing a string of winners on the run, serving with more bite than usual—was even better than he had been at Wimbledon, crushing Rosewall 6-1, 6-0, 6-1.

The devastatingly one-sided result could not alter the fundamental fact that Rosewall had been the runner-up in the two showcase events when he was thirty-nine. No man in the modern era had played as well at that age. Still, the journey was not over, the will was undiminished, his celebrated ball control as artful as ever. Rosewall was No. 6 in the world at the end of 1975 when he was forty-one. In 1977, at forty-three, he won his last tournament in Hong Kong.

"I'm not the biggest guy in the world," reflected Rosewall in 1977, "and I was always told I would probably never have a very long career—that I'd never last physically. But I've been able to prove a lot of people wrong. I still have the desire to play and I'm still happy to train hard and work hard. Tennis has been my life."

Laver could have said essentially the same thing about himself. He, too, always relished the challenge of competition. The difference after Dallas was that Laver's body was not as generous as Rosewall's. He suffered lingering injuries. More importantly, Laver's tactics were not made to last as long as Rosewall's. Be that as it may, both men loom large in the history of the game. Laver is regarded by many astute analysts as the greatest player ever to grace the courts, and Rosewall holds the distinction of playing top-flight tennis for more years than anyone else. Together, they probably contributed more top-of-the-line singles matches than any other duo. Too many of those luminous battles were lost in the wilderness of professional tennis during the 1960s, when accurate records were not kept. In many ways, their 1972 Dallas clash made up for the lost showdowns with timeless vitality.

CHAPTER FIFTEEN

Stan Smith *vs.* Ilie Nastase

WIMBLEDON, FINAL, JULY 9, 1972

The unflappable Smith and the mercurial Nastase gave the capacity Centre Court crowd a dramatic and entertaining battle.

PROLOGUE

They stood at opposite ends of the field in every conceivable respect. Stan Smith grew up in southern California. He graduated from USC in 1969 and was an all-American tennis player. A tall and uncommonly disciplined man, he played the game in a programmed way. At 6'4," he was the tallest champion of his time. With his size 13 shoes and long legs, Smith was an intimidating figure, but nothing came naturally to him. He worked extraordinarily hard to achieve his successes, building his game largely around one of the most potent and productive first serves of his era, backing it up ably on the volley, developing penetrating but not spectacular ground strokes. Smith was a master of restraint who knew how to exploit every opportunity.

Ilie Nastase, on the other hand, had so much virtuosity that he often did not know quite what to do with it. He spent his childhood in Bucharest, Romania, where his father had become a guard at the Romanian national bank. Ilie was one of the most gifted players ever to step on a court. He was primarily a counter-attacker, capable of releasing dazzling passing shots on the dead run from anywhere on the court. He was the first player who could hit top-spin lobs off both sides. He could be quick, and when his mind was clear he could be cunning, but too frequently he found himself in quandaries of his own making.

While Smith was a superb sportsman who refused any invitation to lose his composure, Nastase could come unraveled with surprising ease, needlessly quarreling with linesmen and umpires, berating himself in a variety of languages, tormenting his opponents with his tempestuous behavior. He was a boy disguised in a man's body, snapping unreasonably even when barely provoked, turning from laughter to anger inexplicably. His fellow players seldom knew what to expect next from Nastase, and Nastase's mood swings were so extreme that he was usually hard pressed to understand them himself. As the players prepared for Wimbledon in 1972, the fifth year of Open competition, many of the biggest names in the game were missing. Rod Laver and Ken Rosewall were absent. The 1970-71 titlist, John Newcombe—another of the great Australians—was not there. Arthur Ashe would not be participating. All of these leading players were playing for Lamar Hunt's World Championship Tennis circuit. Hunt and Wimbledon were involved in an unresolved political dispute. As a consequence, too many of the game's finest were not appearing at the premier showcase.

Fortunately for the fans, Smith and Nastase were not linked with WCT and were not forced into that boycott. They were, therefore, seeded first and second at the All England Club. Both men brought strong credentials with them to the grass courts. Smith had progressed significantly over the past five years. In 1968, he had been a member of the victorious U.S. Davis Cup team, joining fellow Californian Bob Lutz to take the doubles in the Challenge Round against Australia. The following year, he surpassed Ashe, Clark Graebner, and Charlie Pasarell to become the top-ranked player in America. In 1969, he had also won the amateur-only U.S. National Championships at the Longwood Cricket Club in Brookline, Massachusetts.

Smith performed solidly in 1970, but that season paled in comparison to 1971 when he collected his first major singles title, toppling Jan Kodes of Czechoslovakia to win the U.S. Open at Forest Hills. He was ranked by nearly all experts in that pre-ATP computer year at No. 2 in the world behind Newcombe, who stopped Smith in five tough sets in the Wimbledon final. Having won Forest Hills the previous September, Smith was moving up. He wanted at least one major title in 1972.

In the 1971 Wimbledon final against the crafty Newcombe, Smith had dropped the first set, but then confidently collected the next two.

He believed he was going to win. He had Newcombe in a critical bind. In 1999, when asked to analyze his 1971 meeting with New-combe, Smith said, "After winning those second and third sets in that final, all I was worrying about was what I was going to say in my victory speech. I ended up losing, and I felt I let that one get away."

Smith made a mistake in underestimating Newcombe's resolve, but his Forest Hills triumph two months later had served to elevate his expectations. Furthermore, he had enjoyed a distinguished first half of 1972, which included four tournament wins on the American indoor circuit. In two of those finals—at the National Indoor in Maryland and the Hampton Indoor in Virginia—Smith had toppled Nastase. His exceptional fast court standards were too much on those occasions for the Romanian, who could compete favorably on any surface but preferred the red European clay where he could demonstrate his ath-leticism to greater effect.

And yet, the questions surrounding Nastase in 1972 were essentially the same as any other year: Could he maintain his emotional stability for two weeks? Would he avoid his usual series of ill-advised alterca-tions? Was he capable of controlling his imagination and signaling to his opponents that he would not surrender to his darker impulses?

His answers to these kinds of questions had not been encouraging earlier that year. Facing the American Clark Graebner in the semifinals at the Albert Hall indoor event in London, he fell into his familiar pattern of self-destruction. Graebner was a muscular man. Tall and strong, he switched back and forth between glasses and contact lenses, and he came to be known as "Clark Kent" or "Superman," depending on his appearance. Graebner was also a formidable player who was ranked seventh in the world in 1968 when he reached the semifinals of both Wimbledon and the U.S. Open. That same year he was the No. 2 American behind Arthur Ashe, and they led the United States to victory in the Davis Cup.

At Albert Hall, trailing 3-1 in the first set against Nastase, Graebner chased a short, wide ball near the net on his forehand side. He was prepared to make the shot when he realized he would have hit a ball-boy who was crouching dangerously close to the court. The umpire, an elderly man somewhat slow to react, realized soon enough what

Graebner had done and he accepted Graebner's request to play the point over.

Nastase should have recognized that Graebner was well within his rights to ask for a "let," but he started muttering, "Why we play let, I don't understand. Why play let?" Graebner won that game to close the gap to 3-2, and at the changeover he earnestly tried to explain to his opponent why he had stopped his swing and, therefore, deserved to have the point played again. Nastase had known Graebner for five years, but now he completely ignored him. As they changed ends of the court, Graebner walked up to the net and made a polite attempt to get Nastase's attention. "Nasty," he called, using his rival's nickname. "Nasty," he repeated. No response.

Finally, frustrated and angry, Graebner climbed over the net, walked up to Nastase at the opposite baseline, and grabbed Nastase's shirt by the collar. Then "Superman" spoke his mind while a quivering Nastase listened apprehensively.

"You got away with this crap against Cliff Richey in Paris with the stuff you pulled on him at The Masters," Graebner warned Nastase, "but you are not going to get away with it against me." He then advised Nastase that he had better stop the gamesmanship or he would take his steel racket and wrap it around Nastase's neck. Graebner walked back over to his side of the net and swept through the following four games to win the first set 6-3. Nastase seemed frozen in fright. After the loss of that set, Nastase walked up to the umpire and announced, "I too scared to play anymore. He say he hit me." Nastase then defaulted by walking off the court. Both players retreated to the locker room and held court in opposite corners with reporters. Tension permeated the air. It took Ion Tiriac to break the stalemate. Tiriac walked to the center of the room, raised his hands to command everyone's attention, then said, "Now I know what to do. I climb over net, threaten my opponent, and I will become champion of the world." The room filled with laughter.

But this was only one among many embarrassing incidents involving the mercurial Nastase, and they were no laughing matter. He was giving away too much ground with his outbursts, and encouraging opponents with his self-defeating actions. At his level of the game—

at or near the top of professional tennis—mental strength and a disciplined temperament were imperative, and Nastase too often was found wanting in both departments.

The Romanian had reached the final of the French Open the previous year before losing to Kodes, and was seeded second behind his conqueror in 1972. But he had the misfortune to meet future champion Adriano Panatta in the first round and he could not handle that demanding assignment. Smith was seeded third in Paris and he advanced to the quarterfinals, bowing in four sets against eventual titlist Andres Gimeno of Spain. Now, at Wimbledon, both Smith and Nastase had ample time to adjust to the English grass courts after their setbacks in France, and they realized their chances were enhanced significantly by the absence of the marquee names playing on the WCT Tour.

THE MATCH

All through the tournament, Nastase was dazzling on the grass courts of the All England Club, and he was calmer than usual. He boosted his morale in the second round when he stopped Graebner—who had beaten him twice before in this tournament—in four sets. In the round of sixteen, Nastase defeated 1971 semifinalist Tom Gorman, a future American Davis Cup player and captain. In the quarterfinals, Nastase maintained his dominance over his future doubles partner Jimmy Connors, routing the American in straight sets. Becoming more proficient with each match, Nastase cut down third-seeded Manuel Orantes of Spain—again in straight sets—to win his semifinal.

Smith, meanwhile, was not playing as skillfully as he could on grass. Compatriot Sandy Mayer pushed him to four rigorous sets in the third round. Journeyman Australian Ian Fletcher took a set off him in the round of sixteen. And, in the semifinals, Smith had to come from behind to win another four-set meeting with Kodes in a repeat of the 1971 U.S. Open final. So the top two seeds had reached the title match as expected, and their clash was precisely what the tournament needed.

By all accounts, it had not been a scintillating fortnight for the men. The women had created considerably more intrigue with the first-ever meeting between the defending champion Evonne Goolagong and Floridian Chrissie Evert, the inevitable world champion in the making. The men had been hit hard by the cavalcade of champions forced away by the WCT/Wimbledon impasse. The fans and players sorely missed Laver, Rosewall, Newcombe, and Ashe. Now it was up to Smith and Nastase to make up for it all with a gripping final-round showdown.

They came through handsomely on that count, but not on cue. Until 1982—when Connors and McEnroe lit up a listless, cloudy day with their fierce five-set final—the men's singles finals were usually contested on Saturday afternoons after the women decided their title matches on Friday. But a hard and ceaseless rain fell on Saturday, forcing a one-day postponement of the Smith-Nastase final. Thus, the pair of twenty-five-year-olds had to wait until Sunday to settle their score.

The delay was disturbing to both competitors, but Smith characteristically handled the matter with equanimity. The traditional champions dinner is held every year on the evening of the men's final, and Smith was not about to be held back by superstition.

Asked in 1999 how debilitating it was to have his final with Nastase delayed for a day, Smith said, "It was hard, and it always is. That is the worst part of sport. Nastase and I had both told the master of ceremonies at the Wimbledon Ball that we would not be attending, but I ended up deciding to go. I rented a tuxedo at 3 o'clock on Saturday, the rained out day of the final.... So I went to dinner with my wife Margie and my friends, Donald and Carole Dell. Then I went to the Wimbledon Ball and cut in on Billie Jean King, who had won the women's title and was dancing with her husband Larry. The British people didn't think that was too appropriate for me to have that so-called victory dance with Billie Jean before I had even won the tournament, but it was spontaneous and the photographers came out while everyone oohed and aahed."

Smith was far from overconfident, but he had a talent for behaving in a relaxed manner no matter how stressful the circumstances. He was undaunted as he stepped on court Sunday afternoon to confront Nastase. As for the Romanian, he had contained himself throughout the tournament, but his high-strung nerves were apparent from the start of the final.

Nastase pressed his American adversary persuasively in the opening set. At 2-2, Smith needed to fight his way out of three break points, but he held on to his serve despite the difficulty. Then at 4-4, the American succumbed. Nastase was making the towering American bend and stretch for almost every first volley, and he was reading his foe's serve exceedingly well. On the fifth break point in the ninth game, Nastase played an effective low, chipped return, and Smith netted the forehand volley. Nastase served out the set in the tenth game, gaining the early one-set lead.

Nastase then became frantic instead of using the first-set success as psychological capital. Although Smith double faulted at break point in the first game of the second set to give his opponent the immediate edge, Nastase was a man with a muddled mind. Despite losing his serve another time, Smith still moved to a 4-2 lead. He closed out that chapter 6-3 and methodically seized the third set by the same score. During this stretch, Nastase seemed a confused and even pathetic figure.

The Romanian stylist was blaming his mounting problems on his rackets. His Italian friend Michele Brunetti was sitting in the first row of the player's section and Nastase frequently called out between points in Italian to Brunetti. At one stage Brunetti and an official from the Romanian Tennis Federation vacated their seats as though Nastase's torment forced them to make some kind of symbolic move. Nastase changed rackets, but no matter what tension he found in the stringing, he was not content.

Smith took little notice of all the fuss and simply pressed on, hoping to finish his business swiftly. He got the early break and served for a 5-3 fourth-set lead. But Nastase halted him there with some tantalizing returns. Nastase was no longer coming apart at the seams. He had suddenly left his woes behind him and was in the process of regaining his touch on the grass. He broke Smith easily again and fought his way to two sets all on a startling run of characteristically flamboyant points.

In the fifth game of the final set—with the score locked at 2-2—Smith squandered a 40-0 lead and had to save three break points before advancing to 3-2. Smith played those pressure points thoughtfully and forcefully. "I was conscious of not trying to play to his pace because he took so little time between points," Smith recalled. Smith deliberately took a few extra but essential seconds longer on the break points to make certain he was ready, and he was. Then at 4-4, Nastase had Smith down 0-30. On that swing point of the match, Smith was as fortunate as he had ever been on any big point in his entire career. He lunged desperately for a forehand volley at full stretch. Making contact off the edge of the racket frame, connecting with wood as well as gut, Smith somehow made a freakish drop volley that fell over for a winner. At that moment, Nastase had every reason to be incensed and disconsolate. Had Smith not made that almost miraculous volley, Nastase would have had him at 0-40, triple break point. Winning one of those points, Nastase could then have served for the match. Instead, Smith moved back to the much safer territory of 15-30 and he held on for 5-4. A predictably dismayed Nastase drifted dangerously. He fell behind in the tenth game at 15-40. But he could still be dogged. He forced Smith to come up with sure winners, and the American could not handle the assignment. Nastase earned an enormous ovation as he held on for 5-5 with some gritty play under pressure. Smith believed that he might be letting it all slip from his grasp, but he served a solid game to hold for 6-5. Then Nastase coasted to 40-0 in the twelfth game, only to find Smith rousing himself. The American struck two winning returns and was also the beneficiary of a double fault from Nastase. It was deuce. Another bruising forehand return from Smith put him at match point for the third time, but Nastase was in tight for a winning volley. Once more, Smith applied the pressure with a clean placement off the forehand, and that gave him match point No. 4. Smith lofted a lob which was much shorter than he would have liked, but it was almost too easy for Nastase. He reached too quickly for the high backhand volley and dumped it into the net. Smith gleefully raised his arms. Nastase stood there, too stunned to realize what had happened. With the crowd applauding emotionally, the Romanian with the long dark hair and the lanky American shook hands. Match to Smith 4-6, 6-3, 6-3, 4-6, 7-5.

It had taken two hours and forty-five minutes for Smith to over-

Ilie Nastase and Stan Smith

come Nastase in the single biggest match of both men's careers. Shortly after it ended, Jack Kramer summed it up succinctly for the BBC television audience. He said, "The better competitor beat the better tennis player today. Stan won this one with character."

EPILOGUE

Smith and Nastase were both featured prominently during the second half of the 1972 season. At Forest Hills—with all of the big names back in business and a much stronger field than Wimbledon—the top-seeded Smith fell in the quarterfinals against his friend and Davis Cup teammate Arthur Ashe (the No. 6 seed) in straight sets. Ashe moved on to the final, where he met none other than Nastase, who was seeded fourth. Ashe and Nastase had a match neither would easily forget.

Ashe seemed well on his way to a second Open title. He was a decidedly better player than he had been in capturing the first U.S. Open of 1968. He was much more certain now of what he wanted to accomplish, and how he wanted to go about getting there. When he took a two-sets-to-one lead and went up a service break early in the fourth against Nastase, Ashe seemed certain to have victory in hand. He was leading 3-1 in the fourth with a break point for 4-1. Nastase had been behaving abysmally, throwing tantrums, spitting, cursing, and abusing the linesmen.

Had Ashe reached 4-1 and gained the insurance break, Nastase would not have recovered. But Ashe missed a backhand return when he had the opening. Nevertheless, he still held on for 4-2. Then Nastase found the range off his graceful topspin backhand, making Ashe miss his suspect low forehand volley. Nastase took four straight games for the set and eventually came through 3-6, 6-3, 6-7, 6-4, 6-3 for his most important title.

When it was over, Ashe put on a rare display of public emotion. He sat in a courtside chair, his head in his hands, fighting unsuccessfully to hold back the tears. In the presentation ceremony moments later, Ashe congratulated Nastase on winning his first major title, and then without rancor he admonished his conqueror, saying, "He is a great player and someday he will be a better one if he learns to control his temper." While Ashe was delivering his congenial advice, Nastase was standing off to his right waving his winner's check while some in the crowd laughed.

Victory on the grass at Forest Hills was a sweet remedy for Nastase's painful failure at Wimbledon. Ashe's despondency lingered for a very long time. Months later, playing a tournament in London, Ashe was asked about the residual sadness of his loss to the Romanian. He declared, "Sometimes I wake up in the middle of the night thinking about that match. All I needed to do was to hold my serve twice from 4-2 in the fourth and I would have had a second U.S. Open title."

A month later in Bucharest, Nastase and Tiriac had the benefit of meeting the United States in the Davis Cup final on their clay courts at home. Because Nastase had been the runner-up at Wimbledon and the U.S. Open champion, the Romanians were counting heavily on him to carry his team to a first-ever triumph. Tiriac had been a celebrated figure longer than Nastase and was a master politician. At the time, he was Nastase's mentor but he would later become the manager for future champions Guillermo Vilas, Boris Becker, and Goran Ivanisevic.

Smith remembers, "Tiriac was telling everybody that the chances of the U.S. winning were about one out of ten. Unfortunately, most of the guys on our team believed him." Even the implacable Smith—a man who seldom sold himself short—had his doubts, especially about his chances of toppling Nastase on the slow, red clay. While Nastase thrived on the slow courts where he could exploit his back-court versatility, Smith often found himself in untenable positions. The surface forced him to make major compromises with his aggressive game. He had to do too much scrambling from the baseline. His powerful presence was unmistakable on any fast surface, but on clay he was a less effective player.

In the opening match of the best-of-five series between Romania and the United States, Smith sensed that Nastase was overwrought. The burden of being the central figure in the proceedings was beyond Nastase. He served for the first set against Smith at 9-8, but played that game poorly. Smith broke him for 9-9 and never looked back. Playing with poise and precision, Smith put the Americans out in front with his 11-9, 6-2, 6-3 triumph over the disgruntled Romanian.

Tom Gorman became the victim of some disgraceful stalling and gamesmanship from Tiriac in the second match, squandering a two-sets-to-love lead and falling in five. Then Smith and Erik Van Dillen cut down the firm of Nastase and Tiriac in straight sets as the Romanians succumbed tamely. On the last afternoon—despite outrageous line calls by the Romanian officials and reprehensible court conduct from Tiriac—Smith ignored the bedlam and halted Tiriac 6-0 in the fifth set to win the cup for his country.

Smith told friends later that night, "I never thought when we came here that I could beat Nastase, and that we would then win the whole thing. It's an unbelievable feeling." His sense of accomplishment traveled well beyond the tennis court. The American squad had lived precariously during their entire stay in Bucharest. A few months before, the Black September movement had threatened the U.S. contingent because, presumably, it included two Jewish players, Harold Solomon and Brian Gottfried. Every precaution had to be taken. As a result, twenty-five Secret Servicemen accompanied the American players, and their captain Dennis Ralston throughout their visit. Ralston and the players ate all their meals in their rooms and took a different route to the courts every day.

At the end of 1972, Smith and Nastase clashed on one more momentous occasion, this time in the final of The Masters indoors at Barcelona. Nastase always seemed to save his most inspired tennis for that tournament—he won it four times in all—and he stopped Smith in a stirring five-set final after the American recouped from two-sets-to-love down. This was the last year before the advent of the official ATP computer rankings, but all the experts concurred at the end of 1972: Stan Smith was unequivocally No. 1 in the world, while Ilie Nastase stood indisputably at No. 2.

Nastase was at his peak. In 1973, he had another banner year. He secured a second major singles championship by taking the French Open in Paris. Seeded second behind Smith, Nastase was so far superior to everyone else that he had no reason or time to become disputatious. In seven clean and impeccable matches, he did not drop a set, crushing Nikki Pilic 6-3, 6-3, 6-0 in the final. He had his share of successes and failures thereafter, but he made it to the top by claiming the Masters crown again, this time gaining the victory in Boston. He won a first rate, four-set final from the "Flying Dutchman," Tom Okker. He was recognized at the end of that year by the ATP computer, and the experts, as the No. 1 player in the world. As for Smith, his 1973 season began in the fashion he wanted. He played perhaps the best tennis of his career from the winter months into the spring. In that challenging span, he recorded six tournament triumphs in eleven appearances, and was a worthy winner of the WCT Finals in Dallas, which remained an elite event. In the Dallas final, he defeated Ashe in four arresting sets.

On that form, Smith seemed destined to retain his ranking. He was so respected after Dallas that the players regarded him almost across the board as the man to beat. Smith lost in the fourth round of the French Open on his least favorite surface in a spirited five-set contest with Okker. He hurried to London to get ready for Wimbledon, but the player boycott on behalf of Pilic prevented him from defending the title he might well have won again.

Smith was seeded first at the U.S. Open, and expected to win his second championship at Forest Hills. He was eager to demonstrate that he still belonged at the top of his profession. Smith was on course when he faced the 1971 U.S. Open finalist and three-time Grand Slam titlist Jan Kodes in the semifinals. Kodes had been outclassed by Smith in the 1971 Forest Hills final, and when the American moved ahead two sets to one on this occasion, history seemed likely to repeat itself.

Smith, however, seemed to lose his authority and took only one game in the fourth set. He recovered and went on to be only one point from the final in the tenth game of the fifth set. With Kodes serving at 4-5 and match point down, Smith was crouched and poised in the advantage court, anxious to make the kind of return that might close out a hard fought battle. The sky was darkening, the remaining light fading rapidly, when Smith tried to make contact with his back-hand return. Kodes's deep serve had taken a bad bounce, and Smith barely got a racket on it. An emboldened Kodes went on to win 7-5, 6-7, 1-6, 6-1, 7-5. Smith was justifiably distraught. Shortly after it was over, he sat on the steps outside the clubhouse at the West Side Tennis Club, looking down at the ground searchingly, wondering how it had happened.

Smith finished 1973 at No. 5 in the world behind Nastase, Newcombe, Connors, and Okker. During that year, he lost two agonizing, final-set tiebreakers to a much improved Connors, including a round-robin defeat in Boston at The Masters. Despite the disappointment of sharing the No. 1 American ranking with the feisty Connors for the year, Smith headed into 1974 full of optimism, still believing he was the better player.

His 1974 WCT results were lackluster compared to 1973. This time, the big man captured only two of twelve events, and had his WCT Finals crown taken away from him by Newcombe in the semifinals. Newcombe toppled Borg in the final, and at that stage of the year—before Connors took over with his Wimbledon and U.S. Open triumphs—Newcombe was seen as the best tennis player in the world.

Trying to reassert himself in his return to Wimbledon, Smith marched to the semifinals and took a two-sets-to-love lead over an evergreen Ken Rosewall, the graceful and indefatigable Australian. Smith served for the match at 5-4 in the third, poised on the edge of a decisive triumph. Surprisingly, the American's volleying let him down and he dropped that critical game. He revived from 0-4 down in the tiebreak to reach 6-5, match point. Rosewall served to Smith's weaker backhand wing and the 1972 champion tentatively drove the ball into the net. The compact thirty-nine-year-old Australian now had the measure of the tall man from the United States. Rosewall prevailed 6-8, 4-6, 9-8, 6-1, 6-4.

That loss marked a pivotal moment in the career of Stanley Roger Smith. Only a single point away from a final-round meeting with Connors, Smith had faltered. As was the case in the Kodes match ten months earlier at Forest Hills, Smith had been wounded—perhaps permanently—by his lost chances. When he lost to the big serving left-hander Roscoe Tanner in the quarterfinals of the U.S. Open—thus depriving himself of another opportunity to confront Connors on grass—the signs were increasingly evident: Stan Smith was no longer the player who had once reached the top.

The following year, in 1975, a severe elbow problem further weakened Smith. He fell in the first round at Wimbledon, then lost in the opening round of the U.S. Open, which had shifted surfaces to the green-gray Har-Tru, known in some circles as "American clay." Smith battled on and as he approached the age of thirty-one in 1977 he had a brief resurgence, pushing Connors into a suspenseful five-set showdown before bowing in the round of sixteen at Wimbledon.

Commenting on the decline in his fortunes, Smith said, "I played my best tennis in 1973 and then I kept playing more and more. I played too many tournaments at that time and lost some zest for the game. But when I look back on matches like the Kodes U.S. Open loss, or Rosewall at Wimbledon the next year, I realize that you have to lose sometimes in situations like that. You have your missed opportunities, but I feel fortunate about doing as well as I did. Being the best in the world for a time makes me proud. And winning Wimbledon over Nastase was the culmination for me of my four goals: making the Davis Cup team, becoming No. 1 in the U.S., getting to No. 1 in the world, and winning Wimbledon, which were almost synonymous at the time."

In the 1980s, Smith was enlisted by the United States Tennis Association to spearhead their player development program, although he was not selected as a Davis Cup captain. In 2011, Smith was named by the International Tennis Hall of Fame to succeed the highly-regarded Tony Trabert as its President.

Nastase had a number of good years left in him as Smith began to descend. The Romanian did not win another major singles title, but remained in the world's top ten from 1974-77, finishing the 1976 season at No. 3 behind Connors and Borg. Nastase had another chance to win Wimbledon in 1976, reaching his second final four years after his memorable meeting with Smith. But Borg routed him in straight sets. He was nearly thirty by then. His best tennis was behind him.

Meanwhile, the Romanian's propensity for foolish imbroglios did not diminish. In 1975, he faced Ashe in a round-robin match at The Masters in Stockholm. Nastase was on the brink of defeat, serving at 1-4 in the final set, down 15-40. With Ashe waiting to receive serve, Nastase resorted to mockery. "Are you ready, Mr. Ashe," he said more than once. The umpire should have admonished him, but timidly backed away.

Ashe took matters into his own hands. He gathered his belongings and left the court in a quiet rage, and said later he viewed his actions as a "citizen's arrest" of Nastase. The tournament committee knew that under ordinary circumstances Ashe should have been defaulted, but they sensibly acknowledged the negligence of the umpire and awarded the match to Ashe. Nastase, regretting the embarrassment, sent Ashe roses as an apology. What is more, he went on to win the tournament by beating Borg. It was his last eminent prize.

The following year—on his way to his last major tournament semi-final at the U.S. Open—Nastase provoked one uproar after another. His second round win over the German, Hans Jurgen Pohmann, was played with so many transgressions that Nastase should not have been permitted to complete the match. He ranted at his opponent and the officials, spat at photographers, and turned the tennis court into something resembling a bullring. A fight broke out in the stands as fans argued heatedly about Nastase's conduct. Tournament referee Charlie Hare had disqualified Nastase during a Palm Springs match six months earlier for much lesser offenses. Asked why he had not removed him from this fiasco of a match, the dignified Englishman replied, "You must understand that what was happening on the tennis court today was a great human drama. And for me to interrupt it and throw Nastase out would have been wrong."

Nastase was at the center of another U.S. Open fracas. In the second round of the US Open in 1979, he faced John McEnroe. The Romanian was in one of his fractious moods during this nighttime clash. Umpire Frank Hammond reluctantly disqualified Nastase for his disruptive behavior, but tournament director Billy Talbert feared a "potential riot" in the stands. He told referee Mike Blanchard to take Hammond's place and continue the match. Play resumed and McEnroe won in four sets. Nastase may have meant no harm, but Hammond's career as a leading umpire was unjustly diminished.

Nastase began playing senior events in the 1980s. In 1996, he ran unsuccessfully for mayor of Bucharest. As it was, he and Smith both concluded their careers with two major singles titles. Both were underachievers in different ways, but Smith at least had done his best with what he possessed. Nastase, on the other hand, willfully provoked controversy while squandering his vast potential.

CHAPTER SIXTEEN

Billie Jean King *vs.* Evonne Goolagong
U.S. OPEN, FINAL, SEPTEMBER 9, 1974

In the last American Championships to be contested on the grass courts of the West Side Tennis Club, King and Goolagong produced some of the most spectacular points ever played in a match of this importance.

PROLOGUE

In a match against an American top-twenty player named Mona Schallau at an obscure Australian tournament, Evonne Goolagong was given an unexpectedly difficult time. She was pressed into a third set. She needed to save several match points. Her followers felt she was fortunate to escape. One of them approached her after the match and asked how she had remained so calm when she confronted match points against her. Goolagong dead-panned, "What match points? I didn't know she had any."

Goolagong's on-court demeanor was markedly different from other modern champions. She was more disciplined and driven than was commonly understood, but was not obsessed with winning big matches or collecting major titles. All through her career, Goolagong was seemingly oblivious to pressure or expectations. She played the game with an old-fashioned mindset, treating every match as an adventure, pursuing her objectives earnestly, yet without much stress.

Born into a poor family in New South Wales, Goolagong was one of eight children. Her father was an itinerant sheepshearer and a descendant of an Aboriginal tribe. As a young girl, she learned to play tennis at the War Memorial Tennis Club next door to her home. When Evonne was thirteen, she went to live with her tennis coach Vic Edwards and his family in Sydney. He became not only her mentor but her surrogate father. By the time she was eighteen, Goolagong was appearing in women's tournaments and making her mark. The following year, in 1971, she was still an unpolished player in many ways, but her brilliance brought her victory at the French Open and Wimbledon.

Many of the leading women—including Billie Jean King—were not present in Paris. Goolagong was seeded third after coming close to defeating Margaret Court in the Australian Open final at the start of that year. In the French quarterfinals, she ousted 1967 titlist Francoise Durr 6-3, 6-0. She lost no sets on her way to the championship match. Determined and confident in the final, she revived from 2-5 down in the second set to defeat countrywoman Helen Gourlay 6-3, 7-5.

Despite recording that first major success of her career, Goolagong was not given a serious chance of winning Wimbledon the next month. She was seeded third again and respected by the experts as a player of long range possibilities. But with Court and King in her path, it seemed certain that Goolagong would not be visiting with British royalty at the end of the fortnight.

That widespread notion was way off the mark. Goolagong was timing her ascent carefully, playing serenely as if in a world of her own. She already possessed several important attributes that carried her gracefully through her career: a versatile backhand ground stroke hit with topspin or slice, an astonishing backhand volley, and a superior backhand overhead to back it up. She also had a first serve of high quality. Her weaknesses then—and for the remainder of her career in tennis—were a short and inviting second serve, and an erratic and unreliable forehand ground stroke.

Exploiting her strengths regularly and not often exposing her weaknesses, Goolagong turned Wimbledon upside down with apparent ease. She stopped the formidable American Nancy Richey 6-3, 6-2 in the quarterfinals. In the semifinals, she accounted for King 6-4, 6-4. That left only Court in her way, and Goolagong came through that match convincingly 6-4, 6-1. Goolagong did not turn twenty until more than three weeks after Wimbledon. Neither she nor her adviser Edwards had anticipated the twin successes in Paris and London. She did not appear at the U.S. Open despite her revised status as a champion.

Over the next couple of years, Goolagong refined her skills, won some significant matches, lost a number of others, and kept growing as a player without changing her attitude. She made it back to the final of the French Open in 1972, losing in straight sets to a better prepared King. She overcame Chris Evert in their inaugural meeting in the 1972 Wimbledon semifinals, taking that celebrated match 4-6, 6-3, 6-4 after trailing 3-0 in the second set. King was waiting for her again and the American posted another victory over the Australian, taking this final by the identical scores—6-3, 6-3—with which she had won in Paris.

Goolagong's performances in 1973 were much the same. She was a semifinalist at Wimbledon, falling in three hard sets to the redoubtable King. Since her big win over the American at the 1971 Wimbledon, Goolagong had lost to her talented rival three times at Grand Slam tournaments. At the U.S. Open, her consistency in the major events was revealed again when she got to the final. Goolagong played with her usual panache, but Court was better on the big points and prevailed in another three set duel.

Heading into 1974, the best players were King, Evert and Goolagong. They were clearly the "Big Three" in the women's game. Goolagong started that season impressively with a victory over Evert. She toppled the Floridian 7-6, 4-6, 6-0 in the final of the Australian Open to secure her first title at that major event. Evert took the French Open title with remarkable baseline strength. At Wimbledon, both King and Goolagong were defeated surprisingly in the quarterfinals. King was ousted by the Russian Olga Morozova. Goolagong bowed out against Kerry Melville. Evert was moving into high gear, and she took the tournament with a convincing win over Morozova in the final. By the time the leading players assembled again two months later at Forest Hills, Evert had not lost since late March. But in a semifinal that began late on a dark, cloudy afternoon and concluded on a bright, balmy Sunday—rain washed out play in between—Goolagong snapped Evert's fifty-five match winning streak with a 6-0, 6-7, 6-3 semifinal victory. That win enabled the Australian to set up a final-round appointment with Billie Jean King.

THE MATCH

King had been consumed for much of that season by the formation of a new league called World Team Tennis, which she had established with her husband's help. She had played that spring and summer for the Philadelphia Freedoms while Goolagong represented the Pittsburgh Triangles. The American's tournament form had been top of the line early in the season when she captured five tournaments. And yet, she had not appeared in Australia, had missed Paris because of World Team Tennis, and had played an undistinguished match against Morozova at Wimbledon. The U.S. Open represented the last chance for King to salvage something substantial from the season, the final opportunity to seize one of the majors. She was seeded second behind Evert, three places above Goolagong. In the semifinals, the feisty thirty-year-old avenged her 1973 defeat by Julie Heldman. That year, King had walked off the clubhouse court in the middle of her round of sixteen match against Heldman, who had complained to the umpire that King was taking too much time between points. Incensed by her opponent's strict reading of the rules, King told Heldman, "If you want it that badly, you can have it."

This time, King had recouped admirably for a 2-6, 6-3, 6-1 win over Heldman. She was not at her best, but was on her way to a higher level. Goolagong was approaching the top of her game. She had settled a score with Melville, winning their Wimbledon rematch 6-4, 7-5 in the quarters before defeating Evert in one of their typically absorbing struggles.

On form, Goolagong appeared to have a slight edge coming into the final against King. That was balanced by the American's grittiness on big points. The two supreme serve-and-volleyers came at each other aggressively from the start. Both exhibited some nervousness in the early games. Goolagong was broken in the opening game, but broke right back. They stayed on serve until King stood at 2-3. She saved five break points. On the sixth, the American served a double fault to hand the advantage to the Australian.

Evonne fully exploited that opening. She held for 5-2, then held again to close out that chapter 6-3. King was not discouraged. Her serve began functioning with increasing efficiency. Her returns became sharper and better directed. Breaking Goolagong at love in the fourth game of the second set, she built a 3-1 lead. King was punishing Goolagong's second serve without hesitation. She held for 4-1 and twice more to win the set 6-3—thus forcing Goolagong into a third set.

That final set was a spectator's delight. There were so many rousing points that the Forest Hills fans sounded at times like an audience from another sport. They could not contain themselves during dramatic exchanges between the two peaking players. Goolagong was superb in building a 3-0 lead, winning twelve of sixteen points in that span, breaking King in the second game. The penultimate point in that game featured Goolagong in full flow. She rolled a top-spin backhand pass down the line to place King on the defensive, then drove another tough top-spin shot off that side, crosscourt. King barely got a racket on the volley. On the next point, a deep, defensive lob from Goolagong backed Billie Jean up on break point, and the American was unable to make the overhead. Goolagong had the break, and consolidated it.

That 3-0 lead was not nearly as large as it looked. King gained more than a measure of pride in the following game. At 0-3, 15-15, she released an inside-out overhead winner off a high, tantalizing lob. On the next point, Goolagong directed a penetrating bounce smash crosscourt and seemed certain to take the point. King chased the overhead and answered with a running topspin forehand crosscourt passing shot produced from far behind the baseline. She had lifted her own spirits and created doubts in Goolagong's mind. Goolagong served at 3-1, 30-15. She double faulted for 30-30, then double faulted again, cautiously pushing that second delivery into the net.

King found the mark with four consecutive first serves to hold at love for 3-3. In her three-game run, she had taken twelve of fifteen points. In responding for a 4-3 lead, Goolagong had large segments of the audience shaking their heads in disbelief. Opening up a 30-0 lead, she reached behind herself for a King lob over her backhand side. Goolagong wheeled around, snapped her wrist, and put the backhand overhead away at an unimaginable angle crosscourt. King applauded with her racket.

King was pressed persistently by Goolagong in the eighth game.

Evonne Goolagong

Twice, the score was knotted at deuce. King needed three game points to hold. She succeeded with nine out of ten first serves and managed to reach 4-4. Both women probed nearly identical weaknesses in each other's games. Goolagong directed deep and wide first serves to King's vulnerable forehand. King had the same plan. Furthermore, King and Goolagong went for each other's forehand volleys if given an option. They had the two best backhand volleys in the business, and their backhand ground strokes were almost equally polished.

At 4-4, Goolagong trailed, 0-30, but won the next three points. King should have advanced to 0-40. She attacked Goolagong's second serve, stationed herself at the net, and had a wide open space available for a forehand volley winner. King deposited that crucial volley into the net. Goolagong got to 40-30 but King took the next two points. Break point down, Goolagong missed her first serve and hung back behind the second. King drove her backhand return cross-court with good depth, and Goolagong netted her reply under pressure.

King was at 5-4, serving for the match. Goolagong followed her return of a first serve in, made a forceful forehand half volley cross-court to put King in a bind, then put her backhand volley past Billie Jean into the open court. At 0-15, King's second serve kicked up too high and Goolagong laced the backhand return at her feet—0-30.

The third point of that game was surely one for the ages. King served-and-volleyed behind the first delivery. She tried an angled forehand volley crosscourt but Goolagong was quickly upon it. Evonne scooped her forehand cross-court, seemingly out of King's reach. As King chased it, another ball fell out of her dress pocket, but in the frenzy no one realized what had happened. King somehow got to Goolagong's shot near the service line and whipped a topspin forehand down the line.

At that stage of the point, the crowd was shouting in excitement. It seemed as if King had the point sealed with her forehand, but Goolagong ran back diagonally across the court and, with her back to the net, sliced a backhand crosscourt. King covered that and, from a deep position, approached down the line off her backhand. Goolagong lifted a remarkable flat lob off the forehand, forcing King back to the baseline again. King ran it down furiously, wheeled around, turned her shoulders, and drove an explosive flat backhand down the line. Goolagong was trapped in "no man's land" but instinctively flicked a forehand half volley crosscourt and retreated to the baseline. King came under her forehand, chipping the approach into the dangerous territory of the Goolagong backhand. Goolagong sent her topspin pass down the line. King had an immense space open for the crosscourt forehand volley. It was right in her range, not too high or low. King made contact. She volleyed over the baseline. The crowd had been bursting with every stroke in that unfathomable rally. When it ended, they rose and cheered both players with wild applause. It hardly mattered who won that point in the end. Both players had triumphed with the wide range of their shotmaking, with their speed and athleticism, with their courage and composure. It was 0-40. Perhaps shaken by her errant forehand volley at the end of that critical point, King missed another volley to drop her serve at love. Goolagong was at 5-5.

King might have been distraught, but she refused to show it. With Goolagong serving at 5-5, 15-15, the Australian missed a forehand volley wide at full stretch. At 15-30, King came in behind her return and confronted Goolagong at the net. A first-rate reflex volley off the forehand was a clean winner and took King to 15-40. She broke on the following point with a forehand crosscourt passing shot winner.

Serving for the match a second time at 6-5, King did not falter. She made three out of four first serves. Goolagong missed narrowly with two passing shots. King held at love to complete a 3-6, 6-3, 7-5 triumph. She had won eight of the last nine points. She had played better tennis matches before, from a purely technical standpoint, but she had never shown more gumption under such trying circumstances. King had captured the championship of her country for the fourth time, and for the third time in the Open Era. In the nature of her victory, she had defined her competitive character. Goolagong had also revealed much about her high personal standards with both her fighting spirit and her reaction to the verdict.

"My greatest high," Goolagong would say years later, "was to hit a ball well, to try to do it perfectly, to try different things with my shots whether they came off or not. I can think back to matches I lost where I played one or two points perfectly, and that gave me a thrill. The most

Billie Jean King

exciting match I ever played was the 1974 U.S. Open final against Billie Jean, and I lost it. What I recall most about that match was standing there in the Forest Hills stadium. Billie Jean and I had just had a great point. I looked down at my arms and there were goosebumps."

EPILOGUE

Ten months later, in July 1975, King and Goolagong met again in a major final. When they stepped out on Centre Court for the championship match at Wimbledon, it was expected by those who had been at Forest Hills that the two rivals would play another splendid match. It did not work out that way at all. King won her sixth and final singles title on Centre Court with a display of disciplined and irresistible tennis. She was flawless in her execution, concentrated in her attack, certain of her chances. Goolagong never found her form. King routed her 6-0, 6-1. Knowing that she would turn thirty-two four months later, King announced that she was retiring from big-time singles competition. She had conquered Goolagong with such decisiveness that it seemed appropriate to retire from singles and devote herself to doubles and administrative endeavors. But that was a promise she could not keep.

Goolagong reached the finals of the 1975 and 1976 U.S. Opens. The tournament had shifted for a three-year period from grass to clay (Har-Tru) courts. With her exceptional mobility, Goolagong was an accomplished clay-court player. Nevertheless, she had the misfortune to meet Evert on a surface where the Floridian was nearing invincibility. In the 1975 title match, Goolagong gave a good account of herself in a 5-7, 6-4, 6-2 defeat. The following year, she lost 6-3, 6-0. For four consecutive years, Goolagong had reached the final of the U.S. Open. Nevertheless, the ranking trio of Court, King and Evert stopped her on all of those occasions.

It was during this lively period that Goolagong's rivalry with Evert had reached new heights. They had staged one scintillating showdown after another in 1976, meeting no fewer than seven times over the course of that season. The best of all those clashes was the Wimbledon final of 1976, when both women were performing powerfully. In their closest ever big-match contest, Evert beat Goolagong 6-3, 4-6, 8-6.

The Australian had her first child in 1977 and missed that season. In the ensuing years, she traveled with her husband and her daughter all over the circuit. She finished 1978 at No. 3 in the world, ended 1979 only one place lower, and remained fleet of foot and gifted on the court. And yet, it seemed likely that Evert and Martina Navratilova had permanently overtaken her. Furthermore, the Californian, Tracy Austin, had emerged, becoming the youngest ever to win the U.S. Open when she was sixteen, in 1979.

Could Goolagong ever come through again to win a major championship? She had won the Australian Open for the fourth time in 1977 over a mediocre field. Winning Wimbledon would be a much taller order. Having lost in the semifinals in 1978 and 1979, she returned in 1980. In a rousing semifinal, the fourth-seeded Australian surprised Austin 6-3, 0-6, 6-4. On the other half of the draw, Evert had toppled Navratilova to join Goolagong in the final.

When the Australian took on Evert that dark, damp afternoon, she played an outstanding match. She coasted to a 6-1, 3-0 lead, then moved on to an impressive 6-1, 7-6 victory. The Australian had secured her second Wimbledon singles title nine years after her first, also becoming the first mother to realize that feat since Dorothea Lambert Chambers in 1914. Goolagong recalled in 1998 her Wimbledon journey of 1980, saying, "I wanted to prove to myself and other people that I could do it. Because of the challenge of coming back after having a baby, I probably worked harder than I had for a long time. I didn't want to have any regrets about my career.... I had been in the final three times since winning in 1971 so I thought in 1980 that I still had a good chance. I had lost to Chris a few weeks before Wimbledon in a three-set final, but I felt quietly confident about Wimbledon. I kept telling myself that I was not going to lose. It was exciting to be out there that entire tournament."

Taking her seventh and final major singles title was inevitably a "last hurrah" for the congenial Australian. Recurring leg injuries made it impossible for her to compete in that territory any longer. She played sporadically for a few more years, and gradually withdrew from competition. She returned in the 1990s to play selected senior events.

King skipped the singles at Wimbledon in 1976 but she came back from 1977 to 1983. In the latter year, she reached her last major semi-final at thirty-nine, losing to eighteen-year-old Andrea Jaeger. Four years earlier, King joined Martina Navratilova to take the women's doubles championship. With that success, she broke the record for Wimbledon titles collecting twenty in all (six in singles, ten in women's doubles, four in mixed doubles). She had shared that record with Elizabeth Ryan. Ryan, at the age of eighty seven, collapsed on the grounds of the All England Club the day before the 1979 doubles final and died on her way to the hospital. King would say with sympathy later, "I think deep down, she didn't want to see her record broken."

King concluded her career with twelve Grand Slam singles championships in her collection and thirty-nine major trophies altogether. But her contribution to the game transcended her triumphs on court. In 2006, she was accorded the highest of honors when the U.S. Open facility was renamed, "USTA Billie Jean King National Tennis Center." While she clearly earned a place for herself among the all-time great players—somewhere among the top ten in the minds of most experts—she made a larger impact as a crusader for causes, as a major leader for women. Nevertheless, tennis fans would celebrate her most for her litany of great performances throughout the 1960s and into the 1980s. In many ways, none of her competitive victories matched her triumph over Goolagong at Forest Hills in 1974.

CHAPTER SEVENTEEN

Arthur Ashe *vs.* Jimmy Connors

WIMBLEDON, FINAL, JULY 5, 1975

Ashe was nearly 32 when he confronted the heavily favored defending champion. This strategic masterpiece was one of the most analyzed matches of the modern era.

PROLOGUE

Walking onto Centre Court at Wimbledon in 1975 for their legend-ary final, Americans Arthur Ashe and Jimmy Connors represented conflicting philosophies and personalities, separated not only by age but by ambition, distinguished not simply by the color of their skin but by the range of their interests. Ashe was African American, less than a week shy of his thirty-second birthday, and in many ways a vast underachiever. He had taken the first U.S. Open in 1968 and the Australian Open two years later, but had never fully explored or ex-panded his talent because his mind too frequently was far away from the confines of the court.

Beyond that, Ashe was the master of restraint. Often a daring shotmaker and superior server, he placed sportsmanship on the high-est plane, and contained his emotions no matter how trying the cir-cumstances. He had been taught by his highly motivational coach Dr. Robert Walter Johnson during his boyhood in Virginia to call any shot even remotely close to a line in favor of his opponent. Johnson also admonished Ashe not to succumb to anger on the tennis battle-field, telling his well-mannered pupil, "Those whom the gods wish to destroy, they first make mad." Ashe carried that message with him wherever he went, never forgetting the value of self control. He was unfailingly polite and dignified, always a cool voice of reason.

Ashe had been brought up in Richmond by his widowed father, who was a policeman, and a strong disciplinarian. He explained to author John McPhee, "I told Arthur I wanted him to get an education and get himself qualified so people would respect him as a human being." It is not surprising that Arthur was an "A" student throughout his schooling.

Connors came from Belleville, Illinois, not far from St. Louis. He was metaphorically a street fighter, unashamedly demonstrative as he moved through his professional career, encouraged from the outset to stand up vigorously for his rights, told not to let anyone or anything get in his way on the tennis court. His mother Gloria—a former player of modest success on the national level—and his grandmother, whom he called "Two Mom," taught him how to play the game.

The two women built his style around solid, flat, ground strokes including a two-handed backhand that became his trademark. Connors left for California in his teens to polish his skills with Pancho Gonzales and Pancho Segura, who gave him the benefit of their experience and lifted him to another level.

The combative Connors looked at life almost entirely through the lens of his tennis aspirations, believing he was born to prove his worth in this particular sport, knowing he could beat back bigger and stronger men with a killer instinct for triumph. As he prepared to play Ashe at the premier tournament of tennis, Connors was close to the peak of his powers. At twenty-two, he was the game's most acclaimed player, the top seed and defending champion at the All England Club. The previous year, he had pursued success in a manner few players have ever known, capturing three of the four major championships, winning a startling ninety-nine of 103 matches, claiming fourteen tournament titles in a steady, dramatic campaign, always intimidating his opponents.

Earlier in 1975, Connors had shown some fleeting signs of vulnerability, most notably in a four-set loss to John Newcombe in the final of the Australian Open on the grass courts of Melbourne. But the left-handed American had restored himself during the following winter and into the spring, rising to extraordinary heights in nationally televised challenge matches against Rod Laver and Newcombe in Las Vegas. Those "Winner Take All" contests—a label later exposed as false although the matches themselves were bruising battles featuring top-flight tennis—drew excellent ratings on television and revealed Connors as authentically, though unofficially, "The Heavyweight Champion of Tennis." He carried himself convincingly like a man who genuinely believed he was larger than the sport he played, strutting around the court as if he owned it, treating even his most revered adversaries as if they were insignificant. He always seemed confident that anyone who confronted him was going to be conquered.

While Connors isolated himself and relished his image as a maverick, Ashe was a universally popular figure among the players and the public. He was challenging himself in 1975 to perform as he never had before, to play his most productive and intelligent brand of tennis before it was too late. Over the course of that season, at a time when most world-class players in his age bracket were gradually descending from eminence and falling short of their former standards, Ashe was moving beyond his chronological age to an unexpected proficiency.

In the months leading up to Wimbledon, he had played perhaps the finest tennis of his career. Among his signature moments that season was a carefully crafted, tactically sound four-set triumph over Bjorn Borg in the championship match of the WCT Finals in Dallas, one of the foremost indoor events of that era. Ashe had come from behind to oust Borg for the title on that well remembered May afternoon. With Wimbledon commencing in less than two months, the win in Dallas over a player of Borg's caliber told Ashe everything he needed to know about what he could accomplish if he maintained his unprecedented drive and discipline.

He had been seeded No. 6, although he had demonstrated over the recent months and years that he could handle all of the men placed above him when he was in form, with the exception of the overwhelming fellow at No. 1.

He had played Connors on three previous occasions, with Connors prevailing each time. In the 1973 final of the U.S. Pro Championships in Brookline, Massachusetts, a surging Connors had stopped Ashe in five tumultuous sets on a sweltering summer day. That was a convincing test for both players which arguably could have gone either way.

Not so in the 1973 and 1974 South African Open finals in Johannesburg, when Connors checked Ashe decisively in straight sets on autumn afternoons one year apart. Those were historic events for Ashe because he was appearing in South Africa where apartheid was enforced. He knew his presence in that country as a proud representative of his race transcended whatever happened in the matches. But his off-court activities and distractions did not diminish his desire to make positive statements in professional combat, and he was fully committed to toppling Connors on the hard courts in both of those tournaments. Connors's ground stroke control and depth had neutralized the power Ashe was able to summon. Most telling, Ashe had been unable to find a suitable answer to Connors's incomparable return of serve.

Ashe took considerable pride in his ability to disconcert almost all of his rivals with the force and variety of his first serve. But in the two Johannesburg clashes—and to a lesser extent in the Brookline battle—Connors had wounded Ashe beyond repair with his searing returns off both sides, taking away Arthur's primary weapon, reading the delivery with crushing effect.

Through the first half of the 1975 season, Connors and Ashe had not competed against each other. They had played on different circuits, Ashe appearing on the WCT tour with the likes of Laver, Rosewall, Stan Smith, and Newcombe. Connors kept himself in the company of much lesser competitors on a circuit run by his tempestuous manager Bill Riordan. Connors had seldom encountered difficulty in these relatively lightweight events, but he was delighted to be the center of attention in every city, celebrating his status as the top player of them all, handling most of his assignments with consummate ease.

Connors had thrived in the relatively relaxed atmosphere of the Riordan circuit, but had marched through the draw at Wimbledon against a much more accomplished cast, demolishing them all without the loss of a set. Meanwhile, Ashe survived some strenuous tests including a four-set win over Borg in the quarterfinals, and a hard fought, five-set contest with 1968 Wimbledon finalist Tony Roche in the semifinals. The tension surrounding the two finalists on Centre Court went well beyond the contrasting paths they took to get there.

The previous year, Connors had been barred from competing at the French Open by the French Tennis Federation along with all other participants in the new World Team Tennis league, an endeavor that the sport's power brokers believed was in direct competition with tournament tennis and, therefore, detrimental to the health of the game. When Connors was prevented from playing in Paris, his absence did not seem to be particularly significant despite his triumph at the start of that season in the Australian Open. But then Connors won Wimbledon and the U.S. Open later in that summer of 1974. His camp made the case that he could have won a Grand Slam if he had been allowed to appear on the red clay courts of Roland Garros, and thus would have become only the third man in tennis history to realize that phenomenal feat.

The combative Riordan convinced Connors to wage a number of lawsuits against the tennis authorities for millions of dollars based on an alleged injustice. Among the many targets of Connors's charges was the Association of Tennis Professionals (ATP). The ATP president was none other than Arthur Ashe. Riordan was an arch political enemy of Ashe's close friend and lawyer Donald Dell, a prime mover behind the inception of the ATP in 1972, and the lawyer for that organization. Furthermore, Riordan was at odds with Jack Kramer, a loyal Dell ally and the first executive director of the ATP.

Connors was too young and politically tone deaf to fully realize what he was doing with what many considered irresponsible lawsuits. By engaging in legal action of that kind against colleagues in a small professional universe, Connors had created an unmistakable distance between himself and most of the people he played against. He found himself— unwittingly or not—caught up in conflicting actions while Ashe stood progressively on the side of the establishment.

And so, as Connors and Ashe took the court, insiders looked at this encounter as much more than another big match between famous tennis players in a major final. It was a philosophical struggle, a meeting of sharply contrasting strategies, a confrontation extending far beyond the lines on the manicured grass.

THE MATCH
When Ashe woke up on the morning of his historic appointment with Connors, he found himself filled with an inner security he could

not fully explain. At breakfast with his friend, Dr. Doug Stein, Ashe revealed, "I have this strange feeling that I just can't lose today."

How could Ashe have been that sure of himself against a great rival he had never beaten? Connors, after all, was blazing. He obliterated the big left-handed server Roscoe Tanner in a straight-set semifinal conquest, returning serve with such awesome consistency and conviction that he appeared to be a player in a league above anyone in the field of 128. The oddsmakers not only picked Connors to defeat Ashe, but many of them predicted that the left-hander would come through decisively without the loss of a set. He was too confident, too cocky, too good.

Ashe was not by nature an overconfident man, not a player prone to an exaggerated view of his chances. He quietly sensed that this was his time. And he knew that he had prepared himself with meticulous care. The night before the contest Ashe went to dinner with Dell—his former captain on the United States Davis Cup team—and fellow players and friends, Charlie Pasarell, Marty Riessen, and Fred McNair. He telephoned his former doubles partner and Davis Cup coach Dennis Ralston for last minute advice. As Dell recalled later, "Arthur brought along that night a list of ten or twelve things he thought would be important for him to do in the match against Connors. He left the dinner with five or six key points which he wrote down on a small piece of paper. At the changeovers when he played Connors, he pulled that piece of paper out of his racket cover and it looked to some people like he was meditating, but he was really concentrating on the five or six key points."

That analytical approach to playing Connors clearly fueled Ashe, but few were prepared for how dramatically he would alter his normal grass court game plan in this supreme effort to throw the heavy favorite off guard. Ashe's strategy was unexpected by his followers. They had grown accustomed to his adventurous, but sometimes reckless, tactics. They had watched him lose many excruciating matches over the years by hurting himself with careless gambles at the wrong times, with questionable shot selection in the crunch, with a low regard for percentage tennis. At one stretch in the early seventies, he had lost sixteen of twenty-two finals.

This time, Ashe unsettled Connors from the outset with a mas-

Jimmy Connors and Arthur Ashe

terpiece of strategic acumen, baffling his opponent with a wide array of spins and speeds, exchanging his usual potent ground strokes for subtle variations of pace, swinging his slice serve wide to Connors's two-handed backhand to pull him off the court, and refusing to allow his adversary any rhythm. Ashe had sweepingly altered his game to suit the opponent and the occasion, displaying a discipline and flexibility in his thinking, cutting into the core of Connors's confidence with an exquisite mixture of chips, dinks, slices, and some of the most superbly crafted backhand underspin lobs of his career. Most surprising of all, Ashe was rarely missing, making astonishingly few unforced errors, and consistently clicking on the low forehand volley, a critical shot that had cost him numerous vital points (and matches) over the years.

The match had commenced shortly after 2 p.m. on a pleasant afternoon, but with Ashe's strategy working sublimely and Connors way off the mark, the first two sets were finished rapidly. Ashe seized them 6-1, 6-1 shocking the spectators with the speed of his progress. The allegedly invincible Connors was induced by Ashe, time and again, to beat himself, and the favorite was obliging. Ashe was exposing the weakness in the Connors arsenal—the low forehand ground stroke—particularly on the approach. Ashe cunningly exploited that shortfall. Connors typically was trying to hit his way out of danger, but his shotmaking was not working.

After Connors held in the opening game of the match, Ashe refused to look back. In the last four games of the first set, he swept sixteen of twenty-one points with a superb display of controlled aggression. With Connors serving at 1-5, 15-30, Ashe chipped one of his teasing lobs off the backhand, directing it over the right shoulder of Connors. All the left-hander could do was tamely poke a high backhand volley back to his opponent. Ashe read the reply easily, driving a forehand passing shot into an open court. His ball control had never been better. The older American sustained his cutting edge in the early stages of the second set. In establishing a 3-0 lead, he took twelve of fifteen points. Connors ended a nine-game slide when he held in the fourth game. He did not collect another in that set, although his play was much cleaner and crisper toward the end as he fought hard in the process of losing a pair of demanding deuce games.

Ashe looked up at the Centre Court clock for the first time during a changeover with his comforting two sets-to-love-lead behind him. He was momentarily thrown off stride by the speed of the match. He thought at that juncture, "Hey, I'm not supposed to be beating Connors so easily. But I couldn't believe it because the clock told me it was only 2:41. I thought it had to be at least 3:15 or 3:20. I really think if I had not looked up at that clock, I would have beaten Connors in straight sets. That snapped me out of a time warp."

Undoubtedly it did. But, conversely, Connors was not willingly going to relinquish his title. He may well have recalled the 6-1, 6-1, 6-4 triumph he recorded over Ken Rosewall in the 1974 final on the same court. Aroused and contentious, Connors had not become a champion without unwavering self confidence. An agitated fan had screamed out during the early stages of the match, "Come on, Connors." Looking up briefly to the stands, Connors snapped back, "I'm trying for Chrissakes."

By the middle of the third set, with Ashe losing some of his edge, Connors at last translated effort into reward. Ashe had inexplicably strayed from his winning playbook, and could not resist the impulse to explode at full force with some flat first serves. Connors answered those deliveries emphatically with returns of the highest order, blasting the ball past Ashe with almost blinding speed and precision. Buoyant and flowing, his spirits soaring along with his game, Connors forced his way back into the match. He dropped his delivery to trail 3-2, then broke Ashe for the first time in the match in the following game. Connors was firing away freely, going for his shots with grunting aggressiveness, aiming almost arrogantly for his targets. Nonetheless, Ashe was making his rival work laboriously for every service game. Connors escaped two break points en route to 4-3, needed four game points to reach 5-4, then saved two more break points in holding for 6-5. In the twelfth game, he broke Ashe once more, advertising his growing intensity with two crackling forehand return winners in a row to seal the set.

The complexion of the contest was changing rapidly as Connors regained his momentum. The 1974 champion moved to a 3-0 lead in the fourth set with a break in the second game, and a fifth set seemed virtually certain as Connors served at game point for 4-1. He was heading inexorably toward the style of play he liked best, recapturing all of his resources in an attempt to overcome the inspired Ashe.

Ashe knew that he faced a crisis. A fifth set would plainly favor an opponent nearly ten years his junior, and he could not afford to allow such a tenacious opponent to regain level ground. Ashe made up his mind to stick assiduously to his original set of tactics, hoping his guile would carry him through in the end.

But could he contain Connors now that the younger man was accelerating? Ashe responded with the imagination required of him. When Connors stood at 40-30 in the critical fifth game, he had served-and-volleyed, drawing his opponent awkwardly into midcourt with a low volley. Ashe came under his forehand and chipped it low over the highest part of the net. Connors leaned to his left, lunged, and poked his forehand volley wide. It was deuce. Two points later, Ashe broke for 2-3, snapping his forehand passing shot with surprising pace down the line, coaxing Connors into an error. He then held for 3-3.

With Connors serving at 4-4, Ashe allowed his adversary only a single point, releasing a cluster of impeccably crafted backhand returns. Now he had a two-sets-to-one lead, a 5-4 advantage in the fourth set, and a chance to serve out the match in the following game. He exploited the same patterns that had already taken him to the edge of an exhilarating victory. Ashe's wide slice serve was unreturnable for 15-0. Connors then sent murmurs through the crowd, moving across the court swiftly, connecting with an astounding forehand passing shot. It was 15-15. Ashe pressed forward behind his first serve, punched a firm crosscourt first volley, and Connors attempted another forehand pass. He caught the net tape; 30-15 for Ashe, two points from the title. Now Ashe intelligently took something off his first serve. His off-speed delivery confounded Connors, who netted a seemingly, simple backhand return. It was 40-15, double match point, and Ashe swung one more wide slice serve to the Connors two-hander, opening up the court for a routine forehand volley. Sweeping five of the last six games, coming through with inspiration and confidence, Ashe secured one of the monumental upsets of the Open Era, toppling Connors 6-1, 6-1, 5-7, 6-4, with the most powerfully persuasive performance of his career.

When he put away that last volley to conclude the contest, Ashe raised a fist in celebration, glancing over to the box behind him where Dell beamed and his wife Carole wept in jubilation. A despondent Bill Riordan walked out of the stands, shocked by the defeat. In the crowded Centre Court, and all over the world, most tennis fans were euphoric in their appreciation of Ashe's triumph. He had silenced the critics who said he could not win the matches of consequence, and had overcome the scrappy, self-assured James Scott Connors when it mattered most.

EPILOGUE

By virtue of that triumph in the world's most prominent tournament, coupled with overcoming Connors in the single most important match of the season, Ashe was universally accorded the No. 1 world ranking for 1975 by the experts. The two top Americans did not meet again that year, and so the Wimbledon showdown took on added significance when the authorities analyzed the best in the business and selected Ashe as the premier player in the world for the first and only time. Connors remained the top-ranked player on the ATP computer because he boasted a stronger week in, week out record than Ashe, but the southpaw failed to collect any of the Grand Slam championships during a frustrating year. Following his losses to Newcombe in the final of the Australian Open, and against Ashe on Centre Court, Connors had one more chance to secure a major prize when he reached the final of the U.S. Open. But in another notable upset, Spain's clay-court wizard Manuel Orantes upended Connors on Har-Tru at Forest Hills after surviving a marathon five-set semifinal the previous evening against Guillermo Vilas, Orantes saved five match points and had apparently exhausted himself with that heroic effort, but somehow he revived the following afternoon and he took an error prone Connors apart 6-4, 6-3, 6-3 for the title.

Ashe later concluded that he had been responsible to a large degree for Connors's problems in the late 1970s. Connors took two more U.S. Opens during that decade—becoming the first player ever to win the tournament on three different surfaces—but he was not the same indomitable player he had been before the Ashe defeat. He revived briefly again with a dazzling run in 1982 and 1983 that included a second championship at Wimbledon and two more U.S. Open successes, but he was no longer the overpowering force he had once been. Connors would not acknowledge the depth of his disappointments in public. After the Ashe loss, he characteristically asserted, "I came in here with my head held high, and I will leave the same way."

As Ashe commented in 1985 on the one decade anniversary of his Wimbledon win over Connors, "I think that had I lost to Jimmy at Wimbledon in 1975, Bjorn Borg might not have gone on to do what he did by winning five Wimbledons in a row and six French Opens. If Connors had beaten me, he might have gone on to beat Orantes at the U.S. Open final. Jimmy might have staved off Borg for a few more years. But losing to me and then Orantes at Forest Hills rattled Connors just long enough for Borg to get in the front door."

As for Ashe, his life was permanently altered by his Wimbledon triumph, a singular success that enabled him to claim a much larger place for himself in the hearts of fans and the minds of historians. He never had another year like 1975, nor did he win another major title or appear in subsequent Grand Slam finals. He lost his last three meetings with Connors to finish with a 1-6 record against his arch foe, but he continued to compete at a remarkably high level into his mid-thirties. In fact, he had some impressive performances when he was thirty-five against the younger brigade of Americans, including a final-round appearance at New York's Madison Square Garden with nineteen-year-old John McEnroe. Ashe had two match points before losing that blockbuster to the young New York upstart.

In the summer of 1979, seven months after his great struggle with McEnroe, Ashe suffered a heart attack only three weeks into his thirty-seventh year. He was still ranked No. 7 in the world at the time and hoped to attenuate his career a little longer, but it was not to be. Four years later, he had another heart attack. In 1988, when he was forty-five, he lost all motor function in his right hand, which led to brain surgery, and the fateful discovery that he had AIDS. He had contracted the disease from blood used during one of his open heart operations, presumably the second, in 1983.

In 1992, Ashe publicly acknowledged his predicament and became an outstanding spokesman for the fight against AIDS during the last year of his life. On February 6, 1993, the illness claimed him and he died at forty-nine, leaving behind a loving wife Jeanne Moutoussamy and a devoted daughter Camera, who was only six. In 1997, the new U.S. Open primary court was appropriately named "Arthur Ashe

Stadium" in his honor.

The Wimbledon match with Connors was a defining moment in his career, a watershed event that touched the lives of countless tennis fans around the world. As Ashe recalled, when asked about the public response to that unique triumph, "I might be standing in an elevator or walking down a street somewhere, and somebody always seems to come up to me and says something about that Wimbledon win. Among whites they say it was one of their most memorable moments in sports. Among blacks, I've had quite a few say it was up there with Joe Louis in his prime and Jackie Robinson breaking in with the Dodgers in 1947. Once a month somewhere, somebody brings up that Connors match to me."

CHAPTER EIGHTEEN

Jimmy Connors *vs.* Bjorn Borg

U.S. OPEN, FINAL, FOREST HILLS, SEPTEMBER 12, 1976

Connors and Borg enlarged their reputations with a clay court engagement of extraordinary rallies and shifting fortunes.

PROLOGUE

When he burst into prominence in the middle of the 1970s, he broke new ground on many surfaces. Sweden's Bjorn Borg carried himself with admirable composure no matter what the score, no matter how dire the circumstances. He had immense appeal to tennis fans worldwide because he maintained unwavering dignity in the public arena. Borg had been brought up by strict parents who taught him to control his emotions. His father won a tennis racket as a prize at a table tennis tournament. He gave the racket to his son, but could not have imagined the consequences of that gesture.

Borg achieved his many successes at a time when tennis was soaring in popularity and attracting colorful rivals who fired the public imagination with their explosive personalities. But Borg was not going to be swayed, even by colleagues whose company he enjoyed off the court. He went about his business entirely on his own terms, building his reputation with the consistency of his character, earning the respect of his peers and the public with his high standards and unfailing sense of fair play.

Borg's arrival as a champion was nourished by his strong code of conduct. He was a persuasive contributor to the evolution of the two-handed backhand along with the Americans, Jimmy Connors and Chris Evert. The impact of this powerfully influential trio in the seventies carried on through the rest of the century as young players everywhere emulated their playing styles and copied their distinctive two-handed shots. Borg's two-handed backhand, however, was a different type of weapon than either of the great Americans possessed. While both Connors and Evert took traditional straight backswings and produced essentially flat strokes with their two-handers, Borg employed his stroke with a contrasting technique.

The stoic Swede was taught to come over the ball with heavy topspin, making his shots dip at the feet of those who dared to attack him from close range at the net. And while Connors and Evert damaged their opponents with their unrelenting depth during rallies, Borg presented other problems to his rivals with topspin trajectories never seen before in the upper levels of the game. What Connors, Evert and Borg all had in common was the stunning deception of their two-handed backhands and all three were nearly impossible to read when they went for passing shots.

Furthermore, Borg had a devastatingly efficient western topspin forehand that many authorities believed was even better than his backhand. And while he never became a first-rate volleyer, he developed one of the best first serves of his era, exploiting that skill with exquisite purpose on grass courts. His preferred surface was clay, where he would wear down his foes with his fitness and ball control. As he came into his decisive meeting with Connors at Forest Hills, he had been gathering momentum in the major events, winning back-to-back French Opens in 1974 and 1975, then defying the predictions of his critics by winning at Wimbledon earlier in that summer of 1976.

Connors, meanwhile, was on a crusade to move back to the top of the tennis rankings he had dominated in 1974. Having lost three of the four major finals in 1975 after he put on twenty excess pounds and drifted into an overconfident style, Connors had rekindled his intensity. He had not played at the French Open, and had faltered surprisingly during a quarterfinal loss to compatriot Roscoe Tanner at Wimbledon, but his form over the course of the year had been increasingly effective. He had defeated Borg twice during his 1976 campaign, ousting his adversary in the final of the U.S. Pro Indoor at Philadelphia, and again on the hard courts at Palm Springs. Altogether, Connors had clipped Borg five consecutive times since losing their first head-to-head duel in a final set tiebreaker at Stockholm in 1973.

His crackling flat ground strokes had been the perfect foil for Borg's severe topspin. The piercing shots Connors made off both wings were too much for the Swede, who was forced frequently into defensive positions during the rallies, and asked too often to produce superb passing shots under pressure as Connors attacked without inhibition on every short ball.

As both Borg and Connors approached Forest Hills, they fully realized the dramatic significance of the occasion. If Borg were to win, he would have taken the two most prestigious tournaments of them all, and his status as the top-ranked player would be established unequivocally among the experts—if not on the ATP computer. As for Connors, the challenge of grasping the championship of his country was in some respects even larger. He did not want to endure a second straight season without gaining a major tournament title, and he wanted to make certain he displayed his most inspired brand of tennis in the tournament he loved like no other.

THE MATCH

Curiously, despite the fact that the Har-Tru clay-like surface seemed much more favorable to Borg with his greater margin for error off the ground, Connors had a much easier time reaching the final. The top seed did not drop a set in six matches on his way to the appointment with Borg. Most impressively, Connors crushed the superb clay-court player Guillermo Vilas of Argentina 6-4, 6-2, 6-1 in the semifinals, with a breathtaking exhibition of back-court skill, punch, and precision. The No. 3 seed Vilas—a left-handed topspin shotmaker reminiscent of Borg—would topple Connors a year later in the Forest Hills final. But he had no chance in this confrontation. Borg, meanwhile, struggled in five-set collisions with No. 15 seed Brian Gottfried, and defending titlist Manuel Orantes of Spain. But when he cut down Ilie Nastase clinically in a straight-set semifinal— repeating his victory over the Romanian in the Wimbledon final two months earlier—Borg demonstrated emphatically that he was ready to conquer a man who had been his superior in their four-year rivalry.

Despite the previous encounters, many thoughtful observers expected Borg to overcome Connors on this occasion. He had lost against the left-handed American on clay courts—at the 1974 U.S. Clay Court Championships and on the same court at Forest Hills in the semifinals the year before—but Borg was clearly the more comfortable of the two performers on the green-gray surface at Forest Hills. Connors was well aware that Borg was not going to give anything away.

Furthermore, Connors realized that a best-of-five-set final favored Borg to some extent on a slow surface. The twenty-year-old Swede thrived in matches where his patience and extraordinary persistence could enable him to prevail. A case in point was his 1974 French Open final against Orantes. Borg had fallen behind two sets to love, but he staged a stunning recovery and eliminated his Spanish adversary 2-6, 6-7, 6-0, 6-1, 6-1. Connors wanted to establish an edge from the start and lock Borg out of the match. The twenty-four-year-old American had the heart and the conditioning to fight Borg convincingly to the finish and stay with the Swede in a five-set struggle, but the longer the match transpired the larger the danger that Connors might falter on his low forehand approach shot. Predictably, Connors went on the attack from the beginning. He broke Borg in the third game of the opening set to take a 2-1 lead, bruising the Swede with a brilliant barrage of flat backhands. In turn, he made two timely visits to the net, concluding that game with a crosscourt approach off his two-hander that Borg could not counter. Borg broke back in the following game with some remarkable retrieving, but the tone had been set. Connors would largely control the tactical agenda.

After Borg cast aside a pair of break points to reach 3-2, Connors resumed command. On his way to 5-3, the American collected twelve of fifteen points, breaking Borg in the seventh game at love. The left-hander then served for the set at 5-4 and did not grant his adversary a single point in closing out the set convincingly. At triple set point, he scampered forward from deep behind the baseline to catch up with a Borg half volley. With one hand, he guided a gentle backhand past Borg. The crowd applauded admiringly.

Borg was behind, but not rattled. He had a game plan and despite his first-set failure, he was going to stay with it. Trying to avoid the Connors backhand at all costs, Borg picked away purposefully at the forehand side. He played a surprising number of sliced backhands crosscourt to break the rhythm of the American. That policy was rewarding. Borg took a 3-1 second-set lead, breaking Connors in the fourth game when the American pressed on a backhand approach and sent it into the net. Borg did not lose his serve in that set. In the ninth game, he served to get even at one set all. At 5-3,40-30, he reached that destination. Connors directed a forehand approach down the line. His timing was flawed, his execution rushed. The shot landed long. Borg had the set.

But the key to the contest was the third set. Connors marched to a 4-2, 40-0 lead. Had he held here and converted on any of his three game points, he would almost surely have closed out the set safely and the entire course of the match might well have been different.

Instead, Connors hobbled himself inexplicably. He was guilty of five consecutive flagrant errors. At 40-0, Borg caught him off guard by rushing the net behind an ordinary backhand approach. Connors drove his passing shot over the baseline. Thereafter, the American was way out of sorts. He netted a high backhand carelessly, then stepped a yard inside the baseline in an attempt to cut off a deep return from the Swede. His low percentage play resulted in a netted backhand volley. It was deuce. Two errant high forehands cost Connors that game and complicated his task. Rather than going to the changeover with the 5-2 lead he urgently wanted, Connors had lost his break and a pleasantly surprised Borg—a master at exploiting unexpected vulnerability from an opponent— was not only back on serve, but very much back in the heart of the match. Borg surged to 4-4 and then had Connors down 0-30 in the ninth game. On that pivotal point, Borg struck his forehand passing shot with heavy topspin down the line. Connors was seemingly stranded. He lunged to his left, volleyed into the clear, then held.

From there, the players proceeded to a crucial tiebreak. After his mid-set collapse, Connors could not afford to come apart again and fall behind two sets to one. As for Borg, emerging from this set with the lead would have given him such an immense boost that even the unrelenting Connors would have been hard-pressed to halt him. So the protagonists put all of their resources into as dramatic a ten minutes as they would ever share on a tennis court together. Incentive was high on both sides of the net, the juices were flowing, the audience of fourteen thousand pulsatingly gripped by every moment of the contest.

A rare Connors double fault—only his second of the match—allowed Borg back to 2-2. When Connors missed a high forehand volley by a whisker, the Swede proceeded to 4-2. Serving the seventh point, Borg was guilty of a forehand unforced error. Connors revived to 4-4 and seemed certain to win the ninth point on his serve. Connors advanced to the net behind an exceedingly deep forehand approach. Borg was on the run. He prepared early, whipped over the ball with moderate topspin on his two-hander and clipped the sideline for a clean winner. Borg had moved to 5-4. At 6-4, 6-5, 8-7, and 9-8, Borg was within a single point of sealing the tiebreaker for the set. True to his cautious instincts, he played not to miss and dared Connors to make the big shots under intense pressure. A composed Connors was up to that task. He attacked audaciously on all four set points against him. Once, his sidespin forehand approach went behind Borg for a winner and the other three times his approach shot was so forceful that Borg could not counterattack with any authority.

In command each time he got up to the net, Connors put away two easy overheads and knocked off a high backhand volley emphatically. After fighting off four set points, Connors was level at 9-9 in this lengthy playoff. From behind the baseline, he sent a searing backhand crosscourt for a clean winner. In a gesture that would become his trademark in the years ahead, Connors pumped his fists as he looked up animatedly toward the sky. Connors came through 11-9 in that tiebreak as Borg tamely missed a backhand. The American had seldom, if ever, been better with his back to the wall. As Connors recalled years later of that frantic sequence of points, "That tiebreaker is probably the best tennis that I will ever play under such pressure conditions."

Having lifted that burden and left it behind him, Connors broke Borg for a 3-2 fourth-set lead and it went with serve the rest of the way. But there remained some last moments of anxiety for the champion. With Connors serving for the match at 5-4, the left-hander directed a forehand volley into a vacant spot for his first match point. Then he followed his serve into the forecourt. Borg's dipping return would have been awkward to volley. Connors let it bounce, then sent a piercing backhand crosscourt and closed in on the net. Borg took his shot on the rise and passed Connors cleanly crosscourt off the forehand. Deuce. Connors was unruffled. He attacked again off a fierce, flat forehand. Borg missed the passing shot. Match point to Connors for the second time. Borg's return this time went deep crosscourt to Connors's forehand. The American's apprehension was painfully evident. He came under the ball and sliced it wide. Deuce again. Once more, Connors pressed forward. Coming in off the backhand, his approach was magnificent. Borg lobbed long off his backhand. Match point No. 3 for the American. The pattern was familiar. Connors got the short ball he wanted. He hit a penetrating forehand crosscourt and came in. Borg tried his patented two-handed crosscourt passing shot. His reply found the net. Match and title to Connors 6-4, 3-6, 7-6 (11-9), 6-4. He had won his second U.S. Open. An instant after Borg missed the final stroke, Connors wheeled around with arms upraised, turning to share his triumph with longtime mentor Pancho Segura, who stood behind the court applauding unrestrainedly.

Afterward, Connors downplayed his long wait for the first major title he had won since his Forest Hills triumph on grass in 1974. "If the sun rose and set only on Wimbledon and Forest Hills," he reflected, "there would be a lot of guys without tans." That was a fair comment, but Connors fully realized that he could not settle for minor triumphs. He had built his reputation on getting the job done when the stakes were high and this triumph over Borg on a landmark occasion was one of the shining moments of Connors's career. His tan that evening was unmistakable.

EPILOGUE

After losing that agonizing battle with Connors at Forest Hills in 1976, Borg was discouraged, but not for long. They did not meet again in an official match until Wimbledon in 1977. In that memorable final, Connors was down 0-4 in the fifth set and Borg had break points to

Jimmy Connors and Bjorn Borg

establish a 5-0 lead. Had he converted in the fifth game, the Swede would likely have taken that final set 6-0. But Connors saved the break points, held for 1-4, and then put on a burst of brilliant shotmaking, reaching 4-4 as an appreciative crowd at the All England Club cheered him on with unreserved enthusiasm. Serving at 4-4, Connors reached 15-0 but a rare double fault "came out of nowhere," as he explained later. The resurgence from Connors was over and Borg quickly collected eight straight points to win 3-6, 6-2, 6-1, 5-7, 6-4. That was the turning point of the Borg-Connors rivalry. After losing six of his first seven clashes with Connors, Borg won fourteen of the last sixteen, including the last ten in a row, for a 15-8 career edge. The critical difference during the last five years of their series was Borg's capacity to deliver unreturnable first serves on big points. He could call on that strength nearly always. In turn, Borg added more elements to his game, demonstrated more flexibility and altered his tactics on the faster surfaces. It was another case of a reversal of fortunes, but their matches remained superb spectacles until the conclusion of their rivalry at the U.S. Open in 1981. In their earlier confrontation in the Wimbledon semifinals of 1981, Connors had played perhaps his best ever tennis against Borg during the early stages, but he could no longer sustain the accelerated pace against the Swede and he bowed 0-6,4-6, 6-3, 6-0, 6-4 in a sparkling showdown.

Connors, however, performed more productively much longer than Borg, who retired from big-time tennis after the U.S. Open in 1981. Connors remained a force until early in the following decade. After beating Borg in that earlier 1976 U.S. Open final, Connors celebrated his last victory over the Swede in the 1978 Open final on hard courts and thus became the only player ever to win a major championship on three different surfaces (grass, clay and hard courts). Borg was constantly cutting Connors down at Wimbledon, adding wins over Jimmy in the 1978 final and the 1979 semifinals before that incomparable triumph in the 1981 semifinals.

Those losses clearly cut into the core of Connors's confidence during big matches. When John McEnroe emerged in the late 1970s, Connors had another nettlesome rival on his hands. From 1979 through 1981, Connors did not capture a single major championship, and as he approached the age of thirty, it seemed entirely possible that he would not capture any more Grand Slam titles. But Borg's unexpected departure after the 1981 season altered everything and Connors was reawakened.

In 1982—for the second time in his career—he was victorious at both Wimbledon and the U.S. Open in the same season. With Borg gone, Connors took a terrific five-set final from McEnroe at Wimbledon and then removed a rising Ivan Lendl in a four-set U.S. Open final only days after turning thirty. The following year, he defended his U.S. Open championship with another surprise victory over Lendl. Over the remainder of the 1980s, Connors gradually declined, but he remained among the top eight players in the world every year from 1973-88. For five straight years (1974-78), he was No. 1 on the official ATP computer. From 1973-84, he did not finish a single year lower than No. 3 in the world.

When Connors had wrist surgery in 1990 at thirty-eight, his time in top-flight tennis seemed certain to be over. But the obstinate left-hander was not through. At the 1991 U.S. Open, he not only celebrated his thirty-ninth birthday, but he strung together a series of inspiring victories and made it to the semifinals before losing to French Open champion Jim Courier. Connors could not help but be reminded—as were countless players and members of the press—of Ken Rosewall's runs to the finals of Wimbledon and Forest Hills in 1974 when the stylish Australian was also thirty-nine. On each occasion Rosewall was overwhelmed by the mighty power of the Connors groundstroke arsenal, winning only eight games in a total of six sets. Eight years later, on the eve of the 1982 U.S. Open, Connors stood in the bright sunlight on the stadium court at Flushing Meadow talking to the Englishman John Lloyd as he prepared to practice. He told Lloyd, "Rosewall more than anyone taught me how important it was to get down low for my groundstrokes. He kept the ball so low all the time that he forced you to keep digging and it was a great lesson for me."

But after his "last hurrah" at the U.S. Open in 1991, Connors wisely rearranged his priorities and, despite sporadic appearances on the men's tour, he moved on to establish a senior tour that revolved largely around him. He remained, as always a ferocious competitor who stood by the statement he made in his prime. "I hate to lose more than I love to win." He carried that attitude with him on the senior circuit, dominating Borg and other marquee players for many years with his overwhelming appetite for success and the fierce combativeness of his play. Observing him on court in his mid-forties, it was hard to imagine that anyone could summon so much energy and enthusiasm.

The joy in putting himself on the line was always unmistakable and he had demonstrated that quality against different generations of great players. When he first came into prominence at seventeen, he had toppled the renowned Roy Emerson at the Pacific Southwest in Los Angeles and had won and lost against the great Pancho Gonzales, one of his early coaches and doubles partners (once) at the U.S. Open. Connors continued his inexorable march to the top when he confronted the Australian superstars Rosewall, Rod Laver and John Newcombe. Then he took on Borg, McEnroe and Lendl in the most colorful rivalries of this career, but it did not stop there.

After his salad days were over, he was not reluctant to struggle with much younger men moving up and through their primes. He had stirring clashes with Boris Becker and Stefan Edberg – routing the Swedish star only a year before Edberg reached No. 1 in the world. And his unflinching latter-day journey even included two meetings with Pete Sampras in the early 1990s. There were times when his behavior was embarrassing, when his crudity toward linesmen and umpires was unacceptably obscene, when his abrasive actions over-shadowed his clean and elegant shotmaking. But despite the complex facets of his personality, Connors was a man the fans could not ignore. The record reveals that McEnroe at his best was a better player, that Borg was superior on the crucial occasions over time, that Lendl won the same number of major championships. But no male tennis player did more than Jimmy Connors to boost the game's popularity. He was an indispensable figure.

As for Borg, after his difficult setback against Connors in their tense 1976 U.S. Open clash, he produced a long sequence of sterling achievements. He won Wimbledon five years in a row from 1976-1980, a feat that had never previously been achieved since the abolishment of the "Challenge Round" system in 1922. Borg was also victorious at the French Open six times between 1974-1981, leading many observers to the conclusion that he was the best men's clay-court player of all-time. He won at least one Grand Slam championship a year for eight consecutive years from 1974-1981, amassing eleven in that span.

In his era, Borg created an almost discernible aura around himself as the unfailingly cool man in a crisis, as the man you could depend upon when the chips were down. He would be beaten during this period by players who peaked on particularly auspicious afternoons, but he seldom beat himself. He was the quintessential match player and a surprisingly adaptable competitor, taking the French Open and Wimbledon in succession for three consecutive years (1978-1980) as he shifted his objectives from the slow clay of Paris to the fast grass of Wimbledon.

CHAPTER NINETEEN

Bjorn Borg *vs.* John McEnroe

WIMBLEDON, FINAL, JULY 5, 1980

In this match of endurance and suspense, perhaps unequalled in its athletic splendor, the Swede and American produced the most gripping tiebreaker ever played.

PROLOGUE

As a new decade dawned in 1980, Bjorn Borg remained the preeminent player in tennis and his mastery of the big points made him virtually unassailable. He had firmly overtaken Jimmy Connors and his majestic performances in the major championships set him apart from anyone else in his field. But in all his time at and near the top of his profession, he had encountered no one quite like John Patrick McEnroe of New York.

McEnroe was a dynamic left-hander with an explosive temperament and a spontaneous style of play that contrasted with Borg's much more meticulous, programmed patterns. McEnroe had grown up in Douglaston, just outside New York City, and had been coached as a teenager by former Australian Davis Cup captain Harry Hopman. While Hopman had worked largely with conventional Australian serve-and-volleyers who seemed to have followed the same systematic guidelines, McEnroe was raised at the opposite end of the spectrum.

His service stance was so fashioned that his opponents saw as much of his back as his face. He seemed dead set against bending his knees when he was up at the net, but he volleyed brilliantly and his touch in the forecourt was often astonishing. His ground strokes were unconventionally well produced. He frequently took the ball on the rise but he was not a big hitter off either side; instead, he was a master at playing off an opponent's pace and rushing them into mistakes with his adroit, subtle variations of speed and direction. Almost across the board, McEnroe broke the rules of conventional wisdom with his approach to playing the game. He was one of the few great innovators ever to step on a tennis court.

McEnroe had a distinguished junior career but it was not until he was eighteen, in the summer of 1977, that he made his mark. That year he went to Wimbledon for the first time, where he had to work his way through the qualifying rounds at Roehampton just to earn the right to make his debut at the All England Club. Even when he won his three qualifying matches, no one expected him to strike a spark in the main event, but McEnroe was rising into another realm as a competitor and the grass court surface was suited to his aggressive serve-and-volley game.

Furthermore, McEnroe's disarming volatility caught the establishment off guard. He seemed to have little respect for the leading players and even less for the officials. He wore what seemed to be a permanent scowl and seldom smiled at his good fortune. No matter how well he was playing, McEnroe seemed incapable of finding satisfaction in his gifted shotmaking. He was so talented that he progressed through the draw at his first Wimbledon with almost bemused assurance, surprised by his success on one level, unimpressed with his opposition on the other. He toppled No. 13 seed Phil Dent, a former Australian Open finalist, in the quarterfinals, then lost his semifinal appearance to Connors in a first-rate, four-set comeuppance.

Nevertheless, McEnroe was now indisputably a rising star. He attended Stanford University for a year, won the NCAA Championships in 1978, then turned professional and went to work with unbridled passion and persistence. By the end of 1978, when he was only nineteen, he became the No. 4 ranked player in the world and he closed that season with a display of impressive poise under pressure. Facing his esteemed countryman Arthur Ashe in the final of the Masters at New York's Madison Square Garden, McEnroe led 5-4, 40-0 in the opening set, then double-faulted three times in a row to allow Ashe back into the set. Ashe pounced on the opportunity and won a tiebreaker to move out in front. Later, in the third and final set, Ashe had two match points with McEnroe serving at 4-5. A deliriously pro-Ashe crowd of seventeen thousand cheered their man vociferously, but McEnroe kept his nerve and went on to win 6-7, 6-3, 7-5.

He seemed to draw upon that outcome over the next three years. In 1979, McEnroe won the championship of his country for the first time. In the semifinals, he cut down the defending champion Connors in three convincing sets, then took apart his friend and fellow New Yorker Vitas Gerulaitis 7-5, 6-3, 6-3 for the title. He had won his first major championship only a few miles from his boyhood home in New York and he had shown that he would be difficult for anyone to handle as the leading players took their talent and ambitions into the 1980s.

Borg, however, was going strong as Wimbledon approached in 1980. In both 1978 and 1979, he had captured the French Open and Wimbledon. He wanted to keep his chances for a Grand Slam alive by winning the U.S. Open in both of those years. He had lost to Connors in the 1978 Open final and to the big-serving American Roscoe Tanner the following year in the quarterfinals. But the month before the 1980 Wimbledon, Borg ruled at Roland Garros on the clay for the third consecutive year, and the fifth time in all, winning the clay court championship of the world without the loss of a single set in seven matches, crushing Gerulaitis 6-4, 6-1, 6-2 in the final.

McEnroe, who had risen past Connors to No. 2 in the world with Borg ahead of him, had lost in the third round at Paris to the Australian Paul McNamee. That may have been a hidden blessing because it gave him more time to adjust to grass courts and prepare for Wimbledon. McEnroe plainly wanted to make amends for his last two Wimbledons, which had paled in comparison to his first in 1977. In 1978, he had lost on an outside court to countryman Erik Van Dillen, a much better player in doubles than singles. For McEnroe, it was a very disappointing five-set, opening-round defeat. The next year he was beaten in straight sets by fellow American Tim Gullikson— who later coached both Martina Navratilova and Pete Sampras—in the round of sixteen. McEnroe was surely a better player than he had shown on either of those occasions. By 1980 he was also more sure of himself as a person and a competitor.

THE MATCH

There was a quiet sense among the cognoscenti all through Wimbledon in 1980 that Borg and McEnroe would meet in the end to play for the title. Borg had become an immensely intimidating adversary for everyone competing on the grass of the All England Club. He was seeking to establish himself as the first man in the modern era to win the game's most coveted crown five years in a row. He had survived so many stern tests on Centre Court that he seemed invincible in that setting. After taking the title without the loss of a set in seven impeccable matches in 1976, he had been stretched to five sets six times in the following three years but had won them all. He was by now the master of the defining moments at the All England Club, a player who treated adversity as a minor annoyance.

McEnroe, meanwhile, was the stylistic counterpart to Borg. No one in the Swede's dominant years at Wimbledon had played a better brand of grass court tennis. Furthermore, McEnroe had demonstrated in his rivalry with Borg that he could compete successfully against the Swede on any fast surface. In their initial battle two years earlier, McEnroe had toppled Borg in straight sets indoors at Stockholm. They had been trading victories and defeats ever since. Borg took their second confrontation at the WCT Richmond event early in 1979, and McEnroe prevailed in a final-set tiebreak a few months later in New Orleans. Borg got back to 2-2 in the series with a 6-4, 6-2 triumph in Rotterdam. McEnroe retaliated with a four-set triumph over Borg in the WCT Dallas Finals in May 1979. Borg made it 3-3 in that summer of 1979 with a win over McEnroe on hard courts at Toronto. Then, in January 1980 at The Masters in New York, Borg got by his tenacious adversary 6-7, 6-3, 7-6.

Coming into Wimbledon, Borg held a narrow 4-3 edge and the Swede had posted two wins in a row in this scorching personal series. Seeded first and second, they took their places in the final as expected. Borg dropped only two sets along the way and was never seriously tested. McEnroe was pressed hard in a five-set, second-round match with the Australian Terry Rocavert, but he struggled from two-sets-to-one down to pull out the victory. In the semifinals, Borg accounted for the unseeded American Brian Gottfried 6-0 in the fourth set, while

McEnroe rallied from 2-4 in the fourth to oust Connors in a high-tension contest 6-3, 3-6, 6-3, 6-4.

McEnroe was magnificent at the start of his eagerly awaited battle with Borg. He glided through the first set 6-1, conceding only seven points in four service games, breaking Borg twice by attacking diligently as Borg stayed back on his second serve. Borg remained cautious and somewhat out of sync in the second set. But he sedulously held on to his serve time and again as McEnroe looked for a way to claim a decisive two-sets-to-love lead. With Borg serving at 4-4 in the second, McEnroe raised the stakes and went after a service break full force.

Three times in that critical ninth game, McEnroe reached break point by pressing forward at every opportunity and volleying with awesome control and touch. Yet on all three of these big break points, Borg produced surgical first serves that were unreturnable. The Swede held for 5-4 and then again for 6-5. Until this juncture, McEnroe had been too much for Borg on serve as the Swede stood 10 to 15 feet behind the baseline to make his returns. But with the New Yorker serving at 5-6, Borg finally found the range with his heavy topspin shots, making them dip at McEnroe's feet as the left-hander came in for the first volley. After McEnroe netted a low backhand approach volley at 5-6, 30-30, Borg was able to make it one set all.

Emerging from that late second set crisis raised Borg's spirits considerably and carried him stubbornly through the third. Borg charged to 3-0, stood firm in a seven deuce game in which he saved five break points to reach 5-2, then served his way smoothly to a 6-3 third-set verdict and a two-sets-to-one lead. Borg was proceeding methodically toward his goal in the fourth set. He broke McEnroe in the ninth game with a plummeting backhand crosscourt return winner, off a trademark McEnroe slice serve wide in the advantage court, and took a 5-4 lead.

He served for the match in the tenth game and proceeded rapidly to 40-15, double match point. As he paused at that moment before attempting to finish his business, Borg seemed certain to prevail in four sets. The clock behind his right shoulder read 4:53 in the afternoon. The match was two hours and thirty-four minutes old. Everything was neatly in place for Borg to enhance his record by vanquishing McEnroe with calm assurance. On the first match point, a deep first serve to the backhand was narrowly off the mark, and then when Borg attacked during a short exchange, McEnroe passed him cleanly down the line off the backhand. A second match point was still available.

The top seed tried to put away a backhand volley but he popped it up slightly and McEnroe advanced to cut it off. On the run, McEnroe released a forehand drive volley past Borg for another winner. The tension was palpable. At deuce, McEnroe forced Borg into a forehand passing shot error and then hit a winning service return. It was 5-5. McEnroe was resurgent. Borg was incredulous. How had it all slipped from his grasp? Why was he still on the court? Could he possibly recoup?

Both players held to set up a tiebreaker. They proceeded to play a sequence of points that enthralled the British audience and kept people around the world in front of their television sets. Both men were so good with their backs to the wall that the fabric of emotion among the fans was torn by conflicting, changing loyalties. The two contrasting competitors raised the level of play far beyond expectation. In this excruciatingly close tiebreak, Borg reached match point with McEnroe serving at 5-6, but the left-hander lunged for Borg's dipping forehand return and produced a brilliant forehand drop volley winner. Borg immediately responded with a vintage crosscourt backhand passing shot and served at 7-6, arriving at match point for the fourth time.

A conservatively played high backhand volley from Borg opened up a wide window of opportunity for McEnroe, who whipped a backhand pass down the line for an outright winner. McEnroe came up with another dazzling passing shot to reach 8-7 and his first set point, only to be halted by a winning forehand return from Borg off a deep first serve.

Then McEnroe stormed in behind serve to knock off a high backhand volley. He led 9-8 but Borg served his way out of that precarious moment and connected with a winning volley of his own. A penetrating first serve deep to McEnroe's backhand forced an error and brought Borg to 10-9—a fifth match point.

Neither man was buckling. McEnroe's service winner to the back-

John McEnroe

hand lifted him to 10-10. Borg's forehand pass beyond the reach of a diving McEnroe gave the Swede an 11-10 lead on serve and a sixth match point. McEnroe was in mid-court when he tentatively struck a backhand approach shot. It clipped the net cord and fell over for a very dicey winner. Internally, Borg had to be distressed by that improbable point, but he concealed his emotions and forced McEnroe into a low forehand volley error with a sharply struck two-hander.

Borg thus moved to 12-11 and a seventh match point. Surely he would seal it all here. But McEnroe rejected that possibility. Borg ran around a return of a second serve and hit his forehand hard with heavy topspin. McEnroe had closed in tightly and his crosscourt backhand first volley was well beyond Borg's reach. It was 12-12. The players now changed ends for the fourth time in this agonizingly suspenseful struggle. McEnroe again came in behind his second serve and punched a forehand volley behind Borg for a winner and a 13-12 lead and, for him, a third set point.

Then Borg came in swiftly behind a deep first serve to the backhand. His backhand volley floated deep toward the baseline. It seemed to be going out, but fell an inch inside the line and McEnroe could not handle the bounce. Then Borg missed a low backhand volley to give McEnroe a 14-13 lead that the New Yorker flagrantly squandered with a forehand volley wide of the sideline despite an open court. Then McEnroe charged to 15-14. A service winner from Borg to the backhand made it 15-15. The players changed sides for the fifth time as the audience lustily applauded both men. Such extraordinary tennis under stress, over so many climactic points, was unimaginable.

Borg served the thirty-first point and failed to "stick" his crosscourt backhand volley. McEnroe easily chased it down and drove a forehand pass into an open space to lead at 16-15. McEnroe served and volleyed again but overplayed a high backhand volley. It was 16-16. Borg missed a forehand return placement by a hair. He was serving at 16-17. Borg charged behind a solid first serve but dumped a forehand drop volley into the net. Centre Court erupted thunderously. The appreciation was non-partisan. Two valiant young men had fought for a glory both deserved. Set to McEnroe 18-16 in a tiebreak that would never be replicated. McEnroe had saved seven match points—five of them in this stupendous tiebreaker. The New Yorker had needed seven set points of his own before he could force a fifth set.

Borg sat in his chair at the changeover understandably dismayed and deflated by his many lost opportunities. A reinvigorated but not overconfident McEnroe reflected briefly on his good fortune. Then both men went back to work. In the opening game of the fifth set, Borg trailed 0-30. He was not going to recover easily if he lost his serve here, not after the demoralizing conclusion of the fourth set. A perfectly placed first serve deep to McEnroe's backhand forced an error and three more solid points lifted Borg out of that bind. He held for 1-0. Now McEnroe trailed 0-40 in the second game. He double-faulted to fall behind break point for the fourth time, but resolutely held for 1-1. At 3-4 in the fifth, McEnroe did it again. Down 0-40, he summoned the best that was left in him and held on gamely for 4-4.

Borg had been through it all now, but he kept plodding on. By the time he reached 7-6, he had finally taken too much out of McEnroe at last. From 0-30 in his opening service game, Borg had won twenty-eight of twenty-nine points on his serve in the fifth set. He had served five love games. He had kept leading his foe into trouble by directing his first serve deep and wide to the American's backhand and McEnroe could not defend himself against that tactic. At 6-7, 15-15, McEnroe was caught off guard by an inside out forehand return winner from Borg. Then Borg's whipped topspin backhand passing shot provoked a netted forehand volley from McEnroe. It was 15-40 and Borg was at match point for the eighth time. McEnroe came in gamely on serve and punched a forehand volley down the middle of the court. Borg lined up his backhand and rifled it crosscourt. McEnroe turned to watch the shot land safely inches inside the sideline. Borg fell to his knees with relief and exultation. After three hours and fifty three minutes—nearly an hour-and-a-half after he had reached match point for the first time—Borg had persevered as only he could.

As Borg walked off the court following his 1-6, 7-5, 6-3, 6-7 (16-18), 8-6 triumph, he was asked by NBC broadcaster Bud Collins where he placed his victory in a historical context. "It has to be one of the best matches I have ever played," he said, "and I think probably the best I have ever played at Wimbledon. I thought after I lost the fourth set

Bjorn Borg

I would lose the match. I was exhausted, especially after losing all of those match points, but I didn't give up."

Nearly two decades later, when he was in New York for a press conference announcing his 1999 induction into the International Tennis Hall of Fame, McEnroe did his best to put this unprecedented match into perspective. Despite the hard reality of losing an epic battle, McEnroe maintained that no match had meant more to him as he looked back on his illustrious career.

"The one thing I hear about the most is the match with Borg at Wimbledon in 1980," he said. "In some ways I would have to pick that. It showed me, and hopefully showed a lot of other tennis players, that in losing, actually that could elevate your status. And even if you are not necessarily the winner every time, if you are part of history like I felt there, it makes it okay. Being part of that match was perhaps the most exciting thing in my career. The vibrations and goodwill I get from people from that match are incredible. It is far and away my most talked about match."

EPILOGUE

Two months after their monumental encounter at Wimbledon, Borg and McEnroe met again in the final of the U.S. Open. For the third straight year, Borg had a chance to win a third consecutive major title and a first U.S. Open. Had he realized that goal, he would have gone to Australia at the end of those years in an attempt to complete the Grand Slam. But it was not to be. He lost to McEnroe 7-6, 6-1, 6-7, 5-7, 6-4 in a bizarre final at Flushing Meadow. It was a contest that did not approach the level of the Wimbledon extravaganza. At the U.S. Open, Borg twice served for the first set but threw it away. Quietly angered by his failure, he was taken apart in the second set by a resolute McEnroe. Before he knew it, Borg was down two sets to love but he slowly worked his way into the match with meticulous determination in the third and fourth sets. By the time he reached 3-3 in the fifth, Borg looked highly likely to succeed. But on the first point of the seventh game, McEnroe approached on a backhand that the linesman called good on the baseline. Borg stood there staring at the official for an exceedingly long moment, but the call was not altered. McEnroe broke him for 4-3 and ran out the match.

A year later, the major championships were essentially a showcase for Borg and McEnroe to display their rivalry and their supremacy. After Borg took a five-set final from an evolving Ivan Lendl at the French Open—making him the first man in history to win at least one Grand Slam title for eight consecutive years—the Swede and the American squared off in the finals of both Wimbledon and the U.S. Open for a second year in a row. At Wimbledon, Borg had made a remarkable recovery from two-sets-to-love down against Connors in the semifinals to lift his winning streak to forty-one matches, but after taking the first set of the final from McEnroe, Borg bowed 4-6, 7-6, 7-6, 6-4.

Two months later, Borg bowed in four sets to McEnroe in the U.S. Open final. He had failed again in New York, falling for the fourth time in a championship match of a major tournament he never won.

When that match was over, the normally imperturbable sportsman was so distraught that he did not stay for the presentation ceremony. He sadly picked up his belongings and left the stadium. Without realizing it at the time, he was in the process of quitting the game. The following year, he obdurately refused to adhere to the rules imposed by the game's governing authorities who wanted him to commit to ten tournaments outside of his Grand Slam participation. Borg had already sharply reduced his schedule in the previous two years. He played a few scattered events thereafter, but never again appeared in a major tournament. His loss to McEnroe in New York was his last match at a Grand Slam event.

Borg would later concede that one of the primary reasons he left the game was his pessimistic view of how he would fare in the future against McEnroe, who had taken away his No. 1 ranking by winning the two most coveted titles in tennis during the 1981 season. Borg believed then that McEnroe was too versatile for him and assumed he would keep confronting his nemesis time after time in the years ahead. But he may have been well off the mark with that assessment. In 1982—with Borg having stepped out of the picture—McEnroe did not retain his major titles. He lost to Connors in a five-set Wimbledon final, then fell to Ivan Lendl in a straight-set U.S. Open semifinal. Connors, the man who had not beaten Borg since 1978, elevated his game brilliantly and won Wimbledon and the U.S. Open in 1982.

McEnroe, for his part, acknowledged that he missed having Borg around to push him on to greater heights. He was not as comfortable as he should have been occupying the lofty terrain as the best player in the world. In retrospect, Borg would almost surely have won at least one major championship in 1982 and perhaps more. But he had lost his taste for tough competition, and once he stopped training as he had for so long, his determination crumbled.

Nearly a decade later, in 1991, Borg plotted a comeback. He was approaching thirty-five by then and he had waited far too long. The ill-advised return to tennis never got off the ground and he was unable to win a match in his main tour appearances from 1991-93. He sensibly stopped playing in the men's game once and for all.

Bjorn Borg had a relatively brief but remarkable career. His footwork and mobility were unsurpassed in his time—and perhaps ever. He gave the game a good name with his dignified demeanor and admirable court behavior. He may well be remembered most for his splendid series with McEnroe. After the 1980 season, Borg led, 7-4, but following the three 1981 setbacks, they stood even at 7-7, and that is how it ended.

McEnroe's best tennis was still ahead of him. He, too, would suffer from a mid-career burnout, but he played successfully into the early 1990s. Somehow it was never the same for the stormy left-hander without Bjorn Borg.

CHAPTER TWENTY

Chris Evert *vs.* Martina Navratilova

AUSTRALIAN OPEN, FINAL, DECEMBER 6, 1981

With the wind blowing unrelentingly, the two great rivals of contrasting styles and temperaments closed out their 1981 campaign with a captivating contest.

PROLOGUE

During the last quarter of the twentieth century, there were no series of matches more engaging than those played by Martina Navratilova and Chris Evert. These clashes pitted a demonstrative, left-handed serve-and-volleyer against a patient, disciplined baseliner. They met in head-to-head competition eighty times between 1973 and 1988. They collided at least four times in every major championship. They battled gamely indoors and out, on slow and fast surfaces, in good and bad conditions, throughout their careers. Their rivalry was regarded by the vast majority of authorities as the greatest in the history of the game—not excluding the men. Others placed their confrontations in an even grander category as the most compelling rivalry produced in any sport. From the outset, the Evert-Navratilova matchup had everything working for it. As Evert herself said when she reflected on the rivalry for this book, "What made it interesting all along was the contrasts between Martina and me. If you have two players with the same kinds of games and personalities, it can be boring and repetitious. But we had so many things about us that were different. She came from Czechoslovakia and I was from Florida. She was left-handed and aggressive. I was right-handed, with a two-handed backhand, and a counterpuncher. I internalized things and she did not. We both brought our own set of fans into each match we played."

The contrasts did not end there. Navratilova was sturdily built and over time became muscular and ruggedly athletic. Evert was known as "The Girl Next Door" and was a model of womanly grace and elegance. Navratilova was often outspoken and emotional; Evert was diplomatic and polite in the public arena. Evert turned her restraint and dignity into enduring attributes; Navratilova used her passion to engender popularity with her audiences. Navratilova would protest questionable line calls genuinely but sometimes caustically; Evert would simply register her disapproval with a stern glare at the officials.

And yet, there were some subcutaneous similarities. Their respect for each other as professionals was visible and sincere. Both women were highly intelligent in person and as players.

They would become better at their craft because of the demands they placed on each other with such different brands of play. Finally, Chrissie Evert and Martina Navratilova stayed at or near the top of their profession for much longer than they could have imagined when they started their climb up the ladder.

Chris was one of five children raised by Fort Lauderdale teaching professional Jimmy Evert, a strict taskmaster. Jimmy Evert was once ranked eleventh in the United States and won the Canadian Championships in 1947. He stressed sound ground stroke fundamentals and a consistency of commitment. Each one of his five children—three daughters and two sons— reached at least the final of a national championship during their junior careers, but Chrissie had the greatest drive and the highest hopes.

She was well ahead of the game during her junior days, moving into women's tennis precociously in her teens. When she was fifteen, she sent signals to the tennis world of her immense promise, toppling world No. 1 Margaret Court in a pair of tiebreakers at a small tournament in Charlotte, North Carolina. Less than a month before, Court had completed a Grand Slam by capturing the U.S. Open.

At sixteen, in the summer of 1971, Chrissie became the youngest ever to reach the semifinals of the U.S. Open. She recorded a string of stirring, come-from-behind triumphs in that tournament. A pivotal victory was her round of sixteen success against countrywoman Mary Ann Eisel. Confronting a seasoned serve-and-volleyer on the fast grass courts at Forest Hills, the Floridian saved six match points in a remarkable three-set win. Although she lost decisively to Billie

Jean King in the semifinal round, Evert had arrived as a celebrated player. By 1974, when she was nineteen, she was the best woman player in the world. She won her first two Grand Slam championships at the French Open and Wimbledon that year. Evert would stay at the top for seven of eight years in that span. She had tested herself against a cluster of commendable rivals through the seventies and into the eighties, winning nine of thirteen matches against Court, taking nineteen of twenty-six meetings with King, and overcoming Goolagong in twenty-five of thirty-eight battles. Other than Navratilova, the only major adversary to cause serious problems for Evert was the Californian, Tracy Austin. Austin was a virtual clone of Evert from the baseline, solid and assertive off both sides, seldom making careless mistakes, always probing for flaws. She would have her career cut short in the early eighties by back problems, but not before she defeated both Navratilova and Evert to establish herself as the youngest-ever U.S. Open women's champion in 1979 at sixteen. Austin took the crown again two years later.

Evert recorded one of the most significant triumphs of her career when she stopped Austin 4-6, 6-1, 6-1 in the semifinals of the U.S. Open in 1980. She had lost to the Californian five consecutive times leading up to that battle. Evert collected her fifth Open title the next day, and restored her confidence and authority with that triumph. She then had an excellent first half of 1981, winning her third Wimbledon singles title and expanding her game under the expert guidance of a new coach, Dennis Ralston, a former U.S. No. 1 player.

Navratilova had developed her game in Czechoslovakia. She was two years younger than Evert, and much more of a risk taker. Her parents divorced when Martina was three. Her father committed suicide when she was about ten, although Martina did not know until much later. Meanwhile, her mother married Mirek Navratil. They lived in a village called Revnice. Martina regarded Mirek as her father—not stepfather. Both her mother and grandmother were versatile tennis players, though they did not make a career of it. Her mother's family lost nearly everything they had during the 1948 takeover by the Communists. Nonetheless, Martina was able to pursue her tennis career. After losing to Evert in the semifinals of the U.S. Open in 1975,

Martina Navratilova

she defected from her native land and took up residence in the United States. By then, Navratilova was already entrenched among the top five in the world.

The athletic left-hander joined Evert to win two major tournaments in doubles, including the 1976 championship at Wimbledon. Over time, they gave up playing as a team because their singles competition took precedence. In 1978, Navratilova came of age when she won her first Grand Slam singles title at Wimbledon. At twenty-one, she rallied from 2-4 in the final set to oust Evert 2-6, 6-4, 7-5. The following year, Navratilova toppled Evert again in the Centre Court final. She was the top-ranked player for the year.

Navratilova seemed to be peaking after enduring a couple of difficult years. She did not win a major title in 1980, and her confidence was wavering in the spring of 1981. During the clay court final at Amelia Island, Florida, Evert was letter-perfect and Navratilova was way out of sync. Evert won 6-0, 6-0. But that loss made Navratilova realize that she needed to get back to work.

It was in that period that basketball player Nancy Lieberman took over as a fitness coach and mentor for Martina, and later in the year transsexual Renee Richards became her tennis coach. As Evert recalled, "I remember Nancy Lieberman coming to Amelia Island and watching me beat Martina love and love. Nancy had an edge and a toughness about her and she influenced Martina with those characteristics. Nancy convinced Martina to get more serious about her conditioning. Right after Martina lost that match to me at Amelia Island, Nancy took her out to the basketball court."

Between then and the U.S. Open, Navratilova trimmed her weight and approached each match with a growing professionalism. As Evert observed, "By the U.S. Open, there was a big change in Martina's body. She was much stronger and fitter. She went through rigorous workouts, changed her eating habits, became a better athlete, and it all helped her tennis. In a sense, she was brainwashed. Nancy Lieberman kept reinforcing that she was the strongest and the best one out there. Together with Renee Richards, they were a very good combination for the fitness and the tennis."

At the U.S. Open of 1981, Navratilova was rejuvenated in many ways. She had become a U.S. citizen after a six-year wait. In the semifinals, she and Evert played a stupendous match, a contest filled with splendid points and brilliantly pursued rallies. Navratilova was behind 2-4 in the final set, but stopped Chrissie 7-5, 4-6, 6-4. They had not played since Amelia Island. The hard courts at Flushing Meadow provided a neutral surface, and both players shined. Navratilova lost a wrenching 1-6, 7-6, 7-6 match against Austin in the final.

As the year came to a close and the leading players assembled at the Australian Open for the last major of the season, both Evert and Navratilova looked at Melbourne as the chance to finish the Grand Slam season on a high note. Navratilova had not won a "Big Four" singles title since Wimbledon two years earlier. Evert wanted to add Australia to her victory list—it was the only major title she had not secured. At Kooyong Stadium on the grass courts of Melbourne, they would confront each other in yet another epic clash.

THE MATCH

The rivalry was eight years old when Martina and Chrissie came into Melbourne. This would be their first meeting at the Australian Open, but they had played many classic matches over the years in and outside the major events. In their overall series, Evert led 29-15. In the Grand Slam events, Evert held a slim 4-3 edge. It was apparent, however, that Navratilova was making sizable strides. She had been beaten in twenty of their first twenty-four clashes between 1973 and the middle of 1978. In that time frame, Evert was much stronger mentally, more consistent off the ground, and better as a match player.

With her comeback triumph over Evert in the 1978 Wimbledon, Navratilova demonstrated a tenacity she had seldom shown before. She would drift away from her finest form again in the years ahead, but on balance she was moving in the right direction. In any case, after their extraordinary U.S. Open battle three months earlier, Navratilova had ousted Evert that autumn in Tokyo. But the week before Melbourne and the "Big Four" showdown, Evert had stopped Navratilova in the grass court warm-up event, winning 6-1 in the third set at Sydney.

Seeded first and third, respectively, at the Australian Open, Evert and Navratilova reached the final without much difficulty. Evert did not drop a set on her way to the title match while Navratilova conceded only one—to the American, Kathy Jordan. The second-seeded Austin was upset by countrywoman Pam Shriver in the quarterfinals; Navratilova accounted for Shriver in a straight-set semifinal.

In their forty-fifth career confrontation, Evert and Navratilova stepped onto the stadium court at Kooyong on a windy afternoon. "I felt going into the match," said Evert, "that Martina had the momentum with her. She was in great shape and I knew she had not won a Grand Slam title for a long time. She had a lot of pride. As a champion, she did not want to go without a Grand Slam title that year. By the time we played at the end of the tournament, the stadium court at Kooyong was pretty chewed up, so your best bet was to get to the net. That also favored Martina."

Nevertheless, Evert stood her ground ably in the first set. She had the best ground strokes of her era, and they served her well on any surface. On both the forehand and her revered two-handed backhand, she hit the ball basically flat with incomparable depth. She kept her returns solid and low when Navratilova charged in behind her heavily spun serve. And no one could disguise the lob better than Evert, particularly off her backhand side.

Martina was on her way to demonstrating that she was the greatest grass-court player in the history of the game. With so many low and irregular bounces, Navratilova's slice backhand approach was a deadly weapon, paving the way for open court volleys and crisp smashes. Her mobility all over the court was strikingly impressive, but she excelled with her lateral movement at the net. There were times when Evert seemed certain to have driven a ball past her on her right side, and yet Martina would lunge with alacrity and make astounding backhand volley winners at full stretch from near the sideline.

Evert knew the importance of a high first-serve percentage when she faced Martina on grass. Chrissie did not want to present Navratilova with the opportunity to chip and charge off her second serve, although she had unflagging confidence in her ability to counterattack. No one could match her in that department. It was not Evert's agility that gave her such an edge on her passing shots off both sides; it was her intuitive anticipation, her unerring court sense.

The first set was fought intensely all the way. Evert had to work harder to hold serve, but her concentration was a strong asset. She knew precisely what she wanted to do against Navratilova from the backcourt, and her execution was nearly flawless. "It was tough playing Martina on grass," she recalled, "but it was predictable. She would hit big forehands and that was her dangerous side because she could do anything and go anywhere with that shot. But her backhand was also a great shot for her on grass because she would keep it so low and deep, and then be on top of the net so quickly that I would have to hit a perfect passing shot. Her serve was versatile and she gave me problems pulling me off the court to my backhand."

Chris Evert

That was essentially the pattern of play. Navratilova applied the pressure; Evert tried to shift the burden back to her rival with her un-canny precision. Navratilova attacked relentlessly on serve and closed in swiftly to the net; Evert answered with a marvelous mixture of passing shots and lobs. The players battled furiously in that first set and were level at 5-5, then again at 6-6. They moved on to the tie-break, and were locked there at four points all.

Evert collected three points in a row to take the tiebreaker 7-4, and it gave her an inevitable lift. She went down a break at 3-2 in the second set, then broke back in the sixth game with pinpoint returns and held for 4-3. She sensed then the possibility of a straight-set win. If she could break in the next game, she would be serving for the match. The soon-to-be-twenty-seven-year-old Floridian was eager to finish the job in style.

Navratilova was not obliging. As Richard Yallop observed in the Melbourne newspaper *The Age*, "Navratilova met fire with fire, pro-ducing her best service game to date, with two winners, and although she was passed twice by Evert's forehand, she held serve with a back-hand volley." Martina was at 4-4 and she was soaring. She granted Evert only two points in the next two games to close out the set and level the match, finishing with an emblematic ace on set point in the tenth game.

The twenty-five-year-old left-hander was ignited by her second-set resurgence. She moved firmly to 2-0 in the third set, having won five games in a row. With Chrissie serving in the third game, Martina reached break point six times. An obstinate Evert would not yield, giving nothing away, forcing Martina to sustain a very high standard of attacking play. The Floridian held for 1-2 after a long and strenu-ous game.

A composed Navratilova resumed her control of the contest. She held on safely for 3-1, broke for 4-1, and held again for a seemingly insurmountable 5-1 lead. "At that stage," Evert said eighteen years later, "you are frustrated. You are so mad that you just find yourself going for your shots more stubbornly. Shots were hitting the lines and I was connecting with the ball as well as I could have."

In a scintillating recovery that captivated the crowd, Evert came back into the match. She held on for 2-5, broke for 3-5, held again, and broke once more. Navratilova had twice served for the match but had never advanced to match point. Evert had displayed her determination when it counted. She was serving at 5-5, looking to complete a spirited comeback, knowing she was on a very good roll.

And yet, she was not convinced she could keep flowing. As she recalled, "Martina didn't panic when I got to 5-5. She just stuck to her game plan and kept trying to get in. She had the attitude that if she was going to lose, she would lose playing her game. By then I think I had probably exhausted my supply of passing shots."

At 5-5, 30-30, Evert served into a heavy wind. She wanted to maintain her length off the ground but did not gauge the wind correctly. She drove a flat forehand long for 30-40. She decided she had to make a move, beat her opponent to the net, and strike from close range. Chrissie came in, but Navratilova worked her way in as well. They had an exchange of volleys, but the left-hander pressed forward to put away a backhand volley.

Navratilova was serving for the match a third time at 6-5. She reached 40-15, double match point, only to squander the first with a netted low forehand volley. Navratilova attacked again, made a remarkable half volley, and forced Evert to miss one last passing shot attempt. Martina Navratilova was the Australian Open champion, defeating Chrissie Evert 6-7, 6-4, 7-5. She had captured the third Grand Slam championship of her career, having defeated her foremost rival and friend on every one of those final-round occasions. Evert had narrowly missed out on an opportunity for a thirteenth "Big Four" title.

EPILOGUE

By virtue of that triumph over Evert in a major final, Navratilova had altered the course of her career irrevocably. Although Evert finished 1981 as No. 1 in the world, for the seventh time in eight years, and Navratilova concluded her campaign at No. 3 behind Tracy Austin, the prodigious left-hander would take over the game in the first half of the 1980s the way Evert had controlled the second half of the 1970s.

In the five years that followed her breakthrough in Australia, Navratilova was beaten only fourteen times. From 1982-86, she won seventy of eighty-four tournaments, including twelve major singles championships. In 1982, the Richards-Lieberman team gave her the regimen on and off the court to make major advances as an athlete. The following year, Richards stepped aside and was replaced by former world-class player, Mike Estep.

Estep—who remained Navratilova's coach through the 1986 season—took full advantage of the hard work done by Richards in the year-and-a-half preceding his arrival. Richards had revamped Navratilova's ground game comprehensively. She urged her pupil to come over the forehand with heavier topspin, providing a platform for Martina to gain greater margin for error with that shot while still attacking. Richards also had worked diligently on the development of a topspin backhand, a shot Martina needed primarily to pass her opponents.

Martina's revamped ground strokes made her less vulnerable from the backcourt. Her forehand remained a potent stroke, but there were days when it went off the mark. The top-spin backhand was still suspect at times, but it made Martina a much better counter attacker. When Estep appeared on the scene in 1983, he tinkered with Navratilova's serve and worked on other aspects of her game, but primarily he devoted his energies to strategy.

Evert's coach Dennis Ralston, meanwhile, was devoting his time to encouraging her to be a more well-rounded player. He added kick to her second serve. He gave her the confidence to take more chances to volley. He helped her develop sting in her smash. He worked with Chrissie to develop a topspin lob off the forehand to match her two-handed backhand topspin lob. Across the board, in subtle and sensible ways, without devaluing her superb ground strokes and enormous consistency, he helped Evert to become a more complete tennis player.

Evert and Navratilova—the two great champions—divided the four major titles between them in 1982. Navratilova won her first French Open and a third Wimbledon; Evert secured a sixth U.S. Open and avenged her loss to Navratilova in a repeat Australian Open final, finally adding that title to her resume. In 1983 and 1984, Navratilova swept six of the eight majors, with Evert taking the other two.

Over that period, Navratilova was virtually flawless in her meetings with Evert. They were in a class of their own as the two best players in the women's game, but from the end of 1982 through the 1984 season, Navratilova defeated her chief rival thirteen consecutive times. The last of those losses was particularly painful for Evert. In the final of the U.S. Open, Evert earned a standing ovation from the capacity crowd at Flushing Meadow when she took the first set from Navratilova.

The crowd sensed a watershed moment for Evert and so did she. Chrissie seemed set to break back for 5-5 in the second set when she had Martina down 15-40. Navratilova stayed back behind a second serve, but Evert was too careful and sent a forehand over the baseline. Her chance was gone. Navratilova prevailed 4-6, 6-4, 6-4. Evert found a vacant room outside the stadium court, where she wept over a golden opportunity lost. "If I had won this match," she lamented to friends, "it would have been the perfect time to retire. I wish I could have done it."

Three months later, Evert captured the last major of the season, taking her second Australian Open title over the tall Czechoslovakian, Helena Sukova. Sukova had toppled Navratilova in a three-set semifinal, ending a record seventy-four-match winning streak by the world No. 1, and preventing Martina from capturing a Grand Slam. This time, it was Martina who was in tears as a significant goal eluded her grasp.

CHAPTER TWENTY-ONE

John McEnroe *vs.* Mats Wilander
DAVIS CUP, ST. LOUIS, JULY 11, 1982

In a rousing Davis Cup match, the veteran McEnroe, and the newly crowned 17-year-old French Open titlist, played the fifth and final match between their nations with a patriotic passion.

PROLOGUE

With the unexpected departure of Bjorn Borg from the major championships after the 1981 U.S. Open when he was only twenty-five, it seemed safe to say that no one of his skill would emerge from Sweden or anywhere else for a long while. But in a peculiar twist of fate, a teenager did emerge from Sweden—almost as if by design—the following year. In 1982, Mats Wilander struck down one established, frontline player after another at the French Open, the tournament Borg had ruled so thoroughly for six of the previous eight years. Wilander, who as a boy played ice hockey along with his two brothers, was the son of a factory foreman. He became a virtual replica of Borg on the tennis court, wearing down his rivals with exasperating patience from the backcourt, coolly sizing up the opposition before systematically dismantling their games. He rarely allowed himself to be thrown off stride by players with a much wider range of experience.

In 1982, Wilander was unseeded at Roland Garros, seventeen years old, and a semifinalist at the recent Italian Open in Rome. He had never won a professional tennis tournament before, though only one year earlier he had been the French Open junior titlist. With a temperament much like Borg's, a two-handed backhand of similar quality, and a flair for match play, he became the youngest ever to take this championship at the time and the first unseeded winner as well. In the round of sixteen, he trailed second-seeded Ivan Lendl two sets to one, but came through in five exhausting sets. Fifth-seeded Vitas Gerulaitis of the United States was his next victim in a four-set quarterfinal. He then recorded a four-set triumph over Argentina's Jose Luis Clerc—the No. 4 seed—in the semifinals. In the final, Wilander completed a startling run by upending third-seeded Guillermo Vilas of Argentina in four sets. Vilas had won the tournament in 1977.

With this cluster of fine wins, Wilander established a place for himself among the world's top-ten players. He also earned the right to represent his nation against the United States in St. Louis that summer when the two countries collided in a Davis Cup quarterfinal. He had shown unequivocally that he belonged among the elite by defeating four of the top five seeds in one stirring sequence on the slow red clay at Roland Garros. After watching that string of unanticipated successes, Don Budge returned from Paris to New York and confessed that he was thoroughly impressed with what he had witnessed. He told a reporter in New York, "You know what this guy Wilander is. He is another Borg. He is just like Bjorn in so many ways."

As the United States-Sweden confrontation neared, John McEnroe was going through a rough patch in his career. Most significantly, he had lost the Wimbledon final to Jimmy Connors in five sets after coming within three points of a four-set victory. That discouraging defeat was fresh in McEnroe's mind as he headed for St. Louis the weekend after Wimbledon. He did not have the luxury of time to heal the wounds of his loss. He had to come right back to represent the United States. He knew how much captain Arthur Ashe and his teammates were counting on him.

The strain of competing at the loftiest levels had clearly taken its toll on McEnroe. His 1981 season demonstrated indisputably that he was a player made for great moments. Not only had he toppled Borg in both the Wimbledon and U.S. Open finals from a set down each time, but he had been the chief architect of the U.S. Davis Cup triumph as well. He had scored a critical five-set victory over Argentina's Jose Luis Clerc in the Cup final at Cincinnati, and joined Peter Fleming to capture a five-set doubles match from Clerc and Vilas. With his tactical acuity and shot selection, McEnroe was considered by many to be the greatest doubles player in the history of the game. In terms of his on court heroics, he had done everything he could possibly have asked of himself, perhaps more.

But the fact remained that he had withstood an untold amount of deep personal pain which must have diminished his successes as he weighed them later in his mind. During the Davis Cup semifinals against Australia, he was coasting along with Fleming, leading two sets to love against Phil Dent and Peter McNamara, when he became embroiled in a needless dispute. Both Fleming and McEnroe railed at their captain Arthur Ashe in an embarrassing courtside episode when the captain refused to intervene on their behalf. Although order was restored and McEnroe and Fleming completed a routine triumph, severe damage was done in the process.

In the weeks that followed, Ashe received numerous letters from leaders in the tennis community urging him to remove McEnroe from the team, believing that was the only remedy for his unacceptable behavior. The letters were responding to a number of incidents, including McEnroe's first-round contest at Wimbledon against Tom Gullikson. He had caused such uneasiness on that occasion that the committee at Wimbledon wanted to disqualify him retroactively for his conduct during that match. ATP Executive Director Butch Buchholz persuaded the Wimbledon officials that they would be making a serious mistake if they took that action. They concurred. McEnroe remained in the tournament and won it. Moreover, Ashe stood by him against many revered members of the tennis establishment because he was convinced McEnroe sincerely wanted to stop demeaning himself by behaving so inappropriately.

In any case, the scars of 1981 were still haunting McEnroe as he stumbled through 1982. This was painfully evident when the Wimbledon title slipped from his grasp against a revitalized Connors. Connors, on the edge of thirty, was an immensely popular player who had left behind most of his troublesome times. He was not only a superb shot-maker but also a brilliant orchestrator of an audience. His gesticulations became a familiar trademark. Arm-raising, fist-shaking, air-punching exhortations brought the crowd to its feet when he needed their support. That was a role which suited Connors's theatricality, but McEnroe was not nearly as skilled or as natural in that posture.

Connors, with the fans whooping, rallied from two sets to one behind and three points from defeat to prevail in five tempestuous sets.

McEnroe was a man in utter misery, knowing he had been out-played, recognizing that Connors was the overwhelming sentimental favorite of the fans. McEnroe's despondency was visible after that loss, and the Davis Cup schedule gave him no time to heal.

THE MATCH

When the Wimbledon finalist and French Open titlist were scheduled to meet each other on the closing afternoon of the United States-Sweden Davis Cup quarterfinal, the players, press and performers were all in accord that McEnroe was the overwhelming favorite. With the two nations deadlocked at 2-2, the intensity surrounding this match was heightened by the circumstances. McEnroe was a renowned Davis Cup veteran who had represented the United States in the 1978 final at Palm Springs, when he took two singles against the British as the Americans completely outclassed their rivals from across the Atlantic. Now in his fifth year of Davis Cup duty for his country, McEnroe had developed a genuine pride in his par-ticipation. That was precisely why he was willing to put himself on the line so soon after Wimbledon, a sacrifice Connors refused to make. He had joined McEnroe the week after Wimbledon in 1981 when they collaborated to oust Ivan Lendl's Czechoslovakian squad at Flushing Meadow.

This time, however, McEnroe's task was more burdensome. He had defeated Anders Jarryd on the opening day, but Wilander brought Sweden to 1-1 with a five-set win over the Californian Eliot Teltscher (or "Teliot Eltscher" as Connors playfully referred to him). McEnroe then took the doubles alongside Fleming to give the United States a 2-1 lead with a straight-set win over Jarryd and Hans Simonsson. When Teltscher was injured, Brian Gottfried had to step in and substitute in the fourth match of the series against Jarryd. Gottfried had once been ranked third in the world, but he was now a few years past his prime. He bowed in straight sets.

The pressure was back on McEnroe to prevent a stunning Ameri-

John McEnroe

can defeat. The match would be played on a medium-fast Supreme Court carpet. McEnroe's chances seemed excellent against the Swedish teenager, who had made his debut in Cup competition against the Russians earlier in the year. Confronting McEnroe in his rookie season representing Sweden was a daunting prospect for Wilander, even if he did mask his emotions in a manner strikingly reminiscent of Borg. Despite playing away from home on a court much faster than he preferred, Wilander demonstrated early that he was not about to surrender passively.

While McEnroe had the advantage of sealing points with relative ease by packaging his first serve with solid first volleys, Wilander had to work considerably harder to hold his place. Spinning the first serve in deep to McEnroe's backhand, he did a fine job of pinning the American deep in the backcourt, forcing him to wait for just the right midcourt ball to attack. Even then, Wilander often had the appropriate answers, finding even the smallest spaces to pass the hard-charging New Yorker at the net with his precise shots off the backhand side.

Wilander moved ahead of McEnroe to take a 3-1 opening set lead before the American broke back. The Swede stayed stubbornly with McEnroe until 7-7, but was broken in the fifteenth game and McEnroe happily served out the set in the following game. The final point featured a classic move from the left-hander. He closed in confidently behind his serve, then opened his racket face purposefully to produce a delicate drop volley off his forehand side. Leaving the burden of that long set behind him, McEnroe escalated his attack and he swept through the second on the strength of two service breaks, 6-2. When McEnroe raced to a 4-2 lead in the third set with four break points for 5-2, he seemed about to complete his mission with swift resolution.

In fact, the battle in many ways had just begun. Wilander's court behavior was virtually identical to Borg's. He was never demonstrative, but he was determined to make a full and forceful effort. As he slid precariously close to a decisive straight-set defeat, his body language was telling McEnroe in essence, "You are going to have to beat me because I won't give this match to you."

Wilander made his move at the right time. He held on for 3-4, then broke for 4-4 at the cost of only a single point. A grinding struggle

Mats Wilander

developed as both men gave all they had to taking the set. It lasted for an astonishing two hours and thirty-nine minutes. A crowd of 15,103 in St. Louis cheered on the American through the marathon set, but Wilander seemed oblivious to the sentiment of the fans. The Swede saved break points at 8-8 and 10-10 with a pair of superb volleys. He plodded on and salvaged a measure of self-respect when he broke McEnroe in the thirty-second game to take the third set 17-15 as the American double-faulted into the net at 30-40. What had once seemed a mere formality was now a tennis match of the highest order.

Quietly buoyant after finally sealing the third set, Wilander had the advantage of starting the fourth on his serve. His counterattacking was increasingly accurate and a somewhat exasperated McEnroe was missing ground strokes with distressing frequency. At this stage, his serve had lost some sting, and the pattern of play was slowing down as Wilander skillfully prolonged the points. The Swede got the break he needed in the eighth game, served for the fourth set at 5-3, and held. He had now rescued himself from a routine defeat to force a fifth and final set, and the momentum was inescapably on the Swede's side.

McEnroe, however, had other notions and still held the bedrock belief that he was going to win. And yet, his tightly strung personality was becoming a problem. After smacking a ball in the direction of a linesman who had given him a questionable call, McEnroe was assessed a point penalty. The violation allowed Wilander to advance to break point, and placed McEnroe two steps from disqualification. Nevertheless, he responded characteristically. He took three straight points with verve, two of them un-returnable serves, and held on for 1-0. He broke Wilander in the following game, but Wilander had not resurrected himself by accident. He broke back in the third game with consecutive backhand placements, held in the fourth, and it was 2-2. With both men competing unyieldingly down the stretch, they got into a holding pattern until 6-6. In that crucial thirteenth game, Wilander reached 15-30 with two fine returns. McEnroe retaliated with two aces down the "T" for 40-30, only to steer a forehand volley out of court. Wilander was two points away from gaining a break, which would have given him a chance to serve for the match. McEnroe had been pushed to his emotional limits.

With the match in such jeopardy, McEnroe somehow composed himself and refused to succumb. He pulled off a magnificent forehand volley into the corner when Wilander appeared to have him beaten with a well-struck forehand pass. At game point for the second time, McEnroe directed a slice serve into his opponent's body. Wilander was handcuffed and netted his response. McEnroe had escaped. He had the edge 7-6. In the following game, the American collected the first point on a net cord service return that fell into the forecourt on Wilander's side, well out of reach. The New Yorker surged to 15-30 by attacking a first serve and following his return in for an emphatic forehand volley winner. The Swede then seemed to have connected with a forehand crosscourt passing shot, but was chagrined when the linesman signaled wide. McEnroe was at 15-40, double match point. Wilander saved the first one with a cleverly placed serve into McEnroe's body. At 30-40, he was set up for a routine forehand crosscourt, a shot he had hardly missed all through the contest. His high trajectory topspin off that side had served as a safety net in rally after rally. This time, however, he did not give himself his customary margin for error. He drove the ball into the net.

McEnroe had won 9-7, 6-2, 15-17, 3-6, 8-6 to give the Americans a 3-2 triumph. It had taken six hours and twenty-two minutes, a record at the time, to complete this unforeseen drama. Both players had tapped into resources only defiance can produce. McEnroe had not lost his nerve when the match seemed to be slipping inexorably from his control. And Wilander had come gallantly close to a major upset on a surface and in a setting he hardly knew.

EPILOGUE

Over the rest of the 1982 season, Wilander reaffirmed his status as a worthy top-ten player. In Barcelona that fall, he repeated his French Open triumphs over Lendl, Vilas, and Clerc to take that tournament title. He finished the year at No. 7 in the world. He had set himself up for a productive future and made the most of it. Altogether, from 1982-88, he spent seven consecutive years among the top ten, the last six in the top four. He expanded his shot making steadily, developing a vastly improved one-handed slice backhand that complemented his two-hander handsomely. He improved his volleying off both sides minimally, but his tactical game was greatly enhanced when he learned to serve-and-volley on fast courts at opportune times.

In that impressive seven-year run, Wilander collected seven major singles championships, including three French Opens, three Australian Opens (on two different surfaces), and one U.S. Open. But while he celebrated many victories in that span, his best season by far was in 1988, when he won three of the four men's Grand Slam titles, a feat last achieved by Connors fourteen years earlier. Wilander in 1988 held back the aggressive serve-and-volley specialist Pat Cash 8-6 in the fifth set to begin the year with a triumph at the Australian Open. Then he won the French Open, overcoming a rising eighteen-year-old Andre Agassi in a five-set semifinal. Then he crushed Frenchman Henri Leconte in a straight-set final, connecting on a remarkable 97 percent of his first serves.

Wilander was upended by the crafty Czechoslovakian Miloslav Mecir in the quarterfinals of Wimbledon, but he more than made up for that defeat at the U.S. Open where he recorded an inspiring five-set, final-round conquest over three-time titlist Lendl. That victory provided the key to Wilander's unexpected rise to No. 1 in the world for the year, as he lifted himself deservedly past Lendl, the man who had occupied that slot for the previous three seasons. In a four-hour-and-fifty-five-minute clash on the stadium court at Flushing Meadow, Wilander deployed a more versatile game plan than Lendl, but he needed courage as well to come through.

The inscrutable Swede led by a set and 4-1, but Lendl rebounded to one set all. Then Wilander led two sets to one, 4-3, 30-0, but Lendl broke back and worked his way into a fifth set. When Lendl held for 3-2 in the fifth and had Wilander at 0-30 in the sixth game, he seemed ready to win a fourth Open in a row and thus repeat his triumph over Wilander in the 1987 final. But Wilander gathered himself for one last surge to the finish line, and he succeeded 6-4, 4-6, 6-3, 5-7, 6-4. He had approached the net no fewer than 131 times (winning seventy-six points) over the five sets, and had connected with 86 percent of his first serves. Wilander was at the peak of his game, and there seemed no reason why he could not contend for major titles and the No. 1 ranking for several years to come.

Oddly, Wilander was through as a frontline player. He slipped to No. 12 by the end of 1989, and played only sporadically thereafter. He did not appear again in the latter stages of a Grand Slam event. He lost his spark and initiative, not anticipating how little would be left of his competitive zeal after reaching the top. He did make a modest comeback in 1995, finishing that season at No. 45 in the world. He was not, however, a formidable player anymore. Asked early in the 1988 season if there was a danger that he might burn out in his mid-twenties as had happened to Borg—a prediction ESPN commentator and former player Cliff Drysdale had made—Wilander answered, "I don't think Borg quit because of his style of play. He won what he thought he should win and then he didn't enjoy playing tennis anymore, so he left. I don't see myself playing at thirty-five like Jimmy Connors. But, for sure, I'll be playing another four, five, six years at least."

Drysdale's vision of the future was sharper than Wilander's. Perhaps if the Swede had taken a few months off after the end of his 1988 campaign, he might have found a way to remain in the upper echelons much longer. Instead, he faded too fast from the center of the tennis universe, and he was missed by fans and players alike. For those who cherished the fierce rivalries between the leading players, the Wilander-McEnroe series was surely a big loss.

In their prime years together on the tour— 1982-87—they confronted each other on twelve occasions with each man prevailing six times. And many of these meetings were in the prestige events. After their initial epic match at the Davis Cup in 1982, Wilander posted victories over McEnroe at the 1983 French Open—winning in four sets after taking twenty-three points in a row at one stage—and again at the Australian Open in a surprise grass-court win later that year. McEnroe routed Wilander indoors at the 1983 and 1984 Masters events indoors at New York. Wilander upended McEnroe at the 1985 French Open in the semifinals, but was defeated by his American adversary on a scorching afternoon later that summer in the semifinal round of the U.S. Open. They had one more major meeting in 1989, when McEnroe ousted Wilander on his way to the semifinals of Wimbledon.

McEnroe's career turned in different directions after his superlative struggle with Wilander in 1982. Despite not winning a major championship that season and losing decisively in the semifinals of the U.S. Open to Lendl, he remained No. 1 in the world for the second year in a row by taking six singles championships, including four consecutive titles at the end of the year when he built a twenty-four-match winning streak. But he fared much better in the big championships of 1983, extending his run as the game's top ranked player to four consecutive seasons.

In 1983, he secured a second singles championship at Wimbledon, and that was the primary reason why he stayed at No. 1. In 1984, he dominated the game in a fashion few have equaled. He was victorious in thirteen of fifteen tournaments, winning eighty-two of eighty-five matches, losing only to Lendl in the French Open final, to the gifted Indian Vijay Amritraj in Cincinnati, and to Sweden's Henrik Sundstrom in the Davis Cup final. In examining the Open Era from 1968-99 when all of the best players competed against each other, McEnroe's 1984 ranks not far behind Laver's 1969 Grand Slam season, and alongside Connors's 1974 when he, too, was nearly invulnerable in winning ninety-nine of 103 matches. McEnroe's most masterful performance was his dissection of Connors in the Wimbledon final. Two years after he lost that agonizing five-set, final-round contest against Connors on Centre Court, he balanced the books by beating Connors with shocking ease 6-1, 6-1, 6-2 in the 1984 title match.

Not since Budge had beaten Bunny Austin in the 1938 final had there been such a one-sided final on Centre Court. It was 102 degrees Fahrenheit that afternoon at the All England Club, and McEnroe's shot making shimmered with the same intensity as the glaring sunlight on court. He was on target with forty-three of fifty-five first serves (78 percent). Facing the game's greatest returner, McEnroe allowed Connors a mere eleven points in eleven service games. Connors was unable to secure a single break point. The match lasted only eighty minutes. McEnroe had released the full range of his talent, tantalizing his countryman with topspin lobs off both sides, delicate drop volleys disguised brilliantly, and passing shots that Connors could not read.

Two months later, McEnroe and Connors collided again in the semifinals of the U.S. Open and this was an entirely different and more competitive match. In five sets, Connors broke McEnroe seven times, but McEnroe still managed to win. He went on to top Lendl in a straight-set final that was almost as impressive as his Wimbledon shutout over Connors. Nonetheless, when the year was over, McEnroe would have traded half a dozen of his thirteen titles to have reversed the result of his French Open loss to Lendl.

He had started that match irresistibly, taking the first two sets, seemingly on his way to a swift success. But Lendl persisted single-mindedly. He won the third, recovered from 4-2 down in the fourth and 3-3, 15-40 in the fifth, and toppled a distraught McEnroe 3-6, 2-6, 6-4, 7-5, 7-5 in a splendid comeback. McEnroe was at a loss to explain how he had failed to prevail, but Lendl had found both the confidence and the power to take the day.

When McEnroe produced the most persuasive tennis of his career at Wimbledon and the U.S. Open later in 1984, he seemed to have many great years ahead of him and was expected to add to his collection of four U.S. Open titles and three Wimbledons. But he was never the same player again, not by a wide margin. He would not win another major championship. When Lendl trounced him in a straight-set U.S. Open final in 1985, both men knew that McEnroe would be hard-pressed from then on. At the end of that season, McEnroe elected to take a seven-month sabbatical from the game.

The time off cleared his mind in many ways as he took care of matters in his personal life, but as a player he did not return with force or conviction. He concluded 1986 at an unimaginable No. 14 in the world, then finished 1987 at No. 10 and 1988 one place lower. In 1989, McEnroe sought a higher level again, reaching the semifinals of Wimbledon, achieving consistently impressive results all year, climbing back to No. 4 in the world. The following year, he reached his last U.S. Open singles semifinal, losing a four-set encounter to Pete Sampras. In 1992, he joined forces with Sampras as the United States regained possession of the Davis Cup. McEnroe and Sampras were victorious in the doubles against the Swiss tandem of Jakob Hlasek and Marc Rosset. Earlier that year, McEnroe made it to the semifinals of Wimbledon before losing to the eventual champion Andre Agassi.

These modest successes were rewarding to McEnroe in the autumn of his career, but he was nothing like the man who had reached five consecutive Wimbledon finals in the 1980s. He was not in the same league as he had been when he won his four U.S. Opens. He had probably not done complete justice to his rare talent despite winning seven major championships, but that assessment must take into account his luminous Davis Cup accomplishments.

In matches he played for the United States Davis Cup contingent, he won forty-one of forty-nine singles assignments and eighteen of twenty doubles matches. It was his intuitive quickness in doubles that gave him a special niche among the great players of his era. Overall, across his entire career, he won even more doubles titles than he took in singles (78 in the former, 77 in the latter). In the major championships, his credits were even greater in doubles as he won five Wimbledon titles (four with Fleming in the 1970s and 1980s, one more with Michael Stich in 1992), and four at the U.S. Open (three with Fleming, one with Australian Mark Woodforde in 1989). Adding the French Open mixed doubles title with Mary Carillo in 1977, he took ten major doubles championships compared to his seven in singles.

In the ultimate analysis, no expert would place him at the top of the list as the greatest ever to play the game of singles. But many would rate him an inspired titan among doubles players, possibly the finest ever. He will be remembered above and beyond anything else as a personality. The most provocative performer of his time, he angered some observers, delighted others, fascinated even more. And he was brutally honest in many cases about himself. After flirting with disqualification at many tournaments over the years, he was finally disqualified officially at the 1990 Australian Open during a fourth-round meeting with Sweden's Mikael Pernfors.

After it was over, he freely admitted that the only reason he had been thrown out of that tournament was his ignorance about the new rules. He thought he would get one more penalty before removal, but he had not been familiar with the new standards. He also conceded some time later that being removed from a match for unacceptable behavior should have happened to him years earlier when it would have been more damaging and instructional.

McEnroe served one year as Davis Cup captain in 2000 before his younger brother Patrick took over that arduous role for a decade. Meanwhile, John McEnroe established himself as one of the premier tennis color commentators in the world, working for a wide range of networks. To this day, he is easily able to detach himself during the matches when he is in the television booth. He is an excellent tennis analyst, offering his pungent and informative commentary to large audiences, primarily in the United States. In his capacity as a broadcaster, McEnroe has continued to give his share of incisive performances.

CHAPTER TWENTY-TWO

Martina Navratilova *vs.* Chris Evert
FRENCH OPEN, FINAL, JUNE 8, 1985

This was perhaps their most absorbing match in a major championship. Out of an incomparable rivalry, spanning 80 matches, none surpassed the suspense and inspiration of this struggle.

PROLOGUE

At the start of 1985, Chrissie Evert was at a crossroad. She had spent the three previous years at No. 2 in the world behind Martina Navratilova. Her thirteen-match losing streak against Martina was an unprecedented sequence of disappointments in her career. Although she had been beleaguered by Tracy Austin during her five-match losing streak against the Californian, those losses had been contained in a brief five-month period. Three of the defeats took place in eleven days in the winter of 1980. No one but Navratilova had plagued her for as long and as thoroughly as Austin.

Martina had lost only three matches in her vintage 1983-84 seasons, recording twelve of her thirteen consecutive victories over Evert in those campaigns. Four of her wins were in major finals, including two at the U.S. Open, one at Wimbledon, another at Roland Garros. The French Open final of 1984 was the most surprising of the showdowns. Navratilova was a 6-3, 6-1 victor on the red clay. She ruled in rallies with verve and spontaneity. She saved her visits to the net for propitious moments and served with great spin and variety. It was arguably the most comprehensive display she would ever present on a tennis court and easily the best slow court performance of her career. She had picked apart Chrissie on the Floridian's favorite surface—a surface on which Evert had amassed an awesome twenty-four tournament, 125-match winning streak from 1973 to 1979. Navratilova went on to win the next two Grand Slam finals over Evert at Wimbledon and Flushing Meadow.

In late January 1985, the two veteran adversaries opened their campaign against each other in the final at Key Biscayne, Florida. Appearing about half an hour away from where she grew up in Fort Lauderdale, Evert snapped the losing streak decisively, defeating her nemesis 6-2, 6-4. But that victory provided only a temporary reprieve from Navratilova's mastery. Martina avenged the loss with two more wins in the finals at Delray Beach, Florida and again in Dallas.

As the two best women players in the world faced the first Grand Slam championship of the season in Paris, Evert remained psychologically stranded by Navratilova. She had lost fifteen of their last sixteen meetings. She realized that the red clay of Roland Garros offered probably her best chance to regain momentum but her pride had been severely wounded by the accumulation of losses.

"I remember how I felt going into the French," she recalled in 1999. "I thought 'Why should this time be any different?' I didn't have much confidence going into the match. Dennis Ralston talked to me a lot about believing in myself, and told me Martina was vulnerable on clay and I could beat her. But as a player you have to believe that yourself and I still had a lot of doubt in me. It was funny in a way because I knew I was a champion, yet I had those lingering doubts that were hard to wipe out of my mind."

THE MATCH

The top-seeded Navratilova reached their final-round appointment without the loss of a set. Navratilova took her semifinal from the tall German Claudia Kohde-Kilsch 6-4, 6-4. Evert knocked out Gabriela Sabatini—the top-spin artist from Argentina—in straight sets.

The time had come for Navratilova-Evert match number sixty-five with Martina leading 33-31 in the career series. This would be their fifth final-round collision in the last six major tournaments. Since Austin had taken the 1981 U.S. Open, Navratilova had won eight of the "Big Four" events while Evert had secured four. No one had threatened their authority during that time.

The morning of the final, the weather was disruptive. A bright sun was shining at dawn, but a few hours later it was pouring rain. The precipitation was accompanied by strong winds sporadically through-out the day.

The conditions changed frequently as the final unfolded. The sun would emerge briefly, then slip behind the clouds, then reappear. The wind whipped across the stadium court at Roland Garros with substantial force for minutes at a time, then subsided, returning again intermittently all afternoon.

The slow court and gusty wind were allies for Evert. Navratilova much preferred the calm conditions indoors with no sun or wind. She could synchronize her service toss, gauge easily how hard to hit off the ground, and punch her volleys without fearing they would float out of her control.

Evert was not daunted by the capricious conditions. She had played all through her youth on windswept afternoons at Holiday Park in Fort Lauderdale, a public facility that was named after her father in 1997. He had worked as a teaching pro there for four decades. Chris-sie's classic ground strokes were groomed on days when the wind be-came something like a third player on the court. She was so adaptable, and her racket preparation was so reflexive, that she kept hitting freely and precisely both with and against the wind. She selected her strokes with tactical effectiveness, making good use of her sidespin forehand, raising the trajectory of her two-handed backhand for more safety, fig-uring out a way to keep the pressure on her opponent without going for too big a shot herself.

The Floridian was ready from the first point onward to accept the challenge of both Navratilova and the wind. Down 15-40 in the opening game of the match, she collected herself quickly. A forehand drop volley winner saved the first break point and then Evert used a sizzling two-hander crosscourt off a short ball for the second. When Navratilova's forehand approach carried over the baseline, Evert was at game point. She lofted a backhand crosscourt lob high into the wind. An apprehensive Martina hit an overhead wide, and Evert had held for 1-0.

Navratilova reached 40-30 in the second game. She took her case to the forecourt but a running forehand passing shot crosscourt from Evert forced Martina into a backhand volley error. Then Evert connected with a backhand return winner into the corner for break point. The next point would produce a pattern repeated frequently for the rest of the match. Navratilova chipped her favorite backhand approach shot down the line to Evert's backhand side. On the run, Chrissie laced another two-hander crosscourt on the sideline. She led 2-0, then held for 3-0.

Martina found her range at that juncture. She worked her way back to 3-3, breaking Evert in the fifth game. Unshaken by Navratilova's recovery, Evert regained the upper hand, took three games in a row, and closed out the set 6-3 with gusto. She had broken serve twice, lost her serve only once, and competed with an equanimity she had not been able to muster for years against Martina.

The No. 2 seed sustained her edge into the middle of the second set. She moved ahead 4-2, 15-40. With success on one of the next two points, she would have served for the match with an extra break in hand. But Navratilova held in that critical seventh game and got back on serve. Evert broke again in the eleventh game and served for the match at 6-5.

Navratilova kept coming forward. She broke Evert to force a tiebreaker. The favorite was highly focused. She sparred well with Evert from the backcourt, served skillfully on the big points and seized the tiebreak 7-4.

Having been on the verge of a straight-set triumph, Evert found herself locked at one set all, needing to start all over again. She was not discouraged by that prospect. "I never gave up mentally in that match," she said. "In many of those losses in my losing streak against Martina, I did not give up, but I thought I lost some of my fighting spirit. This was a seesaw match, but I just played each point as it came and stayed in the moment. I didn't look ahead and I didn't look back."

At the start of the third, Evert shifted to a higher level. She answered a backhand drop shot from Martina with a forehand drop shot winner of her own to hold for 1-0. In the next game, she produced two splendid backhand passing shots on her way to break point, then took the game with a daring forehand drop volley along the sideline.

The fleet-footed Navratilova dashed forward swiftly and had a chance to make the forehand passing shot, but she directed her shot over the higher part of the net and hit the tape. The ball fell back on Martina's side. Evert went ahead 2-0 in the final set.

Chrissie moved to 40-15 at 2-0, seemingly ready to establish a 3-0 lead. Navratilova was steady despite the danger. On Evert's second game point, Martina outlasted the baseline expert in a long rally. Chris netted a backhand to lose the point. Evert had one more game point. Martina drew her in with a backhand drop, then drilled a backhand crosscourt to provoke an errant volley. When Chrissie punched a high backhand crosscourt volley wide at break point down, Martina closed the gap to 2-1.

This was not a day for holding serve, not for either player. In the fourth game, Evert found the range with another beautifully struck backhand passing shot to reach 15-40. She broke for 3-1 when Navratilova overplayed a backhand approach, chipping it long. This time, Evert was absolutely determined to consolidate her break and widen her lead. In a five-deuce game, she persisted and had two game points. But Navratilova broke back for 2-3 with a first-rate backhand pass of her own. Evert had come in on a solid, down-the-line backhand approach, but Martina unleashed a passing shot with topspin. The shot grazed the top of the net, but landed out of Evert's reach for a well-deserved winner.

In the sixth game, Navratilova delivered her best service game of the match. She found her mark with four consecutive first serves and held at love for 3-3. The opening point of that game was a tribute to Martina's talent and ingenuity. She played a backhand drop shot crosscourt to Chrissie's forehand. Sensing that Evert would not be able to do much with that shot, Martina moved into "no man's land" and sent off a perfect backhand volley down the line into a vacant court.

In the seventh game, Evert served at 30-40 after Navratilova had read her passing shot on the previous point, closing in again for a forehand volley winner. Chrissie served deep to Martina's forehand, got the short ball she wanted on the forehand and came in with sidespin to the left-hander's forehand. Navratilova—perhaps thrown off guard by Evert's approach to the net—missed the passing shot. Evert came in again on Navratilova's forehand and elicited another error, then held for 4-3.

Serving in the eighth game, Navratilova proceeded to 30-0 with her trademark serve-and-volley combination, sending her backhand volley crosscourt crisply for a winner. Evert stuck with her task, responding with another stinging backhand passing shot, then reaching 30-30 when Martina hit a looping crosscourt forehand long with the wind at her back. The defending champion came in behind a kick serve to Chrissie's forehand but the hard hit return was too good. Break point. Martina approached the net behind a well-executed backhand crosscourt. Evert was on the dead run. She whipped over the ball with topspin, and Navratilova had no chance to cover it. Evert had moved to 5-3 with a dazzling shot.

Serving for the match a second time, Evert did not miss a first serve in five points. Nevertheless, Navratilova was too good in this game. The left-hander concluded the sixteen-stroke first point with a backhand drop volley winner. An instant before Evert made contact with a crosscourt backhand on the second point, the wind gathered sudden force. Her shot flew inches long over the baseline, making it 0-30.

Navratilova knew she needed to apply the pressure. She came forward confidently, made a penetrating backhand volley crosscourt, and Chrissie netted her forehand pass on the run for 0-40. Evert got to 15-40 with a bold backhand drop volley winner at full stretch, but was broken when Navratilova got some extra bite on her backhand approach. Evert's lob was short. Navratilova devoured it with an overhead from close range.

Martina was back to 4-5 and serving. She passed Evert off the backhand for 15-0, came up with a quick forehand volley winner for 30-0, and passed Chrissie again with another backhand for 40-0. Navratilova then found her mark with a first serve and held at love for 5-5.

As Evert served in the eleventh game, Navratilova continued to attack. Chrissie missed the first serve and then double-faulted as a menacing Martina moved in closer to provoke the mistake. Martina rolled a forehand passing shot with accelerated pace crosscourt. Chrissie barely got a racket on it. It was 0-30. Somewhat shaken, Evert made a rare backhand unforced error for 0-40. After all of her leads, she found herself in a desperate position, triple break point down at 5-5 in the final set.

"At that point," Evert said, "I did not have complete faith that I could win the match but I had so much desire. I still wanted it and the juices were flowing. But I also remember that I didn't have my normal tunnel vision where I would block everything out as I was used to doing. I opened up my senses and was aware of the crowd's response to our tennis. I didn't lose my focus but I allowed myself to enjoy the suspense of the match and the excitement it was bringing to the fans. They were completely involved in that match."

Serving at 5-5, 0-40, Chrissie benefited from a brief lapse from Martina, who drove a forehand topspin crosscourt wide, allowing her rival to reach 15-40. Down to a second serve as she had been on the previous point, Evert took full advantage of a relatively short return from Navratilova. She stepped in as if it were 2-2 in the opening set and directed a two-hander crosscourt. Clean winner. 30-40. The next point was the single most critical exchange of the match.

Navratilova waited for her opening, releasing a well executed backhand drop shot. Evert scampered forward and had to scrape the ball back. Unintentionally, she hit the ball with sidespin. The spin surprised Martina, who lifted her forehand higher than she would have liked. Both women were at the net. Evert needed to make a forceful high backhand volley. She struck it hard and kept it low. Navratilova could not respond. Deuce.

When Martina netted another attempted backhand drop shot, Evert had climbed back to game point. Martina was not yielding. With Evert in the forecourt again, Navratilova chipped a lob over her backhand. Evert chased it down but could not make the play. Deuce for the second time. Navratilova unwisely tried another backhand drop shot. Evert anticipated it early, moved forward rapidly, and drove her two-hander with extra pace for a winner. At game point for the second time, Evert came through as Navratilova netted a forehand approach.

It had seemed certain that Navratilova was going to serve for the match in the twelfth game. Instead, she served to save it at 5-6, knowing that a triple break point opportunity had eluded her. Even so, the left-hander was not unduly rattled. She had come from behind throughout the match. She would try to do that again one more time.

Martina got to the net on the first point, coming in behind a cross-court forehand with good depth. Evert responded with a magnificent backhand topspin lob winner making it 0-15. Martina rallied to 15-15. She closed in on the net again; Chrissie made her stretch for a low forehand volley. Martina handled it reasonably well, but Evert struck a flat forehand pass down the line through a narrow slot. The crowd raised the level of their applause excitedly. It was 15-30. Evert was two points from triumph.

Navratilova got her first serve in, covered the return with cus-tomary swiftness and knifed a backhand volley crosscourt into the clear—30-30. Martina charged in again and sensed Chrissie would go crosscourt off the backhand. She moved forward to cut it off, and her forehand volley was a winner down the line—40-30. Martina served-and-volleyed but Chrissie took the net away from her, coming in behind a forehand crosscourt deep to Martina's backhand. Martina sliced her lob crosscourt. Chrissie could not get back to cover it, but thought it might go long. Both players waited in suspense for the call. Out. Deuce.

Evert looked up at the sky and rolled her eyes, appreciating her good fortune on a big point. Again Martina came in behind her first serve to the forehand. Chrissie's return was low. Martina poked her backhand volley long. It was match point for Evert.

Martina went for an ace down the middle in the advantage court, but her serve landed well wide. The favorite stayed back behind her second serve. On a high ball off the forehand, Chrissie went cross-court but her shot lacked depth. Martina moved into her backhand approach with authority and chipped down the line. Chrissie had a lot of court to cover. She got her racket back early. Martina seemed to have the entire net covered. Somehow, from well outside the sideline, Evert found the space to drive her backhand down the line. Navra-tilova turned, knowing it was over. The passing shot was perfect. In two hours and fifty-two minutes, Evert had triumphed 6-3, 6-7 (4), 7-5.

"Nobody gave me a chance going into that match," said Evert. "I don't think people thought it was going to be an epic Navratilova-Evert match. When I won, that was the happiest I ever felt after

Martina Navratilova and Chris Evert

winning a Grand Slam title. I was thirty at the time and everybody had counted me out. Beating her near the end of my career, when everybody including myself was beginning to doubt if I would ever do that again, was very rewarding. I beat the odds and broke through my negativity. Winning that match with Martina spurred me on. That title alone prolonged my career for another four years. I honestly have never felt better after winning a tennis match."

EPILOGUE

Thereafter, the rivalry took on added dimensions. After Roland Garros in 1985, Navratilova took ten of their last fifteen head-to-head encounters. That is a misleading statistic because Evert recorded two more major triumphs over her foremost opponent. In 1986, back on the same court at Roland Garros, Evert registered a 2-6, 6-3, 6-3 victory over Navratilova to collect a record seventh French Open crown.

That match was of a higher technical quality on a calmer afternoon in Paris. Evert trailed 0-2 in the third before taking six of the last seven games to win the match. For dramatic content, however, it was not as compelling as the 1985 final. In 1988, Chrissie upstaged Martina 6-2, 7-5 in the semifinals of the Australian Open on a hard court. In those latter stages of her career, she had no trepidation about facing Martina. The Roland Garros battle of 1985 had revived her belief in herself.

The 1986 final at Paris marked the thirteenth consecutive year that Evert had won at least one major title, a record for women and men that might well stand forever. Her win over Martina at Melbourne in 1988 enabled Chrissie to make her thirty-fourth and last appearance in a major final. She would lose to Steffi Graf in the German's Grand Slam season. But she would still conclude her career with eighteen Grand Slam titles, setting a standard for consistency that no one has equaled in the modern era of the game. In fifty-six Grand Slam events, she was at least a semifinalist in fifty-two. Furthermore, in nineteen consecutive U.S. Opens beginning in 1971, she never failed to reach the quarterfinals.

She appropriately appeared in her last tournament at the U.S. Open in 1989. In many ways, that was where it all began for her—at Forest Hills when she was sixteen in 1971. On a remarkable Sunday afternoon in the middle of the event, she played one of the great matches of her career, dissecting the fifteen-year-old Monica Seles, 6-0, 6-2. If she had beaten Zina Garrison in her quarterfinal match, Evert would have squared off one last time against Navratilova. She lost to Garrison in straight sets.

"I came along at a good time," said Evert in 1999 as she reflected on her eighteen-year run among the top four in the world. "It was good timing and hard work. I came along at a time when very few players really had ground strokes. You needed to be able to handle pressure and you had to be a great tennis player, but you didn't have to be a great athlete. When people compare players from different eras, I always say you are as good as your competition. It comes down to how hard they push you and that is how good you become. When I beat Monica Seles at that last U.S. Open, I was a better player than when I won Wimbledon the first two times. What I feel great about is that for eighteen years I stayed with the competition. I improved as they improved."

So, too, did Navratilova. She would conclude her career with the same number of Grand Slam singles titles as Evert. Her tally of eighteen was differently distributed. In 1990, at thirty-three, she won a record ninth Wimbledon singles title, defeating Garrison in the championship match. Chrissie was a three-time Wimbledon champion, losing seven of nine times she played Martina on Centre Court, falling five times to the left-hander in the finals. In the end, it was the edge Navratilova had at the All England Club that made the difference in her overall series with Evert.

Navratilova retired from full-time singles play at the end of the 1994 season when she was thirty-eight. Little more than three months shy of that birthday, she very nearly took a tenth singles championship at Wimbledon, losing in three sets to the Spaniard Conchita Martinez. Just as Evert had built a strong case for herself as the greatest clay court player of all time, Navratilova had the all-time supremacy on grass.

Historians will differ in their assessment of the two enduring champions. Navratilova may well have been the most complete woman player in history and the best at the peak of her powers. Evert played the game at a high level longer than anyone who ever competed in the field of women's tennis. Together, their rivalry surpassed any other series of matches between champions, and by a wide margin. At its conclusion, Navratilova had the edge—43 to 37—including victories in 14 of 22 Grand Slam confrontations.

As Evert concluded, "In our era, I felt Martina was the best athlete and the strongest and fastest we had. Physically, she was better than anyone else. In that era, I was the best athlete mentally and maybe the best under pressure, possibly the best match player. When we played each other, it came down to whose strengths were better on that day. She forced me to develop the physical side of my game and made me a better shot maker and athlete. Because of her I was a more versatile, well-rounded player and I improved my mobility. And in my way, I guess I forced her to get stronger mentally.

"On the negative side, the frustrating part for me was that Martina could be very arrogant on the court and that got to me at times. I am sure I got to her at times with my coolness and concentration when she could not read what I was thinking. But on the positive side, it was great that we had one another. If she had not been around, I am sure I would have won more titles, and if I had not been there I'm sure she would have won a lot more tournaments. But I think we would have gotten bored and we would not have had the drive to go to the next level. That is what kept us going."

CHAPTER TWENTY-THREE

Steffi Graf *vs.* Monica Seles

FRENCH OPEN, FINAL, JUNE 6, 1992

Two big hitters battled methodically on the clay of Roland Garros with the outcome uncertain until the closing points.

PROLOGUE

Groomed for greatness on the tennis court, propelled by an obsessive but savvy father, Steffi Graf was a central player in the women's game over the latter stages of the twentieth century. She came out of Germany as a slender teenager, determined to stake her claim swiftly as a champion, admiring but not in awe of those who stood in her path.

Graf was well ahead of the game during her formative years. She turned professional at thirteen in 1982. She had first picked up a racket at the age of four. It had been sawed off for her by her father Peter who created a mini-court inside the house by fastening a cord between two chairs. A year later, she played in the seven-and-under "Bambino" Tournament in Munich. After that, Steffi's mother Heidi drove her to tournaments until her father decided to become a teaching professional at the tennis center in their hometown, Bruhl.

She was only fifteen in 1984 when she took the Olympic demonstration singles title and reached the round of sixteen at Wimbledon the same year. Displaying arguably the most explosive and the best forehand in the history of women's tennis, she moved quickly toward her goals.

In 1985, still only sixteen, she became No. 6 in the world and was a U.S. Open semifinalist. The following season, while rising to No. 3, she played world champion Martina Navratilova in the semifinal round of the U.S. Open and had three match points before conceding defeat in an absorbing struggle. From that moment on, Graf was not to be contained.

She won her first major singles title at the French Open in 1987, lost only twice all year, and became the No. 1 player in the world. In 1988, only nineteen, still far short of her peak, she became the third woman to win the Grand Slam as she garnered the Australian Open, French Open, Wimbledon and the U.S. Open titles. She validated her arrival among the elite by beating Chris Evert in the Australian Open final and Navratilova in the Wimbledon final.

Graf played with triumphant verve, guided every step of the way by her sometimes overbearing but always attentive father. She captured three of the four majors in 1989, winning eighty-three of eighty-five matches. In her three years at the top, she had suffered a mere seven defeats in forty-three tournaments. With Evert retiring and Navratilova beyond her prime, Graf seemed capable of dominating the game for many years and perhaps securing another Grand Slam.

But the quality of women's tennis was enhanced in 1990 by Monica Seles, who challenged Graf for the top ranking. Seles had been born in Yugoslavia, moving with her family to Florida to train at the Nick Bollettieri Tennis Academy when she was thirteen in 1986. Bollettieri, a master motivator, had been the coach for many of the world's leading players. While Seles was at his academy, Andre Agassi and Jim Courier were among the pupils. In future years, Bollettieri would work with Boris Becker. By all accounts, Bollettieri devoted more of his time in the late 1980s and early 1990s to Seles than anyone else.

As Bollettieri wrote of the young Seles in his illuminating book *My Aces, My Faults* (with Dick Schaap), "She worked hard from the moment she stepped on the court. She was tireless, persistent, dogged. From the first ball to the last, she was always focused. She would hit the same shot over and over until she had it down. Not for an hour. Not for a day. For weeks. She would hit nothing but two-handed backhands for two or three weeks, then nothing but two-handed forehands for two or three weeks, followed by nothing but overheads for two or three weeks. She practiced for three or four hours at a stretch. She wouldn't leave the court until she had hit the perfect shot."

After Seles and Bollettieri had a parting of the ways in 1991, Seles insisted he had never been her coach, a baffling stance to all who had watched Bollettieri in consultation with her over the years. But Monica Seles said her father Karolj was her first and only coach.

Karolj had a career as a cartoonist, but saw Monica's tennis as a serious matter. She burst into the top ten during her debut professional year in 1989, finishing that season at No. 6, pushing Graf surprisingly hard while losing a three-set semifinal at the French Open.

Seles was a seminal player, a teenager who shaped and elevated the sport with her revolutionary style. A left-hander, she produced devastatingly potent, two-handed strokes off both sides, going boldly for the lines with every invitation, taking the ball unfailingly on the rise, driving opponents into submission with her unrelenting backcourt attack. She revealed her inimitable talent at the 1990 French Open when she made a stirring recovery to oust Graf. Trailing 6-2 in a first-set tiebreaker, Seles struck back with immense power and courage. She took six points in a row and overcame the German 7-6, 6-4 to collect her first major crown and become the youngest ever to take that title. Graf plainly had a new rival. At the end of that year—after Navratilova had won Wimbledon and Gabriela Sabatini took the U.S. Open—Seles stopped Sabatini to win the season-ending Virginia Slims Championship at New York's Madison Square Garden. While Graf retained her official WTA Tour No. 1 ranking on the computer, Seles overtook the German in the minds of many experts. She did not turn seventeen until the season was over.

The following year in 1991, the "changing of the guard" was ever more apparent. Graf won Wimbledon for the third time with a spirited comeback against Sabatini, after the Argentine served for the match twice in the final set. Seles mysteriously pulled out of Wimbledon a few days before the big event, citing an injury, but refusing to discuss her withdrawal with the media. Everywhere else of importance, Seles was the victor. She took the Australian Open for the first time over Jana Novotna, after Novotna eclipsed Graf in the quarterfinals. In Paris, Seles defended her crown with a well-deserved, final-round triumph over 1989 titlist Sanchez Vicario. And, at the U.S. Open, Seles succeeded for the first time, defeating Navratilova in the final. Navratilova had upset Graf in the semifinals.

As Graf approached the age of twenty-three in 1992, Seles seemed to be soaring above and beyond her, and everyone else. The lefthander was victorious at the Australian Open with Graf injured and absent. As the players focused their attention on the French Open, Seles was an eighteen-year-old competitor who did not often doubt herself. She was controlling the course of the women's game with the same force and persuasion Graf had shown from 1987-89. Seles was seeking a third-straight title in Paris. She had a preference for faster surfaces which gave her greater rewards for the enormous pace of her strokes. But she was more at home on the clay courts of Roland Garros than Graf, who could be her own worst enemy, self-destructing under an avalanche of errors.

After her twin successes in the 1987-88 French Opens, Graf did not sustain her mastery in the next three French Opens. Seles was a shade unlucky losing to Graf at Roland Garros in 1989 before posting a prodigious win over her rival in 1990. All of the signs pointed to another Seles victory on clay. It even seemed possible that Graf would fall before the final. She didn't.

THE MATCH

Both the top-seeded Seles and No. 2 Graf overcame considerable hurdles on their way to a final-round confrontation. In the semifinals, the immensely popular Sabatini did everything short of beating Seles. She delivered an imposing array of heavy topspin shots off both sides to take Seles out of her rhythm in the rallies. She attacked at the right moments, volleying handsomely when she had the openings. She played skillfully to and for the crowd, who celebrated her every move with boisterous approval. Sabatini led 4-2 in the final set. It took all of Seles's resolve to pull her through 6-3, 4-6, 6-4.

Graf got off to a dismal start in her semifinal. She was being outmaneuvered by Sanchez Vicario. The German seemed uncomfortable and troubled. Then, almost abruptly, she found her range and turned it around in a 0-6, 6-2, 6-2 victory over the Spaniard.

It was time for the Graf-Seles rivalry to be renewed. This was their fourth major meeting, with Graf leading 2-1. Seles believed she was the better player. She had not lost in a Grand Slam event since the 1990

U.S. Open. In fact, Seles had won four majors in a row.

In the opening set of the final, Seles seemed to be in another league. Her intensity and immense firepower were evident from the outset. She attacked Graf's stronger forehand wing in the early stages with great precision. In her gallop to 3-0, Seles collected twelve of fourteen points, breaking Graf at love in the second game. Graf's fearsome forehand—a flat, penetrating, go-for-broke stroke—was misfiring and Seles wasn't missing. Seles served an authoritative love game to reach 4-1, then coasted to a 6-2 first-set win behind her boldest hitting.

In essence, Graf had been diminished in the first set, denied the opportunity to dictate the tempo of play. And yet, the fundamental question remained: Could Seles sustain her awesome standards without some sign of vulnerability?

In the fifth game of the second set, with the score locked at 2-2, Graf began raising her game markedly. When Seles served a double fault to give Graf a second break point, the German seized the moment. A series of piercing forehands put Seles on the defensive. Graf gained the break for 3-2 by blasting a forehand that forced Seles into a backhand error.

Graf then appeared to have squandered her momentum. She lost her serve immediately for 3-3 with a pair of backhand unforced errors. Grimly, she fought on. The seventh game stretched into three deuces. Seles escaped two break points before Graf took the third when Seles drove a backhand long. The German had the lead at 4-3 and this time made the most of it.

In another exceedingly hard-fought, four-deuce game, Graf trailed 15-40, saved three break points and held on grimly for 5-3. She closed out that game with two morale boosting shots. First, she angled a backhand approach volley crosscourt with sharp efficiency, then followed with a crushing inside-out forehand winner. Even the resilient Seles was shaken by Graf's furious stand. Serving at 3-5, the top seed was broken at love as Graf accelerated. Set to Graf, 6-3. One set all.

The stellar competitive qualities of both champions were on view all through the stormy final set. After Graf had held easily for 1-0, Seles struggled through two deuces and finally held on her fourth game point, stepping in confidently to drive a forehand down the line

Steffi Graf

for a winner. In the third game, Seles regained the initiative after Graf double-faulted for 0-30.

Graf managed to cast aside three break points, but on the fourth Seles produced an untouchable backhand to get the break for 2-1. Seles needed four game points before she held for 3-1—winning that game with a startling forehand down the line placement that caught the German completely off guard. Nonetheless, Graf was still holding her ground and giving little away. In making it 2-3, the German played an excellent game, including an ace, a forehand winner and a clean smash.

Every game was becoming a statement of authenticity for both players. Neither one was allowing tension to interfere. The two highly charged competitors were going at full force, playing to win, refusing to lose. As Seles held at love for 4-2, Graf was off the mark with three forehands, all of them unforced errors. But both players knew that those mistakes were errors of execution and not of judgment; Graf was not going to beat Seles by being conservative.

At 2-4, Graf was in another precarious position. She served an ace for 40-15, only to miss two first serves in a row. Seles exploited that opening. Graf struck back with a service winner for a third game point, then watched helplessly as Seles clipped the sideline with a forehand down the line. On the next point, Seles sent a series of superbly directed drives off both sides to the distant corners, moving the German around at will, controlling the point from start to finish. Graf ran around her backhand at the end, missed a forehand, and was down break point.

This one was imperative for the No. 2 seed. She could not afford to go two breaks down. She had to stay within range of the front-running Seles. Graf stepped around again and attempted another forehand winner. It worked. Graf finally held on her fifth game point with a service winner. She had closed the gap to 4-3. The effort was swiftly repudiated by Seles, who was feeling the physical strain. She held at love for 5-3, saving her energy for the following game.

With Graf serving to save the match, the battle became even more remarkable at both ends of the court. Four times in that game, Seles stood at match point. On the first of those opportunities, Graf's crosscourt forehand seemed certain to go long as it traveled through the air. When it landed, it hit the baseline and forced a stunned Seles into an error on the backhand. On the second championship point for Seles, Graf attacked unhesitatingly, angled a backhand volley crosscourt, then knocked off a gift overhead close to the net.

One point away from the title for a third time, Seles lost length on her ground strokes and Graf waited for the right ball to wallop her forehand reverse crosscourt for a gutsy winner. On the fourth match point against her, Graf knifed a backhand slice crosscourt and low. It skidded off the court just near the service line and never came up. With the crowd almost entirely on her side, raising their level of support with every shot, Graf held for 4-5 by forcing Seles into an error with an unexpected forehand down the line.

Despite the enormity of that disappointment, Seles was still serving for the match in the tenth game. But she had thrown such a big part of her stamina into the previous game that she was too drained to close out the account in this service game. A rare, wild unforced error off the forehand from Seles put her down 0-15, and another sorely misdirected forehand put her in a 15-30 hole. Graf sensed her chance, breaking serve for 5-5 by pulling a weary Seles off the court with an acutely angled crosscourt forehand.

Graf was soon in a bind again in the eleventh game, serving at 30-40. Seles drove a crosscourt forehand return deep toward Steffi's backhand corner. She thought she had the winner, headed for the changeover, then looked up and was told by the umpire that her shot had been called out. Graf celebrated with a service winner down the middle in the deuce court. Seles followed with an errant backhand, inches over the baseline, making it 6-5 to Graf.

From the enviable position of a 5-3 lead with four match points to follow, Seles found herself serving to save the match at 5-6. She was baffled by her predicament, but undaunted. She served a perfect love game to hold for 6-6. After Seles won the first point outright, Graf helped her with three preventable mistakes. Despite a double fault at 40-15, Graf held serve for 7-6. At 40-30 down in that game, Seles recklessly tried for an outright winner on the return. Her shot landed in the net, not even coming close.

Once more, Seles served to save the match in the fourteenth game. Graf missed a routine backhand return on the first point and netted a backhand drop shot from too deep a position on the last. Seles held for 7-7. From 30-30 in the following game, Graf could not connect with two critical forehands. She drove the first one long off a deep backhand return, then missed the next one from very close in, anxiously overhitting with an open court.

Seles was again back in positive territory, serving for the match at 8-7. She moved to 15-0, then came in for a short forehand. Had she gone crosscourt to Graf's backhand side, she would surely have found a winner for 30-0. But Seles chose the wrong side. Graf recovered, and as Seles backed away from the net, Graf passed her with a backhand. A brilliantly concealed backhand drop shot winner gave Graf 15-30, and she made it to 8-8 when Seles hit an ill-advised backhand drop shot into the net from behind the baseline.

Having served for the match a second time and failed, Seles was

Monica Seles

an exhausted and confused competitor. The next game was crucial for both players. Graf did not miss a first serve. She reached 30-30. She had the Roland Garros spectators cheering her raucously, willing her on. At 30-30, she stepped around her backhand, drove through the forehand, and watched it sail inches long. Seles then went to work, moving Graf from side to side with searing strokes from both flanks. She got a midcourt ball on her backhand, lined it up, and drove it crosscourt out of reach. Graf was stranded. Seles had the break for 9-8.

Seles served for the match again, and reached 40-15. Graf saved a fifth match point with a clean forehand down the line for a winner. It was 40-30. Graf exploded again from the forehand, looking to send it out of reach on Seles's backhand side. The ball caught the tape on top of the net. Then it fell back on her side. Seles was triumphant 6-2, 3-6, 10-8. It had lasted for two hours and forty-three riveting minutes.

Reduced to tears at the presentation ceremony, Graf was overwhelmed by the affectionate crowd that almost carried her to a victory. "I've never played for a crowd like this before. Never," she said. Of Seles, she added, "Even when it's close, even when she's tired, she's going for it. She's tough."

Seles responded in kind, "Both of us deserved to win." No one there could disagree.

EPILOGUE

With Seles the victor at both the Australian and French Opens of 1992, she was halfway to matching Graf's Grand Slam feat of 1988. Be that as it may, she knew that winning Wimbledon would inevitably be a difficult challenge. She had only played on the grass courts of the All England Club twice before, losing in the round of sixteen to Graf in 1989 and falling in the quarterfinals the following year to Zina Garrison of the United States. The skidding, low, grass-court bounces were a major deterrent to Seles's rhythmic, ground-stroking style.

Graf was just the opposite. Her footwork was one of her reliable attributes. Her first serve—a powerful weapon that won her countless free points—was particularly effective on grass. And her slice backhand was a shot made for the lawns, coming through fast and biting, forcing opponents into defensive positions. Seles and Graf—the top two seeds—advanced to the final, their first such meeting outside Paris.

Despite Graf's greater ease on the grass, another titanic battle seemed likely. But their first Centre Court title match did not live up to expectations. Graf's performance was immaculate. She subdued Seles 6-2, 6-1. Seles, however, was devoid of spirit, shaken by accusations made against her by the Frenchwoman, Nathalie Tauziat (a future finalist), and Navratilova (her semifinal victim) that her loud grunting had become unbearably intrusive on court and was breaking their concentration.

Deeply disturbed by the comments of her colleagues—most reporters interpreted the griping of Tauziat and Navratilova as sour grapes—Seles could not muster anything near her customary intensity. Her grunting was unmistakably softer. Her tennis suffered irreparably. Making matters worse, the fifty-nine-minute match was delayed by rain four times. They started at 2 p.m., but it did not conclude until five hours later. By then, the fans were listless. Only a month after the French Open epic, this was a disappointing sequel for the two best players in the world.

Seles recouped remarkably in New York, winning the U.S. Open for the second year in a row, defeating Sanchez Vicario in the final. The Spaniard had ousted an erratic Graf in the quarterfinals. Seles had secured three of the four major championships, replicating her 1991 feat. As was the case in 1991, Graf had won only Wimbledon—no small consolation.

As 1993 commenced, Seles and Graf collided for the third time in four major championships. They met in the Australian Open final. The tennis was played at the lofty level they had reached in Paris seven months earlier. Graf won the first set and pressed her adversary staunchly to the end. Seles succeeded 4-6, 6-3, 6-2 but the match was much closer than the numbers.

The Seles-Graf rivalry of the 1990s was notable, but did not inspire the passion of those who followed the Evert-Navratilova series played during the seventies and eighties. Graf was closing in, gaining confidence, threatening Seles in serious fashion. The feeling grew among the experts that the two combatants would share the most celebrated prizes and that Graf would hold her own with her younger rival.

Both women appeared in Hamburg at the German Open, preparing for the 1993 French Open, which was less than a month away. Seles was playing the Bulgarian Magdalena Maleeva in the quarterfinals on April 30. She was seated in her assigned chair at a changeover when a deranged man came up from behind her with a knife and stabbed her in the back.

The assailant, Gunther Parche, was an obsessed Graf fan who wanted his heroine to regain the No. 1 world ranking from Seles. Seles was rushed to the hospital and was visited by Graf the next day. The two strong-minded women, who so seldom showed emotion during matches, both burst into tears. Graf may have felt some guilt for what happened in her country as a direct result of her crazed fan. She also felt immense sympathy for an opponent she respected above all others.

The wound to Seles's back was minimal; the wound to her psyche was considerably deeper. She would not return to tennis for nearly twenty-eight months. The game lost a unique and admirable player. Meanwhile, Graf came back resolutely into her own. She took the rest of the major championships in 1993. In the French Open final, she recovered from a break down at 4-3 in the third to beat Mary Joe Fernandez. At Wimbledon, she played Jana Novotna in the final. Novotna had a game point for 5-1 in the third, double-faulted, and lost five games in a row. Graf then came through at the U.S. Open in less dramatic fashion, beating Helena Sukova in the final.

The German was indisputably back on top. But it was impossible not to wonder what might have happened if Seles had been able to play. Could Graf have been so secure and successful? Was she simply the beneficiary of a tragedy, or was she destined for these triumphs anyway?

That kind of speculation served no useful purpose. Undoubtedly, Graf's inner game was altered substantially by the absence of Seles. Nevertheless, that could not diminish what she had done. Graf took the first Grand Slam event of 1994 to record a fourth consecutive major championship victory. Thereafter, she faltered and did not win another big title the rest of the year. She remained No. 1 on the official WTA computer for the second year in a row, and the sixth time overall, but her year was less than stellar.

Graf missed the Australian Open of 1995 with an injury, but won the French Open and Wimbledon. As she trained in the summer before the U.S. Open, Seles made a dramatic return to tournament tennis at the Canadian Open. In that tournament, Monica lost a mere fourteen games in five matches and romped smoothly through the field. Her timing was as precise as ever. Her shotmaking remained strikingly self-assured. She looked like the Seles of old.

Coming into the U.S. Open final, Seles was sharper than Graf. She competed with the same all-out authority as she had displayed in Canada. Her ball control was dazzling. On "Super Saturday" at the U.S. Open—after Pete Sampras had beaten Jim Courier, and before Andre Agassi had removed Boris Becker in the men's semifinals—Seles and Graf renewed their rivalry, sharing a court for the first time since the Australian Open of 1993. They staged one of their highest quality encounters. The first set went into a tiebreak. Seles narrowly missed an ace on set point and lost the playoff 8-6. She struck back passionately to take the second set at love, but Graf served splendidly throughout the third set and won 7-6, 0-6, 6-3. The two players embraced genuinely at the net. This had been more than another major tennis match; it had been a healing moment for two young women who had shared a traumatic experience.

With Graf absent again from the Australian Open of 1996, Seles collected her first major crown since 1993 and her ninth overall, taking the title over the German Anke Huber. Then Graf won the French Open and Wimbledon. At the U.S. Open, she took on Seles for the first time since the 1995 title match. In this final, Graf won 7-5, 6-4. Seles—set back by injuries, absent her old gusto—was not nearly as good as she needed to be.

Seles suffered severe shoulder and psychological problems throughout 1996. Some believed she should have taken the time off for surgery. Seles elected to keep competing, and she did so at a reasonably high level. One Grand Slam title and another final in that season was respectable. All the same, her comeback was still in the early stages.

The force of her will and the scope of her talent would be felt by all her rivals in the immediate years to come.

CHAPTER TWENTY-FOUR

Boris Becker *vs.* Pete Sampras

ATP TOUR WORLD CHAMPIONSHIP, FINAL, HANOVER, GERMANY,
NOVEMBER 24, 1996

In an atmosphere resembling a heavyweight boxing match, the German audience cheered Becker thunderously but treated his rival with much respect. When it was over, the players embraced at the net in a rare gesture of mutual admiration.

PROLOGUE

After Gottfried von Cramm drifted out of tournament tennis in the late 1930s, Germany did not produce another world championship player until the arrival of Boris Becker in the middle of the 1980s. Boris was raised in a small German town called Leimen. He dropped out of school to play competitive tennis. His father was an architect who helped to build a tennis center near the Becker home. Though he had played soccer as a boy, Becker was determined to make his mark in top-flight tennis. As a teenager, Becker was notably muscular and fit. Burly and imposing, he was surprisingly mature for his age, on and off the tennis court. Becker burst into greatness when he was seventeen.

Unseeded and unknown to all but the cognoscenti, Becker cut down one veteran performer after another at the All England Club in the summer of 1985. He became the first unseeded, and the youngest-ever, men's singles titlist at seventeen, vanquishing four seeded competitors, and stopping the big-serving South African Kevin Curren in a four-set final. An explosive player in every facet of the game, Becker quickly earned the nickname "Boom Boom," a vernacular tribute to the speed and impact of his shots. He would over time be recognized as one of the strongest servers of the modern era, and probably of all time. Becker's serving style featured a pronounced knee bend, which helped him spring up and out at the ball. He used an eastern forehand grip for his serve, an adjustment few if any of his competitors emulated. Off the ground, his muscle power separated him from nearly everyone else.

Becker won Wimbledon again in 1986, toppling the world No. 1 Ivan Lendl in a straight-set final. In 1989, he took his third crown at the All England Club, securing that championship with a victory over Stefan Edberg, the same player who defeated him in the 1988 and 1990 finals. Later in the summer of 1989, Becker defeated Lendl for his lone U.S. Open title. The win in New York was sufficient for the International Tennis Federation to honor him with the title of "World Champion," although Lendl was ranked No. 1 in the world on the ATP computer. The ATP did not place as much emphasis on the major championships.

The gifted German briefly took his place at the top of the rankings early in 1991 when he halted Lendl yet again in a major final, prevailing in a four-set Australian Open title match. A man of many facets, strong willed and more interested than most of his peers in the world at large, Becker lost some of his zest for the game from 1992-94, only sporadically displaying his best tennis.

In 1995, he recovered his enthusiasm, raised his standards, and was rewarded for his wider commitment. At Wimbledon, he reached his seventh final, defeating Andre Agassi for the first time in six years in a scintillating semifinal match. In an ironic twist, Becker was supported by the presence of Nick Bollettieri as his coach. Three years earlier, Bollettieri had sat in the same "friend's box" and cheered for his longtime pupil, Agassi. The master motivator elected to end his ten-year coaching association with Agassi in 1993, joining forces with Becker the following year, much to the dismay of Andre.

Becker lost the 1995 Wimbledon final to Sampras, and handled his defeat with unusual grace. Paying tribute to a rival he had come to revere, Becker said, "This court used to belong to me in the 1980s. Now it belongs to Pete Sampras." Becker was a semifinalist at the U.S. Open that year. He was back again among the elite. Settled and motivated, he won the Australian Open, at the start of 1996, over Michael Chang, dedicating that triumph to his wife Barbara, who had never seen him capture a major championship.

He injured his wrist at Wimbledon that year and did not return until the autumn segment on the ATP Tour. He was twenty-nine. He had been a formidable force in the game for twelve years. He had conquered the field in Melbourne at a time when many knowledgeable observers believed he could no longer play that well. It had been five long years since he had last won a Grand Slam singles title.

Becker seemed to revive his competitive zeal indoors at the end of 1996. At the Stuttgart "Super Nine" event, he played Sampras in the final and prevailed in a splendid five-set match, recovering from two-sets-to-one down. That triumph was crucial in enabling him to join the field as one of the top-eight players in the world at the season ending ATP Tour World Championship at Hanover. Having missed ten weeks of competition—including the U.S. Open—it was no small feat for Becker to make the roster.

Sampras, meanwhile, was enjoying another banner season at the top. He had endured a year with a wide range of emotions. His friend and coach, Tim Gullikson, had passed away in May. He played the French Open less than a month later, and reached the semifinals at Roland Garros for the first time on the strength of three five-set victories before exhaustion set in. At Wimbledon, he lost for the first time since 1992, bowing in the quarterfinals against Richard Krajicek, the towering Dutchman who went on to win the tournament.

The U.S. Open was a fortnight of heightened significance for Sampras. He had won two major tournaments in each of the previous three years; this was his last chance to salvage one major crown for 1996. In the quarterfinals, he faced the cunning Alex Corretja of Spain. Sampras miscalculated the starting time of the match and did not eat a full meal on schedule. This he would greatly regret.

Corretja forced the favorite to play a match of protracted points, turning the contest into something resembling a clay-court struggle. By the latter stages of the third set, it was apparent that Sampras had little energy left. He trailed, two sets to one, labored to win the fourth, and somehow willed himself into a fifth-set tiebreak. Early in that tiebreaker, he lowered his head behind the court and threw up. The umpire gave him a warning for time abuse.

Sampras was in a terrible bind. He was playing solely on adrenaline and grit, stretching for his shots, making astonishing winners. Between points, he would lean over his racket, shoulders sagging, drained, listless. The New York crowd was chanting, "Pete, Pete, Pete" almost metronomically. Sampras saved a match point with a lunging drop volley for 7-7 in the tiebreak. He followed with an incredible second serve ace, then abruptly, anticlimactically, he won the match when Corretja double-faulted. The crowd stood and cheered both players. At the net, Corretja embraced Sampras, offering generous recognition of an extraordinarily plucky performance.

After a day off, Sampras stopped Goran Ivanisevic and Michael Chang back-to-back for his fourth U.S. Open title. That success carried him through the fall and into Hanover. The Open had been a make-or-break challenge for Sampras, and he refused to be broken. As he headed into Hanover, he had sealed the No. 1 world ranking for the year. He was playing chiefly out of pride, seeking to enhance his standing at the end of the season, knowing that his most obstinate adversary in that setting on a fast indoor court would be Boris Becker.

THE MATCH

As fate would have it, Sampras and Becker were placed in the same round-robin group of four. After Sampras had ousted Agassi in his opening match, he took on Becker in a dramatic showdown. The German—boosted by his win over the American in Stuttgart—overcame Sampras again. He won in two tiebreaks. The first tiebreak was settled by a 12-10 score and the second was seized by Becker 7-4. Sampras had served for the second set, but Becker broke back and went on to victory.

Despite the loss, Sampras still qualified for the semifinals by overcoming his French Open conqueror Yevgeny Kafelnikov. He took on Ivanisevic in one semifinal while Becker faced Krajicek in the other. Both matches were high-quality contests. Sampras edged Ivanisevic 6-7 (6), 7-6 (4), 7-5, surviving thirty-five aces from the Croatian left-hander. Becker withstood a powerful performance from the Wimbledon champion Krajicek, but came through efficiently 6-7 (4), 7-6 (3), 6-3.

The battle of the heavyweights was on. The players walked from their entranceway a level above the court at Messe Halle 2. As they were making their way to the stage, the theme from the movie *Rocky* was reverberating in the arena. In other venues, that kind of a pre-match buildup would have been regarded as nothing more than hype, but not for this encounter.

The thirteen thousand fans and both players were exhilarated by the music and the moment. Here were two of the game's all-time greatest players confronting each other in the final of the most coveted men's event outside the Grand Slams. Becker was buoyant about performing for an audience understandably eager for his success. Sampras relished the challenge of trying to overcome a fellow champion who was at his best indoors in his homeland.

"It is tough playing Boris anywhere, but especially in Germany," Sampras would say later. "He really feeds off the emotion from the crowd. Indoors, I find him extremely difficult to play because he is so powerful and hits the ball so big. I remember telling my coach Paul Annacone right before we walked on the court that this was going to be fun to go out there and hear the crowd going bananas. For me, this is what it is all about."

Sampras took a 9-7 career edge over Becker into this battle. From the start, he knew he was up against an inspired player at the top of his form. Becker served the opening game of the match. Sampras never made contact with the ball. Becker aced him four consecutive times in holding at love. On the first point, he went wide to the forehand. He followed with an untouchable delivery down the middle, then another one out wide, then one more wide to the backhand in the advantage court. The crowd was delirious.

Sampras served a love game himself for 1-1, then had Becker down 0-30 in the third game. Becker blasted his way out of that corner with three unreturnable serves in the next four points. He broke Sampras for 3-1 at the cost of only a single point, producing a forehand return winner, a backhand return placement, and a stinging forehand return at break point that Sampras could not handle. In the fifth game, Becker trailed 15-30 as Sampras found the range with a backhand return crosscourt winner and a stupendous running forehand out of Becker's reach.

Becker responded with two more timely aces and an effective kick serve into the body on the backhand side. The German advanced to 4-1. Both men held at love in their next service games as Becker increased his lead to 5-2. He was playing his best tennis in perhaps seven years, serving prodigiously, striking his first volleys with certainty, returning with power and panache.

At 5-3, Becker served for the first set. Sampras pressed him hard. A forehand service return winner took him to 0-15. A low return set up a backhand pass by the American down the line for 15-30. Becker was composed and ready to deal with the resistance from the American. He served another ace down the middle for 30-30, then benefited from a piece of good fortune.

Sampras drove a backhand passing shot down the line, making the ball dip with top-spin. Becker lunged, made contact off the edge of his frame, and that freakish volley fell over the net. He had hit an accidental drop volley for 40-30. Becker then sealed the set with an amazing winning shot on the run. Racing to his left for a backhand, he snapped it with topspin and left Sampras helplessly stranded. Set to Becker 6-3. The crowd was chanting, "Boris, Boris, Boris."

It took all of Sampras's immense resolve to keep him in the match. He had played a respectable first set, but Becker had simply played maddeningly inspired tennis. Sampras served first in the second set and built a 3-2 lead. He had two break points against Becker in the sixth game. Becker erased those opportunities abruptly. He forced the American wide to the forehand with a deceptive serve to save the first, then delivered a searing ace to escape the second.

At 4-5, Becker served to save the set and held at love with complete assurance. Sampras held for 6-5, employing one of his patented plays. Serving and moving in, he sensed the return would be awkward to volley. The American stopped, took a short backswing, and drove an inside-out forehand into the clear for a winner. Becker was behind 5-6, serving to save the set a second time. He released three more aces in a love game—two of them down the middle in the deuce court—and took the set into a tiebreak.

Sampras was strikingly unruffled during this critical sequence. After Becker aced him on consecutive points for 2-1, Sampras calmly took over. He served and played his first volley deep to the backhand to force a passing shot error, then connected with an elusive first serve to the backhand that Becker netted on the chipped return. Sampras was ahead, 3-2. He reached 4-2 when a slightly miss-hit forehand return pulled the German over to the sideline. Becker's forehand first volley crosscourt lacked penetration, and Sampras whipped a forehand passing shot into the clear space. Becker took the next point with a well-placed wide serve to the forehand.

Sampras got to 5-3 when Becker netted a topspin backhand return off a second serve. He reached triple set point at 6-3 with a percentage play, punching the first volley to Becker's backhand, forcing the German into an error as Becker went down the line. Becker took both of his service points to close the gap to 6-5, but Sampras had a third set point in hand.

The American directed his first serve deep to the German's backhand. Becker lifted his return tamely. Sampras charged in for the backhand volley, sending it down the line safely for the winner, taking the set 7-5 in the tiebreak. Pumping his fists, the world No. 1 sat down for the changeover with a renewed spirit, relieved and delighted to be level at one set all.

In the sixth game of the third set, Sampras served at 2-3, 15-40. He needed two clutch aces to come out of that crisis, holding on for 3-3. Both men were serving prodigiously, finding ways to keep each other off guard. Sampras served at 4-5 and lost only a single point in that game. He reached 5-5 by backing up a big serve with a crisp backhand volley winner crosscourt.

The two titans traded love service games for 6-6. They moved into another tiebreak. Becker revealed a lurking apprehension for the first time in the match. He stayed back behind a second serve and Sampras looped his return high to the German's backhand side. Becker anxiously drove the ball into the net. Sampras played a forehand approach on the next point dangerously close to the baseline. Becker wanted a call but did not get it. Sampras slipped in and deposited an elegant forehand drop volley winner for 2-0. An unnerved Becker complained to the umpire, to no avail.

Sampras soared to 3-0 after a forehand reverse crosscourt winner off Becker's return of serve. Sampras moved to 4-2, but Becker connected confidently with a backhand passing shot down the line to make it 4-3.

Becker again stayed back after his second serve, got the short ball to his backhand, and came in behind a deep approach. He had closed off the court, punching a backhand volley winner down the line for 4-4. Becker missed his first serve, paused, and attempted a deep second serve. The ball was out. Double fault. 5-4, Sampras.

The American served wide to the German's backhand, near the sideline. Becker could not answer. That ace gave Sampras a 6-4 tie-break lead. Sampras now stayed back behind a second serve. Becker rolled his return of serve and came in on the American's backhand. The approach was not sharply hit. Sampras swung freely from low to high, and passed Becker easily down the line. With that shot, he took the lead, two sets to one. His fortunes were rising. In the first game of the fourth set, Sampras found himself in a 15-40 predicament, but he steadied and held on for 1-0. The two players proceeded to 3-3, knowing service breaks would be nearly impossible to find. By the middle of the set, both men were in a kind of rhythm on their deliveries. Sampras held confidently for 4-3. Becker answered with a love game on another ace for 4-4. The American conceded only one point on his way to 5-4.

In the tenth game, serving to save the match, Becker was in trouble. Sampras lined up a backhand passing shot and drove it with unexpected velocity, forcing Becker into a backhand volley error for 0-15. Becker took the next point, but he then netted a crosscourt forehand for 15-30. The American was two points away from the championship. Becker cracked a menacing first serve down the middle and Sampras could not return it—30-30. Becker worked his way in on a heavily sliced backhand approach shot to the Sampras forehand. The American netted the difficult pass. Then the German aced Sampras wide to the backhand. He was alive at 5-5.

Both players held at love to set up a third consecutive tiebreak, with Becker smacking two more thundering aces on his way to 6-6. Inexplicably, the first four points of the tiebreak went against the serve before Sampras broke that pattern to reach 3-2.

Becker took the next three points for a 5-3 lead. Serving on the ninth point, Sampras boldly played his backhand first volley to Becker's forehand side. The German created an acute angle crosscourt. His forehand passing shot looked successful, but Sampras leapt to his right and opened his racket face to bring off a drop volley winner. Becker was still ahead 5-4.

Becker sent a forehand crosscourt wide off a service return hit down the middle for 5-5. When the German was off the mark with another first serve, Sampras hit an extraordinarily deep forehand return. Becker got to it, but Sampras approached behind a sparkling low backhand chip. Becker's attempted forehand passing shot was wide. It was 6-5, Sampras. Match point for the American.

He hit a heavily spun second serve down the middle that Becker could not attack off the forehand, but Sampras rolled a backhand narrowly wide to lose that point. It was now 6-6. The German crowd had lost some of their intensity as Sampras had marched to the edge of triumph. They raised the volume once more as the players changed ends.

Sampras swung his second serve wide to Becker's forehand. The German snapped the return with great pace, forced a weak response from the American, then whipped another forehand for a winner. 7-6 for Becker. Set point for the German.

Becker served-and-volleyed behind a second serve. Sampras dipped a forehand return at his feet. Becker could not handle it. It was 7-7. Becker took control after a stinging first serve to lead 8-7 and reach set point for the second time. Sampras retaliated with an unplayable first serve to the backhand to make it 8-8. The American directed another serve to Becker's backhand, closed in on the net, and put a backhand volley out of reach. Sampras, at 9-8, had a match point for the second time. On his second serve, Becker stayed back and gave Sampras the opportunity to trade ground strokes with him. They had a fourteen-stroke rally. Becker stood his ground. Sampras concluded it by going for too big a forehand. His shot landed well over the baseline. Becker, at 9-9, moved Sampras out of position, then came in on the American's backhand. Sampras netted the passing shot. 10-9, Becker. Set point to the German for the third time.

Sampras was unforgiving on serve, going deep to the German's backhand to tie it at 10-10. Sampras then served-and-volleyed but he played with caution. Becker would not let him get away with it. His backhand pass was a clean winner. Set point number four for the German, 11-10.

Becker stayed back on his second serve, then approached behind a deep crosscourt forehand. On the run, Sampras whipped a forehand crosscourt winner. The crowd sat in nearly silent awe as the score went to 11-11. Becker served a bomb to the Sampras backhand, came in behind it, put away a high forehand first volley for 12-11. Set point number five for the German.

Sampras served and Becker's backhand return was unexceptional, but the American had run out of heroics. He moved around his backhand volley to play an inside-out forehand volley. He opened the racket face too much. The ball flew well out of court. Tiebreaker to Becker 13-11. Set to the German. Two sets all. The fans showered Becker with prolonged applause. Sampras sat quietly at the change-over, reviewing missed opportunities, wondering if he had the will or resources to win the fateful fifth.

Becker opened the final set by connecting on four out of five first serves for 1-0. Sampras double-faulted on the first point of the second game, then netted a backhand first volley to dig a 0-30 deficit for himself. He could not afford to lose this service game. Three unreturnable first serves took him to 40-30 before Becker struck back for deuce. Sampras had a second game point but Becker was reprieved when the American ran around his backhand and caught the tape with a blazing forehand.

It was deuce for the second time. Sampras missed his first serve, but rolled the dice on his second. It was hit as hard and as close to the sideline as his first delivery. Becker's return was wide. Game point for Sampras. When Becker lost a spirited rally, Sampras held on for 1-1. He had survived another crisis.

In the third game, Becker aced Sampras down the middle in the advantage court. It was his thirty-first untouchable delivery of the match. But he followed with two consecutive double faults for 30-30. He held for 2-1, but not before revealing weakness. Sampras served a double fault into the net for 30-30 at 1-2, but he came through this test unscathed after putting away a leaping overhead and then serving an ace. It was all even, 2-2.

Becker served brilliantly in the fifth game, opening with his thirty-second ace down the middle, holding at love for 3-2. The tension was mounting. The fans had high expectations that Becker would complete his task. The players were visibly exhausted, but the suspense seemed unending. Sampras was off target with three out of four first serves in the sixth game, but he held at love as Becker's ground game seemed to unravel.

At 3-3, Sampras probed as much as possible on his returns. He reached 30-30, but Becker used a big serve down the middle to set up a backhand down the line for a placement. He served-and-volleyed forcefully at 40-30, and Sampras netted a backhand down the line pass under considerable pressure. Becker, 4-3.

On the first point of the eighth game, Becker struck his backhand return so deep that Sampras could not play it. A service break would permit Becker to serve for the match. Calmly, Sampras fired a first serve down the middle, making Becker stretch too far for the forehand. At 15-15, Sampras serve-volleyed successfully again, going behind the German with the approach volley. An ace gave Sampras 40-15. Becker saved the first game point, but Sampras made it 4-4 with a sidespin backhand volley provoking an error.

At 4-4, Sampras and Becker invested most of what energy they had left. It was a crucial game. A chipped backhand return from the American was answered by a backhand volley from the German. Sampras was waiting for that response and he flicked a forehand passing shot down the line for a winner. Becker double-faulted for 0-30, but rallied to 30-30.

Sampras again chipped a low backhand return. Becker was a step too slow moving into the forecourt. He punched his forehand volley crosscourt. Sampras was ready. He curled another forehand passing shot down the line for a winner. It was 30-40. Break point for the American. Becker responded with all-out aggression. A first serve deep to the backhand was too strong. Sampras floated his return too high. Becker spiked the forehand volley to reach deuce. Sampras rolled a high return of serve off the forehand down the line. Becker may have had too much time to think. He mishit a backhand crosscourt wide.

At break point for the second time, Sampras seemed in control. Becker had hung back at the baseline. But the American overplayed a forehand. It was deuce again. Becker served wide to the American's forehand and fielded a difficult low return with a backhand volley crosscourt. As Becker retreated to the baseline, Sampras rolled his backhand down the line. Becker did a terrific job reaching that ball and drove a forehand crosscourt. Sampras responded with a flat forehand, but not too deep. Becker had to lunge laterally as he moved forward and his slice backhand found the net.

It was break point number three for Sampras at 4-4 in the fifth. It must have seemed as if he had played several tennis matches on this one long afternoon. He had been out there for nearly four hours. He had lost his serve only once in five sets, but had not yet broken the German's big delivery. He had waged this debilitating battle in a Davis Cup atmosphere, feeling to some extent that he was playing not only Becker but the entire German nation. Pete Sampras knew he was an American competing on his own, not representing his country in any official capacity. More than anything else, he wanted this match as a personal reward for a demanding year.

Becker connected with a first serve to the backhand. Sampras chipped low down the line to Becker's forehand. Becker had to lift the volley but he placed it with good depth. Sampras read it early and propelled his backhand with exceptional topspin. It left his racket and gathered speed. Becker turned. He knew at once that he had lost the game. Sampras had hit a perfect backhand passing shot winner. As a stunned audience applauded politely, Sampras released his tension with a barely audible "Yeah." His fists were clenched. His mind was focused on the next game.

Sampras served for the match in the tenth game. He aced Becker down the middle for 15-0. Becker took advantage of a loose backhand drop volley to reach 15-15, but the American moved to 30-15 with a backhand at Becker's feet. Sampras served to the backhand, played a deep, low volley into the German's backhand corner, and Becker put up a short topspin lob. Sampras was in place, and easily put away a high backhand volley. It had all come down to 40-15, double match

Boris Becker and Pete Sampras

point for the American. Sampras served-and-volleyed. Becker hit a backhand passing shot crosscourt. Sampras lunged but could not make the play—40-30. Sampras missed the first serve, stayed back behind his second, and the two gladiators had their longest and best baseline exchange of the match. Sampras had Becker on the run. He sent a barrage of forehands into the corners and Becker ran them all down. His replies to every big shot from Sampras were powerful strokes of the same high quality.

Having hit Becker with everything in his arsenal, Sampras finally tried a change of pace. He looped a forehand down the line with heavy topspin. Becker now had to generate his own pace. He unleashed a backhand but drove the ball into the net. Sampras staggered briefly behind the baseline, raising his arms and looking as if he might collapse under the weight of victory and the length of the struggle. Becker walked up to the net and leaned over it, a thoroughly depleted figure. Sampras came up to greet him. They embraced for a long moment, and exchanged congratulatory words. In the tennis world of the 1990s, there was no more poignant moment than that.

The electric atmosphere had driven the players to perform at a level they did not think existed. When it was over, Becker said, "I can't play any better than that. It was the most incredible feeling I have ever had walking on a tennis court. That was the ultimate match for me. By the end, I didn't really care who won." (Sampras: 3-6, 7-6, 7-6, 6-7, 6-4.) Sampras was largely in accord. He reflected a month later, "I have never really been in a match like that one anywhere in the world. I have been in my share of U.S. Open and Wimbledon finals but this was very special. You couldn't even talk because the noise was so deafening. It was a huge match for me. Thirteen million people saw the match in Germany, one of the biggest television audiences ever. It was a phenomenal experience.... After I won they gave me a good ovation, which I appreciated. That match with Boris will always stick out in my mind. I have enough money, I have my ranking. It is playing those great matches that matters to me."

British writer Richard Evans has probably witnessed more magnificent men's tennis matches since the early 1960's than any other reporter. He wrote in *Tennis Week*, "Had Boris Becker managed to beat Pete Sampras in one of the greatest matches of modern times, Hanover might never have recovered from its hangover. This was a pulsating encounter between the two best indoor players of their generation."

EPILOGUE

Eight months later, Sampras and Becker clashed again in the quarterfinals of Wimbledon. It was their third Centre Court meeting. Sampras defeated his gifted rival in four sets. When it was over, Becker walked up to Sampras at the net and said, "This was my last match here. I just want you to know it has been a pleasure playing against you." Sampras was astonished by the announcement, and thanked the German sincerely for the compliment. Becker believed then he was on his way out of the game. He did not plan to compete again in the major championships, preferring to stick with one-week tournaments on a part-time basis. Two years later, however, in 1999, the German could not resist returning to Wimbledon one more time. He reached the round of sixteen, but was soundly beaten by Patrick Rafter in straight sets.

Becker had enjoyed a sterling career as a full-time competitor. Between 1985 and 1996, he had finished all but one year among the top six. He had won six major singles titles, had briefly resided at No. 1 in the world, and had shown in particular respects that he was larger than the game he played. He had galvanized tennis in Germany and had become an immensely popular player around the world.

As for Sampras, he moved on from his battles with Becker to conquer other rivals and collect more major titles. In 1997, he won the Australian Open for the second time. At Wimbledon, he was the winner for the fourth time. In seven matches in that tournament, Sampras held serve in 116 of 118 games.

In 1998, the American returned to Wimbledon after an undistinguished first half of the season. At the All England Club, he was revitalized. He won his fifth singles title in six years, besting Ivanisevic in his first-ever five-set major final. He had confirmed that no one in the modern game was better when the stakes were highest. One year later, Sampras did it again. In a devastatingly potent display, he defeated Andre Agassi in a straight-set Wimbledon final. He had triumphed for the twelfth time in fourteen major finals. He had won Wimbledon three years in a row for the second time. He had set a men's record for the century with his six singles titles on Centre Court. One more major tournament and he would break Roy Emerson's coveted record of twelve Grand Slam tournament titles.

Over the second half of 1998, Sampras had gone after a different record. No man had ever been ranked No. 1 in the world for six consecutive years since computer rankings were introduced in 1973. Bill Tilden was the only man ever to achieve that feat in the history of the game. Sampras reached his goal in 1998 after playing six consecutive tournaments in the autumn, pushing himself almost past his physical and emotional limits to remain the best in his profession.

That achievement added substantial weight to the claim that Sampras could be considered the greatest tennis player of all time. His critics argued that the self-effacing American needed to round out his record with a French Open title. His supporters countered that he had been so far superior on faster surfaces that a failure to take the world's premier clay-court championship should not disqualify him. Those who stood on middle ground admired Pete Sampras for his supreme skill and dignity. He was clearly the best tennis player of his generation.

CHAPTER TWENTY-FIVE

Martina Hingis _vs._ Steffi Graf

FRENCH OPEN, FINAL, JUNE 5, 1999

Before a vibrant partisan crowd at Roland Garros, Hingis wanted to win the only major title to elude her grasp, while Graf resolutely sought another major crown in the twilight of her career.

PROLOGUE

Martina Hingis headed into her 1999 Roland Garros title battle with Steffi Graf propelled by a seemingly unshakable confidence. She would not turn nineteen until three months later, but already she had recorded five Grand Slam tournament victories. Having taken her third consecutive Australian Open five months earlier, the Swiss teenager had established herself as a player who was always primed for the occasion. The last time she had not been at least a semifinalist in a major tournament was at Wimbledon in 1996. After relinquishing her No. 1 world ranking to Lindsay Davenport for the 1998 season, she had taken back her place at the top in the early months of 1999. But as she looked forward to her confrontation with Graf on the clay in Paris, Hingis was driven by a larger goal. Roland Garros was the lone "Big Four" tournament she had not captured. She wanted it passionately, was fully committed to taking it, and firmly believed it was her turn to claim the crown.

Graf's inner view was radically different. She came to Paris expecting very little from herself. She had not won a major event since the U.S. Open of 1996. In 1997, her season came to an end after a quarterfinal loss at Roland Garros. Knee surgery was performed on the German immediately following that tournament. Not until Wimbledon in 1998 did Graf compete again in a Grand Slam event. She had lost in the third round there, and bowed in the round of sixteen later that summer at the U.S. Open after securing a morale-boosting title in New Haven the week before.

At the close of 1998, Graf played brilliantly in winning two tournaments and reaching the semifinals of the season-ending Chase Championships at New York's Madison Square Garden. The resurgence was brief. On her way to Roland Garros in 1999, the German's instability surfaced repeatedly. She did not win a tournament. She squandered a 4-2 final-set lead against the surging Serena Williams in the championship match at Indian Wells. She was thoroughly blasted off the court by the advancing Venus Williams at Key Biscayne. Her clay court results en route to Paris were not encouraging.

Graf hoped she could win some matches in Paris to toughen herself up for Wimbledon and the grass courts that suited her game much better. And yet, seeded only sixth, she was surprisingly sharp and solid over the early rounds. Her first major test was against the precocious Russian Anna Kournikova in the round of sixteen. Kournikova had cut down Graf on the grass courts of Eastbourne the previous year. When her big-hitting game was clicking, she had shown just how formidable she could be. In this encounter, Graf recouped from 5-6, 0-40 in the second set to prevail 6-3, 7-6. In the quarterfinals, she stopped the second-seed Davenport in three sets. That set the stage for a semifinal against the No. 3 seed Seles. Graf was apprehensive at the outset, but came on strong for a three-set victory and a well-deserved place in another major final.

Hingis made her way to the final without a hitch. She did not concede a set, defeating defending champion Arantxa Sanchez Vicario of Spain in a one-sided, straight-set semifinal. In that match, Hingis had displayed the full range of her talent. She made some surprise serve-and-volley attacks, catching the Spaniard off guard. She used the drop shot judiciously. She improvised with the lob volley. She used every inch of the court to her advantage. Hingis was close to the top of her game, and was convinced she was going to win the tournament no matter whom she faced in the final. She had completed her semifinal triumph before Graf and Seles stepped on court. Hingis was asked about which woman she would rather play for the title. She did not hesitate. She said she preferred to play Steffi Graf in the final.

THE MATCH

Graf held a 6-2 career edge in her series of matches against Hingis, but that statistic was misleading. Most of those wins had been posted when Hingis was developing her game, and Graf was the best player in the world. Nevertheless, in the year leading up to this clash at Roland Garros, the two champions had each won once against the other. These two matches were played indoors. Graf still had the weapons and the energy to stand her ground against a player eleven years her junior. Be that as it may, the slow court conditions in Paris were much in Hingis's favor. Graf would have more difficulty concluding points with penetrating forehands. She would have to work harder to earn her keep. She would need to make certain her sliced backhand was working at full efficiency. She would need to serve with sting and authority.

Anything less than a top-of-the-line performance from Graf would cause the German to fall short of victory. Hingis had not done herself justice at Roland Garros the previous two years, sliding indifferently to a final-round loss against the Croatian Iva Majoli in 1997, falling almost petulantly in straight sets against Seles in the 1998 semifinals. Despite those failures, there was no logical way to explain why she had not succeeded on a surface that suits her style so well.

At the start of her duel with Graf, Hingis seemed to be saying, "This is my time. This is my tournament. No one—not even Steffi—is going to stop me." The eighteen-year-old was precise and assertive as she broke Graf in the opening game. The Swiss player reached 15-40 by driving her two-handed backhand return deep crosscourt and following it into the net. Graf anxiously sliced her passing shot wide. The German recovered to deuce but hurt her cause with consecutive backhand unforced errors to drop that game. Hingis confidently held at love for 2-0, closing that game with a flourish. A forehand placement lifted her to 40-0, and then she confounded Graf by following her serve to the net, punching a backhand volley into an open court.

When Graf drifted to 15-40 with a double fault in the third game, her chances appeared bleak. It was here, however, that the twenty-nine-year-old realized she had to go for bigger and bolder shots and thus take Hingis out of her rhythm. Steffi released a piercing reverse cross-court forehand that Hingis could not manage with a one-handed backhand stab. The German took charge of the next point, came in forcefully, and put away a smash. It was deuce. Two more scintillating forehands enabled Graf to hold on for 1-2. She broke Hingis easily in the following game, then had three game points for 3-2. Graf sorely needed to maintain her momentum and hold her serve, but Hingis was not yielding. The Swiss girl hit winners on two of Graf's three game points, and provoked a backhand mistake from Steffi on the other. Another errant backhand from Graf—this one unforced—cost her the game. Hingis was back in front, leading 3-2.

Martina's mind was not muddled. She was ably breaking down Graf's weaker backhand wing and preventing Steffi from getting enough opportunities to produce punishing forehands. Hingis took the next two games, breaking Graf again for 5-2. Steffi double-faulted for 15-40, saved the first break point with a potent serve and forehand combination, but surrendered the seventh game when Hingis sliced a forehand that dipped at the German's feet. Graf attempted to half-volley into an empty court, but could not bring it off.

Hingis served for the set at 5-2. She reached 30-30 with an impeccable topspin forehand down the line winner off a short sliced backhand from Graf. Had Hingis applied herself and raised her intensity, she would have closed out the set with relative ease. Instead, she became careless and complacent. An ill-advised drop shot from the Swiss girl served as an invitation for Graf to explode. The German did just that, driving her backhand with topspin down the line. The shot was out of her opponent's reach. Graf broke with a booming forehand crosscourt that Hingis could not control. Reprieved, Graf held at love for 4-5. Her form had been fluctuating, but she kept her resolve.

Hingis, meanwhile, was in a bind. She knew she should already have sealed the set. Serving for it a second time at 5-4, the teenager was strikingly vulnerable. She rolled a two-hander into the net, then double-faulted for 0-30. Then Hingis gathered herself, drove a forehand deep into the corner, and moved in swiftly for a drive volley winner. She proceeded to 40-30 and her first set point. Graf sliced a backhand that clipped the net cord and fell over. It was deuce. Hingis responded remarkably well, defending skillfully from the backcourt, then stepping in with authority to crack a backhand winner.

Graf was not giving in. Her forehand approach was too powerful and accurate for Hingis, who missed a backhand pass. It was deuce for the second time. Martina swung her serve wide with slice to Steffi's forehand, opening up the court for a backhand crosscourt winner. Set point to Hingis for the third time. Graf retaliated once more with all-out aggression. She drove her reverse crosscourt forehand return with great pace. It was untouchable. The score was deuce for the third time. The German seemed poised to make an effective backhand return, only to slice it over the baseline, giving Hingis a fourth set point. Martina whipped a forehand cross-court. Graf was made to play a running forehand at full stretch. She missed. Set to Hingis, 6-4.

Having withstood the challenge of Graf's comeback late in the first set, Hingis started the second set warily protecting her territory. The opening game was hard fought by both players, with Graf determined to establish an early lead and Hingis equally determined to stay ahead. There were three deuces and Hingis needed three break points before she got the early advantage. Martina had altered her game plan, working persistently to pull Graf wide on the forehand side, taking Steffi out of her comfort zone. Rather than allow Graf to control the court with her inside-out forehand, Hingis shrewdly kept Graf on the run with a calculated combination of sharply angled crosscourt forehands and well disguised backhands down the line.

When Hingis held at the cost of only one point for 2-0, she seemed safely back in command, closing in rapidly on the title she coveted above all others. But on the first point of the third game, she lost her bearings. All along, the crowd had been fervently behind her opponent, cheering with wild enthusiasm for Graf, giving Hingis little more than reserved rounds of applause. In a dangerous lapse in judgment, Hingis changed the emotional texture of the match irreversibly. When her forehand return of serve was called out, Hingis irritably questioned the call. Umpire Anne Lasserre got out of her chair and conferred with the linesman, then reaffirmed the decision.

Hingis was not willing to move on and play the next point. She walked around to Graf's side of the court to check the mark herself, a blatant violation of the rules. Lasserre stood by her decision. The Roland Garros capacity crowd of sixteen thousand began chanting,

"Steffi, Steffi, Steffi." Hingis sat down on her chair, waiting for WTA supervisor Georgina Clark to arrive. The crowd was booing Hingis, frustrated by the delay. Hingis spoke with Clark. Hingis—who had earlier been given a warning for racket abuse—was now assessed a point penalty. Graf was rewarded with a 30-0 lead. The German held for 1-2 to the crowd's delight, but Hingis came through with a pin-point forehand cross-court passing shot to reach 3-1.

Despite a 40-15 edge at 3-2, Hingis did not hold. On her second game point, she outsmarted herself with an ineffectual serve-and-volley tactic. Graf read the plan early and responded with a backhand return winner. With Hingis at game point for the third time, the two competitors waged a superb battle of crosscourt forehands. Graf prevailed in that hard-hitting exchange as Hingis faltered in the end. Another damaging crosscourt forehand brought Graf to 3-3. Steffi saved a break point on her way to 4-3. She sensed a chance to take control of the match. So, too, did the animated crowd.

With Hingis serving at 3-4, 30-40, she saved a break point for deuce. Then both players produced the best exchange of the match. In the middle of this tense exchange, Graf angled a drop shot crosscourt off her backhand. The Swiss star answered with a backhand angled sharply crosscourt, which Graf handled with a deep backhand chip down the line. Hingis put up a high defensive lob off the forehand and Graf replied with an indecisive overhead. Hingis had time to set up a strong two-handed response crosscourt. Steffi was stretched low and wide at the net on her backhand side. She tried a drop volley crosscourt, but Hingis read it early. She scampered in swiftly for a backhand down the line. Graf was trapped. She could not make a volley. All she could do was chase the shot down. The ball was almost behind her, but Graf managed to make a wonderful lob over the incoming Hingis. She lofted it crosscourt, deep into the corner, and Hingis was hard-pressed to even get there. She chased it down and managed a high defensive lob. Graf let the ball bounce. Steffi was standing well inside the service line and in the alley. She picked her target, swung hard, and smashed the ball straight into the net. The crowd rumbled a collective moan. Hingis smiled at her good fortune. Graf held her head in despair, astounded that she had lost the point.

Hingis held on for 4-4, then broke a still dazed Graf for 5-4. Hingis lost only the first point of the ninth game, then swept the next four. She got that break with one of her patented backhand down the line placements. Hingis was only a single game away from the championship. She served for the match in the tenth game. Hingis reached 15-0 when her forehand skidded off the baseline and provoked an error from her opponent. The eighteen-year-old was three points from her goal. Then she missed a routine backhand, driving the ball over the baseline, squealing in disappointment over her unnecessary error. It was 15-15. Graf got to 15-30 with a topspin backhand crosscourt pass, then delivered another thundering forehand, rushing Hingis into a backhand error with the force of her shot. When Graf netted a backhand slice, Hingis was back to 30-40, but the teenager's shot selection on the next point revealed that she was both tense and tired. She attempted a backhand drop shot from just behind the baseline. The ball did not clear the net. Graf was level at 5-5.

Graf was revitalized. Hingis was rattled. The fans were galvanized behind the German. Graf took the next two games, sweeping eight of nine points. Graf had the set 7-5. She also had the momentum and the crowd. Graf held quickly for a 1-0 third-set lead, and then Hingis left the court for a bathroom break. Graf followed her rival off the court, but returned long before Hingis. As Graf sat at courtside, the crowd broke into a spontaneous "wave" and Graf joined in the fun. The chants of "Steffi, Steffi, Steffi" echoed around Roland Garros stadium. When Hingis returned with a clean, white outfit, the jeers increased in volume.

With Hingis seemingly devoid of energy and despondent about her lost opportunity, Graf glided to 3-0 in the third. The German had collected six games in a row, winning twenty-four of twenty-nine points in that span. It was apparent that her Swiss adversary was not only depleted but demoralized. She could not comprehend what had happened to her. She had invested nearly all of her resources in an effort to finish the job in two sets. Fighting to salvage her cause in a third set was a task she did not want. Nevertheless, she had too much pride and professionalism to acquiesce. She summoned her waning resolve, moving well and striking the ball with vigor.

When Hingis held her serve for 1-3, the audience responded with a combination of boos and cheers. On the first point of the following game, Graf double-faulted. Hingis pounced. A running forehand winner off a drop shot from Graf made it 15-30. Graf sliced a backhand wide under pressure for 15-40, and Hingis took the next point with another sparkling forehand out of Graf's reach. Hingis had broken back for 2-3. She was leaving her disappointments behind her and getting on with her business.

The next game was pivotal. Hingis slumped to 15-40, but then took the following three points. She was a point away from 3-3. Her shots were flowing again. Her concentration and confidence were reviving. Graf realized she had to raise her intensity and start dictating the tempo again. She moved around her backhand and hit a scorching forehand, sending that shot deep to the Hingis backhand. Martina was on her heels. She was stretched wide, forced to play the stroke with one hand. It was off the mark. The score was deuce. Graf quickly advanced to another break point. She then took a high ball off her backhand and knifed it cross-court, short to Hingis's backhand. Martina was rushed. She could not deal with the low ball, netting a backhand. Graf was at 4-2.

The match was essentially over. Graf and Hingis both knew it. The crowd sensed it. Graf connected with three out of four first serves to hold at love for 5-2. As she walked to her chair at courtside for the changeover, the crowd resumed chanting, "Steffi, Steffi, Steffi."

In the eighth game of the third set, Hingis was a forlorn figure, baffled and frustrated by the crowd's bias against her, infuriated by her earlier wasted chances. She drifted to 2-5, 30-40, match point down. Astounding the crowd and her opponent, Hingis released an underhand serve. She confounded Graf completely with the surprise tactic. Furthermore, she put heavy sidespin on that serve. Graf lunged to make the return, and could only produce a weak shot. She had been pulled so far forward that she had no alternative but to approach the net behind her return. Hingis had no trouble hitting a backhand passing shot down the line that Graf could not cope with.

The hostile fans booed Hingis vociferously believing, as many critics in the media did, that an underhand serve was a shameful display of bad sportsmanship. Graf, however, did not agree. She would say after the match, "I thought it was a hell of a serve. I mean, for her to do it for the first time at match point down was very good. I had the feeling the crowd thought it was an insult. Obviously it shook things up a bit and she won the point. It was a good decision from her point of view."

Hingis got to game point, then missed an awkward low forehand when Graf hit another biting slice backhand. Graf moved to match point for the second time with an unintentional backhand drop shot winner, acknowledging her luck with a wave of the hand toward Hingis. For the second time, Hingis tried the underhand serve, but this one was out. With the fans now baiting Hingis with loud disapproval, the Swiss girl approached the chair umpire, asking for quiet. Graf then walked up to the umpire herself, saying, "Let's play tennis." Order was restored. Hingis produced a conventional second serve. The two players had a brief baseline exchange. Graf sent her last emphatic forehand deep to the Hingis backhand, and Martina meekly netted her response in defeat.

Graf had come through 4-6, 7-5, 6-2 to claim her sixth French Open title, only one shy of the record held by Chris Evert. Hingis had lost her bid for a first championship at Roland Garros. The tennis had been exciting, the theater even better. It was a watershed event for both competitors.

When it was over, a tearful Hingis left the court for the locker room, booed by the sixteen thousand fans in the stadium. They continued to shower Graf with affectionate applause, saluting her spirit and fortitude, recognizing her enduring stature in the history of women's tennis. A few minutes later, Hingis returned to the court for the presentation ceremony, walking arm in arm with her mother (and coach) Melanie Molitor. Hingis was fighting in vain to hold back her tears, consoled by her mother. It was the most poignant moment in a long afternoon.

At the post-match ceremony, Hingis regained some of her composure, speaking in French, congratulating Graf and recognizing her rival as a "great champion." The crowd applauded her warmly, appreciating her grace under the pressure of a shocking defeat. When Graf

Martina Hingis

Steffi Graf

stepped up to the microphone, she was presented with the trophy by five-time former French champion Margaret Court of Australia. It seemed particularly appropriate because Court remained the only woman to win more major championships than Graf, by the slim margin of twenty-four to twenty-two.

"I feel French," was Graf's heartfelt opening remark. "I've played all over the world, but I've never had a crowd like this one—ever."

Later in her press conference, Graf said, "This is the biggest win I've ever had, for sure. I've had a lot of unexpected ones. I have to admit that. But this is by far the most unexpected. I really came into this tournament without belief. This has been incredible. This was one of the craziest matches ever. It had everything."

Hingis was asked if there was one key reason why she lost the match. She replied, "There were a few things. I was not fighting against Steffi only, but the whole crowd, the referee, the line calls. It was not always the way I would like it to be. But if you're better, you win anyway."

Hingis had made many miscalculations. Her actions were inflammatory, inviting the crowd to treat her with increasing disapproval. Nevertheless, the audience was willing to tolerate Graf's excessive questioning of line calls. Umpire Anne Lasserre lost control of the match and did not exert her authority with any conviction. She got down from her chair too many times to check marks and should have set a tougher tone.

In the end, the controversy and the unpredictability added to the drama of the occasion, and made it a more memorable match. Both players had given powerful performances and played inspired tennis. Graf, fired by the crowd, was the victor because of her immense will and her ability to draw upon the resources of past triumphs.

EPILOGUE

Two weeks later, Hingis and Graf came into Wimbledon as the top two seeds. The tennis world eagerly awaited another dramatic meeting between the two champions. But Hingis had still not recovered from her wrenching loss in Paris. And something had gone fundamentally wrong in her professional and personal relationship with her mother. In her opening-round match, Hingis was beaten soundly by an Australian qualifier named Jelena Dokic, a sixteen-year-old ranked No. 129 in the world. Dokic upended the 1997 titlist 6-2, 6-0. The Australian played inspired and inventive tennis, overpowering Hingis from the backcourt, looking uninhibited from start to finish. It lasted fifty-four minutes. Hingis gave a desultory display.

In the press conference following the match, Hingis revealed that her mother had not been with her at the match and had gone home.

She was bombarded with questions by reporters who wanted to know why Melanie Molitor had not been by her side for the first time at a major tournament. Hingis said that she and her mother had mutually decided they needed time apart. She explained, "With this tournament, my mother and I decided to have a little bit of distance from each other to work a little more on our private lives. We'll see how it goes in the future." As she approached her nineteenth birthday in September, Hingis was enduring the inevitable growing pains, coming to terms with a world where nearly everyone expected and almost demanded unbridled success from her year in and year out. Hingis remained a player of considerable importance. She finished 1999 and 2000 stationed at No. 1 in the world. But she never won another Grand Slam championship, concluding her career with five singles majors in her collection. The thirty-year-old German played her ninth Wimbledon final in 1999, scoring an impressive, three-set triumph over the gifted athlete Venus Williams along the way. In the final, however, Graf was unable to repeat what she had done in Paris. She lost to Lindsay Davenport of the United States 6-4, 7-5. Her chance for an eighth singles title on Centre Court was not realized.

Graf announced her retirement in late summer, withdrawing from the U.S. Open. Her career was winding down after eighteen years as a professional. She was the only player—male or female—to win every major championship at least four times.

Graf departed at the right moment, when she was still a great player, but no longer invincible. She had overcome a multitude of injuries, illnesses, and personal stress to become a champion of the highest order. Graf had begun her career competing against Evert and Navratilova. She ended her tenure in the era of Hingis and the Williams sisters. Through it all, she reflected the dignity and competitive resolve that has marked the highest standards of tennis.

CHAPTER TWENTY-SIX

Andre Agassi *vs.* Pete Sampras

U.S. OPEN, SEMIFINAL, SEPTEMBER 5-6, 2001

They confronted each other across a net on no fewer than 34 occasions, on all surfaces, in every setting. But these two American icons never had a match that surpassed this spirited encounter on an idyllic New York evening.

PROLOGUE

After the accomplished pair of champions named Jimmy Connors and John McEnroe had moved into the autumn of their careers in the second half of the 1980's, key leaders of tennis in the United States began to drift into a malaise. It appeared then to most of the authorities that it would be a very long time before anyone emerged to take over the mantle of supremacy from the two enduring superstars. The United States Tennis Association announced the formation of a player development program in 1987 to address the issue of future aspirants to the championship level.

What few people recognized was that the wheels of progress were already in motion. As the 1980's concluded, a promising group of American players reached the upper tier of tennis. The indefatigable Michael Chang became the youngest-ever French Open champion and men's major singles titlist when he won in Paris at 17 in 1989. Jim Courier sealed four major singles titles between 1991 and 1993, triumphing twice at both the French and Australian Opens.

More compellingly in many ways, Andre Agassi and Pete Sampras took their talent to the top with eminently successful runs. Agassi broke into the top three in the world in 1988 at the age of 18, appeared in three major finals during the 1990-91 seasons, and captured Wimbledon majestically in 1992. Unconventional and charismatic, possessed of perhaps the best hand-eye coordination of any player in his time, exploding with supreme confidence one moment and sinking into deep insecurity the next, he fired the imagination of the public like no other player. Andre's father Mike Agassi was a former Iranian Olympic boxer who defected to the U.S. and settled in Las Vegas. When Andre was an infant, his father hung a tennis ball on a string over his crib. By the time Andre was four, the family put a ball machine in the backyard. Mike Agassi estimated that his son Andre, even as a small boy, hit fourteen thousand balls a week.

Sampras was an entirely different personality and player, groomed to reach the highest levels of the game under contrasting circumstances. While Agassi had grown up in Las Vegas—a city that seemed the ideal setting for his brashness—Sampras had his upbringing in California. His father Sam was born in the United States to parents of Greek ancestry. His mother Georgia immigrated to the United States from Greece. They were married in Maryland, where Pete was born. Sam worked for the Department of Defense, but moved to California in 1977 when Pete was almost six years old. It was there that the Sampras interest in tennis began to flower. Sampras's game was essentially free flowing and his ability to hit every kind of shot definitively was apparent early, his natural grace and elegance evident to one and all that saw him play. When he was only a month past his 19th birthday—28 days to be precise—Sampras became the youngest ever winner of his country's championship. He took the U.S. Open with wins over three-time former titlist Ivan Lendl, four-time former champion John McEnroe, and the heavily-favored Agassi.

By then, Sampras had developed one of the best serves in the history of the sport. He had been taught by boyhood coach Pete Fischer to produce different spins—primarily kick and slice—from the same toss position. That lesson in deception was invaluable, enabling Sampras to keep the opposition guessing rather than anticipating. Deuce court or ad court, Sampras was a master at moving his serve around the box tantalizingly.

But the speed of his delivery was an essential ingredient in his success. His motion was pure and economical, graceful and fluid. In effortless fashion, without visible strain, Sampras would serenely serve his way through long afternoons or swift encounters. He backed up his serve with as complete a fast-court game as the sport had yet seen. Sampras had the entire package of skills, but his vulnerabilities when he was a young player were his concentration and his shot selection.

After the 1990 U.S. Open, it took Sampras time to settle into his heady status. He had been seeded only 12th at that landmark event. He thought his time to take a major was at least a year away. He spent a large part of 1991 either injured or, at times, indifferent. But he finished his campaign productively with a victory at the season-ending ATP Tour World Championships in Germany. In 1992, he took his place among the top three in the world, reaching the semifinals at Wimbledon, then the final of the U.S. Open.

His loss in the U.S. Open altered his career irrevocably. Beaten in four sets by defending champion Stefan Edberg, Sampras had served for a two-set-to-one lead before falling. He had been bothered by a stomach virus that had plagued him since the end of his semifinal win over Jim Courier. And yet, Sampras refused to use his ailment as an alibi. He felt he should have taken that Grand Slam tournament final, and detested the taste of failure on such an important occasion. He found that feeling unacceptably painful.

Fueled by a new intensity and ambition, Sampras won Wimbledon and the U.S. Open in 1993, and took over at No. 1 in the world that year. He captured the Australian Open in 1994 and won Wimbledon again. He was beginning to understand his capacity to be the game's dominant performer, to strike down all of his primary rivals with not only the scope of his game but also with the strength of his mind and the size of his heart. But at the outset of 1995, Sampras was faced with the harsh reality of life's darker side. During a riveting quarterfinal collision with Courier at the Australian Open, Sampras broke down in tears. His coach, Tim Gullikson, had been sent home with brain tumors for treatment at a Chicago hospital. When a fan called out early in the fifth set of his duel with Courier and shouted, "Do it for your coach!" Sampras initially concealed his tears under a towel at a changeover, but could not stop when play resumed.

Courier half-jokingly shouted across the net to his rival and former doubles partner that they could continue the match the next day. That did not sit well with Sampras. Angered by what he considered an insensitive goading, Sampras collected himself and won the match after dropping the first two sets. He moved on to the final before losing a hard-fought four-set match with Agassi, who was in the midst of a stretch of disciplined brilliance that he would seldom replicate in his career. Sampras had been ahead 6-4, double set point in the third set tie-break before losing that entertaining contest 4-6, 6-1, 7-6, 6-4.

The great ground stroker from Las Vegas had fallen upon some hard times after his Wimbledon breakthrough in 1992. He had wrist surgery at the end of 1993, a procedure that could have threatened his career. In fact, he came back stronger and more secure than ever, and when he hired the loquacious Brad Gilbert to be his new coach in the spring of 1994, the union proved immensely rewarding. Gilbert was a strategic genius who made Agassi look and think about the game with a seriousness and savvy he had lacked before. Nick Bollettieri had done an extraordinary job of guiding Agassi from his teens through some crucial years as a professional, but Agassi's immaturity meant that too much of Bollettieri's wisdom went wasted.

In any event, aligned with Gilbert, Agassi won the U.S. Open in 1994 as an unseeded player. When he followed up with his big win over Sampras at Melbourne in 1995, he had set himself up for potentially his greatest year as a professional. Agassi seemed well on his way to the final of Wimbledon in July of 1995, bolting to a 6-2, 4-1 lead over three-time champion Boris Becker, fashioning a two-service-break lead in the second set. He seemed to be toying with the burly Becker up until that juncture, but the German battled back with a ferocity he had not shown in years, toppling Agassi in four sets. Sampras then took apart Becker in an impeccably played four-set final for his third singles title in a row on the Centre Court.

Over the summer, Agassi, undismayed, put Wimbledon behind him in a hurry, and proceeded to find invincibility on the summer hard court circuit leading up to the U.S. Open, capturing four tournaments in a row in Washington, Montreal, Cincinnati and New Haven. He marched into the U.S. Open final, riding the wave of a 26-match winning streak. Sampras had not won a tournament over the summer after Wimbledon, but he always looked at the larger picture. It was the Open that mattered to him. He proceeded to stop Agassi 6-4, 6-3,

4-6, 7-5 to win the 1995 U.S. Open. It was a pivotal match for both players, a battle of lasting consequences. They were essentially playing for the honor of worldwide recognition as the best player on the planet, and all of Agassi's summer successes were no longer of value. He had lost the single most important tennis match of the 1990's to his premier rival.

Sampras reflected on his triumph not long after, saying, "It really would have crushed me to lose that match. It is a great effort to get to the final of majors but unfortunately in sports, only one name gets on that plaque. I could see a few weeks after the Open that Andre was deflated and I was still riding high. That was the biggest match of the year for me and one of the biggest in my career. Everyone was talking about Andre being the favorite and saying how well he was playing. To beat him in the final was extra special for me. Andre had given me more problems than anyone else during the year, so to beat him added a lot to winning the U.S. Open. I peaked for the semifinal [with Jim Courier] and the final and everything worked out the way I would have planned it. You have a good, not a great, summer and then leave your best tennis at the U.S. Open."

Over the next two years, Sampras used his big wins at Wimbledon and the U.S. Open in 1995 to inspire more triumphs. He defended his US Open title in 1996, saving a match point in a gut-wrenching quarterfinal against Spain's wily Alex Corretja after becoming ill and throwing up on the court during the fifth-set tie-break in that match. The American crowd roused Sampras with their unabashed loyalty, and he defeated Goran Ivanisevic and Michael Chang over that weekend to hold onto his cherished crown. In 1997, Sampras won his second Australian Open title and his fourth Wimbledon championship.

By then, Sampras had collected ten major championships and was distancing himself from Agassi. Heading into the 1995 Open, Sampras had captured six majors while his rival had amassed three, but the gap was widening considerably. Sampras was unrelentingly professional, a man who never lost sight of his purpose in life, a champion through and through. Agassi was wildly unpredictable, a non-conformist, a tormented individual who frequently struggled to believe that he belonged at or near the top of his profession. In 1996, Agassi had one moment of greatness, taking a gold medal in Atlanta at the Olympic Games. But his year was otherwise a disappointment. He had spent much of 1995 at No. 1 in the world before Sampras wrestled that prize away at the end of the year. By the end of 1996, he had slipped to No. 8.

In 1997, matters grew a good deal worse. He married actress Brooke Shields that year but did not play in three of the four majors. His ranking slipped to an embarrassing No. 141 in the world. But Agassi admirably faced up to his predicament, and played in a couple of minor league "Challenger" events in an effort to raise his game and stock again. He was rewarded for that rededication to his craft, rising to No. 6 in the world, conducting an energetic 1998 campaign. Yet he still was not the same player who had soared through that summer of 1995. In 1999, however, the unpredictable American confounded his critics by capturing his first major title in four years. He had strongly considered skipping the 1999 French Open after suffering a shoulder injury not long before, but Gilbert convinced him to make the journey to Paris.

Agassi had divorced Shields, and his outlook about big time competition was changing again, all for the better. He played his way into surprisingly good form at Roland Garros. Over that fortnight, Agassi was two points from losing to the always tricky Frenchman Arnaud Clement but survived. He was down a set and two service breaks in the second set to defending champion Carlos Moya, but made it safely through that one as well. In the final, he lost the first two sets 6-1, 6-2 but rallied to oust a fine clay court player named Andrei Medvedev in five sets. Inspired by a capacity crowd cheering his every move, finding his range with deeper, more daring and heavier shots from the baseline, Agassi recovered brilliantly to win 1-6, 2-6, 6-4, 6-3, 6-4.

The victory seemed fated. Agassi himself called it "sheer destiny." Agassi had lost the 1990 Roland Garros final to Ecuadorian left-hander Andres Gomez, and was beaten in five sets by Jim Courier in the 1991 French Open final. He knew he should have secured one, if not both, of those meetings. But this time around, in 1999, he seemed to be blessed with extraordinarily good fortune, and made the most of his openings. He became only the fifth man in history to win all four Grand Slam tournaments, and the first to do it on three different surfaces. In this elite category, he stood alongside Fred Perry, Don Budge,

Roy Emerson and Rod Laver. Later, in the next decade, Roger Federer and Rafael Nadal would join that club.

Two weeks later, the leading players assembled for Wimbledon. Agassi was rejuvenated, wanting to become the first man since Bjorn Borg in 1980 to claim the Roland Garros and Wimbledon titles back-to-back. His return of serve was buzzing on the lawns at the All England Club, and his mood was entirely upbeat. A surprising number of authorities picked Agassi to surprise Sampras when they met in the final. Sampras had, after all, won Wimbledon five of the previous six years.

In the first set of the final, Sampras was serving at 3-3, 0-40, but from there he swept majestically to victory, never losing his serve in an immaculate display on the Centre Court, getting the win 6-3, 6-4, 7-5. Sampras and Agassi met two more times on the hard courts over the summer, with Sampras besting his great rival in both Los Angeles and Cincinnati. There was a growing feeling among the experts that they would do battle again in the U.S. Open final. But Sampras hurt his back during a practice session and a herniated disc forced him out of the tournament. Agassi went on to topple Todd Martin in a five-set final. For the first and only time in his career, he not only won two Grand Slam tournaments in a single year, but also finished the season at No. 1 in the world, another unprecedented achievement on his part.

The following year, Agassi captured the season's first major in Melbourne at the Australian Open, overcoming Sampras in a stirring five-set semifinal before removing Yevgeny Kafelnikov in the final. Sampras won Wimbledon that year to hit a milestone in his career. The tournament victory was his 13th at a major, and the American had broken a record he had shared with Roy Emerson of Australia. It was also his seventh tournament triumph on the British lawns, a men's record among all modern players. The last, and only other, man to win seven crowns was William Renshaw in the 1880's, when defending champions only needed to play one match to hold onto to their title, meeting the winner of an "All-Comers" event.

In any event, the triumph for Sampras in 2000 at the world's premier tournament was more than gratifying. It had taken so much dedication for so long, and he had given so much of his heart and soul to realize the goal of winning more majors than anyone else. He had pushed himself so close to his limits, that Sampras understandably lost some of his motivation. He made it to the final of the U.S. Open later that summer. But the 29-year-old Sampras confronted an immensely gifted 20-year-old Russian named Marat Safin. Safin struck down the mighty Sampras 6-4, 6-3, 6-3 with a breathtaking display of unstoppable power from the baseline and on serve. The Russian could do no wrong, playing the match of his career, almost unconsciously disposing of a great champion as if he was playing a casual practice match of little or no consequence.

Sampras—who married the actress Bridgette Wilson three weeks after the Open—concluded that year still among the upper crust, ranked third in the world. Agassi slipped from No. 1 down to No. 6. But while Agassi recaptured some of his old zest in 2001, Sampras for the most part did not. At the start of the year, Agassi rose to the heights of his game once more "Down Under" in Melbourne, taking his seventh career major singles title by winning the Australian Open for the third time. Agassi went on to win at Indian Wells with a straight-set triumph over Sampras in the final, then was victorious in Miami at the event many considered comparable to a "fifth major."

Beaten at Roland Garros in the quarterfinals, Agassi lost a heartbreaker at Wimbledon to the eminent serve-and-volley stylist Patrick Rafter, bowing in five sets to his Australian rival for the second straight year on the Centre Court. Agassi served for the match at 5-4 in the fifth set and led 30-15, but his unwavering opponent bounced back to take the match. Nonetheless, Agassi played well during the summer in toppling Sampras 6-4, 6-2 in the final of Los Angeles.

As the U.S. Open of 2001 approached, Agassi was unmistakably sharper than his old American rival from California. Sampras had hoped to secure a fifth Wimbledon singles title in a row, but a young man from Switzerland called Roger Federer—still only 19—surprised him in a five-set, round of 16 contest. That would be the one and only time the two all-time greats ever collided on the ATP World Tour. The loss to Federer meant that the U.S. Open would be the last chance for Sampras to win a major title in 2001. He was seeking to become the first man in the history of tennis to win at least one major for nine seasons in a row, and Agassi loomed as one of his toughest potential obstacles to overcome in New York on the hard courts.

As fate would decree, Agassi and Sampras—two of the sport's icons who had met in both the 1990 and 1995 finals—were placed in the same quarter of the U.S. Open draw. Agassi was seeded second while Sampras was seeded tenth. They had met in four major finals across their careers, including two title-round showdowns in New York. Agassi was 31. Sampras was 30. They had grown up in the public eye, moving through their teens, into their twenties, and on into their thirties. They were now the sentimental favorites more than ever before. Everyone in the know eagerly awaited another classic confrontation between the two Americans, crossing their fingers that Agassi and Sampras would arrive safely for another memorable appointment, hoping they might witness a golden moment in the lives of both players.

THE MATCH

Both Sampras and Agassi advanced without much difficulty to the round of 16, and on Labor Day they each faced tough opposition. Agassi had to deal with Federer, who was still putting the pieces of his game together. Federer would soon own the most fearsome forehand in tennis, but on this day that shot let him down badly. Agassi picked him apart and exposed Federer's surprising vulnerability off that side in a straight-set victory. Sampras met a man whose game was ideally suited to the hard courts at Flushing Meadows. Patrick Rafter—the No. 6 seed—had taken two U.S. Open titles in 1997 and 1998. His kick serve was tailor made for the DecoTurf surface in Ashe Stadium, bounding up high and allowing the athletic Aussie to spring forward briskly and take command with his outstanding first volley. He had beaten Sampras in a five-set semifinal at the 1998 Open, but on this occasion the American was nearly letter perfect, getting the job done in four sets.

Sampras and Agassi had indeed made it through to the quarters. Agassi—looking to exploit his fitness, hoping he might grind Sampras down in the heat—lobbied for a daytime meeting with Sampras, but the match was scheduled appropriately for the evening when more fans would be able to pack the stadium, and the USA Network could gain a much wider audience during the prime-time hours in the United States. Day in and day out, night after night, year after year, Ashe Stadium is situated in a virtual wind tunnel. The force of that wind can vary, and the game's greatest performers have coped with it regularly, but rarely is wind not a factor, at least to some degree. That is always the challenge for the leading players, to deal with the ferocity of the wind, to control their own destinies rather than be at the mercy of the conditions. But on this idyllic evening, the wind was almost non-existent, allowing Agassi and Sampras to perform uncompromisingly well, to shine brightly and buoyantly under the lights, to produce magic in the calm night air in front of a capacity crowd thirsting for an epic.

From the outset, there was a stirring in the audience well beyond the ordinary. They seemed to sense that they were about to watch something extraordinary unfold right before their eyes. This was the time to celebrate a pair of individuals the sporting public had long admired, to watch their old and familiar heroes play sublime tennis on the hard courts. Sampras had won the tournament four times, Agassi had taken the title twice, and their rivalry was one of the most enduring and important in modern times.

This compelling head-to-head series commenced in 1989, and Sampras held the career edge at 17-14. But Agassi had won their last three skirmishes, all on hard courts. Yet the scales had to be balanced by the fact that Sampras was the best big-match player of his era, and he had spent a career bringing out his most inspired tennis when the stakes were highest. He was not concerned about recent losses to Agassi. He was out to demonstrate, as he had so many times across a sterling career, that he could respond to a big occasion and a moment of consequence better than anyone.

Sampras made his intentions entirely clear in the opening game of the match. He needed to control the tempo of the match with his magnificent first and second serves. There had been no better server during his tenure as a top player, or perhaps ever. No one in his

Andre Agassi

era—or possibly across history—had surpassed Agassi on the return of serve. Moreover, Sampras was an unwavering attacking player who was among the finest volleyers in the game, and the leading man in tennis on the overhead. Agassi, meanwhile, had an incomparable ground game, and was unassailable with his geometric precision from the baseline, his capacity to take utter control of rallies, and his uncanny propensity to threat the needle time and again with his two-handed backhand passing shots.

As always, Sampras against Agassi was a confrontation of very different strengths, of contrasting playing styles, of dissimilar mindsets. Sampras needed to impose himself from the opening bell, and he did just that. He sent four out of five first serves in, aced Agassi twice, and held at 15 in the first game. As he would say often in describing his outlook for a big match, "I was ready to go." So, too, was Agassi. He served an ace to start the second game, and charged to 40-15. But an aggressive Sampras rallied to deuce. At that juncture, Sampras left a topspin backhand too short, and Agassi walloped an inside-out forehand winner, one of his signature shots. When Sampras just missed a backhand crosscourt, the score in the set was 1-1.

Sampras struggled to hold in the third game. He served a double fault to fall behind 15-30, but that was not alarming because Sampras had gone for a huge second serve that happened to land long. He would make more than his share of those huge second deliveries over the course of the evening, so it was well worth it to him to risk double faults in an effort to keep Agassi at bay. Sampras got back to 30-30 but then Agassi laced a backhand pass down the line that Sampras could not handle on the low forehand volley. It was break point for Agassi, but Sampras responded with customary vigor. He cracked a big first serve deep to Agassi's backhand, and the return sailed long. Sampras could not convert on his first game point, but on the second he played a stellar point that he would replicate many times across the contest. Agassi made one of his patented low returns, but Sampras answered with a terrific forehand first volley deep that set up an overhead winner. He had weathered a minor storm, moving on to 2-1 after connecting with seven of ten first serves.

Now Sampras had his chance. He produced a top of the line forehand inside-out winner to reach 0-40 on Agassi's serve in the fourth game. It was triple break point. Sampras realized the size of his opportunity. If he could win one of the next three points, he would break Agassi, move ahead 3-1, try to hold swiftly for 4-1, and the set would be as good as over. But that did not happen. Sampras missed one of his favorite shots—the running forehand crosscourt—and Agassi was back to 15-40. A deep and penetrating crosscourt backhand from Agassi was too much for Sampras: 30-40. On the third break point, Sampras attempted to run around his backhand for a forehand return from the deuce court, but his down the line shot travelled long. From there, Agassi took the next two points for a crucial hold, arriving at 2-2.

Both men had given themselves openings to break, yet neither had succeeded. Sampras served with rhythmic beauty and precision in the fifth game, acing Agassi wide in the deuce court for 15-0, releasing another ace down the T for 30-0, playing a high quality serve-and-volley point for 40-0, and then acing Agassi down the T once more to hold at love for 3-2. This was Sampras at his very best, taking matters entirely into his own hands. But Agassi played a first-rate game on his own serve to make it 3-3, racing to 40-0. After Sampras took the next two points, the two competitors were engaged in a high-velocity back-hand crosscourt exchange, but then Agassi explored another option, stepping around his backhand for an explosive inside-out forehand winner. He had held at 30 for 3-3, revealing in the process that he was in a positive frame of mind, and in full command of his ground game.

Sampras remained unswerving and supremely confident on serve. Although he made only two of four first serves in the seventh game, the masterful American held at love with brio, displaying with gusto the breadth and scope of his attacking game. He was ahead 4-3 after a second love game in a row on serve, but Agassi was not swayed. At 40-30 in the eighth game, Agassi saw something that was awfully familiar. Sampras drove a scintillating flat forehand crosscourt on the run for a winner to reach deuce, and was threatening to get the break that would enable him to serve for the set. But Sampras tried running around his backhand return for a forehand again in the deuce court, and missed. An extremely accurate second serve from Agassi was unmanageable for Sampras. It was 4-4.

The burden was back on Sampras to renegotiate his authority. Serving at 4-4, 40-30, he stuck with his pattern of attack, serving-and-volleying. He seemed set to make another deep and effective first volley, but surprisingly missed it long. Sampras would miss very few volleys of that nature in the entire match. The miscue allowed Agassi back to deuce. Sampras swiftly made amends, sending an ace up the middle at 127 miles per hour to get a second game point. He then went wide in the ad court with an unanswerable first serve. Sampras had traveled to 5-4. Agassi was serving to save the set, but seemed undaunted by the situation. He rolled to 40-0, lost the next point, then served an ace down the T. That display of gumption under pressure made it 5-5.

Unperturbed, Sampras assiduously stuck to his game plan. He held at 15 for 6-5. After Agassi unleashed a spectacular forehand return winner on the first point, he did not get another return back into play. Four straight times, Sampras went to the backhand with his delivery, twice on first serves, twice on second deliveries. Agassi was stymied every time. But Agassi's expression revealed the depth of his determination. He missed only one of six first serves in the following game, and held at 30 for 6-6 with an ace out wide in the ad court. Neither man had secured a service break. The set would be settled fittingly in a tie-break.

Up until 3-3 in that tie-break, neither man lost a point on serve. But then Agassi found himself on the wrong side of an unfortunate net cord. He took a short ball and approached forcefully off his forehand to the Sampras backhand. But Agassi's shot bounded off the net cord and went long over the baseline.

Sampras seized quickly on that piece of good luck. He served his ninth ace of the set down the T in the ad court for 5-3, then swung his slice serve wide in the deuce court to elicit an errant return from an overextended Agassi. Sampras was in a commanding position, leading 6-3, with three set points at his disposal and a chance to take control of the match with a set in hand. But he chipped his backhand return a bit cautiously, and Agassi replied with a thundering inside-out forehand winner. Then Sampras tried for another run around forehand return from the deuce court, and once again missed it wide. Two set points had disappeared for Sampras, but now he would serve at 6-5, looking to seal the set once and for all.

Sampras got his first serve in, going to the backhand side of Agassi. But Agassi had intelligently moved back a few feet to play his return, giving himself more time to play his return low at Sampras's feet. Caught off guard, Sampras hit a weak half-volley, enabling Agassi to move into the court to rip a forehand crosscourt forehand passing shot. Sampras lunged to his right, but had no play on the volley. It was 6-6, and Agassi had staved off no fewer than three set points. Yet Sampras was still serving, with a chance to garner a fourth set point. He came forward as usual behind his serve, and punched a volley to the open court that seemingly put him in good stead. But Agassi chased that ball down and threw up and impossibly high defensive lob. Sampras backtracked, probably expecting the lob to go long. But Agassi's ball control was astounding. His lob landed just inside the baseline, and a discombobulated Sampras played his overhead safely after taking it on the bounce. Agassi then directed his forehand cross-court, and Sampras missed flagrantly off the forehand.

The inspired crowd in Arthur Ashe Stadium was astonished and highly charged, some of them deliriously pro-Agassi, others decidedly pro-Sampras, all enthralled by an absorbing, exhilarating and momentum shifting contest. Agassi served at 7-6 in the tie-break, having won four points in a row, brimming with intensity as he stood on the edge of a startling comeback. But perhaps his intensity was overflowing and counter-productive. As was his tendency when he was too excited in the tight corners of important contests, Agassi rushed. He missed his first serve, hardly paused, and went for too much on his second serve, which was long. Sampras was back even at 7-7, but Agassi immediately made up for his transgression, serving an ace down the middle for 8-7. Sampras missed his first serve, came in on the second, and had to play a demanding forehand half volley off yet another excellent Agassi return. Sampras made the half volley, but Agassi played a solid passing shot. Sampras had it covered. Nevertheless, he missed a forehand volley. Set to Agassi, 9-7 in the tie-break. The crowd applauded both players effusively, appreciating the high quality tennis they had seen in the first set, looking forward to more.

Agassi was almost unstoppable in these situations. After winning the first set at the U.S. Open, he had won 49 of 50 matches across his career, losing only to Ivan Lendl in the 1988 semifinals when he was only 18 and deeply insecure. Sampras was a strong-minded man not given to bouts of self-pity, but he had to be kicking himself internally now for letting that set slip from his grasp. In his vernacular, he had always known how to "put the clamps down." But in this instance he had not driven home his advantage, and Agassi in turn had displayed a match playing maturity and calmness under duress that he had so often lacked on previous combat missions. The combination of Sampras faltering slightly and Agassi competing with such daring assurance in the crunch had altered the complexion of the match.

The early games of the second set were inevitably going to be a somber time for Sampras as he tried to reignite his game, bring back his confidence and raise his spirits. After believing he had the first set under control, Sampras knew now he would have to win three of the next four sets to come away with a victory. In 24 of his previous 31 meetings with Agassi, the winner of the first set had gone on to victory. Against an opponent who made him work so hard, it would be a hard task for Sampras to fashion a win. But the fact remained that Sampras was much tougher mentally than many realized. He had built a reputation for soaring talent and supreme athleticism, for the gifts he brought to the game, for the ease and grace with which he played the sport for a living. But the fact remained that he was a steadfast competitor who relished every chance he had to prove that he could shoulder the responsibility of taking down major rivals not only with his shot making brilliance but also with his immense willpower.

Willpower was precisely what he needed as the second set commenced. Agassi—quietly confident, relieved to be out in front, determined to press his advantage—held at 30 for 1-0, closing out that game with an ace down the middle. Sampras double faulted to start the second game, but did not miss a first serve the rest of that game as he held at 30 for 1-1. Both players settled into a comfort zone on serve in the ensuing games. Agassi held at 15 for 2-1 before Sampras took his serve at 30 for 2-2. Agassi held at 30 by prevailing in a pulsating 18-stroke rally, with Sampras narrowly missing a forehand down the line on the run to end that exchange. Agassi was up 3-2, but Sampras was demonstrating that he was not replaying the first set in the eye of his mind. He held at 30 for 3-3. Neither man was giving away anything. Both were performing with aplomb. The level of play remained uncommonly high.

Agassi was having one of the great serving nights of his career. In contrast to when he was younger, he now went after his first serve at full force, looking to win free points, exploring the possibility of releasing aces, casting aside his old philosophy of kicking the first serve to set up his crackling forehand. He knew that he had to go for his first serve and hit it relatively flat, or else Sampras would blast his returns to the corners and rush him into mistakes and right out of the match. Agassi made good on three of four first serves, and held at love for 4-3. Sampras responded in kind, holding at 30 for 4-4, depositing a forehand first volley into an empty space to close out that game.

Both men fully understood—as did a good portion of the crowd—that Sampras could not afford to fall behind two sets to love. Therefore, his burdens were considerably larger than Agassi's at this stage of the match. One false move, one careless moment, one unlucky net cord bouncing unkindly, and Sampras would almost surely be on his way out of the tournament, while Agassi would be ready to march on into the semifinals and put himself in a position to regain the title he had last won in 1999. Agassi was playing every service game with a ruthlessness, tenacity and purpose that were second nature to him now. He had the luxury of serving first, and could keep making Sampras respond with no margin for error. But Sampras was as serene as ever, unruffled and implacable, in search of a sudden opening to strike gold and regain control of the match.

Agassi plodded on with no hint of trepidation. He held at 30 for 5-4. Now Sampras was serving to stay in the set at 4-5—his margin for error was even slimmer. At 15-0 in that critical tenth game, Sampras served his eleventh ace of the match. The next point was nothing less than stupendous. Sampras was stationed up at the net, seemingly at Agassi's mercy. He guessed right as Agassi sent a forehand pass crosscourt. Sampras displayed his masterful touch at the net, making a remarkable forehand half volley drop shot. Agassi moved forward for an attempted passing shot, but could not pull it off. The crowd celebrated the spirit of both players, applauding vociferously. Sampras held at 15 for 5-5, but Agassi then held at 15 himself for 6-5.

Improbably, Agassi had conceded only eight points in six service games during the second set. He led 6-5. The pressure was back on Sampras, who had to hold just to reach another tie-break. Sampras started the twelfth game with a double fault, his fifth of the night. He trailed 15-30, two points from going down two sets. Sampras connected with a fine first serve, closed in on the net, and made a deep first volley. Agassi hoisted up a lob but Sampras moved back swiftly and athletically, putting away an overhead behind Agassi down the line. At 30-30, Sampras followed his second serve in and had to play a tough low first volley. He punched it down the line, but Agassi got there with good speed and drilled his two-hander down the line.

That passing shot was anticipated by Sampras, but Agassi's backhand clipped the net cord. Sampras easily could have missed his volley under those arduous circumstances, but his reflexes were quicksilver. He angled away a forehand drop volley into the open court, raising his eyes in disbelief over what had just transpired. He realized how close he had been to falling set point behind. Then Sampras, going for another big serve down the T, double faulted. It was deuce. For the third time, he was two points from losing the set. A service winner lifted Sampras to game point, but he double faulted again, his third of the game. Sampras, however, was undismayed. He released another service winner down the middle that Agassi netted on the backhand return. Now he paused, reached back, delivered another exquisitely smooth first serve, and it was an ace down the T. Sampras had been given a thorough and stressful test by Agassi in that game, but had passed it commendably in the end. It was 6-6.

The tie-break opened with a flourish from Sampras. With Agassi serving the first point, he had Sampras on the dead run, and came to the net on his adversary's weaker backhand side. Sampras did not have the time to uncoil with topspin the way he usually did, so he improvised and went with an impeccably struck backhand slice angled acutely crosscourt. Agassi never had a chance. It was a timely winner. Sampras had the mini-break and was up 1-0. He did not waste that opening, serving-and-volleying off his second serve and putting away a high forehand first volley, then swinging his slice serve wide to lure Agassi into a netted return. It was 3-0 for an emboldened Sampras.

Agassi took his next two service points with authority from the baseline, closing the gap to 3-2. Serving the sixth point, Sampras made a terrific forehand half volley off an excellent return from Agassi, and that pickup led to an emphatic overhead winner. Sampras moved to 4-2, then reached 5-2 with a strategically placed wide sliced serve to the forehand in the deuce court. An outstretched Agassi erred on the difficult return. Now Agassi was in a bind, serving at 2-5. He cracked a forehand crosscourt with good pace at a great angle, but he had played into Sampras's hands. Sampras covered the court with alacrity, and clouted a forehand crosscourt with all of his might. Agassi was off balance and ill at ease. There was no way he could reply. He missed the open stance forehand, and Sampras had blasted his way into a 6-2 lead.

Agassi was still serving, but Sampras won a magnificent all-court point, forcing Agassi to run wide for a backhand, then coming in himself on an inside-in forehand. Agassi drilled the forehand passing shot directly at Sampras, who reflexed a backhand volley winner off his belly button. The crowd showered loud applause on the players as Sampras clenched his fists while walking to the changeover. He had won the tie-break 7-2 after moving out of a precarious position in the twelfth game. It was one set all. It would all come down to the best of three sets from here.

Both men remained resolute, although it was now Sampras rather than Agassi who had the upper hand, the brighter outlook and the deeper inner security. As for the fans, they could only be delighted, realizing they would get at least two more sets of this soaring tennis. Two sets had come and gone, and not a single break of serve had occurred. That was a testament to both players. Agassi had made Sampras play one low volley after another. Sampras had come at Agassi with some aggressive returns and chip and charges that would have unnerved almost any other player. But neither American had budged. This was a battle of considerable wills, and each man was executing his game plan impeccably. No wonder they were locked in such a close and compelling showdown.

Sampras had the luxury of serving first in the third set. He bolted in front 1-0 by holding at the cost of only a single point. At 40-15, he served-and-volleyed behind his first serve, and Agassi was prevented from doing much with his return. He got it back, but with nothing on it. Sampras pulled up rather than electing to play an awkward, no-pace volley, and instead let the ball bounce and put away a forehand winner down the line. Agassi responded with one of his best service games of the match, holding at 15, acing Sampras twice, closing out that impressive game with an untouchable delivery down the middle.

Sampras soon found himself challenged significantly by Agassi in the following game. He was down 30-40 after Agassi unleashed successive forehand returns that were too much even for the charging Sampras to handle. At break point down, Sampras missed his first serve, but then caught Agassi off guard with a heavy kicker to the backhand. Agassi could do no more than push the return back, and Sampras had all the time in the world to close in and put away a high backhand volley down the line. His tactical acuity had made all the difference on a very big point. Agassi had not anticipated that serve. At deuce, Sampras pulled off another surprise maneuver, staying back on his second serve. He came in off Agassi's return, approaching down the line off the forehand. Agassi was off balance and he lobbed long. Sampras had held in a critical game, moving to 2-1.

Agassi had his problems holding in the next game. But with the score deadlocked at deuce, Agassi aced Sampras again, his ninth of the match. Sampras brought the game back to deuce again, but Agassi served a tenth ace down the T, and followed with a clean winning forehand down the line that he had set up with an angled forehand crosscourt. They stood at 2-2. But not for long. Sampras held at love for 3-2, pouring in four first serves in a row, setting the tone for that game with an outstanding serve-and-volley combination on the first point, putting away the backhand first volley with textbook craft and precision. Agassi was not to be outdone, holding at love with an ace out wide in the ad court, reaching 3-3 with swift assurance.

The estimable Sampras second serve was the story of the seventh game. He held at 15, but two second deliveries of the highest order were the keys. At 15-15, Sampras produced a 117 mile per hour second serve to the backhand, and Agassi netted the return. At 40-15, Sampras hit the second-serve at 120 miles per hour and, once more, Agassi returned off the backhand into the net. Sampras was up 4-3, but Agassi was in fine rhythm on his own serve, holding at 15 for 4-4, serving another ace in that game. Sampras opened the ninth game with a second-serve ace down the T, and another ace—this one on a first serve—gave Sampras a 30-15 lead. He moved on to 40-30, but Agassi's return was a beauty. He hit it at Sampras's feet, forcing a half volley error. It was deuce.

Sampras had to gather himself here. He was two points away from going down a break and allowing Agassi to serve for the set. Despite missing his first serve, Sampras took charge on the second serve with another unstoppable one. He swung it wide to the forehand, and Agassi netted the return. Sampras aced Agassi wide to the backhand in the ad court. That serve was working particularly well for him. Agassi knew full well how skillfully Sampras served down the T on that side of the court, and was often caught leaning the wrong way as he tried in vain to anticipate his opponent's intentions. Sampras had a 5-4 lead.

He played one of his finest return games with Agassi serving to save the set. Sampras was coming forward purposefully, hoping to rush his rival into mistakes. At 15-15, Sampras got to the net, hit a first-rate backhand volley down the line, and seemed to have the point won. Agassi was imperturbable whenever he was asked to come up with pinpoint passing shots by the aggressive Sampras. He demonstrated his belief in those passing shots here, rolling a forehand crosscourt out of his opponent's reach. An appreciative crowd cheered that play gleefully. They were dumbfounded by the excellence they were witnessing on both sides of the net.

Sampras, meanwhile, refused to back away from his strategy. He approached again on the next point, made a nifty forehand drop volley, and Agassi chased it in futility. It was 30-30. Agassi proceeded to beat Sampras to the net as he advanced to 40-30, putting away a backhand volley, but Sampras approached behind his return and this time Agassi's passing shot missed. It was deuce. Sampras was two points from winning the set again, and he chip-charged off the backhand. Considering the score and the situation, Agassi's backhand passing shot was startlingly accurate. He drove his two-hander cleanly down the line for a winner. Sampras had been absolutely true to his instincts, but Agassi's shot was simply too good. Agassi then kicked his first serve to Sampras's backhand, got the short return he wanted, and drove another two-hander immaculately up the line for a clean winner. Despite the most concerted effort yet from Sampras to get to the net unrelentingly, Agassi bravely had held for 5-5. His counterattacking in that game was out of this world.

Sampras pressed on resolutely, well aware that Agassi was performing with meticulous craftsmanship, mindful as well that this was one of those nights when he would need to reach back with all of his resources to somehow get across the finish line. Sampras dropped only one point on his serve as he took a 6-5 lead. He did not miss a first serve up until 40-15, but then finished off the game with a prodigious second serve down the T to the backhand. Agassi's return went wide. Serving to stay in the set a second time at 5-6, Agassi held at 15 with the kind of poise he had displayed all evening. He started with an ace wide to the Sampras forehand, and was sturdy throughout that game. Fittingly, the two formidable champions—who had sedulously held their serves all match long—moved on to a third tie-break.

It was Sampras who served first in that sequence and he made the most of that advantage, sending a thunderbolt down the T to stifle a lunging Agassi. After missing his first serve on the next point, Agassi overanxiously drove a two-handed backhand crosscourt long to trail 2-0, but bounced back on the following point with a forehand winner down the line. Sampras went for another huge second serve down the T but missed; it was his eighth double fault. But he composed himself immediately, swinging his first serve out wide with slice, punching a sound volley deep, then putting away an overhead without the least bit of hesitation. It was 3-2 for Sampras.

Sampras made a solid return off Agassi's first serve, but Agassi beat himself again on a big point, driving another two-hander long. Sampras had a 4-2 lead, and the inner belief that this tie-break might soon belong to him. He surged to 5-2 with a shrewd tactical play, rolling his forehand crosscourt with a degree of topspin Agassi had not expected. Sampras raised the trajectory of his shot, managing to get that ball up high to Agassi's forehand, drawing an error. Sampras had built a commanding 5-2 lead, and there was no stopping him now. An ace down the T in the ad court propelled Sampras to 6-2, and another ace out wide in the deuce court sealed the set. Sampras had captured the tie-break 7-2, gaining a two-sets-to-one lead with a nearly flawless performance in that sequence.

The outset of the fourth set was a dangerous moment for Agassi. He had fought valiantly, not losing his serve, sparring brilliantly with Sampras from the backcourt. He could hardly have played a better brand of tennis. And yet, here he was, despite all of his stellar play, one set away from elimination. Surely Agassi was perplexed and perhaps disconsolate about his plight, although he revealed no discouragement in his demeanor, and showed no sign of despondency in his body language. In the first game of the fourth set, Sampras realized there was no better time for him to pursue a service break with vigor. He drove a backhand down the line into a vacant corner to reach 0-30. He exploited another flattened out backhand down the line to reach 15-40, provoking a running forehand error from Agassi.

It was double break point for Sampras. With a service break at this juncture, he would be poised to move inexorably toward a victory he had fought for tirelessly and ceaselessly. At 15-40, Sampras chipped and charged off Agassi's second serve, coming in down the middle to deny his opponent any angle for his passing shot. Agassi did not despair, driving a backhand crosscourt winner. At 30-40, he rifled a forehand inside-out winner off Sampras's return. An ace down the T took Agassi to game point, and then he connected for another forehand inside-out winner. From 15-40, his clutch play was nearly beyond description. Just when it seemed as if Agassi might lose faith in himself and perhaps surrender emotionally, he elevated his game immeasurably to hold for 1-0. Buoyed by that courageous stand, Agassi raced to his chair at the changeover, signaling to Sampras that he was going to fight this one out to the very end, saying with his actions that he believed the match was far from over.

Sampras had to be disappointed that he had not been rewarded for an exceptional return game. But he was as disciplined an athlete as tennis had ever seen, and he got right on with his business, holding at love for 1-1, closing out that game with two aces and a winning forehand volley. In the third game, Sampras imposed himself again on Agassi, reaching 0-30. Agassi confounded his critics again, refusing to surrender at another disconcerting moment. A wide serve set up a forehand down the line winner for Agassi to make it 15-30, and another forehand winner took him to 30-30. Agassi aced Sampras out wide for 40-30, and then held at 30 for 2-1. He had been perched on the brink of a gut-wrenching loss, but remained thoroughly in the hunt against the foremost rival of his illustrious career.

Sampras—stretched to deuce in the fourth game as Agassi stepped up the velocity and accuracy of his returns—anticipated correctly that Agassi was going down the line with a backhand passing shot. Sampras covered the line beautifully, delicately depositing a forehand drop volley into a wide open court. At game point, Sampras put his first serve in commandingly, but Agassi's return was low and solid. Once more, as he had done all night, Sampras dug out a stupendous low forehand first volley, sending that shot deep crosscourt. Agassi ran it down, but the Sampras volley stayed so low that there was nothing his adversary could do. Agassi's passing shot landed inevitably in the net. In his entire career, Sampras had probably never put on such an exemplary display on the volley over the course of a long match. Time and again against the best returns that Agassi had to offer, Sampras had not been found wanting.

It was 2-2 and neither player was ceding any ground. Agassi held at 15 for 3-2 before Sampras won his serve at love. In the seventh game, Agassi served fantastically, acing Sampras down the T for 15-0, acing his rival out wide for 30-0, winning the next point after getting another first serve in, then acing Sampras by going down the T. He had served three more aces, holding at love for 4-3. In the following game, another opening presented itself. Sampras stood at 15-30. Agassi made another terrifically low return. Sampras was unflustered, making a deep first volley, forcing Agassi to play a forehand passing shot on the run. Agassi netted that shot as he went over the highest part of the net. He had no alternative but to go in that direction.

It was 30-30, but Agassi then hit a hard forehand return that forced Sampras to miss a volley off his hip. At 30-40, Agassi had a break point. If he could convert, he would be serving to send the match into a fifth set. Sampras did not want any part of a fifth set, not after all he had endured through a long and emotionally draining evening. He knew he needed a first serve, and recognized that the way Agassi was returning he had to make his delivery count. Sampras paused, collected himself, went into his effortless and elegant motion, and released his 21st ace of the night, going wide to Agassi's backhand in the ad court. He smacked two service winners to follow, holding on for 4-4. Sampras surpassed everyone in his era with his propensity to come through unhesitatingly on the very biggest points. He had done it again in this eighth game of the fourth set. When it had mattered most, he had demonstrated why he was the most unshakable champion who had ever lived. Sampras thrived at the moments of consequence, did not back down, never doubted himself in a crisis.

The suspense was leaving the fans in Ashe Stadium in a state of wonderment. The hour was approaching midnight, and only a small percentage of spectators had left the arena. This match was arguably the best contest ever staged on Ashe Stadium, which had opened in 1997. To leave now would be sacrilegious, not only for avid tennis enthusiasts but those sports fans who stumbled upon a classic confrontation between two American superstars who were revisiting their primes when they had supposedly left their best tennis behind them.

Meanwhile, Agassi found himself in serious jeopardy again when he served at 4-4. On the first point of that ninth game, Agassi's shot hit the net cord and hung in the air, long enough for Sampras to scamper forward and steer a forehand acutely crosscourt for a well-disguised winner. Then Sampras took Agassi's second serve and angled his topspin backhand return for another winner to reach 0-30. Agassi recouped to 30-30 but a penetrating backhand down the line from Sampras gave him a break point. He was one point away from serving for the match, and the crowd stirred in anticipation of that possibility. The two protagonists waged a high octane twelve-stroke rally, with Sampras defending as animatedly as he had all night long. But Agassi would not relinquish control of the rally. Sampras drove a topspin backhand long while on the run. Agassi took the next two points to hold on gamely for 5-4.

Sampras had narrowly missed another chance to break, but his spirit was not broken. After double faulting to 15-15 in the tenth game, Sampras was three points from a potential fifth set. He gathered himself, sent a slice serve out wide in the deuce court, and it was an ace. 30-15 for Sampras. He took the next two points to hold easily, and surged back to 5-5. Agassi held at 15 for 6-5, before Sampras moved out in front 30-0 in the twelfth game. Agassi rallied to 30-30 when Sampras double faulted for the eleventh time, but Sampras was unbending. He released his 23rd ace—a second serve at 118 miles per hour down the

T—and that lifted Sampras to 40-30. On the next point, Agassi kept his return exceedingly low, forcing Sampras to play a forehand half volley as he came in behind his serve. Sampras directed it deep crosscourt, just inside the sideline. It was an outright winner, and in many ways that shot was symbolic of an entire night's work for Pete Sampras. Agassi had performed with verve and brio, making one piercing and dipping return after another. But Sampras had more than stood his ground; he had backed up his serve immaculately.

The fourth set was locked at 6-6. Another tie-break was about to unfold. The players had been on court for over three hours. And the fans had enjoyed every minute of it. The audience recognized that if Sampras were to win the upcoming tie-break, he would be the victor, and the contest would end right then and there. They had marveled at the magic that seemed to be in the air, and realized that both players had moved beyond themselves to an ineffable level. What Sampras and Agassi were doing was playing from inspiration and memory, suspending time, celebrating who they were and what they could still produce on a tennis court. The fans were deeply appreciative. They rose to their feet to give the players a thoroughly deserved standing ovation, a prolonged round of applause that was their way of thanking the performers not only for this particular match, but for the breadth and scope of their careers. It was a moment to relish for both men, one that would surely remain in their hearts and minds irrevocably.

As Sampras said in a 2012 interview conducted for this book in early 2012, "What I always think about when I look back on that match was that standing ovation we got right before we started the fourth set tie-breaker. Everyone just stood up at that moment and for about five seconds it took me out of the match. I thought, 'Wow, this must be looking pretty good to these fans.' Both of us had been through so much as competitors and it all sort of came to a head at that moment as the fans stood up and applauded us. It was like they were saying, 'These are two great Americans and we might not see this again for the next ten, twenty or even fifty years'. They just showed their appreciation and it felt great to hear that."

But a critical sequence of points was about to begin, and Sampras and Agassi had to leave aside the sentimentality of the crowd and get on with their skirmish. At 1-1 in the fourth set tie-break, Agassi made the first significant move. Sampras pulled him wide with the deuce court slice serve that had been so unanswerable most of the night, but this time Agassi was on to it. He drilled a forehand return down the line, hit it low and hard, and made it impossible for Sampras to control a backhand half volley. Agassi had the mini-break for 2-1. The next two points would be crucial. Agassi went to 3-1 by winning a crackling 16-stroke backcourt exchange. Sampras had set himself up for a sitter off the forehand, but had too much time to weigh his options, and missed badly.

Agassi served deep and wide to the Sampras forehand on the following point. Sampras realized he could not make an aggressive return, blocking the ball back down the middle. Agassi thought he had an opening for a forehand-inside out winner, but he tightened up and made an expensive error. Rather than serving at 1-4 and being three points away from the unwelcome territory of a fifth set, Sampras was back in business at 2-3. He stepped up to this moment majestically, and with two swings of the racket he had moved ahead in the tie-break. First, Sampras aced Agassi wide to the backhand in the ad court for 3-3, and then he aced him down the T at 128 miles per hour for a 4-3 lead. That was his 25th ace of the match, and his most important.

The pendulum of pressure had swung back onto Agassi's side of the net, and the native of Las Vegas knew the odds were now against him. His miscalculation on the next point was damaging to his chances. He tried to attack off Sampras's return, but was trapped in "No Man's Land" as he played a defensive forehand half volley. Agassi was between a rock and hard place. If he chose to approach the net behind that shot, Sampras would have probably passed him with ease. So Agassi exercised his other option, retreating toward the baseline. Sampras had his topspin backhand down the line all lined up. He hit the ball soundly and sweetly, and gave himself plenty of margin for error, making a clean winner for 5-3. A flustered Agassi still managed to get his first serve in on the next point. He came forward and had the court wide open for an angled backhand drop volley, but his insecurity at the net—a career long issue—surfaced at the worst possible time. Agassi's volley landed just wide.

Sampras was right where he wanted to be, serving at 6-3, triple match point. Not a soul in the stadium believed he would not end it on one of the next two points. He went down the T with a percentage oriented first serve, not attempting to hit an ace but looking to take control with his first volley. He punched that backhand volley down the line, and it looked sufficient to put Sampras across the finish line. Agassi, however, was not ready to say goodbye. He rolled a forehand pass sharply crosscourt, making the ball dip decidedly as it went over the net. Sampras was caught slightly off guard, missing a low volley from close range. The crowd stirred, but Sampras was still serving with a 6-4 lead, his destiny remaining in his own hands.

The audience in Ashe Stadium was beside themselves, with the Sampras camp anxious for him to underline his supremacy with an ace, and the Agassi constituency apprehensively hoping for another signature return from the incomparable counter-attacker. While the fans expressed themselves freely and raised the volume of their appreciation, Sampras paced around the baseline, preparing himself for what would hopefully be the last serve he would hit all night. He went for his trustworthy slice serve wide in the deuce court, but it landed in the alley. He paused, and then double faulted into the net, a clear sign of anxiety. The fans were now overflowing with emotions as Agassi served at 5-6. He had already cast aside two match points against him. Could he erase a third?

Agassi missed a big first serve, and then spun the second delivery predictably to the Sampras backhand. Sampras was not going to take an unnecessary chance with so much at stake. He chipped down the middle without much depth, keeping the ball reasonably low. Sampras saw Agassi moving in to attack off the forehand, and was leaning to his right, ready to cover the open court on his forehand side. Agassi's split second decision was to go behind Sampras with an inside-out forehand. Sampras saw that, and was shifting his weight to get back in position. But Agassi's assertive attempt failed. His forehand found the net. A euphoric Sampras grinned widely, raised his hands, and made his way up to the net to shake hands with his revered rival. Sampras had won in three hours and 36 minutes, and it was now

Pete Sampras

12:14 a.m. on the morning of September 6th. They briefly embraced, and Agassi sportingly told Sampras, "Win this thing," meaning that he hoped the man who had just ushered him out of the event would go on to take the tournament.

Reflecting on his triumph in 2012—more than a decade after the contest—Sampras said, "It is rare in tennis when two guys are playing great at the same time. I was doing what I do really well that night, and Andre was solid as a rock and wasn't making any errors. So we just got into this dogfight. Physically I felt like I was doing more of the work because of the stopping and starting with my serve-and-volley, so I was feeling it in my legs a little bit at the end of the match. Andre was mentally very strong that night. It was two great players playing really well and it resulted in one of the best and most dramatic matches that I was ever a part of. People to this day still ask me about that match. It was ironic that it was a quarterfinal but people were ready for this match and I felt both of us lived up to it."

Sampras won his next match, toppling Marat Safin in straight sets. Sampras had knocked out the three men—Rafter, Agassi, and Safin—who had secured all of the Open titles since his last triumph in 1996. Rafter had won the tournament in 1997-98, Agassi was the victor in 1999, and Safin was the defending champion. In the final, Sampras sought to end one of the most impressive runs ever at the Open with a victory over the fleet-footed Australian Lleyton Hewitt. The year before, Sampras had ousted Hewitt in the semifinals, but this time around he was devoid of the sparkle that had characterized his game over the course of the fortnight. Hewitt returned serve magnificently in a straight-set win over Sampras.

But the fact remained that Sampras had celebrated a spectacular tournament, and his win over Agassi was among the finest moments of his illustrious career. They had never played simultaneously at a loftier level against each other. They had produced what many considered the best match ever at the U.S. Open. They had joyously shared in a masterpiece of a match, and it was a contest that would linger forever in the minds of all who were there to witness it.

EPILOGUE

Sampras would have liked to build on his uplifting U.S. Open and finish the year strong, but his wish was not granted. A shoulder injury late in the year was a factor as Sampras finished 2001 at No. 10 in the world, the lowest he had ended any season since 1989. Agassi's consistency kept him near the top, and he concluded that campaign at No. 3. Agassi married women's all-time great Steffi Graf a few months after his epic Open loss to Sampras. As they approached 2002, Sampras was fueled more than anything else by his skeptics. He was going to end his career on his own terms, and was convinced he could win at least one more major before he was through. He did not care what his critics believed; he knew that he could revisit his former glories and triumph again when it mattered.

And yet, Sampras did not fare well across the first half of 2002. The low point of his year came at Wimbledon. Seeded sixth, he was put out on Court 2 against lucky loser George Bastl of Switzerland. Sampras had not played on an outside court at the All England Club in many years, and the environment and setting was like a foreign land to him even though Wimbledon itself had long been his home abroad. Sampras rallied from two sets down on a desultory day for him and got to a fifth set, but suffered an agonizing upset. Nonetheless, he refused to dwell on that setback, and pointed toward the next major in New York.

By the time he arrived at Flushing Meadows, the No. 17 seed Sampras was mired in a thirty-three-tournament drought, having not won a tournament of any kind since his Wimbledon triumph of 2000. In the third round, he overcame 1997 Open finalist Greg Rusedski in five hard sets, and the British left-hander insulted him by saying he was a step slower and not the Pete Sampras who had won thirteen Grand Slam tournaments. Sampras brushed aside the comments from Rusedski, but it seemed to rankle him in the best possible way. It had taken a lot of gall for Rusedski to speak so disrespectfully. Sampras was dismissive, but he was a prideful man who wanted another prestigious prize more than anything else.

In the fourth round, he stopped No. 2 seed Tommy Haas. He then cut down countryman Andy Roddick, who would win the tournament the following year. That straight-set triumph—the highest quality match he had played in a long while—carried him into the semifinals, and he then stopped the Dutchman Sheng Schalken. In the final, fittingly and perhaps fatefully, Sampras played Agassi, who had removed the top-seeded Hewitt in the penultimate round. Agassi—the No. 6 seed—was expected by many in the know to beat Sampras for the first time in four U.S. Open meetings. He had enjoyed a terrific season, winning four tournaments including Masters Series crowns in Miami and Rome, setting a high standard of consistency. In turn, his win over world No. 1 Hewitt was proof that Agassi was in sparkling form. Sampras would need to bring out the finest colors of his game to stop Agassi in the championship match.

He did just that. Sampras was virtually letter perfect in sweeping past Agassi over the first two sets. He lost a close third set but closed out an immensely gratifying victory 6-3, 6-4, 5-7, 6-4. He served thirty-two aces, struck the forehand mightily, volleyed with panache, and rose ably to the occasion. He had beaten Agassi for the twentieth time in thirty-four career meetings, for the third time without a loss in a U.S. Open final, and for the fourth time in five Grand Slam final-round duels. He had more than answered the skeptics, and rewarded himself with a fourteenth major. In the months that followed, he thought long and hard about whether or not he wanted to play any longer on the ATP World Tour. In the end, after a great deal of soul searching, he made up his mind to retire. He had won the last match of his career against Agassi, capturing his final major with a title round win over the same player he had ousted to take his first. He realized that there could be no better way to put the finishing touches on a scintillating career than to beat his biggest rival on a large occasion in the final of his country's Grand Slam event. A year later, on the same court in Ashe Stadium, Sampras officially announced his retirement at a poignant ceremony.

Agassi, however, was still surprisingly driven to succeed, as if to make amends for wasted years in his twenties. At the start of 2003, he took his eighth and last Grand Slam crown in Melbourne, winning the Australian Open at thirty-two. He rose to No. 1 in the world on the ATP Rankings, the oldest ever to reside in that post since the computer rankings were established in 1973. Two years later, in 2005, Agassi reached his last Grand Slam tournament final in New York at his 20th U.S. Open. After a string of five-set victories over Xavier Malisse, James Blake and Robby Ginepri, he confronted Roger Federer in an electrifying contest. After losing the first set, Agassi won the second and moved ahead 4-2, 40-30 in the third before he lost in four sets to the world No. 1. At thirty-five years and four months old, Agassi was the oldest men's Grand Slam tournament finalist since Ken Rosewall got to the U.S. Open final in 1974.

A year later, Agassi wrapped up his singularly captivating career at the U.S. Open. He announced at Wimbledon—where he lost in the third round to a 20-year-old Rafael Nadal—that he would retire in New York. Playing through debilitating pain in his back and hips, Agassi managed to win two matches in Ashe Stadium, including an exhausting and exhilarating contest against Australian Open finalist Marcos Baghdatis in the second round. But he bowed out in the third round against Germany's Benjamin Becker. He addressed the crowd afterwards in a tearful speech.

At thirty-six, Agassi stood in Ashe Stadium and bid farewell to a public that had watched him play in three different decades. It was reminiscent in some ways of Sampras in 2003, when he broke down in tears while speaking to the New York fans at his retirement ceremony. Both champions had celebrated more successes at other venues. Agassi had won four of his eight majors in Melbourne. Sampras shined more at Wimbledon than anywhere else with his seven championships, two more than he had won in New York. But the two Americans who fought so many memorable battles at the Open—most importantly their 2001 epic—had both seen fit to bid farewell in that setting.

That was entirely appropriate. They had been linked together in so many ways as rivals. They had been so different in fundamental respects, yet these two enduring American champions had both given the tennis fans in New York an awful lot to shout about. Sampras and Agassi were, after all, the centerpiece players of their generation.

CHAPTER TWENTY-SEVEN

Jennifer Capriati *vs.* Justine Henin
U.S. OPEN, SEMIFINAL, SEPTEMBER 5, 2003

A highly-charged American and an unwavering Belgian collided on an exhilarating New York evening in a contest neither would ever forget. It was a stupendous clash between two stalwart competitors.

PROLOGUE

Perhaps no woman player in the modern game of tennis has been subjected to more hype and speculation than Jennifer Capriati. Born in New York, she was the daughter of Stefano Capriati, a former Italian soccer player. The Capriati family settled on Long Island, but moved to Florida when Jennifer was four. She had already started playing tennis as a three-year-old, guided by a family fully invested in Jennifer's future as a tennis player. In her early years, Capriati—who was introduced to the sport and originally taught by her father—benefitted immensely from the coaching expertise of Jimmy Evert, the father and coach of the renowned Chris Evert.

From the outset, Jennifer Capriati's prowess on the courts was unassailable. She developed a potent ground game, featuring a flat and classic forehand and a reliable and productive two-handed backhand. Over time, her serve became a strength, and her ball control was always remarkable. She was so far ahead of the game that her junior career was over almost before it began, culminating in 1989 when she established herself as the youngest ever to secure the French and U.S. Open junior crowns. For Capriati, the stage was clearly set for an outstanding professional career.

On March 5, 1990, twenty-four days shy of her fourteenth birthday, Capriati turned professional and reached the final of her debut event at Boca Raton, Florida. Capriati made some inevitable strides as a top flight competitor, becoming the youngest ever French Open semi-finalist in 1990, reaching the semifinals of Wimbledon and the U.S. Open in 1991, and startling most learned observers with a final-round triumph over none other than Steffi Graf at the 1992 Olympic Games in Barcelona. That gold medal win at the Olympics was a milestone, but a determined Capriati did not win a Grand Slam championship during that impressive yet unfulfilling stretch.

Thereafter, her struggle to find an identity as an athlete with more than her share of burdens and the unbearable weight of almost impossible expectations caught up with her. Capriati had a series of personal setbacks—including an arrest for marijuana possession—and her disillusionment kept her away from tennis. Capriati had finished 1991-93 stationed among the top ten in the world every year, but her boosters out among the public wanted more. In her darkened state of mind, that was impossible. In 1994, Capriati played only one match all season and in 1995 she did not compete at all.

And yet, her love of the game and her sense of self were gradually restored. She burst back into the world's top 25 in 1996. After a few disappointing seasons, she got back to No. 23 in 1999, and the following year she finished at No. 14, reaching the semifinals of the Australian Open during that stellar 2000 campaign. Now Capriati was ready to play the game as she never had before, to bring out a maturity and completeness in her play that was previously unattainable. The results were staggering. In 2001, she took the first two Grand Slam championships of the season, ousting Martina Hingis in the final of the Australian Open in straight sets, overcoming Kim Clijsters of Belgium 1-6, 6-4, 12-10 in a crackling French Open final after four times drifting two points away from defeat. Back in Melbourne at the start of 2002, Capriati defended her Australian Open crown audaciously on an oppressive afternoon, rallying gamely from a set and 0-4 down and later saving four match points on her way to a stunning 4-6, 7-6 (7), 6-2 triumph over an overwrought Hingis.

In the span of twelve months, Capriati had captured no fewer than three Grand Slam singles titles. Meanwhile, she realized a longtime ambition by reaching No. 1 in the world during the fall of 2001. She ended 2002 at No. 3 in the world, and as she approached her confrontation with Justine Henin at the 2003 U.S. Open, her standards remained high, her desire to prevail at the majors undiminished. In other words, Capriati remained in the forefront of the game at twenty-seven, and was seeded sixth at the Open, where she had once been on the verge of a popular triumph in her country's national championship. In 1991, at fifteen, she had performed with unbridled passion and extraordinary courage against an unswerving Monica Seles.

On that occasion, Capriati twice served for the match before bowing in a final-set tie-break to her illustrious rival. In 2001, a full decade later, Capriati had made it back to the penultimate round, falling in a straight-set showdown with Venus Williams. But now, coming up against the industrious and enterprising Henin, having moved to a loftier level of the game, Capriati was carrying herself like a woman who believed her time to get on the victory board in the capitol of American sports entertainment could be no better than now.

As for Henin, she had her own reasons for looking forward to this encounter. Born in Liege, Belgium, she had endured a rough childhood. Her mother, a French and history teacher, died when Justine was only twelve. Many times in the years before her death, Francoise Rosiere took her daughter on the short trip to Paris to watch the French Open, opening up the windows of Justine's mind to a time when she might lift that trophy at the world's premier clay court championship. Henin progressed rapidly through the juniors, building an enviable record that set her apart from the vast majority of her competition. In 1996, she secured the prestigious Orange Bowl 14-and-under title; the following year, she was victorious at the French Open junior championships when she had just turned fifteen.

At the outset of 1999, Henin, still only sixteen yet plainly ready to head out into the wider world of women's tennis, turned professional. It did not take her long to make substantial inroads. She found a place for herself among the top 50 in the world in 2000, and then surged into the world's top ten at No. 7 in 2001. That year she made it to the semifinals of the French Open, and at Wimbledon she went farther. In the semifinals, she took on Capriati in the semifinals on the fabled Centre Court. Capriati had already ruled in Melbourne and at Roland Garros, and when she took the first set from Henin convincingly at Wimbledon, the American was only three sets away from a third consecutive major, a feat that would have allowed her to pursue a Grand Slam a few months later at the U.S. Open. But Capriati could not maintain her progress against Henin on the grass, and the Belgian recouped thoroughly for a three-set win.

Henin lost the final at the All England Club to Venus Williams in three sets, but her growing awareness of herself and her potential was surfacing. She knew now that she had the game, the drive and the temperament to win major championships. She realized that the biggest prizes were no longer out of her reach. She understood that supreme dedication to a craft would take a great player to the land of the elite. And so Henin kept honing her game, which was exemplary in many ways. The Belgian stood at only 5'6," which made her a diminutive figure in her sport. Capriati, for example, was 5'8," but across the first decade of the 21st century in tennis, more and more leading players stood at least close to six feet tall.

Yet Henin did not let her relatively small frame diminish her chances to compete at the highest level. Henin's 2002 season was slightly disappointing, with her best showing at a major occurring back on the lawns of Wimbledon, where she advanced to the penultimate round before losing to Venus Williams again. But in the season leading up to her monumental clash with Capriati at the 2003 U.S. Open, Henin soared to another level above and beyond where she had ever been before. She rose to No. 2 in the world over the course of the season, and captured her first major at the French Open, toppling countrywoman Clijsters in a one-sided final. But it was her semifinal with Serena Williams at Roland Garros that everyone would recollect for a lot longer.

In that stirring contest, Henin was in a serious bind against her American rival. In the third and final set, Serena was serving with a 4-2, 30-0 lead. Williams released her first serve, but the Belgian put up her hand to signal that she was not ready. The umpire never saw Henin hold up her hand, so he thought it was a first serve fault. Williams was understandably unhappy. But Henin never walked over to the umpire to acknowledge that she had indeed raised her hand. That meant Williams had to regroup and prepare to hit a second serve. From that juncture, she lost five of the next six games, and Henin rallied admirably and deservedly to take the match 6-2, 4-6, 7-5.

Both players later were in accord that the incident had not altered the outcome of the match. Henin had won it fair and square. But the television images of that moment lingered long after the battle was over. Time and again, viewers watched as Henin put up her hand while the umpire's head was turned in the other direction. It was not as if the incident had cost Williams that point; she still led 4-2, 30-0 in the third set. Having to hit a second rather than a first serve on a red clay court was not a terrible hardship. But the image of Henin suffered considerably from that unfortunate moment. She had been regularly celebrated for her quiet ferocity as a competitor and her astonishing resilience, but fans were preoccupied by what many considered "bad form" on Henin's part for not going out of her way to tell the umpire what she had done. Had Henin acknowledged her gesture, Williams would have been allowed another first serve, and there would have been no controversy.

In any event, Henin had a first major in her collection. She would lose handily to Serena Williams in the semifinals of Wimbledon, as the American went on to record a fourth victory in the last five Grand Slam events. The grass was not tailor made for Henin's game. She was a complete player who operated largely from the backcourt. Her signature shot was clearly her glorious one-handed backhand. Off that side, she could come over the ball with an aggressive brand of topspin, hitting through the ball beautifully, hitting winners almost at will. She used her inside-out forehand to open up all kinds of avenues to unleash her sparkling backhand. Moreover, although she did not come to the net frequently, when she did so, it was with authority. Her technique on the volley was excellent. On top of that, Henin's first serve was ever improving. Her placement and deception with the serve were impressive. In many ways, Justine Henin was the tennis player's tennis player, a consummate professional, a fine athlete, and a champion through and through. Both Henin and Capriati were very good value for money, two terrifically clean hitters of the ball, a pair of formidable individuals, and a couple of excellent competitors. Everyone looked forward to their semifinal meeting in New York, which promised to be a match that would captivate the galleries from beginning to end.

THE MATCH

There was never much doubt that the No. 2 seed Henin and No. 6 Capriati would make it to this eagerly awaited semifinal appointment. On her way to the showdown, Capriati dropped only one set in five matches. Henin was even more convincing, casting aside her five opponents without losing a set. They had met five times prior to this duel under the bright lights in Arthur Ashe Stadium. Henin had been victorious in three of those contests, but all of their head-to-head matches had been settled in three sets, demonstrating that the playing field was relatively level whenever they played each other. Both women were so adept at taking command from the baseline and shaping the outcome of their skirmishes that the margin between victory and defeat was inevitably thin.

As the match unfolded, it seemed as if Henin's wider range of strokes and shot making verve would propel the Belgian through the opening set. From the opening bell, she wore the look of a seasoned professional who knew precisely how she wanted to go about her business. She conducted herself with that familiar strong-willed disposition, that purposeful manner, that sense of quiet authority. Although she did not break Capriati in the opening game of the match, the Belgian planted a few seeds of doubt in the American. Capriati was behind 15-40, and it took a considerable amount of resolve for the American to fight back. She swept four points in a row. She directed her baseline aggression at Henin's more suspect forehand side, drawing a pair of mistakes from the Belgian with calculated precision. Then Capriati served an ace at 113 miles per hour down the T, followed by a big serve that set up a big forehand. Henin was forced into another error and Capriati had a tenuous 1-0 lead.

Despite that minor setback, Henin quickly settled into a groove, sweeping four games in a row. Henin raced to a 40-0 lead in the second game, and eventually held at 30, taking the initiative away from Capriati, winning that point with an outright winner off the forehand, a shot that was set up beautifully by a backhand driven with tremendous depth. At 30-30 in the third game, the two competitors produced a riveting 27-stroke rally, an exchange filled with variety and supreme flat ball hitting. Henin prevailed to garner a break point, which she converted when Capriati approached from too far back in the court off the backhand. The American directed that approach crosscourt, dangerously going to the strength of her adversary. Henin was ready, rolling her passing shot at Capriati's feet. Capriati was trapped, netting a backhand half volley under duress.

Now Henin was off and running. She easily held at 15 for 3-1 despite a double fault at 30-0. The fifth game appeared to be crucial for both players; Henin wanted and needed an insurance break, while Capriati desperately sought to keep the score close and her chances in that set alive. Capriati was ahead 40-15, but Henin took charge to bring the score back to deuce, connecting with a dazzling forehand down the line winner, hooking the ball into the corner from outside the alley. Then Henin unleashed another brilliant running forehand, driving this one crosscourt with surprising pace, rushing Capriati into an error. Capriati proceeded to fend off two break points in this stirring three deuce game, but Henin was unbending. She earned a third break point, and did not waste it. Capriati missed her first serve and then produced a relatively short second delivery. Henin pounced, driving a topspin backhand return down the line for a clean, bold and breathtaking winner. Henin was accelerating, up two breaks, headed inexorably toward a first-set victory. She looked absolutely unstoppable.

Or so it seemed. Capriati, of course, had other notions. The sturdily built American was always defiant in the face of adversity. One of Capriati's great virtues was the capacity to gather her resources whenever she was down, and fight with higher intensity and deeper concentration to recover. At 1-4 and two breaks down in the first set against a player of Henin's stature, Capriati knew full well that she must play every point as if it was match point. Henin was not in the habit of giving anything away. It would be up to Capriati to take this one away with an inspired and unrelenting display of big hitting and top-of-the-line defense from the baseline.

So the 27-year-old went assiduously to work. Henin could sense as she served the sixth game of the first set that Capriati was coming

Jennifer Capriati

at her without hesitation. In her own way, and on her own terms, Capriati was raising the stakes, lifting her game decidedly, showing the Belgian that she believed the set was far from over. With Henin serving at 4-1, 30-30, Capriati fittingly made her move. She pulled Henin way out of position on the Belgian's backhand side, and then stepped in boldly to make a forehand drive volley winner to the open court. Now at break point, Capriati hit a shot short and low, drawing the Belgian into the forecourt. Henin tried to dig out the low ball, but did not succeed, sending her forehand inside-out approach long.

Just like that, Capriati shifted the momentum of the match slightly yet unmistakably back in her favor. Although she was still down a break, the American was revitalized, back in a state of optimism, visibly more confident. But much hard work remained for Capriati. The seventh game went to deuce three times. Both players were competing honorably. The New York crowd was fervently and vociferously behind Capriati. Henin understood their sentiments, but quietly attempted to tune them out, to let her magnificent ball striking do the talking for her, believing she could dampen the enthusiasm of the audience with a timely burst of brilliance. Yet Capriati was not only inspired but also flowing freely. After that third deuce, she released a scorching flat forehand crosscourt that Henin could not answer. Now at game point for the third time, having saved one break point, Capriati won this pivotal game with a body serve into the forehand, eliciting an errant return from the cramped Belgian.

Henin recognized that the set was slowly slipping from her grasp. Knowing that was the case, she played the 4-3 game on her serve with fury. There were four deuces in that eighth game. The Belgian had three game points, but Capriati obstinately took those opportunities away, wisely biding her time until her opponent overplayed her hand. On the first game point, Henin drove a topspin backhand down the line that flew long in the increasingly arduous wind. Henin drove a forehand approach shot narrowly long on her second game point. Looking to catch her adversary off guard, Henin served-and-volleyed on her third game point, but Capriati adjusted instinctively, keeping her return admirably low. Henin netted her forehand first volley. Henin had aced her way out of one break point, but Capriati broke through on her second opportunity, driving her two-hander with excellent depth to draw an error from Henin.

It was 4-4. The crowd was overjoyed by the American's resurgence, shouting their approval unambiguously, applauding thunderously. In the ninth game, Capriati trailed 0-30, but aced Henin down the T on the next point. She went to 40-30, but Henin rallied to deuce with a wonderfully struck flat backhand approach that was too much for Capriati to handle. From deuce, Capriati kept her growing command of the biggest points. She stifled Henin with a service winner to the backhand, and closed out that game when Henin missed an aggressively played forehand return into the net.

Capriati had secured four games in a row. Improbably, she was out in front at 5-4 on serve. That surge was clearly taking its toll on Henin. Externally, the Belgian remained implacable, but internally she was surely distressed and dumbfounded by the reversal of fortunes.

Serving at 4-5, Henin lost the first point, netting a forehand on the 13th stroke of an absorbing baseline exchange. Henin recovered to 15-15, but she did not fool Capriati when she went for a backhand drop volley. Capriati scampered in swiftly and rolled a forehand passing shot crosscourt for a winner. At 15-30, Henin did not get enough velocity on her overhead, and Capriati responded with a low passing shot. Henin's half volley sat up invitingly for Capriati, who ignited the crowd with a backhand passing shot winner struck accurately down the line. At 4-5, 15-40, Henin was down double set point, and out of ideas. She went for an inside-out forehand approach, and missed it long. Set to Capriati 6-4. The fans erupted, many rising to their feet to salute the comeback of Capriati, who had somehow captured five games in a row to seal the set.

The first set had consumed fifty-nine grueling minutes in the cool night air of New York, with the wind blowing capriciously. Capriati had taken the lead, but she was well aware of Henin's propensity to leave even her deepest disappointments behind her and then navigate her way with temerity to victory, however long it took, whatever was required, no matter how bleak her prospects appeared to be. Henin was the ultimate competitor, a warrior through and through, a woman of rare inner strength and stability. She may have been apprehensive, but for Justine Henin overcoming hard obstacles was simply a way of living.

Capriati, meanwhile, needed to guard against a letdown after her flourish at the end of the opening set. But she lost her serve in the first game of the second set with a double fault and a cluster of unforced errors. Henin, however, returned the favor in the second game, squandering a 30-0 lead. Both players settled down from there. Capriati held at love for 2-1 before Henin held at 15 to make it 2-2. Capriati then held at 15 for 3-2, and had a break point in the sixth game. Henin displayed flexibility to save herself there, slicing a backhand down the line, coaxing a forehand crosscourt mistake from Capriati. Henin held on for 3-3, but Capriati still had the upper hand. She held easily at 15 for 4-3, and then swiftly advanced to 0-40 on Henin's serve in the following game. Henin saved the first break point with an ace, but pulled a forehand crosscourt wide on the next point as Capriati defended steadfastly during that critical exchange.

Now Capriati was ahead 5-3, serving for the match, within striking distance of her first U.S. Open final. The task here was to play each point with a combination of aggression and control, avoid unnecessary mistakes, and stick with the winning pattern that had taken her so close to victory. But Capriati was too aware of the score, too conscious of the situation. She double faulted on the first point of that ninth game, fell behind 15-30, but made it to 30-30. She was two points away from one of the biggest wins of her career. She poured her heart and soul into the next point, and seemed to have Henin entirely at bay. The American hit a terrific forehand pass on the run, and Henin needed to make an exceedingly difficult forehand half volley. With startling ease and poise, Henin finessed that ball delicately over the net. An astonishing and courageous half volley drop shot winner had taken Henin to break point. Now Capriati lofted a lob over Henin to take the net away from her opponent, but the Belgian retaliated with a perfectly placed lob over Capriati's head. Capriati chased it down but could not get the ball back into play.

With those two spectacular clutch points in a row, Henin had at least temporarily rescued herself from a straight-set defeat, but the fact remained that Henin was still serving just to stay in the match. At 4-5, Henin stood at 15-30, two points from elimination again. Her majestic backhand came through for her magnificently at that juncture, as Henin angled a topspin winner acutely crosscourt. At 30-30, Henin crowded Capriati with a second serve into the body, setting up a first rate forehand approach shot. An off balance Capriati netted her passing shot attempt. Now Henin came up to play an elegant backhand drop volley with sidespin. Capriati managed to reach that shot, and tried to pass Henin, but the Belgian's anticipation was uncanny, and she punched a backhand volley winner into the clear. It was 5-5.

The American had three times been within two points of victory, but the score was locked at 5-5. Capriati must have been reeling from emotional discomfort, yet she plodded on. In the eleventh game, she got to 40-30 on her serve but lost the next three points as Henin found her range off the backhand. Serving for the set at 6-5, a reinvigorated Henin connected with four consecutive first serves, produced two remarkable winners (including an astounding inside-out overhead win-ner off a deep lob from Capriati), and held at love. With a flourish, true to her code of never giving up, proud of her resolve, Henin had manufactured a stunning recovery.

But a third and final set was still to come, and Capriati realized she would have a second chance to rouse the crowd, raise her game, and carve out a victory. And yet, the third set did not start well for the American. She had two game points to hold serve, and saved a break point. But then, with Henin at break point a second time, the Belgian sparkled. Capriati had come in to play a well-executed inside-out forehand volley. Henin moved across the court with her typically fine footwork, stayed low, took small steps, and timed her topspin back-hand passing shot immaculately. The Belgian angled that shot sharply crosscourt, leaving the American helpless at the net. Henin had hit a startling winner, and she had the break for 1-0.

Henin had collected five games in a row from 3-5 down in the second set, and was looking increasingly sure of herself. She advanced to 40-30 at 1-0 in that final set, but Capriati attacked behind a backhand return crosscourt, forcing Henin to miss a passing shot. Henin had a second game point, only to miss a routine inside-out forehand. Capriati fought tenaciously, and broke back for 1-1. She had weathered a serious storm. She held on for 2-1 in a deuce game with an ace down the middle in the ad court, and suddenly the shape and feel of the match had been altered. The fans were fueling Capriati, cheering her on unabashedly, giving her a shot of adrenaline every time she needed it.

Henin was losing conviction in her forehand, and Capriati was playing to that side whenever possible. Capriati was driving through the ball beautifully off her forehand side, and she was winning more than her share of the longer rallies. With Henin serving at 1-2, 30-30, Capriati out-dueled her adversary in a 25-stroke exchange when Henin drove a forehand long. Henin saved one break point, but Capriati earned another with a shining piece of business. Henin punched a forehand volley crisply crosscourt, but Capriati cracked a forehand passing shot on the dead run down the line, jumping for joy when she saw her shot land safely for a winner. Then Capriati applied some pressure, forcing Henin into a running forehand wide. The American was up 3-1 in the final set, ascendant once more, buoyed by the grow-ing effusiveness of the audience.

Twice in the fifth game, Capriati was pushed to deuce, but she went back to the pattern that was working so well for her over the course of the set. In a crosscourt forehand exchange, Capriati gained the upper hand. Henin blinked first. It was 4-1 for Capriati. Serving at 40-30 in the sixth game, Henin outperformed the American in a brilliant 18-shot exchange. At the end of that gripping rally, Capriati drew Henin in with a short backhand chip, but Henin answered with a sidespin backhand, luring Capriati into a passing shot error. That was inventiveness off the top shelf. Henin held on for 2-4.

Capriati then put in three out of four first serves, opening the seventh game with a swing volley winner off the backhand, closing it with a forehand inside-out winner, holding commandingly at love to reach 5-2. Capriati raced to her chair at the changeover, eagerly awaiting the chance to close out a remarkable account. Not long after, Henin appeared to be on the edge of despair. In the eighth game, she led 40-15, and then lost the next point. At 40-30, after missing her first serve, she started cramping, and then missed a backhand wide. It was deuce, and Capriati was back in that elusive territory: two points away from winning the match.

Henin knew this was no time for caution. She drilled a forehand crosscourt approach that landed right smack on edge of the baseline for a winner. There were three more deuces in that game. Three more times, Capriati was tantalizingly close, within two points of a triumph. But Henin drove a terrific backhand down the line to force Capriati into a running forehand error. Capriati missed another tough running forehand on the second chance, and Henin swung her first serve wide to Capriati's forehand to win the last of those critical points. After four deuces, Henin held for 3-5.

Despite those elusive opportunities, Capriati still served for the match a second time when she led 5-3 in the third. At 15-15, Henin threw in a biting backhand slice to set up a topspin winner off that side. Her perspicacity and self-assurance were striking. Henin broke through at 15, and was back to 4-5. In the tenth game, the score went to 30-30. For the eighth time, Capriati was within two points of victory. They had an absorbing 19-stroke rally that Henin concluded with a forehand down the line winner. In the middle of that point, Henin had pulled off a nearly impossible shot. Capriati had blasted a backhand down the line that should have been unanswerable, but Henin had somehow lofted a deep lob into the corner to stay in the point, eventually shifting from defense onto offense.

Capriati had given Henin every conceivable chance to miss, but Henin refused the invitation. The demonstrative American was understandably rattled, baffled, and infuriated. She was playing well enough to beat just about any woman in the world, but Justine Henin was no mortal in her business. The Belgian was not unlike a boxer who had been sent to the canvas innumerable times, yet kept getting back on her feet and throwing blockbuster punches of her own. Henin held for 5-5 at 30. Capriati's consternation was almost palpable. Yet she steadied herself, held at 15 with an ace for 6-5, and fashioned another all-consuming bid to put this match in her victory column.

With Henin serving at 5-6, the 21-year-old Belgian found herself near the end of her physical limits again. Her cramps returned as she served at 15-15, and the Belgian lost that point with a forehand crosscourt error. It was 15-30. Henin once again refused to miss, and Capriati went for an audacious forehand down the line winner, but her shot went narrowly wide. At 30-30, Capriati was two points from victory for the tenth time, but only for an instant. Henin aced her down the T. The Belgian's first serve at 40-30 was sufficient to induce a forehand return mistake from Capriati. Fittingly, this match would end in a final-set tie-break, which would have been impossible at any other major. The U.S. Open is the only Grand Slam event to allow tie-breaks in the third set of women's matches and the fifth set of men's contests.

On the first point of this pivotal sequence, Capriati saw a good opening to get to the net, but Henin made her play a very demanding low backhand approach volley, and Capriati could not clear the net with that shot. Henin had the immediate mini-break at 1-0, and made the most of it. Capriati's normally trustworthy two-handed backhand let her down on the next two points as consecutive mistakes allowed a disciplined and concentrated Henin to stretch her lead to 3-0. Capriati closed the gap to 3-1 by clipping the line with a backhand crosscourt passing shot. But Henin made it 4-1 with a double mini-break when Capriati's flat forehand flew off her racket and travelled long.

Henin was distancing herself from Capriati. The Belgian reached into her wide arsenal and drove a backhand down the line, drawing a forehand crosscourt in the net from a beleaguered Capriati. Henin was up 5-1 and serving, but Capriati saw no reason to surrender. She came forward purposefully and produced a winning forehand volley, executing that shot superbly. Capriati then served at 2-5, knowing she had to secure the next two points. That did not happen. Henin approached the net behind a backhand crosscourt, followed with a solid backhand volley crosscourt, and Capriati lobbed long off the backhand. Henin was ahead 6-2, quadruple match point.

The Belgian gambled on the next point, going for a backhand top-spin winner up the line, netting that shot. With Capriati serving at 3-6, Henin tried for another backhand down the line winner that was not in the cards, hitting that one wide. Capriati had saved two match points, and was serving at 4-6, still in with a chance. She came in on Henin's forehand, but the Belgian was ready to counter attack with typical preparation and ball control. Henin went down the line and kept the ball low, forcing Capriati to net a backhand volley. Henin had recorded a singularly impressive triumph over a keynote rival, somehow eclipsing Capriati 4-6, 7-5, 7-6 (4) in three hours, gaining the win under adverse circumstances in front of a partisan crowd heavily favoring her opponent. Henin had overcome one Jennifer Capriati, the frenzied nighttime crowd, two bouts of cramps, and whatever demons were surely invading her mindset, to reach her first U.S. Open final. That was no mean feat.

For Capriati, the defeat was devastating in many ways, deeply wounding, even bewildering. She had been on the edge of winning the match so many times that to come out second best in such a scuffle was almost more than she could bear. A short time after the match, she said in her press conference, "You have to give her [Henin] credit for the way she was feeling, to stay out there and win. But I definitely feel I had the match in my hands, and it was my match to win."

A few moments later, she added, "When I came off the court, I just

Justine Henin

felt the whole world was coming down on me. My heart was being ripped out. It was a great match and I gave it all I had. She did, too."

Asked how long the defeat would linger in her mind, Capriati replied, "I really don't know. There's some losses that stay with you forever, the same as the wins."

Henin reflected, "In the first set I think it was a very high level of tennis. I was leading 4-1 but Jennifer was playing very well. I was playing unbelievable. And then the crowd gave her a lot of support. It wasn't easy for myself in the first set, but I stayed very calm...Then she was leading me 5-3 in the second set. That was the key of the tournament, 30-30, I come to the net. It's a big save I did at this point. In the third set I was cramping. I wasn't able to think at all because I thought the match was over many times. It was an amazing feeling [to win]. Unbelievable."

As astonishing as it was that Henin bested Capriati in the semifinals, it was even more remarkable that she returned to Ashe Stadium less than 24 hours later and took apart Clijsters 7-5, 6-1 in the championship match to capture her first U.S. Open. Henin's recuperative powers in pulling off that improbable feat were stupendous.

EPILOGUE

On October 20, 2003, Henin moved to No. 1 in the world by virtue of her two major title wins that season and a record of unparalleled consistency on the WTA Tour. Her success rate thereafter was befitting a woman of her high standards and wide range of ambitions. In 2004, Henin was hindered significantly by poor health, and her ranking dipped to No. 8 at the end of that year. Nonetheless, she did collect a third major singles title, upending Clijsters in a hard-fought, three-set final at the Australian Open in Melbourne. The following year, the Belgian collected a second French Open singles crown at Roland Garros, but her productivity in 2006 and 2007 was of a more sustained level of excellence. In those two years, she played seven of the eight Grand Slam events, reaching at least the final in all but one of them, adding three more major titles to her swiftly growing collection. She was the indisputable No. 1 player in the world both years, and her

2007 campaign was particularly gratifying for the Belgian, who won 10 of the 14 tournaments she played, including a fourth French Open in five years and her second U.S. Open.

Henin had won seven majors. She was driven by the most powerful of private engines to succeed as an enduring and far reaching champion. There seemed no good reason why she should not remain at or near the top of her sport for a very long while, moving up the historical ladder of tennis year by year, beating her opponents into submission with her penetrating ground strokes, unflappable demeanor, and supreme mental toughness. And yet, she commenced 2008 indifferently, losing badly to Maria Sharapova in the quarterfinals of the Australian Open. Her form did not improve much across the winter and on into the spring.

And then, in a startling development only two weeks before the 2008 French Open, Henin announced her retirement from the game. She was just a few weeks shy of her 26th birthday. She had won all of the Grand Slam events save Wimbledon, where she had twice reached the final. She explained that her competitive fires were no longer burning as brightly as was once the case, that her body could no longer take the incessant pounding. She walked away from the game she had played so brilliantly, leaving the tennis world distressed and perplexed by her decision. Why would she leave without exploring the complete boundaries of her game? No one really knew. Few could even begin to understand her choice. Everyone lamented her departure.

But Henin reconsidered after being away for nearly two years, and returned to tennis in 2010. Her comeback was celebrated everywhere she went, and the women's game benefitted enormously from her reemergence. Henin's tennis at the outset was inspired. In her first tournament back, she got to the final in Brisbane, Australia and had a match point before losing to Clijsters. On she moved to the Australian Open. Entering that event as a wildcard, Henin marched all the way to the final, pushing Serena Williams to three sets in the title round. It seemed certain that she would be in the thick of things at the majors all year long.

And yet, Henin lost some of the spark that had marked her initial return. She was surprisingly upended by the Australian Samantha Stosur in the fourth round of the French Open, and her 24-match winning streak at Roland Garros came to an end. At Wimbledon, she suffered a right elbow injury during a fourth-round loss to Clijsters. That injury proved to be much more serious than most observers originally thought it would be, and Henin did not play tennis again in 2010. Discouraged by the injury and what it would take to compete again on her own terms with her old consistency and physicality, she announced her retirement again not long after a disconcerting third-round loss to Svetlana Kuznetsova at the 2011 Australian Open. This time, the evidence was convincing that she was really leaving the game permanently, which seemed a shame to those who believed she deserved to play longer. She left with her seven majors and 43 WTA Tour singles titles overall, but the fact remained that she belonged among the all-time greats in tennis. Small of frame but large of heart, she gave the game everything she had and was sorely missed when she departed.

As for Capriati, the agonizing loss to Henin at the 2003 U.S. Open was one of her last appearances in a match of great consequence. She finished that season at No. 6 in the world, and played on in 2004 at a reasonably high level, finishing that year at No. 10, losing her last head-to-head contest with Henin at the season-ending WTA Tour Championships in Los Angeles. She did not win a tournament in 2004 but enjoyed a very good year at the majors, stopping Serena Williams to reach the semifinals at Roland Garros, reaching the quarterfinals of Wimbledon, and making it back to the semifinals of the U.S. Open for the fourth time with another triumph over Williams. For the third time in those four years, Capriati was beaten in a bruising penultimate round match. She faced Russia's Elena Dementieva on a ferociously windy day in Ashe Stadium and lost in a final-set tie-break again after serving for the match.

Capriati was still only 28, seemingly capable of at least two or three more impressive years, still a tennis player of the front rank. But, after finishing her 2004 season with a 6-0, 6-1 quarterfinal loss to Vera Zvonareva, Capriati—without realizing it at the time—had played the last tennis match of her professional career. Lingering problems with her shoulder requiring surgeries and other ailments prevented the Floridian from competing again. Perhaps she was slightly unfulfilled by losing out on more years of top flight tennis, but Jennifer Capriati could reflect upon a career that was immensely successful. She had her three major singles titles. She secured the No. 1 world ranking. She appeared in her first major semifinal in 1990 and her last in 2004, and that was proof that she was an enduring and significant champion.

Capriati played a good many great matches across an outstanding career, striking down the likes of Monica Seles, Gabriela Sabatini, Steffi Graf and Serena Williams. She was unbeaten in three major singles finals. She was a winner. But perhaps her greatest performance ever was the riveting skirmish she waged with Justine Henin at the U.S. Open in 2003. In the final analysis, that loss was ultimately as much a triumph of the spirit as any match Jennifer Capriati ever contested.

CHAPTER TWENTY-EIGHT

Serena Williams *vs.* Maria Sharapova

AUSTRALIAN OPEN, SEMIFINAL, JANUARY 27, 2005

The two most ferocious female competitors of their era clashed on the hard courts of Melbourne in a blockbuster of a battle that was suspenseful, hard fought and compelling. Both players produced tennis that boggled the minds and raised the spirits of an exhilarated audience.

PROLOGUE

The rise to immortality of Serena Williams as a tennis champion of the highest order was not only improbable, but probably should have been next to impossible. Along with her renowned and older sister Venus, Serena was taught the game by a father who had no background in tennis whatsoever. He learned to play by looking at instructional videos, watching the sport on television and reading tennis publications. Richard Williams and his wife Oracene Price went totally against the tide of conventional wisdom and raised their daughters to be champions entirely on their own terms. As former British Davis Cup player and captain John Lloyd once said, "Serena and Venus getting to the top at No. 1 and No. 2 is the greatest story in the history of the game. Here were these two kids coming from an underprivileged area in California with a father who never played and learned tennis from a book, and they made good on his prediction that they would be the two best players in the world one day. How can there be a bigger story than that? They don't get as much credit as they deserve. I would say that not only is this the greatest tennis story ever, but it is the most incredible story in all of sports."

Serena and Venus were raised near Los Angeles in Compton, California, a city with a substantial African American population. Richard Williams found some important voices in the tennis community to help him with the development of his daughters as players, including Paul Cohen, a leading teaching professional who had worked with John McEnroe and Harold Solomon. But Richard was the driving force behind Serena and Venus, a man with a show business flair who relished going against the establishment and proving that the path to success is up to those who pursue it.

Richard Williams made one major decision that critics wrongly believed would be his undoing. He took his daughters out of junior competition in 1991. Venus was approaching the age of eleven while Serena was not yet nine. Venus had already been the No. 1 ranked junior in Southern California in the 12-and-under division, winning sixty-three consecutive matches. Serena had taken utter control of the 10-and-under tournaments. They could have gone on at least for a few more years as unstoppable forces in the junior marketplace, striking fear in the hearts of their rivals, building confidence every step of the way. But Richard Williams had other ideas. He told esteemed tennis writer Joel Drucker the reason for his different and controversial point of view.

Richard Williams said, "I was sick of all of those competitive parents and kids and no one caring about their children's education. I wanted my girls to be smart first. That matters more than making tennis players."

Later, he would wisely send Venus and Serena during their formative years to Florida, where they trained under the expert eye of Rick Macci, one of the nation's leading teaching professionals and a strong-minded individual who understood sound mechanics as well as anyone. Macci had a staff of top quality players and professionals who would get on the court with the Williams sisters daily and hone their skills. The girls were extraordinary athletes who kept improving by leaps and bounds. Venus turned pro at fourteen in 1994. In 1997, at seventeen, Venus got to the final of the U.S. Open as an unseeded player ranked No. 66 in the world.

Venus Williams established herself initially as a front line player, but it was Serena who got on the board first at a major. She captured the U.S. Open singles title in 1999, upending Switzerland's guileful Martina Hingis, who had toppled Venus in the 1997 title match. Serena had turned pro in September of 1995, but did not break into the world's top 20 until 1998. Her 1999 triumph at Flushing Meadows was not startling, but still unexpected. She was seeded seventh, but knocked out the top two seeds (Lindsay Davenport and Hingis) to thoroughly earn her crown.

Venus Williams, however, was still better than her sister at that time. In 2000 and 2001, she won both Wimbledon and the U.S. Open, defeating Serena in the first "Prime Time" final at the Open. But Richard Williams had outspokenly proclaimed that Serena would be superior to Venus, and his prescience was remarkable. Serena burst into her own in 2002, sweeping the last three majors of that season in a blaze of glory. In 2003, she opened the year with a triumph at the Australian Open. That achievement of winning four majors in a row—a feat equaled only by Maureen Connolly, Margaret Court, Martina Navratilova and Steffi Graf—was dubbed a "Serena Slam," and Serena mastered Venus in all of those championship matches. After losing to Justine Henin in the semifinals of the 2003 French Open, Serena bounced back emphatically to win her second straight Wimbledon singles title, halting Venus in a three-set final.

But Serena Williams slipped to No. 3 in the world by the end of that year after needing a knee operation over the summer. She had been gone for eight months by the time she returned to competition in 2004, but was clearly not performing with the same overwhelming blend of power and panache. Seeking a third straight singles championship on the lawns of the All England Club, Serena was completely outplayed and even overpowered by a 17-year-old who was seeded at No. 13. Her name was Maria Sharapova. Her poise and professionalism for one so young was extraordinary to say the least. Sharapova confronted Williams with almost no inhibition and a deep core inner belief. The Russian prodigy triumphed 6-1, 6-4 to collect her first major championship, and Serena Williams never quite knew what had hit her.

Sharapova was born in the town of Nyagan in Siberia, Russia. When Maria was two, she moved with her mother Yelena and father Yuri to Sochi. Her father struck up a friendship of sorts with Aleksandr Kafelnikov, the father of Yevgeny Kafelnikov, a future world No.

1 and French and Australian Open victor. Aleksandr Kafelnikov presented Maria with her first racket when she was only four. Thereafter, Maria practiced regularly in a park with Yuri.

At the age of six, Maria attended a clinic in Moscow conducted by Martina Navratilova, who recommended the Nick Bollettieri Tennis Academy to the aspiring Russian. Yet the finances of that venture were not easy for Sharapova's family. They went to the U.S in 1994 when Maria was seven, although Yelena Sharapova had to wait another two years to join them due to visa restrictions. Yuri Sharapova took on the most menial of jobs—including dishwashing—to support his daughter's tennis education. In 1995, Maria signed with International Management Group, and they agreed to pay her tuition fee of $35,000 to attend the Bollettieri Academy. At nine, Maria Sharapova was able to join the Academy, and from there her career took off.

Sharapova—who would grow to be 6'2"—had predictably first rate junior results before turning professional on her fourteenth birthday in 2001. By the end of 2003, she was already ranked No. 32 in the world. That year, she made it to the fourth round of Wimbledon, where she lost narrowly to her countrywoman Svetlana Kuznetsova, a formidable player who would win the U.S. Open in 2004 and the French Open five years later. Sharapova was on her way, and more than aware of what she could do as the 2004 season unfolded. Like Serena Williams, she was an exceedingly big hitter of the tennis ball, a product of the modern game who blasted away relentlessly off both sides but never recklessly. Her ball striking was commanding and almost metronomic, and although her mobility was suspect in some ways, her heart was so large that she refused to concede a point unless a ball was well out of reach.

Sharapova concluded 2004 at No. 4 in the world. Her exploits immediately after her dramatic breakthrough at Wimbledon were not as impressive, but she did end the year on a very high note, capturing the WTA Tour Season-Ending Championships in Los Angeles, edging Serena Williams in the final of that prestigious event in three tumultuous sets. After a brief off-season, both Williams and Sharapova headed "Down Under" for the Australian Open, the first major of the new year. It was a time when both players looked to assert themselves.

Williams had not won a major since the 2003 Wimbledon, and wanted to re-establish her supremacy. Sharapova was eager to deliver on the promise she made so gloriously in 2004, to prove that she belonged among the elite, to show the world her authenticity.

THE MATCH

Sharapova arrived in Melbourne as the No. 4 seed. Her form as she approached this semifinal contest with Serena was not very convincing. In three of her five matches, Sharapova was made to go the full three sets by determined adversaries. Unheralded American Lindsay Lee-Waters took the first set from an apprehensive Sharapova in the second round before the Russian struck back with typical gumption to win 4-6, 6-0, 6-3. The Italian Silvia Farina Elia—the No. 15 seed— gave Sharapova a difficult time before Maria pulled away 4-6, 6-1, 6-2. In the quarterfinals, Kuznetsova took advantage of another slow start from Sharapova, winning the opening set. But with her usual spunk, Sharapova recouped again to prevail 4-6, 6-2, 6-2. The bad news was that Sharapova was struggling, but the good news was that she never panicked when she was down in those contests.

Williams had a much smoother run to her penultimate round collision with Sharapova. The American dropped only ten games in six sets over the first three rounds. In the round of 16, she had some problems with the always capable Nadia Petrova, dropping the middle set before carving out a three-set triumph. And so the match that everyone in the game's cognoscenti had anticipated so eagerly was all set. Williams had won their first head-to-head showdown at Miami the year before in straight sets, but had suffered those consecutive losses to the Russian at Wimbledon and Los Angeles. Given that background, this was a match that was nearly too close to call, and both players knew that even if they performed at peak efficiency, they could still lose. This one had blockbuster written all over it.

Serena's serve was universally regarded as the best in women's tennis. Her smooth service action, reliable toss, and excellent weight transfer were fully on display as she held at 30 in the opening game of the match. She connected with five of six first serves, and recovered from 15-30 down with three straight service winners. That was no simple task against Sharapova, who returned serve with a ferociousness not many players could match. Sharapova was a superb counter-attacker who was quick to read her opponent's intentions. She was particularly forceful and dynamic on second serve returns. You produced weak and short second deliveries at your own peril when Sharapova was on the other side of the net.

Sharapova's first serve was quite a weapon itself. She used her height and reach to get good velocity on her serve, and could win more than her share of free points with the pace and accuracy of that delivery. But she was pressed hard by Williams in the second game of the match. Sharapova was up 40-15, but Serena took the next two points with a blazing forehand return winner and a thundering inside-out forehand winner. Sharapova missed her first serve at deuce, but Williams went for an aggressive backhand return and missed it. Sharapova held on for 1-1 with a well-directed body serve to the forehand that Serena sent back into the net.

In the third game, Williams made only three of six first serves, and double faulted to put herself behind 15-40. Sharapova sensed her opportunity—and took it. At 30-40, she got great depth on her crosscourt forehand and forced Williams into an error. Sharapova had a quick service break, and made it count, holding at 30 for 3-1. The key point in that game was at 30-30 as Sharapova out-dueled Williams in a forehand to forehand exchange, drawing an error from her uncomfortable opponent. Serena's forehand—always the make or break stroke in her arsenal—was letting her down flagrantly at this juncture. Sharapova directed nearly every shot she could to that side.

Perhaps preoccupied with her less than stellar execution off the forehand, Williams was broken at love in the fifth game. Serena opened that game with a netted forehand off another deep shot from Sharapova, but then made a glaring unforced error off a backhand down-the-line return from Sharapova. Another fundamentally flawed forehand from Williams put her down 0-40 and Sharapova ran out that game confidently. Williams drew Sharapova in with a short slice, but the Russian handled it well, directing her backhand down the line to make Serena run. Williams was off the mark with a forehand passing shot. The American was two service breaks down at 1-4.

Sharapova had to fight through two deuces in the sixth game, but on her third game point she held on for 5-1 by unleashing a scorching inside-out forehand, making Serena miss a backhand under considerable duress. To the layman, the set appeared to be over. Sharapova had two breaks in hand, a 5-1 lead, and a depth of conviction that would be tough to remove. But Williams has never been fond of making concessions. She went right back to work, holding at love with an ace wide in the ad court to make it 5-2. Even if this set looked like a lost cause, Williams did not want to allow Sharapova the luxury of serving first in the second set. In any case, Sharapova was magnificent in serving the first set out at 5-2. She commenced that game with an ace out wide in the deuce court, rolled to 40-0, lost the next point, then aced Serena down the T at 40-15 to close it out in style. After so many poor starts over the first five rounds, Sharapova had taken the measure of her formidable rival with thirty minutes of top of the line tennis. Who could blame Williams if she was unduly worried?

Her anxiety was not helped at 30-30 in the opening game of the second set. Sharapova laced an exquisite backhand down the line, applying more pressure on the vulnerable Williams forehand. Serena missed her shot long and a eupeptic Sharapova yelled "Come On!" to urge herself on. At break point, however, Sharapova did not exploit her opportunity to go up an immediate break in the second set. She tried going behind Williams with an inside-out backhand, but missed that important shot wide. It was the right kind of a mistake—an aggressive miss if you will—but it was costly. Williams seized on that error, releasing a trademark backhand drive volley winner down the line as she approached the net. Serena followed with a service winner to the backhand, holding on gamely for 1-0.

Sharapova got on ably with the job at hand, holding at 15 for 1-1. Both players held relatively easily to bring the score to 2-2. Williams' forehand unprovoked mistakes were diminishing, her serve was picking up decidedly, and her intensity was ever apparent. At 2-2, Williams was ahead 40-30 when she double faulted, but she held on from there, ending that game by approaching on the Sharapova backhand, eliciting a backhand passing shot error from the harried Russian. Williams

Serena Williams

had plainly raised her standards in the second set, but she still had not broken Sharapova in the match. Sharapova kept that record intact. At 2-3, she had a 40-15 lead, but narrowly missed a running forehand crosscourt, and then Williams followed with a forehand winner.

This was dangerous territory for Sharapova. If she lost her serve here, Wiliams might well accelerate and find another gear in her game. But Sharapova held on as Williams unluckily drove a return that hung on the net cord but refused to go over. Then Williams came forward and bungled a forehand volley off a backhand pass up the line from Sharapova. It was 3-3. In the seventh game, Sharapova moved to break point, threw up a first-rate lob, but was stymied as Williams put away a spectacular inside-out overhead for a winner, showcasing her astounding athleticism in the process. After two deuces, Serena held for 4-3 with an ace down the T and a service winner out wide.

Trouble was brewing for Sharapova in the following game. She trailed 15-40. Losing one of the next two points would be a blow from which the Russian might not recover. Williams would be serving for the set with a strong wind of momentum behind her. Sharapova fully understood what was at stake. She struck a terrific forehand inside-out that Williams could not handle. At 30-40, Sharapova hit a nearly identical shot off the forehand that was called in. The Hawkeye replay system—which would become a fixture in the game at tournaments starting the following year and thus allow the players to challenge calls—was not yet used except for broadcast purposes. On the ESPN telecast, Hawkeye showed that Sharapova's shot was clearly out, but that was of no use to Williams, who was infuriated.

Williams should have been right where she wanted to be, leading 5-3, serving for the set, building up belief in herself. Instead, it was still 3-4, deuce on Sharapova's serve. Nonetheless, Williams won the next point to reach break point, but Sharapova wiped that chance away with another huge forehand as she went behind Williams. Serena tried in vain to make a sliced backhand, but did not succeed. Sharapova took the next point, and then at game point she made three stupendous gets, playing phenomenal defense before an exasperated Williams netted a backhand down the line. It was 4-4. It was getting late for Williams. Sharapova seemed both unbreakable and unshakable. In the ninth game, Williams fought valiantly through four deuces. She had four game points but could not fend off a resourceful Sharapova. After the last of those deuces, Sharapova caught Williams in her tracks with yet another sizzling forehand that was unanswerable. Now at break point, Sharapova scampered ably to her left to strike a backhand passing shot at an acute angle, making the ball dip sharply crosscourt. Not even a diving Williams could catch up with it.

Sharapova's persistence had rewarded her with a chance to serve for the match at 5-4. She had broken Williams for the third time in the match. She had still not lost her own serve even once. She was conducting herself with immense poise. As she sat at the changeover after that crucial ninth game, Sharapova had every reason to believe in herself and her chances. She was four points away from a second final-round appearance at a Grand Slam event. She had come through admirably on the grass against Serena at Wimbledon the previous year. Why would she not be encouraged about trying to serve out this Australian Open semifinal match in a few moments?

But that next game was—at least from Sharapova's standpoint—a debacle. She got her first serve in on the first point, but drove a two-hander down the line over the baseline. It was not the way to start off such a critical game. At 0-15, Sharapova was caught off guard by the pace of Serena's inside-out forehand return, and was pressured into an error. Sharapova made it back to 15-30 but then Williams drilled a forehand down the line and Sharapova gave her familiar loud grunt as she tried to reply with a two-handed backhand. She netted that shot to fall into a 15-40 predicament, then double faulted. Sharapova had lost her serve at 15, making only one of five first serves. Her serve had finally been broken, and it had largely been Sharapova's own fault. It was 5-5.

Williams was energized. She connected with four out of five first serves and held at 15 with an ace down the T. The complexion of the contest had been altered immeasurably. Trying to save the set at 5-6, Sharapova did manage to get five of six first serves in, but she had lost her competitive edge and her sense of inner calm. At 30-15, she pulled a two-handed backhand wide and then indecisively missed a backhand down the line. It was 30-40 and Sharapova was set point down. The tide had turned in the space of ten consequential minutes. Sharapova needed to strike back at Williams boldly now, or else she would find herself in a third set. The Russian was set up comfortably for an inside-out forehand. That shot had been one of her primary attributes throughout the battle. She went for it again, but misfortune struck at the worst possible time—the shot landed barely wide. Set to Williams 7-5.

And so Williams had recovered from close to the brink of defeat, making it back safely to one set all, staging one of her patented comebacks that had become almost second nature to the prideful American. Yet there was a lot of tennis left to be played. There was a rude awakening for Williams in the first game of the final set. Clearly, Sharapova was fighting back with renewed fury. In breaking Serena at 15 for a 1-0 third-set lead, Sharapova's depth and weight of shot was striking.

But Maria—despite the fact that she did not miss any first serves—was immediately broken at love by an unwavering Serena, who then held at love for 2-1. The American had swept eight points in a row. But Sharapova gathered herself admirably and held easily for 2-2. Both players held routinely to make it 3-3. And then Sharapova found some daylight just when she needed it in the seventh game.

Williams was ahead 3-3, 30-15 when her forehand let her down. Sharapova made Serena dig out a low ball and Williams was not up to the task. 30-30. The two great players then had a crackling sixteen-stroke exchange that Sharapova won with a forehand winner off a hanging net cord shot from Williams. Sharapova made a typically deep return of serve at break point, and Williams chose unwisely to run around her backhand for a forehand that just wasn't there. She drove that shot long. Sharapova had taken the critical seventh game to move ahead 4-3 in the final set, once more placing herself within striking distance of a victory she wanted with every fiber of her being.

The Russian was brimming with confidence, sensing that this was her moment. She poured in four straight first serves—including an ace for 30-0—and held at love for 5-3. Now Serena was serving to stay in the match, but she handled that situation remarkably well, holding at 15 with a service winner. A deeply concentrated Williams missed only one first serve in that game. She was not going to bow out tamely. Sharapova would have to beat her, because there was no better player in the modern world of women's tennis under extreme pressure than Serena Williams. That was when she so frequently seemed to bring out her best stuff, raised the level of her game significantly, imposed her will with a force and persuasion that was inimitable.

At 5-4 in that final set, Sharapova served for the match a second time, having collected herself across the third set with a dignity and determination that were rare in her trade. At 30-30, Sharapova used a big serve to set up a piercing backhand down the line. An apprehensive Williams netted a forehand. Sharapova at last had made it to match point. She crunched a forehand crosscourt, but drove it long. A service winner wide to the forehand in the deuce court gave Sharapova a second match point. Maria missed her first serve and hit the second delivery with slight caution. Williams refused to let her opponent get away with that, cracking an inside-out forehand return winner unhesitatingly. Another slice serve wide from Sharapova provoked a return error from Williams, and so the Russian had earned a third match point.

The crowd in Melbourne was exhilarated by both players, but they seemed more in Maria's corner at this moment, knowing how much she had endured over the last couple of hours. The two players traded some big punches in the next rally, a high quality, pulsating ten-stroke exchange. But when it mattered most, Williams again had the gumption to go for a daring shot. She stepped in and pounded an inside-out forehand winner behind Sharapova. At deuce again, Sharapova—understandably anxious after three match points had eluded her—pressed. She drove a forehand into the net off a high deep ball. Then the Russian followed with a running forehand down the line that travelled long.

Williams had done it again, breaking back forthrightly for 5-5. She had summoned the best and bravest tennis that she had to offer when a single mistake or misjudgment would have sent her off the court with a bruising defeat. Williams played immaculately in the next game, holding at love for 6-5. Her sense of urgency was apparent to one and all who watched this stirring contest. The audience braced itself for another onslaught from Williams in the following game. She had not come from so far back to fail. Yet Sharapova surged to 40-15 at 5-6 before Williams brought the score back to deuce. Sharapova demonstrated that her resilience and temerity were just about the equal of Serena's. She swung her slice serve wide to open up the court for another inside-out forehand. Williams ran that shot down, but her two-hander at full stretch found the net. The gutsy Sharapova closed out that game on the next point with a terrific first serve down the T that coaxed a backhand error from Williams. The pendulum was swinging again. 6-6.

Sharapova threw herself passionately into the next game, looking for another break, hoping for another chance to serve for the match. She reached 30-40, but the fearless Williams attacked her way out of that point, coming in on Sharapova's forehand, putting away an overhead off a short lob from her opponent. Sharapova earned a second

Maria Sharapova

break point, but Williams erased that one with a wide serve leading the way eventually to a forehand winner. Nevertheless, Sharapova reached break point for a third time as the Australian audience gasped with every tantalizing point down the stretch. Sharapova had control of the next rally, but the American's defense was astounding. Sharapova lost the initiative and drove a forehand long down the line.

Williams knew no bounds with her competitiveness. She jumped joyously after winning the next point with a forehand swing volley winner into the clear. Serena and Maria had been out there for two hours and thirty-three minutes of exhilarating yet taxing tennis, but Williams now looked fresher than she had for a long while. She went to the net again on the following point and Sharapova missed an arduous backhand passing shot. Williams had moved to 7-6 in this suspenseful final set. With Sharapova serving at 6-7, 15-30, the Russian played a backhand drive volley at a short angle crosscourt. Williams anticipated that shot with uncanny skill and her backhand pass down the line found a wide open space.

Having been behind for so much of this enthralling tennis match, Serena Williams was now up double match point with Sharapova serving at 15-40 in the fourteenth game of the final set. Serena drove her return deep, got a short ball from Sharapova, and then with one last swing of her racket on her two-handed side, Williams laced a clean winner with uncanny control. She had won one of the most captivating matches of her career, eclipsing Sharapova 2-6, 7-5, 8-6. Two years earlier on the same court, she had rallied spectacularly from 1-5 down in the final set against Kim Clijsters, taking that skirmish after saving three match points. But winning this one over Sharapova was an even higher achievement. Fittingly, Williams battled back again in the final, stopping Lindsay Davenport 2-6, 6-3, 6-0. She had commenced 2005 commendably. Serena had set herself apart in the history books with yet another distinction, establishing herself as the first woman in the "Open Era" to collect two major championships after being down match points during the course of the events. The last woman to realize that feat was Margaret Osborne duPont of the United States, who did so at the French Championships of 1942 and then again at the U.S. Championships six years later.

EPILOGUE

The rest of 2005 did not go so well for Williams after her brilliant start in Melbourne, when she captured a seventh career Grand Slam singles championship. For the first time in seven years, she did not finish among the top ten players in the world, falling to No. 11. After the Australian Open, Williams did not win another tournament all year long. Hampered by injuries, she played only twenty-eight matches across an abbreviated season. Both ankle and knee injuries kept Williams largely out of circulation. Still bothered by her ailments, Williams had a miserable 2006, competing in only four tournaments, missing two of the four majors, slipping to No. 95 in the world.

But at the outset of 2007, Williams restored her pride with one of her most astonishing career accomplishments. Ranked only No. 81 in the world, she secured her eighth major in Melbourne, knocking out six seeded players in the process, crushing Sharapova 6-1, 6-2 in the championship match. This was Williams at her most willful and obstinate, at the top of her intensity level, securing a major she really had no business winning. She was at least ten pounds overweight. She was drawing on her reservoir of desire, her fighting spirit and her experience as the best big match player of her era, knowing she needed all of that to compensate for her lack of fitness. Before her brilliant performance against Sharapova in the final, she lived dangerously. Petrova was up 6-1, 5-3 in the third round over Williams before the American escaped. Israel's Shahar Peer pushed Serena to 8-6 in the third set in the quarters. And yet, she kept inventing ways to win on days she should have lost.

Serena moved back to No. 7 in the world at the end of 2007 and that set the stage for a first rate year in 2008. She climbed back to No. 2 in the world, won four tournaments including her third U.S. Open, and was impressive across the board. Her biggest disappointment was undoubtedly a final-round loss to "Big Sister" Venus at Wimbledon. But she avenged that defeat in the Wimbledon final of 2009, knocking out Venus in the championship match. She also captured her fourth Australian Open that season. She was demonstrating increasingly how much the majors meant to her and how deeply she cared about her place in history.

Over the first half of 2010, Williams was setting the pace at the majors again, taking her fifth Australian Open, and coming through at Wimbledon for her fourth crown on the revered Centre Court. In the semifinals of that event at the All England Club, she saved a match point against the elegant Russian Elena Dementieva, then crushed Vera Zvonareva of Russia 6-3, 6-2 in the final. For the third time in her career, Williams had battled back from at least one match point down in the fortnight to pull off a major title. That was stupendous. Meanwhile, she moved ahead of Billie Jean King into sixth place on the all-time leader list for the women at the Grand Slam events, collecting a thirteenth crown. Only Margaret Court (24), Steffi Graf (22) Helen Wills Moody (19), Martina Navratilova and Chris Evert (18) had won more singles majors, and Williams seemed determined to close in on the leaders.

But she could not compete again in 2010 after Wimbledon after suffering a bizarre injury to her right foot. Hoping to rejoin the WTA Tour at the start of 2011, she was hit even harder by a pulmonary embolism. Not until Eastbourne in 2011 was Williams able to reappear on the WTA Tour. She lost in the third round at Wimbledon, but over the summer raised her game considerably, winning two tournaments on her way to the U.S. Open, then sweeping through the draw in New York into the final without losing a set. But she was beaten in a major upset by Samantha Stosur in straight sets after an angry outburst during the match directed at the umpire Eva Asderaki for a ruling against Serena early in the second set. She raged a few times at Asderaki with disturbing venom.

Serena's conduct seemed to be a flagrant attempt to manipulate the crowd and distract her opponent on a day when nothing was going her way. This was all the more regrettable because it called to mind Serena's last appearance at the Open two years earlier, when she hurled insults and anger at a lineswoman. In that instance, Williams was in a semifinal contest with Clijsters. The Belgian had won the first set 6-4. Serena was serving at 5-6, 15-30 in the second set. She was called for a second serve foot-fault, and then raged at the lineswoman, looking as menacing as she ever has, losing all reason.

To be sure, it was the worst possible time to be called for a foot fault, because it put her down 15-40, double match point. Her body language was very threatening and Williams was obscene as she tried to intimidate the official. Fittingly, Williams was assessed a point penalty for her unacceptable behavior, which cost her the match. Clijsters had won 6-4, 7-5. The saddest part of both the 2009 and 2001 Serena incidents at the U.S. Open was her refusal to offer a gracious apology for her actions.

Be that as it may, it was apparent—despite the shocking loss to Stosur in the U.S. Open final which constituted only her fourth defeat in seventeen major singles finals—that Serena Williams was on her way back to the top of the game, and ready to make her presence known on the premier stages of the sport many times in the next couple of years. Williams turned 30 at the end of September in 2011, but because she had taken so many extended breaks from the sport, she seemed fully capable of remaining in the forefront of the game for at least three or four more years. Her climb through history was apparently not over.

Sharapova, meanwhile, was one of the most enduringly popular female athletes in the world. After her semifinal loss in that landmark match with Williams at the 2005 Australian Open, Maria had a solid year with a quarterfinal appearance at Roland Garros followed by semifinal showings at Wimbledon and the U.S. Open. That was a sign of good things to come. In 2006, she was ranked second in the world and was at her ruthless best in taking apart Justine Henin in the U.S. Open final to capture a second career major title. That year, she also got to the semifinals of the Australian Open and Wimbledon as well.

In 2007, Maria made it back to the Australian Open final where, of course, Williams dismantled her with a career signature performance. And yet, the following year, Sharapova shined brightly in Melbourne. She came through on the hard courts there to take a third career major title. She did not lose a set in the fortnight, crushing Henin in the quarters, the crafty Jelena Jankovic in the semifinals and the charismatic Ana Ivanovic in the final. Sharapova's serve was the cornerstone of her game, carrying her to the title unfailingly. But she eventually needed shoulder surgery, which contributed largely to her woes in 2009 and 2010, when she never made it past the quarterfinals at a major.

And yet, Sharapova, despite long absences to deal with ongoing shoulder problems, despite setbacks that would have thwarted lesser player many times over, despite all of the difficulties she encountered, resolutely plodded on, and in 2011 had a terrific season in many ways. She won the Italian Open on the red clay in Rome, taking that estimable crown on her worst surface over Stosur. She got to the semifinals of the French Open and appeared in her first Wimbledon final since her victory over Williams seven years earlier. Sharapova lost to the gifted left-handed shotmaker Petra Kvitova, but her perseverance at twenty-four was remarkable.

Maria Sharapova is much like Serena Williams in many ways. They are the two toughest and finest competitors in the modern era of the women's game. They know no bounds in their pursuit of their highest goals. They leave no stone unturned once they step on a tennis court. A shining moment for both competitors was surely their best ever clash against each other at the Australian Open of 2005. At that time, it seemed as if Sharapova could impose not only her will but her game on Williams, stay with the American and even outperform Serena from the baseline, and keep her adversary at bay with the quality of her serving. Yet over time, Williams figured out what she needed to do against Sharapova, and more and more the American exploited her opponent's relative lack of foot speed and athleticism. Moreover, she refused to allow the Russian to dictate from the back of the court.

By the end of 2011, Williams held a commanding 7-2 lead in her career series with Sharapova, having won six head-to-head contests in a row over the Russian. In that span, Williams conceded only one set. Perhaps the matchup simply worked in the American's favor. Somehow Williams seemed to always elevate her game when she took on Sharapova across the years. The fact remains that Sharapova approaches every match with a champion's mentality, looking for reasons to win, refusing to allow herself excuses to lose. Say the same for Serena Williams. No matter what happens with either Williams or Sharapova from here on in, this much is certain—they are headed for the International Tennis Hall of Fame, and when they are inducted, the fans in Newport, Rhode Island will shower them with the kind of enthusiasm and respect reserved only for players who have changed the face of the sport with both their playing styles and personalities.

CHAPTER TWENTY-NINE

Roger Federer *vs.* Rafael Nadal
WIMBLEDON, FINAL, JULY 6, 2008

The Swiss maestro and a dynamo from Spain produced a Centre Court masterpiece that will live forever in the hearts and minds of all who witnessed an astonishing spectacle.

PROLOGUE

They came upon us from different parts of the world, developed contrasting styles of play and became immensely popular individuals because they comported themselves so commendably. Spain's Rafael Nadal was left-handed and an indefatigable workhorse who operated predominantly from the backcourt with a brand of heavy topspin that was revolutionary in its impact on the game. Switzerland's Roger Federer was a classic stylist, elegant to his core, an artist who turned the tennis court into a private canvas to showcase his shot-making sparkle and versatility. Nadal was an incomparable warrior, a ferocious competitor who struck fear into the hearts of his rivals with his unbridled intensity.

Federer, of course, was cut from another cloth. His competitive appetite was every bit as large as Nadal's and his obsession with being the best as crucial in his list of objectives as Nadal's need to surpass everyone else. Yet Federer went about his business with misleadingly casual ease. He practically had no pulse and always seemed unruffled no matter what the situation. Even in the longest and most strenuous contests, through hard-fought matches played across long afternoons over vast stretches of time, Federer remained inscrutable, seldom if ever revealing his innermost emotions. Nadal was demonstrative while Federer was more understated and mellow. Nadal's mannerisms reflected the life and death nature of his intense battles on the court. He wore many of his emotions on his sleeve, particularly when he was closing in on victory. Federer's demeanor was utterly calm. He presented himself as the champion of serenity, the master of understatement, and an individual who knew how good he was and saw no need to flaunt it.

Born in Basel, Switzerland, Federer grew up in the suburbs of that city. His father, Robert, was Swiss, but his mother, Lynette, came from South Africa. Robert Federer worked for a chemical company in his homeland, but decided to emigrate to South Africa when he was 24 to work there for his company—Ciba. Lynette was a secretary at Ciba, which had offices located in Kempton Park, an extended suburb of Johannesburg. There she met Robert Federer and a courtship began.

Robert Federer had become interested in tennis and he took Lynette to a club in Johannesburg to get her acquainted with the sport. In Switzerland, he had been a regionally-ranked player. Lynette was quickly enamored with the game and became a member of the Swiss Inter-Club team after she and her husband moved back to that country in 1973 and got married. She went on to teach juniors at her club, worked at the ATP World Tour event in the credentials office at Basel, and took to the sport with considerable passion.

Out of that environment, it was not surprising that their son Roger would start playing tennis as a kid. Lynette would bring him out to the courts when he was an infant of one-and-a-half to expose him to her favorite sport, and when he was three-and-a-half Roger hit a tennis ball for the first time. At four, Roger Federer's affinity for tennis was strikingly apparent. At that age, he could hit twenty to thirty balls in a row, displaying the almost ineffable ball control that would define his play later on.

Roger liked playing other sports including skiing, wrestling, skate boarding and swimming. But his feelings about tennis went deeper and he devoted himself increasingly to that endeavor. When he was eleven in 1992, he captured his first Swiss National title—the 12-and-under Indoor Championships. Six months later, he secured the Swiss National Outdoor 12-and-under crown. He had still been interested in soccer up until that time but gave it up to put more time into his tennis. Federer would attend the Swiss National Tennis Center along with only seven other boys and four girls.

369

He kept on winning, taking more national titles in the Swiss 16-and-under division in 1996; the following year he was the victor at the Swiss National Indoors and National Outdoor Championships in the 18-and-under division. Yet even when he was still fifteen, Federer was branching out into some men's events and was already ranked No. 86 in Switzerland among the men.

Through his junior years, Federer was a high strung competitor, throwing more than his share of temper tantrums and tossing rackets. Even at seventeen, and perhaps slightly beyond, he could be a volatile character on the court, a fact that would be almost incomprehensible to those who have watched him compete with such equanimity across almost his entire pro career. What was difficult for Federer in coming to terms with his talent and temperament was that he could not tolerate losing. At fifteen, he told René Stauffer—the author of *Roger Federer: Quest for Perfection*, "I know that I can't always complain and shout because that hurts me and makes me play worse. I hardly forgive myself on any mistakes although I know they are normal." Federer paused, and then told Stauffer almost wistfully, "One should just be able to play a perfect game."

Gradually, Federer grew into his composure, and the consistency of his successes was one cure for his temper. Federer closed out his junior career in 1998, winning the Wimbledon junior title, reaching the final of the U.S. Open juniors, and taking the prestigious Orange Bowl in the 18-and-under category. At the end of that year, he garnered the highly coveted No. 1 ITF world junior ranking. He turned professional the same year but only played five matches. The next year he played his first two career majors, losing in the opening round of the French Open (to 1997-98 US Open champion Patrick Rafter) and falling in the first round of Wimbledon as well.

But Federer still rose to No. 64 in the world at the end of that 1999 campaign. In 2000, he advanced to No. 29. He was improving by leaps and bounds. From his early days as a junior, Federer had loved experimenting with different shots and his gift for making astonishing winners was always evident. In 2001, he made headlines around the world when he toppled Pete Sampras on the Centre Court of Wimbledon in the fourth round, ending the American's 31-match winning streak at the world's premier event with a gritty five-set victory. Federer attacked much more then than he would in subsequent years, serving-and-volleying regularly on his first delivery, coming in often on his second. Federer was still a work in progress, but he was moving up the ladder spectacularly, concluding that year at No. 13 in the world.

Federer had an impressive 2002 season, rising to No. 6 in the world. He won two tournaments and performed admirably across the board, although he fell short of his goals at the majors, never advancing beyond the fourth round at a Grand Slam event that season.

Everything changed dramatically in 2003. That year, he won his first major title at Wimbledon, upending Andy Roddick with sheer brilliance in the semifinals and stopping the big serving Mark Philippoussis in the final. Federer finished that year at No. 2 in the world behind Roddick. But Federer's sense of self was now growing steadily and irreversibly. The redoubtable Federer clearly believed that his time had come to take over the game comprehensively and he was going to make the most of it.

From 2004 to 2007, he celebrated the finest four-year sequence in the modern history of the men's game. In that golden stretch, he was virtually untouchable, winning eleven of the sixteen majors. In three of those four years—all but 2005—he garnered three of the four major championships, losing only at Roland Garros on the clay. Federer's overall match record during that period was impossibly good—he was 315-24 for a winning percentage of .929. Moreover, he was victorious in 42 of 64 tournaments that he played. Yet even Federer could not quite keep up with Federer. In the first three of those years—2004-2006—he was 247-15 for a winning percentage of .943. Only in 2007 did the soaring Swiss maestro seem to come down to earth, capturing only eight of sixteen tournaments and 68 of 77 matches. But the fact remained that he collected all but one of the majors and added the season-ending ATP World Tour Championship title to his triumph column.

There was a good reason why Federer's hold on the sport loosened to a degree in 2007. At long last, he was faced with sterner opposition, the kind he needed to define himself more fully, the type that the public needed to better understand who he was and how he responded to pressure. The previous three years he had exploited his mastery over a field that was surprisingly weak in the upper tier. The combination of his own genius and the vulnerability of so many other leading players had brought about Federer's utter dominance. But one man had been a serious problem for Federer from the very beginning when they first clashed in 2004. He was a left-hander with a heart that could only belong to a champion. He respected Federer immensely but was not afraid of him. Above all else, he believed in himself. His name, of course, was Rafael Nadal.

Nadal was born in Manacor, a small town of about 40,000 located on the edge of Mallorca. Nadal started playing tennis at age four. His family lived in an apartment that was located opposite the town tennis club. From his home he would walk to the red clay courts and train with his Uncle Toni Nadal, who was known as the "resident coach." Nadal was an impassioned soccer player as well. In fact, like Federer, he loved all sports that involved a ball. As Nadal recounts in his autobiography, *Rafa*, published in 2011, his Uncle Toni remembers that Nadal initially (but not for long) found tennis boring.

In the popular lore, it has long been reported that Uncle Toni strong-armed his nephew into playing tennis left-handed. Yet Rafael Nadal refutes that notion in *Rafa*. "I've seen reports in the media that Toni forced me to play left-handed and that he did this because it would make me harder to play against. Well, it's not true. It's a story the newspapers have made up. The truth is I began playing when I was very small, and because I wasn't strong enough to hit the ball over the net, I'd hold the racket with two hands, on the forehand as well as the backhand. Then one day my uncle said, 'There are no professional players who play with two hands [off both sides] and we're not going to be the first ones, so you've got to change.' So I did, and what came naturally to me was to play left-handed. Why, I can't tell. Because I write with my right hand and when I play basketball or golf—or darts—I play right-handed too. But in football [soccer] I play with my left; my left foot is much stronger than my right.... This was definitely not something that Toni, in a moment of genius, thought up."

In any event, Rafael Nadal—nourished by Uncle Toni (a modestly successful, low-level pro tennis player)—developed a healthy and insatiable appetite for tennis. His parents were instrumental as well in the shaping of Rafa as a boy, with his transition into adulthood, in the molding of his character. Sebastian Nadal, his father, was a successful businessman who today is involved in the glass business. He insisted when Rafael was young and still playing on a soccer team that his son always congratulate the competitors on the other squad after a defeat. He wanted Rafael to learn how to handle losses with dignity.

Yet Rafa despised the taste of losing. It didn't matter whether it was tennis or soccer, cards or a casual game in his garage—he had trouble digesting any kind of defeat. But always there were relatives to help him deal with both ends of the competitive spectrum. Another uncle, Miguel Angel, was a championship soccer player in his nation, a revered sporting figure. His mother, meanwhile, provided a softer yet invaluable touch. Ana Maria Parera was an unfailingly supportive parent. She had grown up in a family immersed in the furniture business. Her guidance in instilling strong values in Rafael was far reaching and critical.

When Rafa was nearing his thirteenth birthday, he still played soccer regularly—or football as they called it in Spain. He had once dreamed of playing that game for a living. But he knew he had to decide which one he would seriously pursue. Nadal chose tennis and his instincts were excellent. In 1997, he became Spain's national 12-and-under tennis champion. Three years later, in 2000, he was crowned national 14-and-under champion. And from that juncture, shaped largely by his task-master Uncle Toni, driven by his own thirst for success on the highest level, he took off on a momentous journey.

He officially turned professional in 2001 when he was only fifteen, and won his first ATP World Tour match in his hometown of Mallorca, defeating veteran Ramon Delgado. By the end of 2003, at seventeen, Nadal stood almost unnoticed among the world's top 50. He played on the victorious Spanish Davis Cup team in 2004, toppling Andy Roddick in four sets, becoming the youngest player ever to take a singles match for a victorious nation in a Davis Cup Final. That was also the year he first collided with Federer. In an early-round match at the prestigious Masters 1000 event in Miami, Nadal upended Federer 6-3, 6-3.

It was in 2005 that Nadal surged into much greater prominence. He secured eleven titles on the ATP World Tour that season, including his first French Open title in his Roland Garros debut. In the penultimate round, in a contest that started late in the afternoon and stretched into a damp evening, Nadal cut down Federer in four sets, and then went on to oust Mariano Puerta of Argentina in the championship match, taking the title in another four-set showdown. Nadal had won 24 matches in a row on clay, the surface that most suited his heavy topspin artillery.

Yet Nadal was still not ready to compete at the same level on other surfaces. That would come in time. Nevertheless, Nadal finished 2005 at No. 2 in the world, stationed right behind Federer. The following year, the Spaniard made impressive strides across the board, and not only on the dirt. He surprised Federer to win the hard court title in Dubai. He caused Federer a lion's share of pain on the clay court circuit, stopping the Swiss in the finals of Monte Carlo and then Rome, taking the latter contest after saving two match points in a classic five-set showdown that went to 7-6 in the fifth set. At Roland Garros, Federer was gunning for a fourth consecutive major title, and his first on the red clay of Paris, but Nadal halted him once more in a come-from-behind four-set win in the final.

At Wimbledon, no one was surprised when the three-time defending champion Federer arrived safely again for the final, but Nadal's emergence as a genuine threat on the grass at the All England Club was unexpected. The Spaniard was two points from losing to the dangerous fast court player Robert Kendrick of the U.S. in the second round, but thereafter he found his range and performed commandingly. He would lose in a four-set final to Federer, but the Spaniard had recorded a triumph of sorts just by advancing to the championship match.

Nadal remained at No. 2 in the world. In 2007, he secured a third French Open title in a row with another four-set triumph over Federer in the final, and he won 70 of 85 matches that season. Most importantly, he nearly defeated Federer in the Wimbledon final. This time around—in stark contrast to the 2006 meeting—Nadal looked entirely comfortable confronting the Swiss on the grass. He played the match largely on his own terms and the standard of play on both sides of the net was outstanding. They went to a fifth set. Twice in the early stages of that set, Nadal had 15-40 on Federer's serve, but he could not exploit his chances. Federer pulled away to win 6-2 in the final set, but in many ways the die had been cast. Nadal had irrefutably demonstrated he could threaten Federer on any surface.

When it was over, a despondent Nadal, overwhelmed by the most emotionally jarring setback of his career, broke down weeping in the locker room, reflecting that he might have lost his one and only chance to win the tournament he wanted more than any other. But Uncle Toni brought both clarity and reason to his distraught nephew, making the young man understand that he would have his share of chances to be the victor on the lawns of the All England Club. Uncle Toni's forthright candor was just what Nadal needed to hear at a time of despair.

As 2008 commenced, neither Nadal nor Federer took the first major of the new season. Serbian Novak Djokovic—a gifted, somewhat controversial, always compelling character from Serbia—delivered strongly on the promises he had made the previous year, when he had toppled both the Spaniard and the Swiss to win in Montreal, and then reached his first U.S. Open final before losing to Federer. On that occasion, Djokovic had wasted five set points in the first set and two more in the second, bowing in straight sets to the Swiss. But four and a half months later, Djokovic knocked out Federer in a straight-set semifinal and then got the title in Melbourne by removing the dynamically athletic Frenchman Jo-Wilfried Tsonga, who had produced an almost unconscious gem to oust Nadal in a brilliantly crafted straight-set semifinal.

Nadal came alive during the clay court season, sweeping through the fields in Monte Carlo, Barcelona and Hamburg, ousting Federer in two of those three finals. At Roland Garros, the Spaniard was irresistibly good, claiming his fourth French Open in a row, crushing Federer 6-1, 6-3, 6-0 in the final. Federer had struggled through the entire first half of the year, winning only one minor title, taking the clay court crown in Estoril before his pasting at the hands of Nadal. But then the Swiss restored some of his pride and a measure of his confidence by winning the grass court event in Halle.

Federer was determined to re-establish his supremacy at Wimbledon, where he had not lost a match since 2002. Nadal was equally committed to winning his first championship on the grass, especially after the near miss of 2007. There was a growing feeling among most authorities that Federer and Nadal would meet for the third year in a row in the Wimbledon final, replicating their feat of confronting each other in the last three French Open title round duels. Federer, of course, had lost all three skirmishes in Paris. Nadal was determined to avoid that fate in Great Britain.

THE MATCH

Federer sought to peak each and every year for Wimbledon. The grass courts suited his brand of play to the hilt. To be sure, he had altered his playing style decidedly from his early years at the shrine of tennis. He hardly ever served-and-volleyed on the lawns now, choosing to use his highly underrated first serve—surely the most accurate, smoothly delivered and deceptive in the men's game—to set up his devastatingly effective and potent forehand, long known as the finest in tennis. But Federer's incomparable footwork, court positioning, inclination to go forward at the propitious moments, and capacity to control his surroundings, made him the era's towering grass court player.

He had not lost on the lawns since 2002 and his five Wimbledon singles titles in a row had not been achieved by accident. Federer felt virtually unbeatable whenever he walked through the gates at the All England Club and set up his Centre Court office there for a fortnight every single year. Despite his slump in 2008, he fully expected to recover his winning ways with another triumph in Great Britain. He swept into the final without the loss of a set, ousting—among others—old rival and 2002 titlist Lleyton Hewitt, and the last man to beat him there, Mario Ancic. In the semifinals, Federer turned in a distinguished performance to defeat Marat Safin, a two-time Grand Slam tournament winner who had saved a match point three years earlier on his way to a five-set triumph over Federer in the Australian Open semifinals. In plain and simple terms, Federer was back in form, confident and eager to break Bjorn Borg's modern men's record by making it six in a row at the world's most highly coveted event.

Nadal, however, was playing remarkably good tennis as well. He dropped only one set in his six matches, surviving a tense contest with the talented Latvian Ernests Gulbis, a free-wheeling shot maker with immense power, good touch on the drop shot and a big serve. Gulbis stretched Nadal far and wide but the Spaniard was the decidedly better match player, coming through in four tough sets. Otherwise, Nadal was almost entirely comfortable and sharp over the fortnight, particularly when he took apart British No. 1 Andy Murray in a straight-set quarterfinal demolition. He then accounted for the German Rainer Schuettler in a straight-set semifinal. Although Nadal was well below the upper level of his game in that contest, he still came into the final in the right frame of mind, ready to make amends for his losses to Federer on the Centre Court the last two years, excited as always about the opportunity to test wills and skills with Federer, with whom he was making history of a high order every time they stepped on a court. This was their eighteenth meeting and Nadal had an 11-6 lead in their series.

The players had been expected to walk out on court around 2 p.m. for their eagerly awaited final, but the British rains had intervened, and they did not make their entrance until 2:23, with the warm-up—or " knock up" at it was called in Great Britain—starting at 2:29. The sky remained dark and cloudy, although the sun would emerge faintly and periodically. It was an essentially cool afternoon, but Nadal and Federer were such popular and luminous sporting figures that they lit up the day just by showing up. The Centre Court crowd greeted them both with full-blooded applause and genuine affection. They soon would be ready to get on with the proceedings, with the tension in the air almost palpable. The sense of anticipation among observers was almost off the charts and sports fans in every corner of the globe paid more than casual attention to tennis in the sport's premier theater. There is no tournament like Wimbledon—it is the Kentucky Derby of tennis—and the annual showdown between Federer and Nadal sweepingly captured the imagination of the universal public.

When the battle commenced, shortly past 2:36, the first point was a dandy. The players traded baseline punches for fourteen magnificent strokes. At the end of that exchange, Federer elected to cast aside his topspin backhand and went instead to his slice. On the grass, the sliced backhand is always a good option because the ball hugs the court and stays so low. But Nadal handles that tactic remarkably well. Despite his extreme western grip, he manages to get beneath the ball and still sweeps over the top of it with his inimitable brand of topspin. In this case, he flattened out the stroke beautifully, driving his shot immaculately down the line for an outright winner. What a beginning! Yet Federer dismissed that moment in his mind briskly. He took the next four points, holding at 15 with an ace down the T.

Both men knew that the first serve of Federer would be one of the keys to the outcome of the contest. Nadal had to find a way to neutralize his adversary and make some telling returns, send the ball back deep, hold his ground on the returns. But the Spaniard also needed to set a certain tone on his serve as well. He would, as always, direct most of his service traffic to his rival's backhand. That strategy might be predictable, but Nadal is a percentage player who sticks with what works until his opponent forces him to alter his thinking. Nadal held at 30 for 1-1, connecting with four out of six first serves. Federer missed two backhand returns and Nadal took another point by unleashing a patented forehand crosscourt that elicited a miss-hit topspin backhand wide from an unsettled Federer. That point symbolized Federer's fundamental problem whenever he played Nadal. The Spaniard's greatest strength—the crosscourt topspin forehand hit with utter conviction—played into the weakness of Federer on the Swiss maestro's backhand side. Nadal's propensity to get that shot above Federer's shoulders on the backhand—even on the grass—was a pattern that Federer would be hard pressed to answer.

In the third game of the match, Federer's estimable serve let him down tremendously. He made only one of six first serves. At 30-30, Nadal rolled his forehand to the backhand of his opponent and unsurprisingly drew the error. The Spaniard had earned the first break point of the match and he was unwilling to squander it. Federer missed his first serve and spun the second to Nadal's backhand. Nadal sent his return deep down the middle. Federer was backed up by that return and made to feel uncomfortable. He nearly swung and missed, perhaps thrown off stride by an irregular bounce. The depth and high trajectory of Nadal's shot was too much for Federer. Nadal had the quick, early break, moving swiftly to 2-1. He then raced to 40-0 on his own serve, but Federer strung together four terrific points in a row. Included in that sequence were a winning backhand half volley flicked down the line by the Swiss, a forehand volley winner exceedingly well produced, and some marvelous baseline probing from the Swiss. He now had a break point to get back to 2-2, but Nadal met that moment with strong-minded purpose. He flattened out a backhand crosscourt and Federer was caught off guard by the accelerated pace. The Swiss missed a forehand. Nadal needed two more game points, but eventually held on for 3-1 as Federer erred on another topspin backhand return.

Federer surely was disconcerted about his missed chance, but he pressed on without any hesitation. At 1-3, he held at love, throwing in four first serves in a row, closing that game with an ace out wide in the ad court. But Nadal retaliated in his own fashion, missing only one first serve in the next game, holding commandingly at 15 for 4-2. Three times in that sixth game, Federer missed off the backhand in different ways, and once Nadal passed his adversary impeccably with a cross-court backhand. The two competitors were now fully engaged in a quest to win the critical opening set. Federer may have been down a break, but he was playing some spectacular tennis. In the seventh game, he took a 40-15 lead with a stellar serve-and-volley point. He served wide to Nadal's backhand in the deuce court and the return came back low. Federer bent his knees impeccably and his winning forehand first volley was outstanding.

Back to 3-4 was Federer, but Nadal—serving with new balls—was not ceding any ground. He poured in every first serve in the eighth game. At 40-15, Nadal pushed his opponent wide with an inside-out forehand and the Swiss drove a forehand down the line long. Nadal was up 5-3. Yet Federer remained focused. In the ninth game, he enjoyed his finest serving of the set, holding at love with three service winners and an ace. He did not miss a first serve in that game. Federer was going to make Nadal work hard. He knew how arduous his task would be if he fell behind a set against the sport's premier front runner.

Nadal served for that first set at 5-4 and Federer came at him with tenacity, temerity and the will of a champion. Federer reached 15-30 by going wisely on the attack, approaching deep, knifing away a backhand volley winner. Nadal took the next two points for 40-30, earning his first set point. But Federer took control, driving his famed inside-out forehand with trademark pace and accuracy. He had Nadal on the run. The Spaniard's forehand clipped the net cord and hung in the air for an instant, allowing Federer the extra time to roll a backhand winner crosscourt. Federer advanced to break point with another scintillating forehand volley winner set up by a softly hit approach that allowed the Swiss to close in tight on the net. Federer knew full well he had to keep moving forward whenever he could. He had to make Nadal pass him now, with the set on the line.

One point away from squaring the set at 5-5, Federer did indeed approach the net, coming in on Nadal's backhand. Nadal drilled his two-hander down the line, making Federer play a defensive backhand volley down the middle. Nadal had time to step around and blast a forehand as hard as he could. Federer was slightly off balance. Nadal's shot had too much pace and a burdensome spin. Federer's backhand volley went long. Nadal followed with an ace down the T in the deuce court, his first of the match. That set up a second set point for the Spaniard, but Federer released a dazzling inside-out forehand. Nadal could only try to scrape the ball back with underspin from an open stance. Nothing doing. It was deuce for the third time. Federer was finding his range completely off the forehand. He laced another inside-out forehand to the Nadal forehand to coax an error.

For the second time, Federer stood at break point in his intensified effort to make it back to 5-5 and keep himself in a set he wanted badly. But at that essential moment, Federer lost faith in himself. He tamely chipped a backhand return off a second serve into the net. He had let Nadal off the hook with that moment of glaring timidity. Federer then lost control of a backhand down the line with the wind at his back. Nadal had advanced to set point for the third time. He quickly sealed the set this time as Federer netted a routine topspin backhand. Set to Nadal 6-4. He had made good on twelve of fourteen first serves, but still had to fight through a four deuce game before he closed it out.

Yet Nadal had been the mentally tougher player, seizing his chances, holding his nerve when it mattered. Federer had played hard and brilliantly, but it was Nadal who deservedly held the upper hand with his greater consistency.

At the start of the second set, however, Federer was back on song, holding at love for 1-0, serving another ace in that game. The Swiss proceeded to break Nadal for the first time in the match to make it 2-0. The Spaniard had recovered from 0-30 to 30-30, but Federer then went to break point with a forehand down the line approach hit with the kind of depth that not even Nadal could handle. The Spaniard raced to his left but was off the mark with a forehand pass up the line. Break point for Federer. A shift in momentum was at hand. Here was a chance for the five-time defending champion to alter the course of the match. At break point down, Nadal sent his forehand approach down the line, perhaps a tactical misjudgment. Federer moved gracefully to his right and whipped a forehand pass crosscourt. Nadal had no chance. It was a winner. Federer was euphoric, breaking into a fist pump, exhilarated about his prospects.

Buoyed by his breakthrough in the previous game, Federer held at 30 for 3-0. He opened that game with an ace out wide to the Nadal backhand in the deuce court and played a solid and thoughtful game. After Nadal held easily to make it 3-1, Federer was unstoppable on serve in the fifth game, producing a service winner, two aces and a well-conceived approach to the net to hold at love for 4-1. Federer had virtually everything going his way and seemed certain to find his way back to one set all with his markedly improved serving and returning. He was orchestrating points adroitly, keeping Nadal largely off guard and elevating his game more than marginally.

But while Nadal is an unassailable front runner, he is only slightly less daunting when he is playing from behind. The Spaniard realized he was only down one break. In his mind, a 4-1 deficit is simply an obstacle to overcome, a challenge to be met. He held at 30 for 2-4. Now it was time for Federer to serve with new balls in the seventh game. But the wind was gathering strength, and that may have nullified his advantage with the new balls, which added bite to his delivery. At 30-30, Federer served down the T to Nadal's forehand, shifting from his more regular and successful wide serve to the backhand. Nadal's return was relatively high and not all that deep. Federer saw an opening. He went after his inside-out forehand at full force, hoping to produce a winner. But he drove that crucial shot wide. Nadal was at break point. Federer attempted a short backhand down the line approach, low and near the sideline. Nadal was ready, driving a backhand passing shot right back up the line, making Federer go for a difficult backhand volley down the line. Federer hit that shot wide.

Nadal was ever the opportunist. He had climbed back on serve to 3-4. Yet he, too, was severely challenged by the wind, and pressed hard by a determined Federer. The eighth game was hard fought. Federer garnered a break point. If he could succeed here, he would serve for the set. But Nadal's fierce intelligence took him out of danger. The Spaniard aimed his first serve to the forehand side of Federer, into the Swiss player's body. Federer was crowded and netted his return. Nadal rallied to 4-4 when Federer sent a forehand swing volley long and followed with an errant backhand return.

This ninth game was the time when Federer needed to reassert himself on serve, but he fell into an immediate bind. Federer missed three first serves in a row on his way to trailing 0-40. He made it 15-40 with a forehand winner, but Nadal gained command of the next point. He put Federer onto defense, and the stretched out Swiss sliced a forehand meekly down the center of the court. Nadal seemed to hold the ball on his strings forever before drilling an inside-out forehand winner. He had broken at 15 for 5-4 and would now be serving for a two-sets-to-love lead.

With Nadal serving at 5-4, 30-30, umpire Pascal Maria—one of the top officials in all of tennis—called the Spaniard for a time violation before the Spaniard hit his second serve. To be sure, Nadal often ventured beyond the twenty-second limit between points, but seldom was called for that infraction. Maria picked a questionable time to impose that warning, but Nadal took it in stride. Federer approached off the forehand to the Nadal backhand and had the Spaniard on the run. Nadal realized his customary topspin-two-handed backhand would be tough to pull off under these circumstances, with the wind such an important factor. So he went instead to a backhand slice pass crosscourt and controlled it brilliantly, making a startling winner. It was set point for Nadal, but Federer sent a vicious backhand slice across the net. Even Nadal could not answer that shot, netting a forehand.

At deuce, Nadal made one of his rare strategic missteps. He tried a sidespin forehand drop shot but it floated well wide, and so Federer had moved to break point, giving himself a chance to recoup to 5-5. Federer's forehand return off a body serve was a good one and Nadal had to make a tough pickup. Federer sensed his chance to attack, coming in on Nadal's backhand. Nadal's backhand pass down the line was a beauty, forcing Federer to retreat. Nadal shifted from defense to offense in an instant with a crackling forehand down the line. On his next shot, Nadal ripped his forehand crosscourt, and a beleaguered Federer could not handle a backhand slice. Nadal was back to deuce and he surprised Federer again with a kicker to the forehand. Federer's return went long, giving Nadal a second set point. Nadal pounded another forehand crosscourt, which Federer tried to answer with a topspin backhand down the line. That gamble failed. Nadal had the second set 6-4. He had a two-set lead. No one had rallied from two sets to love down in a Wimbledon final since two of the renowned "Four Musketeers" collided in 1927. In that all-French final, Henri Cochet toppled Jean Borotra 4-6, 4-6, 6-3, 6-4, 7-5. Nadal had only once been beaten after building a two-sets-to-love lead and that was against Federer at Miami in 2005. He did not want to experience that kind of humiliation again now, not in the final of Wimbledon, not with Federer again standing on the other side of the net, not with so much at stake in the most important tennis match the Spaniard had ever contested.

The skies were darkening as the third set unfolded and both players were well aware that more rain was bound to come their way. Yet they tended to their knitting quite well. Federer opened the set with authority, holding at love. Nadal retaliated with an easy hold of his own. At 40-30 in the second game, Federer elected to run around his backhand on a second serve return. He went inside-in. The notion made sense. But the Swiss missed that shot wide as Nadal moved to 1-1. Federer, however, was in his groove again, holding at 15 for 2-1 with an ace out wide in the ad court followed by a service winner.

Rafael Nadal

The battle was still very much on.

Nadal fell into a 15-40 deficit in the fourth game, but he escaped with typical perspicacity. A body serve set up a forehand crosscourt winner. Then Federer narrowly missed a backhand crosscourt. Nadal quickly collected two straight points from there, holding on gamely for 2-2. Federer answered that bell by holding at love for 3-2, connecting with three of four first serves, finishing off the fifth game with a first rate serve-and-volley combination, taking Nadal's return and sending a first volley into an open court. Once more, in the sixth game, Nadal wandered into some rough terrain. He was down 15-40 again, but the Spaniard stood up to the challenge. His kick serve to the backhand drew an errant return from Federer. Federer followed with a bad mistake, netting a topspin backhand return off an inviting second serve.

Federer sorely wanted a service break here. He garnered a third break point and charged the net behind a well struck forehand crosscourt approach. Nadal kept his backhand pass low. Federer could not make the volley. The Spaniard fought through three deuces and held on tenaciously for 3-3. Federer had converted only one of twelve break points, while Nadal had exploited three of his four break points against the Swiss. In the seventh game, Nadal made it to 0-40 on Federer's serve. Both men knew it: a break for the Spaniard at this juncture would almost certainly carry him to a straight-set victory. The chips were on the line.

Federer was staring into adversity, but did not blink. He stepped around his backhand and sent a penetrating forehand deep to Nadal's backhand, forcing an error. The Swiss hit a service winner wide to the backhand for 30-40. And then Nadal wasted a glaring opening. Federer's second serve sat up high. Nadal went for his forehand return, but sent it inexplicably into the net. Two more admirable first serves from Federer were un-returnable. Federer had bravely held on for 4-3 with five points in a row from 0-40 in a clutch display. Although Nadal then held at 15 for 4-4—putting all five first serves into play and backing it up skillfully—Federer was still in a match he could have already lost. In the ninth game, Federer aced Nadal for 30-0, but then double faulted. It was his first double fault of the match, and his first since the fourth round. He then missed a backhand down the line, committing his 25th unforced error of the day, thirteen more than the strikingly consistent Spaniard. But Federer composed himself, threw in two more penetrating first serves, and held at 30 for 5-4.

It was 4:52 in the afternoon. The match was two hours and fourteen minutes old, but now it was halted by rain. The players were off the court for eighty minutes. Nadal was serving to save the set in the tenth game at 4-5. He played every point with understandable caution, recognizing that one false move could swiftly cost him the set. Nadal raced to 40-0 but Federer took the next two points and then reached deuce as Nadal double faulted off the net cord. Nadal was two points away from losing the third set, but an inside-out forehand forced an error from Federer. After Federer got back to deuce again, Nadal managed to hold on. He served to Federer's forehand in the deuce court and the Swiss mishandled an awkward return. Nadal took control of the next point, and Federer erred on a running backhand. 5-5. Federer and Nadal held easily to make it 6-6—both men closed out their service games with aces.

A tie-break would settle the outcome of the third set. Federer went ahead 1-0 with a 125 mile per hour ace down the T. Nadal—bearing down hard—took his two service points for 2-1, but Federer was now rhythmically in sync. He aced Nadal wide to the forehand in the ad court, then aced him down the T at 128 miles per hour. He was up 3-2. Federer got the mini-break he wanted for 4-2, running around his backhand for a brilliant forehand return, rushing Nadal into a backhand mistake. Federer's return on the next point was right where he wanted it, and Nadal's reply was relatively weak. Federer was set up for his signature shot, the inside-out forehand. He rifled it away for a winner, reaching 5-2.

Federer missed a running forehand crosscourt, but then a service winner wide to Nadal's forehand lifted the Swiss to 6-3, triple set point. Nadal had no intention of acquiescing. He punched a high forehand volley into an open court, then served hard to Federer's forehand in the deuce court, eliciting a netted return. Federer had one set point left at 6-5. He paused, picked his spot, and aced Nadal wide to the forehand. Set to Federer, 7-6 (5). Of the six points he served, four had been aces. That had been the fundamental difference between the two staunch competitors in that critical sequence; Federer had seldom if ever served that stupendously in a tie-break. The serve had kept him in the match, giving him a fighting chance against his incomparable rival.

On they went to the fourth set, with Nadal still feeling good about his chances, and Federer beginning to believe he could stage an astonishing recovery. Nadal had the advantage of serving first in the set, and held at 15 for 1-0. His strategic serving in that game was impressive. He kept Federer guessing with his location, and his execution off the ground was impeccable. Federer struck back boldly, holding at 15 himself without missing a first serve. On the first point of the third game, Nadal flicked back a deep backhand crosscourt from Federer, but the Swiss still had an avenue to get to the net. His backhand topspin approach down the line was a great one, but Nadal drove an impossibly difficult two-handed pass crosscourt for a winner. He held at 30 for 2-1 but Federer took his serve at 15 for 2-2, releasing his sixteenth ace of the match for 40-0.

The tennis in this set from both men was nearly letter perfect. Nadal got five consecutive first serves in and held at 15 for 3-2, and then made Federer work hard in the sixth game. Federer had 40-15 but the Spaniard took him to deuce. Federer did not buckle, taking the next two points to deadlock the score at 3-3, closing that game with a service winner out wide to Nadal's forehand in the ad court. Nadal seemed not to worry about Federer's exceptional serving. He kept his focus on his own delivery and the need to back it up with gusto off the ground.

The Spaniard held at love for 4-3, missing only one first serve. He was navigating the match skillfully, holding quickly every time and forcing Federer to reply under increasing duress. Yet Federer had not won 65 matches in a row on grass without good reason. He held at 30 for 4-4. At 30-30, he implemented another deadly accurate first serve wide with slice, opening up the court for his trustworthy inside-out forehand, which he drove into the clear for a winner. An inside-out forehand approach at 40-30 from Federer was too much for Nadal. It was 4-4.

Nadal picked on Federer's backhand persistently in the following game, holding at the cost of only one point. The one point he dropped was a stunning backhand winning pass from Federer that raised chalk on the sideline. Nadal had moved to 5-4 and Federer was soon serving to stay in the match. At 0-15, Federer went in on the Nadal backhand behind a backhand topspin down the line, but the Spaniard made a sparkling passing shot winner up the line. Federer was down 0-30, two points away from a four-set defeat. But he put on his thinking cap to take the next crucial point. Rather than swinging his slice serve wide to Nadal's backhand as he had done so frequently, Federer came down the middle with his delivery and Nadal uncomfortably missed a forehand return.

Federer remained in a precarious zone at 15-30, but pounced on a short return from the Spaniard and cracked a forehand winner. At 30-30, Nadal went for something extra on his two-handed backhand crosscourt, but drove the ball long. A few moments later, Federer seized the initiative once more, striking an immaculate forehand inside-out winner. From the stark danger of 0-30, Federer had collected four points in a row for 5-5. That was unmistakably grace under pressure. But Nadal remained quietly intense, totally concentrated and imperturbable. He held at 15 for 6-5 without missing a first serve again. At 40-15, the Spaniard confounded Federer with a wide serve to the forehand, a tactic that had become increasingly significant as the match progressed. But, serving to stay in the match a second time, Federer was unruffled. He held at 30 with authority. As was the case in the third set, the fourth would be settled in a tie-break, a sequence Federer could not afford to lose.

The Swiss grabbed a quick mini-break, taking the first point. Nadal leaped for a high backhand volley and sent it crosscourt. But Federer read it beautifully and measured his forehand pass masterfully. It whistled down the line for a winner. The Centre Court crowd cheered with unrestrained vigor. Federer's fans sensed his chance to control the outcome of the tie-break. But Nadal answered immediately. His return of serve was so deep that Federer's reply was much too short. Nadal stepped in for a routine forehand inside-out winner for 1-1. Federer pressed on the following point, driving a forehand inside-in wide into the alley.

In an instant, Nadal had changed the chemistry of this crucial sequence. He was brimming with confidence now, serving an ace with a wide breaking short slice for 3-1, then a service winner into Federer's body on the forehand that hit the line and bounced capriciously. Nadal had a 4-1 lead, and was three points away from a victory that had been his dream for many years. Federer took the next point on his serve to close the gap to 4-2, but Nadal then coaxed Federer into a 15-stroke rally, the kind that the Spaniard relishes. On the last shot, Federer attempted a backhand down the line behind Nadal that went wide. Nadal had an insurance mini-break and a 5-2 lead.

The Spaniard served the next two points, knowing full well that he could close it all out right then and there. Perhaps he was too conscious of the score, too keenly aware of the situation. Nadal's second serve down the T clipped the net cord and landed wide. He had double faulted. Federer glanced subtly in Nadal's direction, sensing that his opponent might be filled with apprehension with the title so close to his grasp. Nadal's first serve on the next point was safe. Federer made a good return and then jumped all over a forehand, forcing Nadal into an off-balanced backhand error. Now Federer was serving improbably at 4-5. Rather than being out of the match altogether or at least triple match point down, Federer was back on serve in the "breaker."

The Swiss had gone from pessimism to optimism in the space of a few minutes. He served wide to the Nadal backhand to set up a forehand winner, then cracked an un-returnable first serve to Nadal's forehand. Federer had collected four points in a row, and was rewarded for that gigantic effort with a set point as the Spaniard served at 5-6. Federer needed to be aggressive here, but not reckless. Nadal wanted to make Federer earn this point. The Spaniard was in his "refuse to miss" mode. They rallied for eighteen strokes and Federer finally went for broke with an inside-out forehand from near the center of the court. He hit it cleanly, but missed it wide. Despite all the jarring things that had just happened to him—starting with his double fault—Nadal had been courageous with his back to the wall.

At 6-6 on Nadal's serve, Federer's forehand approach travelled long, and Nadal at long last had a match point. But Federer was serving at 6-7. His wide ad court delivery was unstoppable. Nadal barely touched it. 7-7. Federer then pulled Nadal wide and approached to the open court on the Spaniard's forehand side. Nadal raced across the court, laced a forehand up the line, and struck pure gold. Federer had the line covered but the ball blazed by him, landing inches inside the sideline. The Spaniard was ahead 8-7. Nadal had given himself a second match point, but this one would be on his serve. He deliberately swung his slice serve wide to Federer's backhand. The Swiss chipped his return short, near the service line. Nadal was poised to win Wimbledon as he drove his forehand approach crosscourt to Federer's weaker side. But the Spaniard played that shot too conservatively. He did not get enough pace on the approach. Federer unhesitatingly drove a gorgeous topspin backhand pass down the line into an open space for a winner. It was 8-8.

The two men were commendably matching each other moment to moment, shot for shot, like a pair of prize fighters refusing to hit the canvas no matter how many times they landed telling punches. The Wimbledon fans were getting up off their feet with frequency, astonished and overjoyed by what they were witnessing. The players were reaching back with every resource they had, playing the game with unimaginable verve and spontaneity, pushing each other to the hilt. Nadal was still serving at 8-8, but Federer was reinvigorated. He made a fine return off a first serve, sent Nadal on the run with an inside-out forehand and the court was wide open. Federer drove his forehand out of Nadal's reach for a winner.

The Swiss was at 9-8, at set point for the second time. He spun his second serve down the middle to Nadal's backhand. The Spaniard drove his return long. Federer jumped joyously as he saw the ball go out, looking over at his corner with amazement about what he had just done. Federer had saved two match points, climbing out of a dark corner, sending himself into a fifth set with a burst of momentum. Nadal was not discouraged, but he had lost two tie-breaks in a row, and his lead had evaporated. It was now two sets all and Nadal had the added burden of serving from behind in the final set against a surging adversary who had not lost his serve since the end of the second set. Had Federer fashioned this kind of a comeback against anyone else, he would be just about home free. But Nadal was his sport's toughest and most durable competitor, unshakable to his core, a tennis player with the heart of a lion.

Federer started the fifth set in style. He held at 30 for 1-0, closing out that game with an excellent approach shot setting up a classic backhand volley winner. Nadal held at 30 for 1-1 despite missing his first serve on the last three points. At 1-1, Nadal had a chance to make an impression on Federer's serve. A double fault from Federer—one of only two he would hit in the entire match—allowed Nadal back to deuce. Nadal was in a favorable position to hit a big forehand, but drove it long. Nadal made it to deuce a second time with a backhand drop shot winner, but Federer was not to be swayed, connecting with a forehand crosscourt winner before Nadal netted a backhand return off a second serve. 2-1 for Federer.

Nadal held on easily at 15 for 2-2 after losing the first point of that game. Federer was taking considerable risks because he had no alternative, but his forehand misfired twice, and Nadal came up with an inside-out forehand winner of his own. In the fifth game, Federer served an ace for 40-30, but lost the next point. It was deuce. And yet, at 7:54 in the evening, after three hours and fifty-four minutes of play, after so much gallantry on both sides of the net, the match was suspended again for half an hour. When Nadal had left the court for the first rain delay during the match, he had been in an advantageous position, up two sets to love, on serve in the third. Now he was locked at two sets all, and the match was on serve at 2-2 in the fifth set. But neither player wanted to stop at that point, and they realized that only a limited amount of light was left to fill the day. With no tie-breaks played in the fifth set, there was no guarantee that this match would be completed in one day.

As soon as play resumed, Federer was primed. From 2-2, deuce, he promptly smacked two aces in a row, both down the T. Nadal conceded only one point on his way back to 3-3, but Federer's serve was unanswerable in the next game. The Swiss held at love for 4-3 with an ace down the T. Serving in the eighth game, Nadal was tested severely by a determined and unwavering Federer. The Swiss advanced to break point with a thundering forehand winner down the line. He was one point away from moving to 5-3, and a chance to serve for the match. Nadal chose a body first serve into Federer's hip on the forehand. The tactic was a big success. Federer could not get much on the return. Nadal drilled his inside-out forehand to the open court, and Federer was hard pressed to even get the ball back into play. Nadal swooped in, let Federer's short lob bounce, and put away the overhead commandingly.

Nadal then challenged Federer with another inside-out forehand, and the Swiss drove a forehand well wide. At game point, Nadal swung his slice serve wide, got a short return from Federer, and whipped a forehand winner crosscourt behind Federer. From break point down, Nadal had taken three clutch points in a row to arrive at 4-4. Federer connected with only two of six first serves in the next game, but produced a timely ace for 40-15 and held at 30 for 5-4. Nadal was returning well, searching for chances, bearing down hard. But Federer was serving unreasonably well at this stage. The Spaniard walked to the changeover after the ninth game, knowing he would be serving to stay in the final when play resumed.

That tenth game was filled with tension. At 30-15, Nadal tried a backhand slice, but Federer was all over it, going for an aggressive forehand that rushed Nadal into an error. Here was Nadal, serving at 4-5, 30-30, two points from a five-set defeat after having led two sets to love. He served to Federer's backhand down the T and the return came back short. Nadal approached confidently with the crosscourt forehand and Federer's lob was long. At 40-30, Nadal went to the sliced serve wide, and a stretched out Federer responded with a short return. Nadal moved in with no inhibition whatsoever, and cracked an inside-out forehand winner. It was 5-5. Nadal had survived another crisis.

Now the Spaniard would get his chance. With Federer serving at 15-30 in the eleventh game, the Swiss invested in the daring strategy that had paid so many dividends for him over the last two sets. He directed a forehand inside-out, but Nadal got a good jump on this one, and curled a forehand winner up the line on the run. That spectacular shot took Nadal to double break point. Federer went for an ace down the T at 127 miles per hour, and pulled it off. It was 30-40. He saved the next break point on a miss-hit from Nadal, struck another sizzling forehand winner, and then drew a mistake from Nadal. Four consecutive points for Federer from double break point down. The Swiss was ahead 6-5.

Nadal served to stay in the match a second time in the twelfth game. At 40-15, he caught Federer off guard again with a kicker to the forehand. Federer's return was long. Nadal had made it back safely to 6-6. Federer was twice extended to deuce by Nadal in the thirteenth game but the Spaniard never got to break point. Federer was purposeful and sound at those moments. He held on for 7-6. Serving the next game, Nadal had 40-30 when he approached the net. Federer put up a short lob that Nadal tried to demolish, going crosscourt with great force on the overhead. But Federer "stayed home" as they say in the trade. He somehow managed to loft another backhand lob down the line over Nadal's head into the corner, and his touch was exquisite. Nadal retreated swiftly to the baseline with considerable intensity, tracking the ball with every step he took. He then wheeled around and played an overhead on the bounce to Federer's backhand. Federer chipped his shot conservatively and Nadal promptly stepped in for a forehand inside out winner. It was 7-7. The exhilarated crowd—astounded by the greatness of both competitors, not really wanting either man to lose, torn by their conflicted emotions—erupted.

The light was fading fast now. It was past 9 p.m. and the players knew the next changeover would almost surely be the last one. With Federer serving at 15-30, Nadal got hold of a backhand crosscourt, going behind Federer for a startling winner. The Spaniard was at double break point again, in striking distance of serving for the match. Yet every time he got within a whisker of achieving that long awaited service break, Nadal was denied by an adversary who refused to let go. Federer served an ace wide to Nadal's backhand in the deuce court. He was back to 30-40, and then he surged to deuce when Nadal missed an off balance passing shot. Nadal earned a third break point, but Federer's determination knew no bounds. He served wide to Nadal's forehand in the ad court and the Spaniard barely made contact on the return. Deuce again. The Spaniard was totally immersed in the moment. He wanted to make Federer keep coming up with gems. Nadal would make no donations. In the next rally, Federer looked for an opening for a forehand inside-in winner after running around his backhand. He netted that critical shot. Federer was facing his fourth break point of the fifteenth game in the final set. He drove a forehand approach down the middle, but the shot was long. Nadal had at last broken to take an 8-7 lead.

There could be no doubt in either player's mind that the next game would be the last one they would play that evening. The sky was steadily darkening over the Centre Court. Nadal would be serving for the match in the sixteenth game, and would either walk away in triumph, or come back the next day to complete a contest that would inappropriately turn into Russian roulette. He had lost his serve only once in the match. Nadal served with new balls and apprehensively drove a forehand long to fall behind 0-15. But the Spaniard resolved to go on the attack. He swung his slice serve wide in the ad court and came in behind it.

For the first time in the entire match, he was serving-and-volleying. Federer's return came back right where Nadal wanted it and the Spaniard punched his backhand volley crosscourt for a winner. At 15-15, Nadal cleverly served wide to Federer's forehand and the return was relatively short. Nadal drove his forehand crosscourt approach with conviction and closed in tight on the net to put away a forehand volley down the line.

Nadal was at 30-15, two points from victory. Perhaps wanting to avoid chasing balls around the baseline in the greatly diminished light, Nadal went to the net again, but his forehand volley was unremarkable. Federer laced a backhand topspin pass down the line. The ball might well have gone long if Nadal had let it go, but the Spaniard took no chances and missed a backhand volley. He lost the point for 30-30, but took the next one when Federer pulled a backhand wide crosscourt. Nadal had arrived at match point for the third time. He sliced his first serve wide to the backhand, but it did not break that sharply. Federer came over the top of his return and drove it majestically crosscourt. Nadal scampered to his left but had no play. Federer's backhand was breathtaking. He was somehow still alive. It was deuce.

Nadal served wide to Federer's forehand in the deuce court, with a devilish kicking spin and good velocity. Federer was late on his return

Roger Federer and Rafael Nadal

and had no chance to keep it in play. Nadal thus stood at match point again, for the fourth time. A short rally ensued. Federer was stationed near the middle of the court, inside the baseline. He was looking to come in off the forehand, but drove the last shot of a glorious battle into the net. Victory had come to Nadal 6-4, 6-4, 6-7 (5), 6-7 (8), 9-7 in four hours and fourty-eight minutes, the longest Wimbledon final ever.

The final ball was struck at 9:16. Nadal had withstood a gallant and inspired comeback from Federer. He had overcome his foremost rival, ending Federer's 40-match winning streak at the world's premier tennis tournament, winning his first Wimbledon under the most trying of circumstances. The two men greeted each other with genuine affection at the net. Nadal left the court to share his most rewarding triumph ever with his family, including a beaming Uncle Toni, the architect of his success in so many ways.

In the media center after the match, journalists gathered to assess the historical significance of the epic they had just witnessed. They recollected the Borg-McEnroe Wimbledon final of 1980 and wondered how this one stacked up against that. There was no immediate consensus but the feeling grew in the hours and days that followed that Nadal-Federer had perhaps surpassed Borg-McEnroe and now could be considered the greatest tennis match ever played.

EPILOGUE

Later that summer of 2008, Nadal travelled to Beijing and won a gold medal at the Olympic Games, adding that highly valued title to the two Grand Slam events he had captured in Paris and London across the season. But the Spaniard's bid to secure the U.S. Open Championship for the first time failed. Mentally and emotionally spent, devoid of his customary spark on the court, unable to summon the will to perform at his best on the hard courts, Nadal was ousted in the semifinals by Great Britain's talented and versatile Andy Murray. Federer's hard court summer had been abysmal by his standards. He had lost in the second round at the ATP Masters 1000 event in Toronto, and then fell in the third round at Cincinnati in another Masters 1000 tournament. James Blake upended Federer in the quarterfinals of the Olympics, the first time the Swiss had ever lost to his American rival.

The saving grace for Federer during that stretch was taking a gold medal at Beijing in the doubles with countryman Stan Wawrinka, but that seemed like a very small consolation prize for Federer as he came to New York. By then, Nadal had taken away the No. 1 world ranking from the Swiss. Federer's confidence level was abnormally low.

But he found his form and benefitted from Nadal's unexpected loss to Murray. In the final, Federer beat Murray in straight sets. He had won his fifth consecutive U.S. Open, replicating the feat he had realized at Wimbledon the year before. No man had ever managed to capture five titles in a row at the two most prestigious tournaments before in the history of tennis.

Yet Nadal—despite his setback in New York—was clearly the best player in the world that memorable season of 2008. Across the first five months of 2009, he grew even more into that status. At the start of that year, he surpassed Federer in another classic confrontation, winning in five sets over the Swiss in an emotional final at the Australian Open. Nadal had defeated compatriot Fernando Verdasco in another five-set clash a few days before in the semifinals, and that battle had lasted five hours and fourteen minutes. To recover with so little rest and beat Federer to win his first Australian Open crown was another career defining moment for Nadal. In the space of less than eight months, he had stopped Federer in three Grand Slam tournament finals held on three different surfaces. To say the least, that was no mean feat.

Heading into the French Open that spring, Nadal seemed certain to remain at No. 1 in the world indefinitely. He had won five tournaments in 2009 already, and was shooting for a fifth French Open title in a row. But his knees were betraying him and the Spaniard encountered Robin Soderling of Sweden, who was plainly in the zone when they met at Roland Garros in the round of 16. Soderling produced one of the biggest upsets of the decade when he halted Nadal in four sets. Nadal had been the overwhelming favorite in Paris, but suddenly the event was wide open. Federer had lost to Nadal in three consecutive finals. Now his primary obstacle was out of the way. Federer reacted to the absence of Nadal accordingly, although he struggled. The German Tommy Haas was one point away from serving for a straight-set, round-of-16 win over the Swiss before Federer made one of the great clutch shots of his career, an inside-out forehand winner at 4-4, break point down in that third set. Federer recovered boldly and obstinately for a five-set victory. In the semifinals, he rallied from two sets to one down to beat the tall Argentine Juan Martin Del Potro, a big hitter with a rapidly evolving game. That set the stage for Federer to complete a career Grand Slam when he knocked out Soderling in a straight-set final. The triumph also placed Federer in a tie with Pete Sampras for the all-time men's record of fourteen major singles titles. He would head to Wimbledon later that month in search of more history.

Nadal, meanwhile, was at bay. Not only was he worried about his knees, but his parents were going through a divorce. The Spaniard was in the doldrums, his spirit largely broken by the excruciating pain he was experiencing both on and off the court. He returned over the summer but was not the same player, losing emphatically 6-2, 6-2, 6-2 to Del Potro in the semifinals of the U.S. Open. The rest of the year was essentially a downcast time for Nadal as he tried to regain his equilibrium and find the zest to compete with the same emotional energy that had been his hallmark.

In 2010, Nadal did just that. Nadal built his game and his psyche back up and even beyond his old standards. He took back his French Open crown, capturing the Roland Garros title for the fifth time in six years, dissecting Soderling in a straight-set final. At Wimbledon, he returned to the scene of his 2008 triumph and played magnificently, taking that title for the second time with a straight-set dismantling of Tomas Berdych in the final. Most important of all, Nadal was victorious at the U.S. Open, completing his career Grand Slam by virtue of a four-set, final-round triumph over the Serbian Novak Djokovic, the captivating Serbian who would take over the game sweepingly in 2011. Nadal thus joined Don Budge, Fred Perry, Roy Emerson, Rod Laver, Andre Agassi and Federer as the only men ever to win all four majors.

The Spaniard had another very good year in 2011, garnering his sixth French Open title with a final-round triumph over Federer. The two great rivals met for the eighth time in a final at a Grand Slam event, with Nadal the victor in four sets. He had beaten his Swiss opponent for the sixth time in those eight critical meetings. But it was Djokovic's year. The Serbian thwarted Nadal every time they clashed across the season, defeating the Spaniard in six finals, most significantly at Wimbledon and the U.S. Open.

Nonetheless, Nadal would not turn twenty-six until June of 2012.

He would surely make his presence known in the latter stages of majors for many more years. He never underestimated a rival. He had always displayed immense admiration for Federer no matter how many times he beat him on big occasions. He would be no less respectful of Djokovic, or anyone else. There would surely be more celebratory moments for Rafael Nadal, the greatest competitor of his time, probably the best competitor of all time. But no matter what is in store for the Spaniard as he finishes a phenomenal career, it seems certain that the match he will recollect and cherish above all others will be the Wimbledon final of 2008, when he beat Roger Federer in a battle of such enthralling beauty and unimaginable majesty that it could not have been scripted.

CHAPTER THIRTY

Andy Roddick *vs.* Roger Federer
WIMBLEDON, FINAL, JULY 5, 2009

A year after his historic duel with Rafael Nadal on the fabled Centre Court, Roger Federer returned for a another epic final-round contest against his old rival Andy Roddick. Clashing for the third time in the final of the world's premier event, they gave sports fans a match for the ages.

PROLOGUE

The emergence of Andrew Stephen Roddick as the world's best tennis player and a Grand Slam tournament champion was timed exquisitely. Diehard followers of American tennis had grown accustomed for a good many years to celebrating the achievements of Pete Sampras and Andre Agassi. And yet, Sampras had wrapped up his storied career in 2002. Although Agassi remained in the forefront of the game and competed until he lost early at the 2006 U.S. Open, he realized he was playing on borrowed time as he moved past his prime and into his mid-thirties. By then, Roddick had arrived in the forefront of the game, and had attracted his own constituency of fans. In 2003, at twenty-one, he captured the U.S. Open title, saving a match point in a five-set semifinal triumph over Argentina's formidable David Nalbandian, casting aside Spain's Juan Carlos Ferrero (Agassi's semifinal conqueror) in the final. Roddick finished that year at No. 1 in the world. He thoroughly earned that distinction by virtue of his consistency across the season, his professional integrity, his durability as a competitor, and his first-rate work ethic.

Roddick was born in Omaha, Nebraska on August 30, 1982. His father, Jerry, was a businessman and investor and his mother, Blanche, a school teacher who later became the director of the Andy Roddick Foundation, which was started in 2001 and raised about ten million dollars over the next twelve years. When Andy was four, the family moved to Austin, Texas. Seven years later, they moved to Boca Raton, Florida, where Roddick graduated from Boca Prep International School. His primary focus was tennis from a very young age. Yet Roddick and his friend and eventual U.S. No. 1 Mardy Fish—classmates at Boca Prep—both played high school basketball.

Roddick had a highly successful junior career, culminating in 2000 when he won the Australian and U.S. Open 18-and-under events. He was the world's top-ranked junior that season. Andy's brother John helped lead the way for his younger brother. He was an All-American tennis player for the University of Georgia from 1996-98. John Roddick started his own tennis academy later on, and even assisted his brother as a coach for a time. His guidance was invaluable.

Andy Roddick was a quick learner, a good athlete, a fine student of the game. Even during his brilliant 2000 campaign as the world's leading junior, he made serious inroads playing pro events, becoming the youngest player of that season to finish among the top 200 in the world when he was eighteen years and three months old. Roddick rose to No. 158 at the end of that year, and never looked back. In 2001, he had a fantastic first full year as a professional, winning forty-two of fifty-eight matches, taking three ATP World Tour titles, reaching the quarterfinals of the U.S. Open, and rising to No. 14 in the world. Roddick made his Davis Cup debut for the U.S. that season as well. The following year, Roddick returned to the quarterfinals at the U.S. Open, won fifty-six of seventy-eight matches, and finished at No. 10 in the world. The steady progress he made in 2001 and 2002 clearly gave Roddick the sense of self he needed for his banner year in 2003, when he garnered six tournament titles, secured his first major, and leaped to the top of his profession.

Roddick had been guided from the middle of 2003 by Brad Gilbert, who had worked so successfully with Agassi from 1994 until 2002. From the time that Gilbert took over, Roddick performed with growing command and efficiency. Gilbert joined forces that year with Roddick at Queen's Club in London for the Wimbledon tune-up event. Roddick saved a match point in a semifinal win over Agassi and went on to take the title. He then made it to the semifinals of

Wimbledon before losing to a sublime Roger Federer, but resumed his winning ways on the hard court circuit, winning tournaments in Indianapolis, Montreal and Cincinnati before his landmark victory at the U.S. Open. In that initial span with Gilbert providing astute council, Roddick had won five of the seven tournaments he played, and that stretch paved the way for Roddick to take over at No. 1 in the world at the end of that season.

He finished 2004 at No. 2 in the world, surpassed only by Federer. The Swiss bested the American in a four-set Wimbledon title match, the first time they would meet on that final-round occasion. Roddick and Gilbert would end their partnership when that season concluded. A year later, the crucial moment for Roddick was again in the final of Wimbledon, as Federer took him apart in a straight-set final. Federer had stopped Roddick three times on the lawns of the All England Club, twice in the final round. Gradually over this phase of his career, Roddick drifted away from the recipe that had made him so imposing on his way to becoming the No. 1 player in the world.

In those halcyon days of 2003, Roddick had built his game around a prodigious first serve, one of the biggest deliveries the sport had yet seen. His first serve was released explosively and with uncanny accuracy. He could find the four corners of the two service boxes with extraordinary regularity, and he backed up his cannonball first serve with a second serve that was a nightmare for opponents to handle. Roddick's kicker always landed deep and bounded up high, forcing adversaries to make contact above their shoulders from uncomfortable positions. The serve was the cornerstone of his game, the weapon that set him apart. Aesthetically, Roddick's delivery was not in a league with the serves of Pete Sampras or Roger Federer. But it was mechanically magnificent, and seldom did Roddick have a bad day on his serve.

In those days, Roddick also possessed one of the most fearsome forehands in tennis. His forehand did not have the artistic value or the meticulous craftsmanship of Federer's forehand, but Roddick's was a blockbuster of a shot. Like Federer, his inside-out forehand was an essential shot in his repertoire, and Roddick flattened that shot out for scorching winners whenever possible. The combination of the serve and the forehand made Roddick who he was.

Over time, he diversified his game admirably, went to work diligently to improve his volley, found the right avenues to get to the net. But by 2005, he had largely lost his knack for boldness off the forehand, slipping into self-defeating conservatism by covering the forehand with too much topspin, allowing opponents who once had been at the American's mercy to stay in rallies that had once been Roddick's province. The American's firepower had been diminished significantly, and the reduction in power had been of his own choosing.

In 2006, over the summer, Roddick appointed Jimmy Connors to be his coach. Connors was out of touch in many ways with the modern players and their tactics and methodology, yet he understood the psyche of a champion, knew how to motivate Roddick, and recognized how he could get the most out of his charge. The eight-time Grand Slam tournament champion had spent five consecutive years (1974-78) at No. 1 in the world. Connors was inspired by what he believed he could do to push Roddick on to greater heights. His goal was no different from Roddick's—the full pursuit of another major title. Roddick was seeded ninth that year at Flushing Meadows. He took advantage of a good draw, and made it to the final with a four-set victory over the Russian Mikhail Youzhny, who had upset No. 2 seed Rafael Nadal. Only one man stood between Roddick and a second major championship. His name, of course, was Roger Federer.

Federer and Roddick were locked at one set all and 5-5 in the third before the Swiss swept eight out of nine games to break the contest wide open, winning 6-2, 4-6, 7-5, 6-1. Roddick had fought gamely for a long while, but in the end Federer ran him into the ground by moving the American skillfully from side to side, orchestrating points to his own liking until he would uncork another outright winner. For the third time against Roddick in a major final, Federer was simply the superior player, too crafty and versatile, too much of a magician, too good for Andy Roddick. Yet Roddick had made up some ground after falling out of the world's top ten in July before his September resurrection. Roddick, who had finished every year from 2003-2005 amongst the top three in the world, was back up to No. 6.

He remained in that identical position at the end of 2007 after parting ways with Connors. He had gone to the semifinals of the

Australian Open but failed to advance that far at a major the rest of the year. His 2008 season was largely a disappointment as Roddick fell to No. 8. But he joined forces at the end of that year with a coach who may well have been the best in the business. Larry Stefanki had boosted both Yevgeny Kafelnikov and Marcelo Rios—a pair of difficult personalities—toward their achievement of holding the No. 1 world ranking. He had coached John McEnroe. He had used his brilliant and agile mind to help Tim Henman reach the top five in the world.

As 2009 commenced, Stefanki was determined to get Roddick back into more of an aggressive mode, to keep his player out of unnecessarily long rallies and get him taking charge of his own destiny again. Stefanki had found the right combination of encouraging pep talks with Roddick coupled with a healthy blend of constructive criticism. Roddick's results were solid but unspectacular in the early season. He won the indoor title in Memphis, advanced to the semifinals of Indian Wells, went to the quarters of Miami. But the American sensed he might be on the upswing, and so did Stefanki.

Federer, meanwhile, had turned his year around sweepingly at the end of the clay court circuit. He had upended Nadal in the final of the Masters 1000 Madrid event, a day after Nadal toiled for four hours and three minutes, saving three match points in a semifinal victory over Novak Djokovic. Then Federer had made his history in Paris, winning the French title that had long eluded him. That unexpected win carried him into Wimbledon with renewed optimism. A year earlier, Nadal had become the first man since Bjorn Borg in 1980 to win Roland Garros and Wimbledon back to back. Federer has his heart set on replicating that achievement. He headed into Wimbledon buoyed by his recent triumphs, ready to make amends for his heartbreaking loss to Nadal the year before on the Centre Court, expecting to produce his best at the tournament he valued above all others. As for Roddick, he drew on his history of successes on the British grass. He, too, approached Wimbledon in a good frame of mind.

THE MATCH

With Rafael Nadal injured and unable to defend his title on the lawns of the All England Club, Federer became the clear favorite to regain the crown he had swept from 2003-2007. Federer was invigorated after winning at Roland Garros to realize a career Grand Slam. He was back at the shrine of the sport, eager to perform in a setting he cherished. Federer was seeded second because Nadal had withdrawn after the official draw ceremony, but his status as the favorite was beyond dispute. The Swiss dropped only one set on his way to the final—dropping a third set tie-break against the gifted German Philipp Kohlschreiber in the third round before reigniting quickly to take the fourth set 6-1—and produced his customary level of high caliber grass court tennis all through the tournament. In the semifinals, he accounted for No. 24 seed Tommy Haas in straight sets, prevailing with relative ease after his harrowing escape against the German at Roland Garros the previous month.

Roddick took a while to find the upper level of his game. He was pushed to four sets in his first three matches, but played with clearer conviction in a straight-set triumph over No. 20 seed Tomas Berdych, who would reach the final the following year. In the quarterfinals, Roddick needed all of his resolve and grass court acumen to oust 2002 champion Lleyton Hewitt in five tumultuous sets. That earned the American a meeting in the penultimate round with the No. 3 seed Andy Murray, a 22-year-old bursting with determination, hoping to become the first British man to reach the final since Fred Perry celebrated a third consecutive title run in 1936. Most in the cognoscenti believed Murray's crafty playing style and top notch return of serve would carry him past the big serving American, but Roddick picked apart Murray in four sets for his best win of the year.

When Federer and Roddick walked on court for their title round showdown, a bright blue sky sparkled above them. It was an idyllic, balmy afternoon, and there would be no need to put up the new retractable roof that had been completed in time for the 2009 event. That was ironic. A year earlier, Federer and Nadal were competing not only against each other, but they were also battling the elements, and trying to beat the rain. This time around, the atmosphere was more celebratory, more befitting such a big occasion. Sitting in the Royal Box behind the court—eagerly awaiting the Federer-Roddick duel—were the enormously popular all-time greats Rod Laver (four times the Wimbledon singles champion) and Bjorn Borg, who had captured five titles in a row from 1976-80. Alongside Laver and Borg was the artistic Spanish champion Manuel Santana, the 1966 Wimbledon victor.

But the larger buzz around Centre Court was created by the late breaking news that seven-time Wimbledon champion Pete Sampras was on his way out to the arena to join Borg, Laver and company, and watch his friend Federer try to break the record they shared. Both icons owned fourteen Grand Slam singles championships, but Sampras had believed for a while that Federer was destined to surpass his total at the majors, and the American was convinced that the Swiss was worthy of the honor. Sampras had flown to London from his home in Los Angeles, and he arrived early in the first set. As he took his seat in the Centre Court, Sampras waved to the fans, and received a generous and heartfelt round of applause.

The bright sunshine and heat were arguably a good omen for Roddick. The warmer the weather, the faster the ball travels through the air. Roddick's serve would be an even more potent weapon than usual in these conditions. When he had lost to Federer in the 2004 and 2005 Centre Court finals, they had played on relatively cool days. On the first of those occasions, Roddick and Federer were locked at one set all but the American had built a 4-2 lead in the third set. Rain intervened. Federer rallied for a four-set triumph. The next year, the day was essentially cloudy and cool. That was surely in Federer's favor as Roddick's explosive serve was slightly diminished in the cooler air.

Now, on this exquisite afternoon, with his heart set on taking his first major since the 2003 U.S. Open, Roddick went right to work. On the first point of the match, he unleashed a devastatingly potent first serve down the T at 135 miles per hour. Federer had no play on the return. After Federer drew even at 15-15 with a dipping topspin backhand passing shot down the line that was too much for Roddick to handle, the American aced Federer down the T at 136 miles per hour. A huge second serve was unmanageable for Federer, lifting Roddick to 40-15. He held at 15 with another ace, this one at 137 miles per hour down the T again. Roddick had connected with four out of five first serves, uncorked two aces, and released two more unanswerable serves. It was the kind of start he surely wanted. But Federer would not be upstaged. His first serve was not as big as Roddick's, but his placement, execution and capacity to disguise his location were at least the equal and perhaps superior to the American's. Federer aced Roddick out wide for 15-15, aced him down the T for 30-15, and held easily at 15, letting Roddick know that he would make no concessions.

Roddick rolled to 2-1 by holding at love, closing that game with a pair of service winners. It was at the changeover after the third game when Sampras took his seat in the Royal Box. Federer briefly greeted the thirty-seven-year-old American, but quickly turned his attention back to the task at hand. He fluidly released four first serves in a row for a love hold, acing Roddick twice to make it 2-2. Roddick would be tested for the first time on his serve in the following game. The American missed a difficult low backhand volley down the line to make the score 40-30, but he counter-attacked skillfully to close out that game. Federer attacked behind an inside-out forehand, going to Roddick's weaker backhand side. Roddick was undaunted, driving his two-hander down the line for a winner. 3-2 to the American.

Although Federer missed three out of five first serves in the next game, he still held at 15. Swiftly, calmly, assertively, Federer was even at 3-3. Yet Roddick was in a marvelous groove on his serve. He was finding the corners with overwhelming pace and control, and coming at Federer unhesitatingly. Roddick went five-for-five on first serves in the seventh game to hold at 15 for 4-3. The serving from both competitors was first class. Federer held at 15 for 4-4, acing Roddick down the middle in the deuce court with radar-like precision. Roddick retaliated forcefully, holding at love for 5-4. He opened that game with an ace at 137 miles per hour down the T, and added another ace and a service winner. He did not miss a first serve.

Federer was serving to stay in the set, but he remained unflappable, holding at love with four consecutive neatly concealed first serves in a row. The Swiss then made his move on the receiving end. With Roddick serving at 5-5, Federer got to 0-30. Roddick sent a body serve into Federer's backhand side to elicit a mistake, and then fired a service winner down the middle at 133 miles per hour. Federer garnered a break point at 30-40, only to chip a backhand return off a second serve wide. Federer challenged the call, but the Hawkeye replay system verified that the call was correct. Hawkeye had become a crucial part of big time tennis starting in 2006 at the U.S. Open, allowing the players to have bad calls overturned by a computerized image that was flashed on a big screen in the stadium, usually within ten seconds or so of the challenge.

In any case, after Federer's lost challenge, it was deuce. Roddick gained the advantage, but Federer rolled one of his gorgeous backhand passing shots down the line to bring it back to deuce. Federer garnered a second break point opportunity, but Roddick erased that with a thundering service winner to the backhand, cracked at 138 miles per hour. Federer was sinking his teeth deeply into this game, knowing a service break here might propel him through this set and well beyond. The Swiss approached off the forehand, deep to the Roddick backhand. The American netted the pass. Federer was at break point for a third time. He approached again with the forehand down the line, and there was no call on the baseline. Roddick thought the ball was out. He challenged. The replay vindicated the American. It was deuce for the fourth time.

Federer remained resolute, rifling a forehand winner immaculately out of Roddick's reach. Federer blocked a forehand return on his fourth break point, and it was called long. Federer disputed that decision, but the replay went against him. It was deuce for the fifth time. Federer made a surprising forehand unforced error, then netted a forehand passing shot under extreme pressure. Roddick had held on for 6-5 with courage, discipline, and a sprinkling of good fortune. But he had persevered.

Federer knew that tennis could comprehensively test a man's patience. He had four times been within one point of serving for the set, and perhaps gaining a momentum that he would not give back. Yet here he was, serving at 5-6, needing to hold just to reach a tie-break. Federer fell behind 15-30, served an ace wide to Roddick's backhand in the ad court, and then his anxiety became evident. The Swiss missed a backhand slice wide, and found himself improbably at set

Roger Federer

point down. Roddick was poised for the next point at 30-40, ready to make the most of it. He drove his two-handed backhand flat down the line, and Federer was made to play a running forehand. Federer was more dangerous whenever he could move around his backhand to play the inside-out forehand. Forced to hit the forehand on the run, he was a considerably more vulnerable. He drove that shot wide. Set to Roddick, 7-5.

As the second set began, Roddick was fully aware how much he needed to be in the lead. Coming from a set down in a Wimbledon final against a rival who had beaten him in eighteen of twenty career confrontations would have been a daunting and perhaps impossible task. Federer was revered among his peers as a virtually unstoppable front runner. His habit after winning the first set in major finals was to soar to another level. This was his 20th appearance in the final of a Grand Slam event. In the previous nineteen, he had taken the first set fourteen times, and had lost only one of those contests—to Nadal at the 2006 French Open. But on the five final-round occasions at the premier events when Federer did not capture the opening set, he had come back to record a triumph only once—against Roddick in the 2004 Wimbledon final. Federer was underrated as a competitor, far tougher and more resilient than many realized. But the fact remained that he had built his reputation more on his propensity to move in front and never look back.

Roddick wasted no time asserting himself in the second set. He held at 15 for 1-0, taking the last two points of that game with aces down the middle. Federer responded impressively, holding without the loss of a point. The standard of serving on both sides of the net remained outstanding. Roddick double faulted to trail 15-30, but swept three points in a row for 2-1. Federer coasted to 2-2 with another love hold. Roddick moved to 3-2, conceding only one point on his delivery, but Federer countered with a routine service game, holding at 15 to make it 3-3. Neither man was ceding any ground. This was grass court tennis the way it was meant to be played. There had been a good deal of talk in recent years about the grass courts playing slower at the All England Club, but Roddick and Federer were making the surface look awfully fast the way they were conducting this skirmish.

Roddick surged to 4-3, holding at 15, closing that game with his ninth ace of the match. Federer swiftly climbed to 4-4, holding at the cost of just one point. The pattern continued as the two resolute competitors fought on almost imperiously. Roddick again held at 15 to reach 5-4. Briefly, Federer seemed apprehensive as he served to save the set in the tenth game. He double faulted for 30-30, and suddenly was two points from trailing two sets to love. But Federer went to his familiar pattern of play, swinging his first serve wide with slice in the deuce court, setting up a forehand winner behind Roddick. At 40-30, Federer stupendously angled a backhand chip passing shot winner in response to a Roddick forehand drop shot down the line. With that dazzling shot ending a sparkling 23-stroke rally, Federer stood at 5-5.

The inevitability of a tie-break was increasingly apparent. Roddick held again at 15 for 6-5. In his six service games across the second set, he had conceded only seven points. Federer was even more statistically proficient. He served three more aces to hold at 15 for 6-6. In his six service games, the Swiss had allowed Roddick only five points. A tie-break it would be. Federer had always thwarted Roddick when they had collided in tie-breaks throughout their careers—he held a commanding 12-3 edge in those critical sequences. But the Swiss was in an uncomfortable position as he headed into this one. If Roddick prevailed, he would be up two sets to love, and the American would have been just about unbeatable from there. Federer needed this tie-break more than Roddick did, or so it seemed when it commenced.

Roddick served first, and his adrenaline was flowing. He released a 143 mile per hour service winner to Federer's backhand, easily provoking an errant wide return from Federer. Federer got his first serve in on the next point, but then his forehand flew long off Roddick's return. That was clearly a mistake caused by nerves. Federer followed with an unstoppable first serve, but Roddick had a 2-1 lead with a mini-break. He expanded that lead in a hurry. First he unleashed a service winner to Federer's forehand in the ad court, then he aced the Swiss on the next point. Federer challenged that call, but Roddick had hit the line. It was 4-1 to the American.

Federer missed a first serve and a backhand crosscourt exchange developed. Roddick then redirected a backhand down the line, catching Federer off guard. The Swiss missed a running forehand. Roddick was up 5-1. Federer took his next service point to close the gap to 5-2, but the American was in a commanding position, and he would serve the next two points with a chance to close out the set right then and there. Roddick came forward to punch a forehand volley winner up the line. He was ahead 6-2, quadruple set point. Roddick served deep to the Federer backhand, and the Swiss response was a chipped backhand return down the middle. Roddick inexplicably chose to slice his backhand down the line without much depth at a time when he could have been aggressive. Federer ripped a forehand crosscourt to take Roddick off the court. The American played a fine forehand down the line. Federer gambled, stepping forward to flick a backhand half volley crosscourt. His timing was impeccable. Clean winner for the Swiss.

Now Federer was serving again at 3-6, but he was still triple set point down. But his inspirational shot on the previous point had given Federer renewed hope. He threw in a service winner to the backhand, followed by an ace wide to the forehand. Federer had saved three set points, but Roddick had one left, and it was on his own serve. He missed his first serve, but got good depth on the second. Federer went with the short, chipped backhand return, forcing Roddick to come forward. That tactic had worked regularly for Federer against Roddick over the years. Roddick would usually be at his mercy as Federer drew him in and then passed him at will. But not this time. Roddick dug out the low ball, approaching to his adversary's forehand. On the run, Federer's down the line passing shot was not struck cleanly. The trajectory was high. Federer was off the court. He was in a desperate plight.

But Roddick had a moment of indecision. It crossed his mind that Federer's passing shot was going long. He was not sure whether or not to hit his backhand volley. The hesitation was deeply wounding. With no conviction, he reached for the high volley and missed it flagrantly. It was one of the most colossal blunders of his tennis career. He had the line covered. The court was wide open. Even a mediocre crosscourt angled volley would have sealed the set for the American. But now it was 6-6, and a revitalized Federer changed sides of the net

delighted that he was still alive in the tie-break. Roddick was still serving as he switched ends of the court. He missed another first serve.
Ineffectually, Roddick approached behind an inside-out forehand. Federer alertly rolled a backhand pass at Roddick's feet. The American
had no play on his backhand half volley. Federer had astonishingly
collected five points in a row from quadruple set point down. Now
he was serving for equality at one set all, with a set point of his own.
He sliced a backhand crosscourt, wanting to give Roddick a chance to
miss. Roddick obliged, driving a two-handed backhand long. Federer
had stolen the set, winning the tie-break 8-6, demoralizing Roddick in
the process, raising his own spirits immeasurably.

The enormous lift Federer got from salvaging the second set carried over into the third. He served an ace down the T at 125 miles per
hour, released another ace at 111 miles per hour down the middle for
30-0 and held at 15 for 1-0. Roddick must have been reeling from the
previous ten minutes, realizing that a chance to seize control of the
match had inexplicably eluded him. But he held on at 15 for 1-1, getting
on admirably with his business. But Federer was serving sublimely.
He held at love for 2-1, making all four first serves, hitting two aces.
Roddick would not be upstaged. He won his serve at love for 2-2,
twice acing Federer down the T in the deuce court. But after Federer
easily advanced to 3-2, Roddick was in trouble on his own delivery,
and in danger of losing the set quickly.

The American served in the sixth game and was down break
point. He realized that if Federer converted on that opportunity, the
Swiss would move to 4-2, with a chance to make it 5-2 in no time flat.
But Roddick stifled Federer with an excellent body serve to the backhand. Federer could not make the arduous, awkward return. After
two deuces, Roddick held on at a crucial juncture for 3-3. Thereafter,
it was a server's paradise. In his next three service games, Federer did
not lose a point, connecting with 10 of 12 first serves, releasing three
more aces. His rhythm was remarkable, his placement unwavering,
his execution magnificent. Roddick was almost as impressive, winning
twelve of seventeen points on serve, producing four aces. At 5-6, he
was down 15-30 but aced Federer down the T and then took the next
two points.

Back were Federer and Roddick in another tie-break, with the winner having the luxury of a two-sets-to-one edge. At 1-1, Roddick tamely netted a backhand slice approach to fall behind a mini-break. Federer pounced, driving a forehand passing shot winner crosscourt, pulling Roddick wide again with his slice serve to the forehand, drawing an errant return from the American. Federer was up 4-1, bursting with confidence. He ran around his backhand to rush Roddick into an error with a sizzling forehand. It was 5-1. Federer was two points from taking the set.

Roddick acquitted himself well here. An inside-out forehand winner got him back to 5-2, and he took the next point with essentially the same shot. Federer was still serving at 5-3, and he went to the short backhand slice. Roddick had to come in on Federer's terms. He chipped his backhand approach down the line, but Federer was playing chess. He knew what Roddick was going to do before Roddick did. Federer whipped a forehand passing shot crosscourt for a winner, advancing to 6-3, triple set point. Roddick fought obstinately and took the next two points on serve, and so Federer served at 6-5. He directed his delivery to Roddick's backhand, read the return perfectly, and drove a forehand crosscourt for another winner. Federer had the set, taking the tie-break 7-5. He skipped toward his chair at the changeover, elated by his revival, knowing he was one set away from a sixth Wimbledon singles title.

Given the way Federer had served in the third set—winning ninety-six percent of his first serve points and seventy-eight percent on his second—Roddick would have been justified to be despondent at the outset of the fourth. But he was a thorough professional, highly charged and deeply emotional, durable and unswerving. And then suddenly and unexpectedly, Roddick found an opening. Federer was serving at 1-2, 15-30 in the fourth set. Roddick came to the net, and Federer tried an inside-out forehand passing shot. Roddick anticipated easily and punched a backhand volley winner down the line. Federer served an ace at 127 miles per hour down the middle for 30-40, but Roddick remained at break point. He kept his backhand passing shot low, and Federer could not get enough "stick" on his volley. Roddick struck another backhand pass, sending this one up the line. Federer could not handle a low forehand volley. Roddick had broken Federer for only the second time in the match, building a 3-1 fourth-set lead. He was pushed to deuce in the following game, but he improvised with a forehand half-volley drop shot, forcing Federer into a passing shot mistake. With Roddick at game point for 4-1, Federer missed a forehand on the run.

Federer realized he would probably be taken into a fifth set, but he also recognized that he had to impose himself again on serve. He did just that. At 1-4, he held at 30, serving three aces. Roddick went to 5-2, holding at 30 with a clutch ace down the T. At 5-3, he served for the set. Federer predictably raised the stakes just a little bit higher, and Roddick found himself down 0-30 after Federer laced a dazzling forehand winner down the line. The American took the next point when Federer missed a backhand pass. Roddick attacked again, and Federer miss-hit a forehand pass long. At 30-30, Roddick was stretched out. He scraped the ball back low with slice, and that defensive ploy worked. Federer mishandled another forehand. Roddick had collected three crucial points in a row, and now stood at 40-30, a point away from a final set. He smacked a first serve deep to Federer's backhand, and the backhand chipped return floated long. Somehow, after the jarring events of the second set, after losing the hard-fought third set, Roddick had battled back gamely to admirably bring about a fifth set.

And yet, despite his poise and tenacity, Roddick had a burden to bear in the final set; Federer would be serving first. That was a distinct advantage to the Swiss. To be sure, Roddick had broken Federer twice in the match and had not yet lost his own serve, but serving from behind in the fifth and final set of a Wimbledon final is no simple task. Rafael Nadal had done that the year before when he toppled Federer, but usually the man serving first in a fifth set of a major final is the last man standing. Federer took his serve at 15 in the first game, missing only one of five first serves. Roddick then drifted into trouble. At 0-1, 30-30, he made an excellent approach shot but Federer's reply was an ineffably flicked backhand passing shot winner that barely clipped the net cord.

Now break point down, Roddick walloped a big first serve down the T, and the pace was too much for Federer, who missed a blocked forehand return. Roddick then aced Federer at 138 miles per hour down the middle, and he held for 1-1. The two steely competitors battled on gamely, looking largely untouchable on serve. Federer held at 15 before Roddick won his serve at love. It was 2-2. Federer, however, was flowing even more freely at this stage than Roddick. He aced Roddick three times in a love game—twice down the T and once out wide—and held at love for 3-2, but Roddick drew level at 3-3. Federer moved to 4-3, hitting two more aces to lift his total to thirty-three, holding at 15. Roddick went five for five on first serves in the eighth game, holding at 15 for 4-4.

Federer was in a zone now, the master of his own serving universe. He served three more aces and held at the cost of only one point for 5-4. In his last three service games, Federer had won eight of his twelve points with aces. Yet Roddick did not despair. Serving to save the match at 4-5, he held at love with an ace and a forehand winner consecutively for 5-5. But Federer charged to 6-5 with an easy hold at 15, acing Roddick two more times, both down the T in the deuce court with Roddick leaning to cover the wide delivery. Federer now had no fewer than 38 aces. Roddick, however, had not lost faith in himself. He held at 15 for 6-6 with a brilliant running backhand passing shot down the line.

At last Federer seemed human again in the thirteenth game. He did not serve an ace. Roddick took him to 30-30. But the Swiss took the next two points calmly from there. Roddick made his way back to 7-7, but Federer swiftly advanced to 8-7. He won that game not with spectacular serving but with the virtuosity and completeness of his game. At 15-15, Roddick threw up a terrific defensive lob, making Federer retreat from the net to the baseline. Federer let the ball bounce, turned for his overhead, and sliced around the outside of the ball, going down the line for a remarkable winner. Then he put away a textbook backhand volley winner crosscourt, and sent out an unstoppable serve. This was Roger Federer at his very best.

Roddick, however, was right up there with his opponent in lofty territory. He opened the next game with an ace down the middle, and won his serve at 15 for 8-8. The American had served to stay in the match four times, and had not been found wanting. Now he played a terrific return game. With Federer serving at 15-30, the Swiss unloaded on a forehand inside-out approach, making Roddick chase that shot far and wide to his backhand. Roddick hooked his winning backhand passing shot down the line and into the corner. That startling play took Roddick to 15-40, double break point. All he needed was one of the next two points, and the American would then be serving for the match.

Federer knew he had to play his best brand of percentage tennis. The Swiss swung another slice serve wide, and Roddick steered a forehand return long. At 30-40, Federer served big and wide to Roddick's backhand. All the American could do was pop the return back into play, defensively and high. Federer saw the ball hanging, and refused to let it bounce. He stepped in for a forehand drive volley, and put it away emphatically for a winner. That was a gutsy shot at a propitious moment, and Federer never hesitated. At deuce, he served to the Roddick forehand again, and the return went long. It was game point for Federer, and soon he was ahead 9-8 when Roddick sliced a backhand approach long.

Roddick had lost a golden opportunity, not through his own ineptitude but because Federer had raised his game when it counted. But Roddick held easily for 9-9, losing only one point in a stellar game. Federer had just come off a perilously close service game, but now he held at 30, serving two more aces in moving to 10-9. The Swiss had forty-one aces. They were coming in clusters. Roddick simply could not read his opponent's first serve on either side of the court. But the American made it back to 10-10, connecting with all five first serves in that game. Federer delivered ace No. 42 in the next game as he held for 11-10 at 15.

Every time Roddick walked to a changeover, he understood that he had no alternative but to hold his serve. He had no margin for error left. Federer was doing his job exceedingly well, and now Roddick had to respond in kind. The American served at 10-11 and went ahead 40-15, but Federer brought the score back to deuce. The Swiss was two points away from that record breaking 15th Grand Slam title. Roddick reached back and fired a first serve at 127 miles per hour to the Federer backhand. Federer chipped the return into the net. Roddick reached back again and cracked a 133 mile per hour thunderbolt to the forehand. Federer sent another return into the net. Roddick had survived, holding for 11-11. But every time Roddick stood up to the immensity of the occasion, Federer took it all up a notch. Federer went to 15-0 at 11-11 and then aced Roddick down the T, aced him wide to the backhand, and aced the American a third time in a row to hold at love for 12-11. How much more psychological punishment could Roddick take?

The American's combativeness was boundless, his spirit indomitable. Roddick was playing this tennis match as if his entire life depended on it. He did not seem to care how many times he had to fight from behind. All that mattered to Roddick as he battled with such ferocity was to take it all one moment at a time, one point at a time. His lost opportunities were apparently forgotten. At 11-12, the American held at love, opening that service game with an ace, following with two more unstoppable serves. He did not miss a first serve on his way to a 12-12 deadlock. Then Roddick created an opening. He had Federer at 15-30. His boosters believed that Roddick might be on the verge of a seminal moment. But Federer had other notions. With three swings of the racket, the Swiss travelled to 13-12. He aced Roddick down the middle for 30-30, aced him wide in the deuce court for 40-30, and aced him wide again for the hold. Federer now had forty-eight aces for the match. Once he sensed impending danger, Federer declared his greatness with striking clarity.

Roddick was pressed hard again by Federer as the American served at 12-13. Roddick led 40-15, but Federer got back to deuce, putting himself two points away from a triumph that would live irrevocably in his heart and mind. Roddick searched inside his soul, refusing to surrender. He blasted an excellent first serve to Federer's backhand, and the Swiss was stymied. Roddick took the next point with a typically high quality second serve that induced a netted chip backhand return from Federer. 13-13. Federer made good on only two of four first serves in the twenty-seventh game, but still held at love, releasing his forty-ninth ace in the process. He was ahead 14-13. Roddick drifted to 15-30 in the following game, but he was unflagging. Roddick attacked, punched a backhand volley crisply down the line, and Federer netted a forehand pass up the line. The American then produced consecutive service winners. He had held at 30. The score was 14-14.

Federer's demeanor—always one of his largest attributes—was unaltered. Whatever he was feeling or thinking remained hidden from public view. The man was implacable. He held at love, finishing off that game with his fiftieth ace and a superb first serve down the T that a stretching Roddick could not handle. Federer marched to 15-14. Fatigue seemed to be closing in on Roddick. He had held serve an astonishing thirty-seven consecutive times. Federer had not yet broken him all afternoon, and on into the early evening. As brilliantly as Federer had served, he had fleetingly lost his command, late in the first and early in the fourth set. Roddick had managed to exploit those few chances. But Federer had labored all across more than four hours without breaking Roddick. The weight of that failure had to be considerable for the Swiss.

Roddick looked in slight disarray as he served the thirtieth game. He trailed 0-30, but three first serves in a row—all un-returnable—put Roddick back out in front at 40-30. This was a game point for 15-15. But a backhand unprovoked mistake from the American took Federer to deuce. Roddick gave himself a second game point with a service winner to the backhand, but the depth of Federer's return was enough to coax a backhand long from Roddick. It was deuce for the second time. Federer masked his emotions in his inimitable fashion, comporting himself with dignity, wondering if he could at last find a chink in Roddick's armor. Yet Federer's play was passive. He was understandably not sure how to proceed. He needed to stay in an aggressive mode, but wanted to discover if Roddick might falter at a critical moment. Federer chipped his return shot, luring a weary Roddick in. The American did not get up to the ball in time. His approach sailed long.

Despite a gallant and career surpassing effort from Andy Roddick, Roger Federer was at match point. A short rally unfolded, but on the fifth stroke of the exchange, the American faltered, miss-hitting a forehand well over the baseline. A jubilant Federer raised his arms, jumped for an instant, allowed his inner feelings to emerge. Federer had made history of a high order once more, winning the longest men's final—in terms of total games played—ever played on the Centre

Andy Roddick and Roger Federer

Court, serving a career best fifty aces, somehow eclipsing Roddick on a day when the American outplayed him in many ways. Federer's mental toughness had been the separating factor between the two players in the end. He had achieved his record fifteenth major with a narrow triumph in an epic four-hour sixteen minute duel of seventy-seven games. The final set was also the longest ever played in a title round contest at the shrine of the sport. Sampras, Laver and Borg applauded the two players appreciatively.

The long journey from California for Sampras had ultimately been worth it. He had been there in person to watch Federer break his record, a gracious gesture for the American to make. He congratulated Federer afterwards, demonstrating no resentment, reaffirming his respect for a player he held in the highest regard. And yet, while Sampras was delighted that Federer had prevailed, he was also very sympathetic to Roddick. He fully understood his fellow American's immense pain in the aftermath of a contest that seemed headed into the Roddick victory column.

Speaking of his trip back to Wimbledon, Sampras said, "It was the right thing for me to do to go. I wanted to be there out of respect for Roger. The fact that we are pretty good friends certainly added to it. Being back there brought back a lot of great memories for me. Seeing Roger break the record made people ask me if I was rooting against him, and I really wasn't. I think all of us—Laver, Borg and myself—were kind of wanting Andy to win the match because it would have been his first Wimbledon title. Andy was working so hard and sitting behind him we could see the strain on his face, while Roger always looks so cool. Roddick was so close and he just slipped for about fifteen seconds in the second-set tiebreaker and that gave Roger a bit of breathing room.

"We all felt bad for Andy," Sampras continued. "This was his one shot really to be assured of a Hall of Fame career. To beat Roger on that court would have solidified his career. It is not that he hasn't had a very good career, but winning Wimbledon over Roger would have added a ton to what he has been able to do, and he came up just short. At the same time, Roger has been a great champion. I have said many times that if somebody is going to break my record I would like it to be him. So it was a great moment for the sport having myself and Rod and Bjorn all there in the Centre Court to see it. You won't have many moments like that in tennis."

EPILOGUE

The loss for Roddick was indeed deeply and perhaps permanently wounding. He had played probably the match of his life, and yet he had lost. It was a defeat that would have lasting implications. At the end of that summer, Roddick lost to his big serving compatriot John Isner in a fifth-set tie-break in the third round of the U.S. Open. He closed that 2009 campaign back in familiar territory, stationed at No. 7 in the world. Roddick had enlarged his reputation immeasurably by virtue of his heroics during his loss to Federer at Wimbledon. In many ways, that loss paralleled John McEnroe's agonizing setback against Bjorn Borg in the 1980 Wimbledon final. For years, even decades, McEnroe came upon people who were so moved by his performance that July afternoon that they did not recollect that he lost the match. In their minds, he had triumphed.

And so it was with Roddick. He had done everything but win against Federer, who had stopped the American for the fourth time without a loss in the final of a Grand Slam event. As Roddick tried to move beyond his deep disappointment, public sentiment was on his side to a degree he had never felt before. Almost everywhere he went, fans yearned for Roddick to be rewarded somewhere, somehow, with another major title. And yet, not much changed in 2010. He completed that season at No. 8 in the world, his ninth in a row among the top ten. But he did not advance beyond the quarters at the four majors. That was disheartening.

Roddick was held back often in that period by injuries and illnesses, and the pattern continued in 2011. He had another disappointing season, marred by his absences, hindered by the lack of continuity in his tournament play. Roddick fell out of the top ten in the world, finishing the year at No. 14. He was now in his thirtieth year. He remained a threat at the majors, but seemingly time had passed him by. Roddick had much for which to be proud as he approached 2012. He had finished one year in his career at No. 1 in the world. He had won a major singles championship. He had led the United States Davis Cup team to a long awaited triumph in 2007, the first time the Americans had won the Cup since 1995. The case for his eventual inclusion at the International Tennis Hall of Fame was substantial, but even his biggest boosters could feel his record did not do him justice. Roddick's backbreaking defeat against Federer at Wimbledon in 2009 was as valiant a performance as he had ever given in a loss, but it was a singularly bruising setback.

Federer, meanwhile, went to the 2009 U.S. Open in search of a third consecutive major singles championship. He sought to become the first player since Rod Laver to take Roland Garros, Wimbledon and the U.S. Open in succession. The Swiss came remarkably close to realizing that substantial goal, a target that Nadal hit the following season. Federer got to the 2009 U.S. Open final, and served for a two-sets-to-love lead over Argentina's towering and overpowering Juan Martin Del Potro. Federer lost that second set, but took the third. In the fourth set he was within two points of securing the title. But Federer did not succeed. Del Potro thwarted him in five sets. The fact remained that Federer had reached the final round of every major in 2009, which was no mean feat. He garnered the year-end No. 1 ATP World Tour ranking, the fifth time in six years he had earned that distinction.

At the start of 2010, Federer captured the Australian Open, taking that title for the fourth time, collecting a sixteenth major title. But the rest of the year was not productive for the Swiss. He lost in the quarterfinals of the French Open to Robin Soderling, the same man he had bested for the title the previous year. Federer had gone at least as far as the semifinals in a record twenty-three straight men's Grand Slam events before that loss. Soderling had never beaten him before. At Wimbledon, he fell in the quarters again, this time at the hands of the big-hitting Tomas Berdych. Most distressing of all, Federer had two match points against old rival Novak Djokovic in the semifinals of the U.S. Open with the Serbian serving at 4-5 in the fifth set. Djokovic escaped to win that match.

Federer's struggles continued in 2011. Djokovic upended him in a straight-set semifinal at the Australian Open. He stunned Djokovic in the semifinals of the French Open, ending the Serbian's forty-three-match winning streak before losing to Nadal. But the Swiss squandered a two-sets-to-love lead in the Wimbledon quarterfinals against the dynamic Frenchman Jo-Wilfried Tsonga. It marked the first time that Federer has ever lost at a major tournament after leading two sets to love. At the U.S. Open, lightning struck for the second time. In a semifinal collision with Djokovic, Federer served for the match at 5-3 in the fifth set, moving to 40-15, double match point. Djokovic released a startling and screaming forehand return winner crosscourt, hitting that shot with all his might, taking a big chance because he knew he was in a serious bind. Djokovic saved a second match point and swept four games in a row to win 7-5 in the fifth set, a virtual replication of his 2009 victory over Federer.

Federer turned thirty in August. He had done it all, dominated the game with grace, elegance and the skills of a supreme artist. He had performed so prodigiously that more than a few authorities considered him the greatest tennis player ever to pick up a racket. But he was struggling. The Swiss won his opening tournament of 2011 in Doha, but was beaten in twelve consecutive events thereafter. His slump ended fittingly at the tournament in Basel, Switzerland, where he claimed the crown in his hometown for the fifth time. Federer had slipped from his No. 3 world ranking down to No. 4, the lowest he had been graded since before he won his first Wimbledon in 2003. But his late season form indoors was outstanding. After his Basel victory, he took the Masters 1000 crown in Paris, and then swept through the field in London to secure a record sixth Barclays ATP World Tour Championships, moving back to No. 3 in the process after claiming seventeen match victories in a row.

Federer's quest for success on the highest level was not gone. Roger Federer had nothing left to play for besides pride, a quality he had in abundance. He had become the father of twin daughters on July 23, 2009 after marrying his longtime companion Mirka Vavrinec on April 11 of that year. Federer's life had presented him with other options, different priorities, a wider range of possibilities. But tennis was still his overriding passion, a profession that consumed him, a sport he cherished. Roger Federer may have moved into the autumn of his career, but his pursuit of the game's highest honors was unwavering, his professionalism enduring and admirable, his standards still exceedingly high. More than anything else, Federer had become singularly compelling, bringing out the best in his chief rivals, driving himself as rigorously as ever.

CHAPTER THIRTY-ONE

Rafael Nadal *vs.* Novak Djokovic

AUSTRALIAN OPEN, FINAL, JANUARY 29/30, 2012

In the longest Grand Slam tournament final ever played, the sport's two top-ranked players stretched each other nearly beyond their limits with an encounter "Down Under" that raised the morale of everyone with the good fortune to witness a spectacle unlike any other.

PROLOGUE

Growing up in the Republic of Serbia, the gifted Novak Djokovic began playing tennis when he was only four. He was born in that nation's capital of Belgrade. The country was not known as a tennis mecca. Those with bright prospects had to find the right kind of guidance, be exposed to individual coaches who could take them to the next level and display enormous potential to be noticed. And so it was with Djokovic.

His parents—who later ran a pizza restaurant—had no background in tennis. Novak's father, Srdan, and his mother, Dijana, had met on the ski slopes. Both were good competitive skiers and they hoped Novak might follow along the same path. She worked in that field as an instructor. But Novak demonstrated early on that he had an affinity for tennis. At six, he was inspired by watching Pete Sampras win Wimbledon. He joined a summer tennis camp in Belgrade that year run by Jelena Gencic, who had worked in the past with Monica Seles and Goran Ivanisevic when they were kids.

Gencic became a central figure, working with Djokovic for years on his tennis, teaching him larger lessons about life, guiding him however she could. As Novak Djokovic told S.L. Price of *Sports Illustrated* about the role Gencic played in the nurturing of his tennis, "[She was] my second mother. The base of everything I have on the tennis court, and a lot of things off it, is from her. She took care of my life in general: What I was doing in school, what I was having to eat and drink. We were listening to classical music together. She wanted to teach me how I should behave on the court, how professional I should be."

To Gencic, it was readily apparent that Djokovic might be destined for greatness on the courts. Those with keen eyes for the nuances of tennis saw something extraordinary in Djokovic. But Novak was a good judge of his own capabilities and how best to structure his game. At seven, he switched from a one to a two-handed backhand after realizing he was troubled by high balls to that side.

When Novak had turned ten and was devoting himself with fervor to his tennis, Srdan Djokovic was telling those who crossed his path that his son would one day become the best tennis player in the world. Novak progressed steadily and impressively through the juniors, becoming the No. 1 ranked player in the 14-and-unders and again in the 16-and-under division. He was single-minded and obsessive about his pursuit of the sport, looking for any edge he could find to improve. But financially it was very difficult for the Djokovic family to provide for Novak and his tennis. At one point, Srdan considered having his three sons switch nationalities and play under the British flag. Novak's two younger brothers—Marko and Djordje—were both fine tennis prospects. But Novak believed deeply in his heritage, put his weight behind continuing to play for Serbia, and that is the way it was.

Meanwhile, Novak's life beyond the lines of a tennis court was complicated and, at times, even frightening during his upbringing in Serbia. Across the 1990's, Serbia became embroiled in conflicts with Slovenia, Bosnia and Croatia, and engaged in ethnic cleansing when President Slobodan Milosevic was in power. In 1999, when Novak was twelve, a NATO coalition led by the United States bombed Belgrade for just over eleven weeks. Growing up under that kind of strife and extreme apprehension was a character building experience for Djokovic. He saw his country experience significant change for the better as he got older, including holding democratic elections.

Novak Djokovic never forgot that he was a product of his nation. He would always feel an extraordinary responsibility to Serbia and a pride in being one of its most prominent citizens. In 2011, when he was riding high and dominating men's tennis comprehensively, he sought the advice of his boyhood hero Pete Sampras. Djokovic wanted to pick the American's brain on what it took to handle the pressure of being the game's greatest player and how best to handle the burdens that went along with achieving that status.

Sampras was struck by Djokovic's deep devotion to his nation. "He talked a lot with me," Sampras explained, "about growing up in Serbia and trying to be a good role model. I think he feels a big responsibility to carry the sport in his country."

That was apparent from the beginning. In any event, Djokovic built largely on the platform of his early successes. After setting the pace in the juniors, he turned professional when he was only sixteen and gradually got his bearings in the tougher world of men's tennis. And yet, when he was still only eighteen, Djokovic cracked into the top 100 on the ATP computer, winning eleven of twenty-two matches that 2005 season. Djokovic concluded that year at No. 83 and realized he was headed toward bigger and better things.

Unsurprisingly, the 2006 season represented an even larger breakthrough for Djokovic in his evolution as a professional tennis player. He ascended to No. 16 in the world and reached his first quarterfinal at a major in Paris before losing to Rafael Nadal on the clay of Roland Garros. He won two ATP World Tour titles, captured an impressive forty of fifty-eight matches and found a level of comfort in the big leagues that was admirable.

It was in 2007 that Djokovic surged into the forefront of the sport and gained a wider following for his qualities not only as a champion in the making but for his capacity to entertain. He secured five singles titles that season, reached his first major final at the U.S. Open and soared to No. 3 in the world. That summer of 2007 was a buoyant time for the inimitable Serbian. It was then that he took his first Masters 1000 championship, upending Nadal and Federer back to back for the crown in Montreal. It seemed entirely possible that he would be ready to step up and take the U.S. Open title a few weeks later.

He very nearly did. Djokovic captivated the galleries in New York over a compelling fortnight. He faced Federer in the championship match and led 6-5, 40-0 in the first set. He had five set points in that game but was stymied by a resourceful and opportunistic Swiss Maestro. Djokovic fell in a first set tie-break but fought back to garner two more set points in the second. Once more, the singularly composed and confident Federer escaped and then went on to record a straight-set triumph. Djokovic had been outplayed on the big points by Federer, losing his bid to put his name up there among the elite as a "Big Four" tournament winner.

Yet Djokovic won the hearts of a wide range of fans for his humor and irreverence. After his quarterfinal victory over Spain's Carlos Moya, the congenial Serbian was interviewed by Michael Barkann on USA Network. He had the spectators in Arthur Ashe Stadium and those sitting at home enraptured with his brilliantly accurate impersonations of fellow players including Nadal and Maria Sharapova. He had entered another realm as not just a swiftly emerging tennis champion but also as an entertainer. New York was buzzing with sports aficionados who were thoroughly taken with Djokovic as a personality.

As 2008 commenced, Djokovic followed up commendably on his competitive exploits of the season before. He collided with Federer again in the semifinals of the Australian Open, but this time he was the more self-assured man on the big points. Djokovic halted the defending champion in straight sets and toppled the gifted athlete Jo-Wilfried Tsonga in a four-set final. At twenty, he had come through at a major for the first time. His authenticity as a tennis player of the highest order could no longer be disputed. Djokovic was among the elite, and the only lingering questions about him revolved around whether or not he could replicate his success "Down Under," and rise again to the heights when it mattered on other big occasions.

Painfully for the Serbian, he struggled to measure up to his highest standards. Djokovic advanced to the semifinals of the French and U.S. Opens later in 2008, but was defeated by Nadal and Federer respectively. The following year, he was twice a quarterfinalist at the majors, and he reached the semifinals at the U.S. Open, falling in the latter event to Federer. But the Serbian was found wanting too often when it really counted. His frustrations grew, and he carried himself to a large degree with considerable insecurity, as if he did not think he belonged in the territory of the best in his business.

And yet, Djokovic's hard work and professionalism remained essential virtues. He was determined to find higher successes in 2010, but they were hard to come by. Djokovic was a quarterfinalist at the Australian and French Opens, and he reached the semifinals of Wimbledon. The U.S. Open that season marked a pivotal point in his career. He nearly lost jarringly to countryman Viktor Troicki in the second round, trailing two sets to one, falling behind a service break in the fourth set. On a stifling day in Arthur Ashe Stadium, Djokovic escaped with a five-set triumph. On he went to the semifinals, where he took on Federer for the fourth year in a row on the hard courts of Flushing Meadows.

At 4-5 in the fifth set, Djokovic was twice down match point, but he saved both with daring and gutsy tennis, making a spectacular forehand swing volley winner behind Federer, followed by a forehand ground stroke winner driven magnificently into a vacant corner. Djokovic prevailed 5-7, 6-1, 5-7, 6-2, 7-5. But he was beaten in a four-set final by Rafael Nadal, who joined the career Grand Slam club with that victory.

At the end of that year, Nadal upended Djokovic in London during the round robin at the season-ending ATP World Tour Championships. The Spaniard finished 2010 with a 16-7 lead in his head-to-head series with Djokovic. He had never lost to his formidable rival at any of the four major events. The Spaniard headed into 2011 with deep convictions. He had enjoyed the finest year of his career and was quietly convinced that at his best no one in the world could stay with him in a big match. Nadal thought 2011 could be as celebratory a time for him as 2010 had been.

But the Spaniard was caught off guard—along with just about everyone else—by the transformation of the Serbian. In some ways, Djokovic had set the stage for a landmark season in 2011 by leading Serbia to their first ever Davis Cup championship at the end of 2010. Spurring on Serbia in the great international team competition was immensely gratifying to a player who cared so much about the welfare of his country. His countrywomen Ana Ivanovic and Jelena Jankovic had followed his lead with towering triumphs of their own. Ivanovic had become the first ever Serbian to secure a Grand Slam singles championship when she won the French Open in 2007. Jankovic had concluded 2008 as the No. 1 ranked female player in the world.

Yet Djokovic was destined for larger achievements. He commenced 2011 with a spirited campaign at the Australian Open, dropping only one set in seven matches, eclipsing Andy Murray in a resounding straight-set final for his second Grand Slam championship. Djokovic had become unstoppable. He would win seven consecutive tournaments and forty-one matches in a row into June before losing in the penultimate round of the French Open to Roger Federer. John McEnroe had opened his 1984 campaign by taking forty-two matches in a row, but his scintillating streak did not include a Grand Slam title. He was the first to concede that Djokovic's unbeaten span had been of larger value than his own.

In any case, it was the redoubtable Nadal who was scarred the most by Djokovic as the Serbian blazed through 2011 so unhesitatingly. Djokovic had never toppled Nadal from a set down across their careers, but he realized that feat in the 2011 final of Indian Wells. A few weeks later in Miami, Djokovic retaliated from a set down again to stop Nadal in a debilitating hard court contest in the Florida heat. As if to add insult to injury, Djokovic bested Nadal twice in clay court finals thereafter, beating the sport's all-time best performer on his favorite surface in straight-set finals at both Madrid and Rome. Nadal had never been beaten by Djokovic on clay until these two setbacks.

Nadal had never endured anything like this in his life—not even close. Four times in a row, Djokovic had handed him final-round defeats. But after Djokovic—who had four days off following his fourth round win at Roland Garros before meeting Federer—lost to the inspired Swiss, Nadal moved past Federer in a four-set final at Roland Garros for his tenth major singles title. Many astute observers sensed that the Spaniard would strike back boldly if he met Djokovic in the final of Wimbledon at the All England Club, where Nadal had not lost a match since he dropped a five-set final to Federer 2007.

They underestimated Djokovic. The Serbian cut down Nadal in a four-set grass-court final on the Centre Court. No longer did the surface or the circumstances matter when Djokovic collided with Nadal. The Serbian simply had the upper hand in the rivalry. The two gladiators squared off again at the end of the summer, meeting in the U.S. Open final. Djokovic was masterful once more, stopping Nadal in four sets for his third Grand Slam title of the season, joining Nadal (2010), Federer (2004, 2006, 2007), Mats Wilander (1988), Jimmy Connors (1974) and Rod Laver (1969) as the only men to secure three majors in a single year during the Open Era. Laver, of course, had taken all four in 1969 for the second Grand Slam of his esteemed career.

Djokovic would finish 2011 with an astounding 6-0 winning record over Nadal and a commanding 4-1 edge over Federer. He won seventy of seventy-six matches during the landmark year, captured ten singles titles altogether and distanced himself from everything and everyone else. Nadal had to settle for three tournament triumphs in all of 2011, the fewest he had won in any year since 2004, when he was only eighteen and still residing outside the top fifty in the world. Had Djokovic not been there to confront him almost everywhere of consequence in 2011, Nadal surely would have taken a lot more titles. Nadal finished 2011 as one of the top two players in the world for the seventh consecutive year, yet he found himself far behind Djokovic, the game's new presiding officer.

As 2011 closed, Djokovic was now a decidedly better player than he had ever been before. He was fitter, he had gone on a gluten free diet that cleared up most of his allergies, and his poise under pressure was striking to behold. He was at the height of his powers. He had wandered into difficulty with his game for much of 2009 and into the middle of 2010. Djokovic was sporadically prone to damaging mistakes off the forehand, and he tampered with his serve, much to his own detriment. His once smooth delivery became discombobulated and stiff-armed. His fluidity disappeared and he was not getting his racket into the "back scratch" position. But in 2011 his serve was once more a consistent strength and his forehand was more versatile and better than ever. He had no weaknesses.

Djokovic understandably faded toward the end of 2011 after losing only twice through the U.S. Open. His last four defeats were in the autumn, when he ran out of energy and ambition. But that left Djokovic less depleted with the 2012 season approaching.

As for Nadal, he was also spent after the U.S. Open, but at the end of the year he made one last push, leading Spain to victory in the Davis Cup. Nadal took the clinching match in four hard sets over Juan Martin Del Potro at home on clay. He hoped to use that triumph to propel him into 2012, to remove the many seeds of self-doubt that Djokovic had placed so clearly in his mind all across 2011, to start anew and impose himself again as only he could. For Djokovic, 2012 represented an opportunity to reaffirm for one and all that he was simply a great player trying to move beyond himself to an even loftier level of the game.

THE MATCH

Djokovic and Nadal arrived in Melbourne for the Australian Open primed for another major, revitalized after a brief yet crucial off season, eager to assert their authority at the start of another season. Both moved through the early rounds with total assurance. Against his first three opponents, the Serbian conceded only ten games in nine impeccable sets. Former world No. 1 Lleyton Hewitt took a set off Djokovic in the fourth round, but victory was never in serious doubt for the No. 1 seed as he marched through in four sets. The tenacious David Ferrer made Djokovic work hard in the quarterfinals, but could not prevent a straight-set triumph for the favorite.

But the defending champion was precariously close to bowing out in a magnificent semifinal contest against Andy Murray. Djokovic had swept past Murray in the Australian Open final a year earlier—winning in straight sets—but this time around Murray came into his duel with Djokovic in a much better frame of mind. He had hired eight-time major tournament victor Ivan Lendl as his new coach and Lendl had joined forces with his new pupil a few weeks earlier in Brisbane. Lendl's presence in Murray's courtside box in Melbourne was clearly beneficial to the British competitor. Murray's deeper composure over the fortnight was strikingly evident. Lendl's influence with Murray was a major storyline at the first major of 2012.

Djokovic was in control at the outset against Murray, taking the first set comfortably. But Murray began stepping up the pace significantly off his forehand side and he won the next two sets, saving three set points in the third. Djokovic took the fourth easily and charged to 5-2 in the fifth as Murray faded physically. Yet Murray battled back gamely to 5-5 and the British player had three break points in the eleventh game before Djokovic toughed it out 6-3, 3-6 6-7 (4), 6-1, 7-5 in four hours and fifty minutes of crackling tennis. The Serbian was back in the final after a stellar display of mental toughness.

Nadal blitzed through his first four matches without the loss of a set, but was in jeopardy against No. 7 seed Tomas Berdych in the quarterfinals. Having dropped the opening set in a tie-break, Nadal was down set point in the second. But he climbed out of that corner and raised his game tremendously across the last two sets, winning 6-7 (5), 7-6 (6), 6-4, 6-3. In the semifinals, Nadal confronted Federer for the twenty-seventh time in their illustrious career series. It was only their second meeting in a semifinal at one of the Grand Slam events; all of their other skirmishes at major events had been in finals. Nadal was down a set and a break, but he recouped with growing vigor and raised his record with the Swiss to 18-9 overall and 8-2 at the majors by virtue of a 6-7 (5), 6-2, 7-6 (5), 6-4 victory.

And so the stage was set for the two best players in the world to meet in a third consecutive Grand Slam final. Since "Open Tennis" had commenced in 1968, there had never been three major finals in a row contested between the same two men's competitors. Nadal and Djokovic were worthy of such an honor. They had been the most dedicated of champions, leaving no stones unturned in their pursuit of the sport's highest honors, preparing for each and every major with urgency and passion. Both the Spaniard and the Serbian wanted this particular Australian Open crown very badly. Nadal was determined to erase the harsh memories of losing so many times to Djokovic in 2011, while Djokovic had his heart set on proving that he could maintain his mastery of the game and perhaps perform even more prodigiously.

The Djokovic-Nadal championship match in Rod Laver Arena started just after 7:30 on a comfortable evening, giving the players a reprieve from the heat of Melbourne that reflects so powerfully off the hard courts. Having lost such a large degree of confidence from suffering so many losses against his chief rival, Nadal understood the importance of establishing a lead in this contest and doing everything possible to come out on top in the first set. Nadal had the benefit of two days off after his semifinal with Federer, while Djokovic had taken on Murray a day later. Nadal knew that Djokovic could well be physically and emotionally fatigued after his marathon duel with Murray and the Spaniard realized that he had to play the first set as if it was the fifth. Winning that opening set was imperative for Nadal.

Nadal burst out of the blocks purposefully. The Spanish lefty had plainly taken a long, hard look at his setbacks against Djokovic in 2011, and was committed to making some alterations in his game this time around. In that string of defeats against Djokovic the year before, Nadal had been thwarted by the Serbian in some fundamental ways. Nadal's trademark topspin forehand crosscourt—the bread and butter shot in his repertoire, the stroke that could break down every other player's backhand—was no longer working against Djokovic. The Serbian's two-handed backhand had become increasingly formidable and he was remarkably adept at handling high balls off that side. So he had largely taken the crosscourt forehand away from Nadal.

Moreover, Nadal had another tactical problem when he met Djokovic. His crosscourt backhand no longer measured up to Djokovic's stellar forehand crosscourt. Djokovic had demonstrated that he could drive that forehand with topspin, adding some sidespin as he came around the outside of the ball. He used that shot to pull Nadal off the court and to get the Spaniard out of position. Nadal's two-handed backhand was now more likely to break down than Djokovic's vastly improved forehand, which had let the Serbian down in his younger days. Djokovic had once been vulnerable to higher balls on his forehand and would press in the tight corners of close contests. But by the time he collided with Nadal in Melbourne at the outset of 2012, the Serbian had virtually no weaknesses off the ground.

That meant Nadal had to revise his thinking and reshape his game in some respects. Nadal made it abundantly clear on this occasion that he would do several things differently. He would make a more concerted effort to run around his backhand to blast aggressive inside-out forehands. He would try to go up the line more off his backhand to surprise Djokovic and to flatten out that stroke whenever he could.

He would take his forehand up the line to make Djokovic play arduous running forehands. Nadal also believed he had to serve with more variety and precision. So the Spaniard elected to go for considerably more body serves, and when he served down the T in the deuce court, Nadal aimed much closer to the center service line to make Djokovic stretch as wide as possible.

From Djokovic's standpoint, the choices were not as complicated. He would essentially play his game, swinging his first and second serves wide to Nadal's weaker backhand wing in the deuce court, controlling rallies from the center of the court with his flatter strokes off both sides, driving through his two-handed backhand crosscourt relentlessly to rush Nadal on the forehand, directing his two-hander down the line selectively to keep the Spaniard honest. Tactically speaking, Djokovic had less to think about than Nadal. His job was to control the tempo of the contest, to wear Nadal down with his pace and precision and to play the match largely on his own terms. That would be no mean feat for Djokovic, but he had shown across the previous ten months that this match-up was in his favor.

In the opening game of the match, Nadal had a small opening to break. Djokovic served at 15-30 after consecutive errors from the Serbian, one off each side. But Djokovic stepped in to release a beautifully timed inside-out forehand for a winner to knot the score at 30-30. He swiftly took the next two points as Nadal missed an aggressive forehand down the middle and then was off the mark with a forehand return as Djokovic got extra kick on his second serve. Djokovic had held on for 1-1, but Nadal struck back at him forcefully, holding at love. He commenced that game with an ace and missed only one first serve in that game.

Once more, Nadal did his utmost to negotiate a service break. He provoked an error from Djokovic by implementing a clever sliced backhand down the line and then sent a blazing forehand down the line for an outright winner. It was 0-30. Djokovic calmly took matters into his own hands, approaching with a forehand down the line to elicit a passing shot error from Nadal, then acing his adversary out wide in the ad court. Djokovic swung his slice serve wide to set up a forehand winner down the line and followed with a sizzling forehand that Nadal could not answer. Djokovic had swept four points in a row from 0-30 to move ahead 2-1, but Nadal promptly played an excellent service game, holding at the cost of only one point. From 0-15, he cracked a forehand winner up the line, followed by a winning overhead, followed by a pair of service winners. It was 2-2.

The fifth game was strenuous for both competitors. It went to three deuces. Djokovic missed only four of twelve first serves. But Nadal was unrelenting. Djokovic served an ace for 40-30, but the Serbian missed an inside-out forehand wide, taking the ball too close to his body. Nadal garnered a break point and he attempted to step inside the baseline to take his second serve return earlier. He drove his backhand long off an effective kick serve, but the Spaniard had at least let Djokovic know that he would explore that option. Djokovic moved to game point with an ace, but missed with a two-hander long. Then Nadal added velocity to his backhand down the line to coax an error from the Serbian. At break point down, Djokovic approached down the line off his backhand, but sent the shot long. The break belonged to Nadal. The lead was 3-2 for the Spaniard.

And yet, a one-service-break lead against Djokovic is never safe. He had been widely acclaimed as the man with the best return of serve in tennis. With the incomparable elasticity of his body and his propensity to stretch in any direction to make seemingly impossible returns, Djokovic was not going to lose his self-conviction simply because he had fallen slightly behind in the set. Nadal served in the sixth game and was under constant stress. That game featured five deuces. Djokovic had two break points. Nadal needed four game points before he could hold on. On the last of those deuces, Nadal used a body serve to the backhand to set up a forehand inside-out winner and then he sent a backhand up the line that was unmanageable for Djokovic, who lunged for a backhand, missing it wide.

Nadal had advanced to 4-2, but Djokovic was ceding no ground. He held at 15 for 3-4 despite missing four out of five first serves. Twice in that seventh game, Djokovic produced winners off the forehand. In the eighth game, Djokovic kept Nadal working inordinately hard again. There were three deuces. Nadal had a game point that would have given him a 5-3 lead, but Djokovic's deep backhand return was too good. On the third and last break point against him, Nadal was overcome by apprehension, netting an inside-out forehand for his most glaring and damaging mistake of the set. It was 4-4. Djokovic drifted to 0-30 on his serve in the ninth game, but he swept four points in a row to move out in front 5-4, methodically picking Nadal apart.

Nadal had lost three games in a row from 4-2. He was now serving to stay in the set at 4-5. This was a moment of consequence for the Spaniard, who had put forth such an obvious effort to take the opening set. But here he was, four points away from falling behind by a set, knowing how daunting his task would be if he did not find a way to halt Djokovic's momentum immediately. Serving in the tenth game, Nadal was ready to meet a critical moment. He did not miss a first serve. He was composed and strategically sound. Nadal held on at 30 for 5-5. A terrific body serve kept Djokovic at bay and Nadal created an opening for a forehand down the line winner. Another fine body serve elicited an errant return from Djokovic. Then a deep serve to the backhand was too much for Djokovic to handle. Nadal had given himself the cushion of a 40-0 lead. Although Djokovic collected the next two points, Nadal bravely ran around his backhand on a deep ball to that side and drove an inside-out forehand for a clutch winner. He was back to 5-5.

In the eleventh game, Djokovic moved to 30-15, but Nadal's flat backhand crosscourt opened up an avenue for a forehand inside-out winner. A scorching forehand up the line from the Spaniard provoked a forehand error from the Serbian and Nadal gained the service break when Djokovic missed a backhand long. Nadal served for the set at 6-5 and surged to 40-15, double set point. Djokovic connected with a terrific inside-in backhand return winner off a second serve and then the Serbian effortlessly drove a two-hander deep crosscourt to provoke an error from Nadal.

The score was deuce and Nadal was under almost palpable strain again on serve. Nadal was unwavering. He took control of the next point off the forehand and drew an error from Djokovic. At set point for the third time, Nadal went with another first rate body serve to the backhand and Djokovic sent a backhand return long. In eighty demanding minutes, despite a spirited comeback from Djokovic, after

Rafael Nadal

a few missteps of his own, Nadal had prevailed in the opening set 7-5.

In 133 of 134 previous matches at the four major events, Nadal had lost only once after winning the first set, falling against David Ferrer at the 2007 U.S. Open. His status as a great front runner was unarguable. Djokovic realized precisely what he was up against. To win this tennis match, he would need to play at least three more sets and perhaps four. Against just about any other opponent, coming from a set down in a big match at a major would not be out of the question for the Serbian. He had battled back ferociously from two sets down to oust Roger Federer at the 2011 U.S. Open, saving two match points in that confrontation.

But this was Rafael Nadal, the most physically imposing player in tennis, a competitor unlike any other, a man with a heart of gold and a mind of steel. He was right where he wanted to be. The burden was on Djokovic to climb back into the match, to stop Nadal in his tracks, to show the world why he had moved to the top of his profession. In twenty-five of twenty-nine previous meetings between Djokovic and Nadal, the player who had captured the first set was the victor in the end. But Djokovic at this moment was not interested in historical patterns. He was now the ultimate professional and he fully understood that he had to take it one point, one game, and one set at a time. His growing resilience as a competitor was among his finest traits.

Djokovic created a chance for himself to swing the match back in his favor. He held serve comfortably in the opening game of the second set and then had Nadal at 15-40 in the second game. But the Spaniard performed admirably at that juncture. He whipped a forehand inside-in winner off a short ball, then forced Djokovic into an error to reach deuce. Nadal closed out that game on his second game point with an ace. He had rallied to 1-1, but Djokovic now was gaining the upper hand and elevating his level of play decidedly. He held on for 2-1 and went full force after a break in the following game. Nadal served at 30-40 in the fourth game. Djokovic came forward and punched a low forehand volley down the line, clipping the baseline with that immaculate shot. He was ahead 3-1 and he swiftly held at 30 for 4-1. Djokovic was closing in on winning the second set.

The Spaniard served an ace for 40-15 in the sixth game and held on at 15 for 2-4. But Djokovic remained in command, holding at 15 for 5-2 with a forehand drop shot winner set up by a deep forehand down the line. Djokovic nearly sealed the set in the eighth game, garnering a set point with Nadal serving at 2-5. But Nadal erased it with an alert piece of business, making a delayed approach behind a forehand curling deep to the Djokovic backhand. Djokovic sliced his backhand long. Nadal held on after three deuces for 3-5. But the Serbian was now serving for the set at 5-3 and he built a 40-15, double-set-point lead.

An enterprising Nadal saved the first set point with a penetrating crosscourt forehand that Djokovic could not handle and wiped away the second with an outright winner off the forehand. At deuce, Nadal got away with a poorly executed drop shot that sat up invitingly for Djokovic, who seemed to have a wide open avenue for a passing shot. But Nadal read it perfectly and punched away a forehand volley for a winner. At break point down, Djokovic double faulted. Improbably, Nadal was back on serve, still in the set, still in with a chance to establish a two-set lead.

At 4-5, the Spaniard went to 40-30, one point away from a 5-5 deadlock. But Djokovic—in danger of losing a third straight game and perhaps squandering a big opportunity—remained uninhibited. He made an aggressive return of serve and then cracked an inside-out forehand with outright authority. Nadal was pulled off the court and he understandably missed a running forehand down the line. At deuce, Djokovic's return down the middle was a sitter for Nadal, but the Spaniard elected to go to the Djokovic backhand with a forehand approach. Djokovic easily anticipated that move and his down the line passing shot was a clean winner. Now set point down, Nadal sensed that Djokovic was ready to attack a second serve return. The Spaniard went for something extra on his second serve, but double faulted long. Djokovic had willed his way through that game and had broken at a propitious moment. It was one set all.

Nadal had staged a remarkable second set comeback, but it was to no avail. Djokovic had still not played his finest tennis and yet he had found a way to win the set with his heart and his mind rather than the quality of his shot making. He was clearly relieved and exhilarated to be back on level terms. The boost he got from salvaging that second set carried Djokovic right on through the third.

Djokovic started that third set commendably, holding at love. Al-though Nadal managed to hold for 1-1 after three deuces, it was appar-ent that Djokovic was more inspired and decidedly more confident than his opponent. Djokovic held at 30 for 2-1 with another unstop-pable inside-out forehand. With Nadal serving at break point down in the fourth game, the two warriors had a taxing exchange from the back of the court, lasting twenty-one high quality strokes. Nadal missed a forehand wide by inches as he sought to hit a winner. The Serbian was up 3-1, and he held commandingly at love for 4-1, releas-ing three service winners and an inside out forehand winner, connect-ing with all four first serves in that game.

The match had already consumed three hours and the two unwav-ering competitors were only in the middle of the third set! Nadal held on for 2-4, but Djokovic had soared to another level while the Span-iard seemed disheartened. In the seventh game, Djokovic held at love, closing out that game with a backhand down the line winner. With Nadal serving at 2-5, Djokovic broke at love, finishing that game with a devastatingly potent forehand winner down the line, as if he wanted to underline his supremacy with that dazzling shot. Djokovic had won eight points in a row to take the set 6-2. He had won sixteen of eighteen points on his serve in that set. He was ahead two sets to one.

Djokovic looked in many ways like the fresher and fitter man. Nadal was in a terrible bind, hoping to find a way back into the match, knowing that Djokovic was not going to provide any help. The Spaniard's bright beginning had largely been washed away by Djokovic's masterful play from the backcourt and by the Serbian's wider range of options.

And yet, Nadal's temerity has always been one of his primary virtues. Djokovic knew that Nadal's reservoir of pride surpassed anyone else the Serbian had ever confronted. Nadal would inevitably fight on indefatigably and it would be up to Djokovic to remain ascendant while keeping Nadal from finding another gear. That would be much easier said than done. Neither player could feel entirely comfortable at this stage of a bruising encounter, although Djokovic had bolstered his self-conviction by taking a two-sets-to-one lead.

Djokovic opened the fourth set on his serve, surging to 40-15 with an ace out wide in the ad court. But Nadal stretched that game to two deuces before Djokovic held on for 1-0. The players had been at it for three hours and twenty two minutes. Djokovic, however, seemed to have more in reserve at this stage. After Nadal held at 30 with an ace down the T in the ad court to reach 1-1, the Serbian poured in four straight first serves, released a pair of aces and held at love for 2-1. Nadal answered that challenge forcefully, holding his serve at 15, getting all five of his first serves in, closing out that game with another top of the line inside out forehand that was unmanageable for Djokovic.

Nadal held for 2-2 with relative ease. With the Serbian serving in the fifth game, Nadal reached 15-30, but the Spaniard became timid, netting a sliced backhand when he could have come over the ball with topspin. Djokovic took a 40-30 lead with an exceptionally well placed sliced serve wide, provoking an errant return from the Spaniard.

Nadal then went for an adventuresome forehand down the line and sent it well long. It was 3-2 for Djokovic.

The Spaniard—recognizing that one break of serve against him now could be fatal—was bearing down hard. Ahead 30-0 in the sixth game, he double faulted wide down the T and then Djokovic made it back to 30-30. On the next point, Nadal moved swiftly from defense to offense, moving around his backhand for a heavyweight inside-out forehand. Djokovic had to play defense, netting a sliced forehand. Nadal then opened up the court with tactical acuity, angling away a backhand crosscourt, travelling to 3-3 after that winning stroke.

And yet, Djokovic was apparently not unduly worried. After netting a backhand drop shot to fall behind 0-15 in the seventh game, he swept four points in a row, moving to 4-3 as Nadal netted an aggressively played forehand return. The Serbian—afforded the luxury of serving first in the fourth set—was applying scoreboard pressure on Nadal. Nadal found himself having less and less margin for error the deeper he went into the set. He served in the eighth game and Djokovic came after him with guns blazing, going for it all. The Serbian fully realized that by breaking Nadal here, he would have the opportunity to serve for the match.

Djokovic opened that critical game with a scintillating two-handed backhand winner up the line. He then unleashed a forehand with interest, placing Nadal in an uncomfortable position on his backhand side. The Spaniard erred. Djokovic was at 0-30. Sensing he was on the verge of triumph, Djokovic took utter control once more, driving a forehand down the line for an outright winner. He was at triple break point for 5-3, five points away from a second straight Australian Open title, within striking distance of the crown. But Nadal was majestic with his back to the wall. He crunched an inside-out forehand winner from well back in the court for 15-40, produced a service winner wide to Djokovic's forehand for 30-40, and measured a backhand down the line immaculately on the next point, finding the corner for a winner with Djokovic leaning in the wrong direction.

It was deuce. Nadal had entered another zone with his emotional energy. He aced Djokovic down the middle for game point and caught the Serbian off guard with an excellent first serve to the forehand that was unreturnable. From 0-40, Nadal had collected five points in a row, playing inspired tennis, taking the right kind of calculated risks, halting Djokovic just when it seemed certain the Serbian was going to break him. Nadal boldly held on for 4-4. The match was three hours and fifty-nine minutes old, but rain was falling. Play was halted for nearly ten minutes.

Djokovic admirably resumed his business with no hint of trepidation. The Serbian held at love for 5-4 with a spectacular forehand winner down the line. He was conducting himself like the thorough professional he was and Nadal was again in an awkward corner, serving to stay in the match, facing the best returner in the game of tennis. Nadal lost the first point of that tenth game and stood three points away from a four-set loss. But he was unbending on the next three points, going to Djokovic's stronger backhand side and succeeding every time. At 40-15, the explosiveness of Djokovic's game was more than Nadal could contain. Djokovic sent a tremendous forehand down the line to set up a forehand winner crosscourt. It was 40-30. Djokovic was three points away from the title, but Nadal's sharply angled backhand crosscourt was more than his opponent could handle. 5-5.

Nadal took Djokovic to 30-30 in the eleventh game. He played the percentages with so much at stake, swinging the slice serve wide, coaxing a short return from the Spaniard, then stepping in for a clean winning backhand down the line. This was Novak Djokovic at his very best, calm and purposeful, in utter control of himself and his destiny, ready, willing and able to handle the pressure of a crucial moment. He won a lengthy baseline exchange to hold on for 6-5, with Nadal overcooking a backhand at the end of the rally.

For the second time, Nadal served to stay in the match and here he was nothing less than a towering champion. Serving wide to Djokovic's forehand on the first point, he forced a netted return from his adversary. A solid backhand crosscourt from Nadal led to a forehand down the line long from Djokovic. He charged on to 40-0 and held at love with an inside-out forehand winner to the open court. That was class. That was character. That was Rafael Nadal rising to a critical moment commandingly. It was 6-6.

Nadal had prevailed in six of his previous eight career tie-breaks against Djokovic, but this was one was the most important he had ever played against a rival who had become a vastly improved big point player and a man who no longer buckled under pressure. Neither player lost a point on serve until 3-3 in this sequence. Now Djokovic seized the initiative, stepping around for an inside-out forehand, taking Nadal off the court with the weight and precision of his shot. Nadal had to go for a very difficult running forehand down the line and could not make it. Djokovic had gained the mini-break, pulling ahead 4-3.

Clearly, Djokovic felt himself closing in on the finish line. He swung freely on the following point, connecting with a brilliant forehand inside-in winner. The world No. 1 was two points away from the title for the first time, leading 5-3 in the tie-break, serving with a chance to reach triple match point. Djokovic had control of this pivotal point, but Nadal refused to give anything away. Djokovic saw some daylight, going for a forehand winner up the line. He missed it narrowly wide. Nadal had just averted a deficit even he might have been hard pressed to counter.

Nadal served at 4-5 and was forced onto the defensive again by the power and accuracy of the Serbian's up-tempo ground game. But the Spaniard's instincts were spot on. He sliced his backhand low and short down the line, making Djokovic dig out a difficult shot. Djokovic elected to take it on his forehand, but he missed with an inside-out forehand. Nadal was back on level terms at 5-5 and still serving. He was both smart and gutsy, going wide to the forehand with a terrific first serve. Djokovic's return went wide down the line. Nadal had moved ahead 6-5, fighting back valiantly to win three points in a row, standing improbably at set point.

Djokovic served the twelfth point, composed himself laudably, and put his first delivery in. He seemed to have control of the point, but his aggressive forehand inside-in landed wide. Nadal had taken the tie-break 7-5, sending the appreciative Australian fans into a delirious state. The Spaniard was so relieved and so excited by taking the match into a fifth set that he went down to his knees as the audience cheered on both men unabashedly. Djokovic had seemed to have every advantage and opening he needed to win the fourth set. He had served first and was not broken. He had built a 5-3 lead in the tie-break. He was striking the ball with ferocity, clinical efficiency and fearlessness. Yet Nadal—gradually raising his game, serving with more speed and accuracy, playing the biggest points better—had earned that set with his gumption, growing intensity and a singularly positive spirit.

Nadal and Djokovic had moved into uncharted territory. In eight previous best-of-five-set appointments, they had never gone to a fifth set. Nadal had been victorious in six of those meetings, but Djokovic had prevailed in the last two. Yet this would be as comprehensive a test of character as Djokovic had ever confronted. He had already been stretched to his limits by Murray in a debilitating semifinal showdown and now he found himself in a fifth set against a man who had always thrived under those circumstances. In eighteen career five set contests, Nadal had been the victor fifteen times, losing twice to Federer and once to Lleyton Hewitt. The last time Nadal had lost a five-set match was to Federer in the 2007 Wimbledon final. And yet, Djokovic had a surprisingly good five-set record himself. He had won fourteen of nineteem battles that had gone the distance. That was no mean feat.

The central problem for Djokovic was that a sleeping giant named Nadal clearly was revitalized. The Spaniard fully realized how close he had come to bowing out in four sets. He viewed the fifth set as a privilege. Nadal could almost feel the winds of momentum blowing at his back and propelling him forward. He lived for opportunities like this one. Yet Nadal recognized that the Djokovic of 2012 bore little resemblance to the Djokovic of old. In years gone by, the Serbian had a tendency to surrender when he traveled close to the edge of physical exhaustion. The newly matured Novak Djokovic was willing to push himself above and beyond what he once thought was possible. He may not have been happy about the necessity of a fifth set, but he would deal with it.

Nadal performed terrifically in the opening game of the final set. He started with an inside-out forehand winner before Djokovic answered with a forehand return winner for 15-15. But then Nadal, falling back, released a thundering forehand inside-out winner, a startling shot that was measured at 101 miles per hour. The Spaniard double faulted wide down the T to make it 40-30, but then aced Djokovic with a sliced serve wide to hold for 1-0. Djokovic swiftly got back to 1-1, holding at 15, bolstered decidedly by an ace down the T for 40-0.

But Nadal seemed driven by private engines as powerful as a tennis player ever possessed. He held commandingly at love for 2-1. The Spaniard did not miss a first serve. Djokovic could not get a return back into play on the last three points. In the fourth game, Djokovic's deep fatigue was unmistakable. On the first point of that game, Djokovic tamely sent an inside-out forehand into the net. His legs were plainly buckling. His feet were not moving properly. He seemed to be wavering. But the defending champion aced Nadal wide in the ad court for 30-30. Despite more wobbling, Djokovic moved to 40-30 by approaching forcefully on the Nadal forehand to force an error. The match was exactly five hours old. Djokovic reached back with his dwindling resources, cracked a backhand up the line and coaxed Nadal into a mistake. Djokovic's tenacity and temerity were the twin virtues keeping him in the match.

It was 2-2. Nadal had been given an opening in the previous game that he had not been able to exploit. Yet he remained unflappable. Djokovic struggled in the fifth game as his legs seemed to turn to jelly. Nadal served another ace for 40-0 and held at love for 3-2. In three service games across the fifth set, Nadal had won twelve of fourteen points. As Djokovic prepared to serve in the sixth game, he stretched his legs. He took a 30-15 lead, but the depth of Nadal's two-handed backhand crosscourt caused Djokovic to miss off his forehand side. At 30-30, Nadal put on a stupendous display of defense. His deft work from the baseline eventually earned Nadal the point, as Djokovic drove an inside-out forehand wide.

It was break point for Nadal. He did not squander it. The Spaniard changed the direction of the rally, firing a sizzling forehand up the line. Djokovic chased it down, but his crosscourt forehand reply went long. Nadal was exhilarated to be up 4-2 in the fifth set. He had never lost a match in his entire career from a service break up in a fifth set. He was one of the great front runners the sport had yet seen. Moreover, the Spaniard had much more spring in his step than the Serbian at this stage.

Both players knew the seventh game of this final set would be critical. If Nadal could hold, he would take a commanding 5-2 lead and it would be a tall task for Djokovic to fight his way out of that dark corner. But if Djokovic could break back immediately, he could change the complexion of the contest decidedly and he just might re-invent himself and rediscover a way to win. Nadal went ahead 30-15. Djokovic approached on the Nadal forehand and the Spaniard went down the line with his passing shot. Djokovic attempted a forehand drop volley crosscourt, but his shot sat up invitingly for Nadal, who got to the ball in plenty of time to roll his two-handed passing shot up the line for a winner. Djokovic was stranded helplessly on the other side of the court.

But Nadal hit the passing shot too fine and did not give himself enough margin for error. He missed it a few inches wide in the alley. Instead of a comfortable 40-15 lead, Nadal found himself in the more tenuous territory of 30-30. The commentators on ESPN and Tennis Channel instantly recognized how that point might alter the flow of the match. On ESPN, the astute Darren Cahill—a former player and a highly-regarded coach who had worked with Andre Agassi—said, "Novak's got that look back in his eyes that we've seen so many times in the last twelve months." Cahill was saying that Djokovic believed again that he could win. Cahill's colleague Chris Fowler reinforced that notion, pointing out, "A gift like that can help spark a comeback."

Martina Navratilova's analysis of that crucial moment was much the same on Tennis Channel. She asserted, "Oh, he'd [Nadal] like to have that one back. Is this a turning point back for Djokovic?"

Nadal served at 4-2, 30-30. Although he is a seemingly unshakable character, he had to be at least a bit apprehensive now. Djokovic pitted his strength against Nadal's, driving a deep and penetrating crosscourt backhand to Nadal's forehand corner. The Spaniard tried to defend, but could not cope with the pace thrown at him. He netted the forehand. At 30-40, he missed his first serve, then went wide with slice on his second serve. Djokovic's backhand return was magnifi-cent. He hit it deep with immense power. Nadal tried to answer with a forehand down the line, but he drove his shot long.

Djokovic had improbably broken back for 3-4. He lost the first point of the eighth game, but then swept four in a row, picking apart Nadal's backhand throughout that game. It was 4-4. The first point of the ninth game was one of the finest in the match, lasting thirty-two strokes, featuring depth, speed, accuracy and supreme athleticism from both combatants. At the end of that exchange, Nadal changed pace, slicing his backhand softly down the line. Djokovic drove a backhand long and fell on his back in wry amusement. The two players had taken their level up a notch in the sixth hour of a monumental struggle and the Serbian had stepped outside of himself in appreciation of the moment.

Djokovic netted a backhand drop shot to give Nadal a 30-0 lead, but Djokovic battled back to 30-30. A service winner from Nadal made it 40-30 for the Spaniard, but Djokovic captured two points in a row. It was break point for the Serbian. Nadal took his time and then sliced his first serve wide at an acute angle, forcing Djokovic to net a one-handed return. Nadal valiantly held on from there to reach 5-4.

Djokovic had made such a gallant bid to turn the match around, but here he was, serving to stay in the match in the tenth game of the final set after five hours and thirty-three minutes. Nadal was four points away from victory, but Djokovic revealed no insecurity whatsoever. He commenced that game with a forehand winner, built a 40-0 lead, double faulted, but held at 15 with an astonishing forehand crosscourt winner that landed in front of the service line and just inside the sideline. Djokovic was on level terms again at 5-5.

The Serbian had found another gear, while Nadal's intensity and speed had diminished. In the eleventh game, the score went to 30-30. The Spaniard defended brilliantly, but missed a forehand crosscourt as Djokovic kept him on the run. At break point down, Nadal stepped up the pace on his crosscourt backhand to provoke a forehand long from Djokovic. It was deuce. Nadal's forehand down the line landed wide and he was behind break point for the second time. Nadal—perhaps thinking he could draw Djokovic forward—chipped a backhand down the line, but his timid shot found the net.

Djokovic had captured four of the last five games. He was ahead 6-5, serving for the match, hoping to win the Australian Open for the third time, looking to stop Nadal for the seventh time in a row. He took a 30-0 lead, but lost a remarkable rally by driving a forehand crosscourt long. Then the Serbian came forward. Nadal threw up a defensive lob.

Novak Djokovic

Djokovic bungled his overhead completely, sending that weary smash into the net. At 30-30, Nadal put up a wall on his side of the net, retrieving brilliantly as he raced from corner to corner. He found an opening to seize the initiative, flattening out his backhand down the line. Caught off guard, Djokovic erred, netting his two-hander.

And so Nadal had arrived at break point, in striking distance of a 6-6 deadlock. Nadal tried to gain the upper hand with a run around forehand return, but could not get enough on the shot. Djokovic took control, drove a backhand crosscourt and rushed Nadal into a forehand error down the line. At deuce, Nadal's backhand bounded off the net cord, but landed unluckily wide. The Serbian had come from a set down. He had rallied from 2-4 down in the final set. He had taken all of the punishment a player must accept if he is going to prevail against Rafael Nadal in a marathon duel. He had done everything he could possibly have asked of himself, and now he was at match point, only one point away from the fifth Grand Slam singles championship of his career.

Djokovic served with pinpoint precision down the T, eliciting a short return from a stretched out Nadal. The Serbian moved swiftly into the court, saw a window of opportunity for an inside-out forehand and took it. He kept the shot low, hit it hard and directed it close to the sideline. It was magnificent, an outright winner for Novak Djokovic. He had somehow defeated Rafael Nadal in the longest ever Grand Slam tournament final, winning 5-7, 6-4, 6-2, 6-7 (5), 7-5 in five hours and fifty three minutes. The best tennis of this history-making confrontation was played in the fourth and fifth sets, with many of the most absorbing baseline exchanges taking place during the sixth hour of the landmark battle.

Nadal's performance in defeat was exemplary. He was buoyed by giving himself a chance to win after so many stinging defeats against the estimable Djokovic. Nadal said, "I think we played a great tennis match. It was, I think, a very good show. I enjoyed being part of this event and this match. Important thing for me, during all of 2011, I didn't play much like this.... I am not happy I lost the final but that's one of the losses that I am more happy [about] in my career."

The Spaniard was very complimentary about the quality of

Djokovic's returns all through the contest. "Is something unbeliev-able the way he returns, no? His return is probably one of the best in history. I never played against a player who returns like this. Almost every time."

Djokovic shared Nadal's appreciation for being part of an impor-tant chapter in the history of their sport. "I think it's probably the longest final in the history of all Grand Slams and just to hear that fact makes me cry, really. I'm very proud to be a part of this history. I'm a professional tennis player. I'm sure all of my colleagues would say the same—we live for these matches. We work every day. We're trying to dedicate all of our life to this sport to come to the situation where we play a six hour match for a Grand Slam title. We took the last drop of energy that we had from our bodies."

EPILOGUE

Djokovic and Nadal had given the tennis world a gem as the 2012 campaign at the majors commenced. These two remarkable individu-als had raised the profile of the sport sweepingly, taking tennis to a level of physicality that would once have been unimaginable. From the French Open of 2010 through the Australian Open of 2012, they had split the eight major championships over a compelling span. The upper reaches of the game had seldom been more captivating. Both men were still in their mid-twenties, hoping to add substantially more to their resumes. Nadal had collected ten major titles before becoming the first man in the Open Era to lose three Grand Slam tournament fi-nals in a row—all to Djokovic. The Serbian's Australian Open triumph over Nadal gave him half as many majors as the Spaniard.

The Spaniard's boundless quest to find the right solutions to suc-ceed again against Djokovic was admirable. His 16-7 lead in their per-sonal series had been cut to 16-14. But Nadal was a warrior through and through. He accepted the size, scope and sheer enormity of his challenge in trying to topple the Serbian. As for Djokovic, he had be-come as tough a match player and as resilient a competitor as anyone in his trade. He was at the height of his powers, enjoying the battle-field more than he ever had, relishing the chance to raise his historical

STEVE FLINK

stock even more.

Both Djokovic and Nadal were, however, fully aware of the number of formidable rivals who surrounded them as they moved through 2012 and beyond. Federer remained an outstanding player and a champion fully committed to winning more majors. Andy Murray—born exactly one week before Djokovic in May of 1987—was driving himself inexorably toward greater accomplishments. The Frenchman Jo-Wilfried Tsonga was an aggressive player with one of the best serves in the game and the speed and athleticism to strike down anyone. Juan Martin Del Potro—so impressive in overpowering Nadal and Federer to win the 2009 U.S. Open—had the capacity to reestablish himself as a strong contender at the majors. And great prospects like Australia's Bernard Tomic and the Canadian Milos Raonic were out there on the horizon, ready to step forward and claim large prizes when given the chance.

Be that as it may, Novak Djokovic and Rafael Nadal stood majestically as a pair of all-time greats who remained single-minded in their pursuit of hard-earned prizes and the kind of success reserved only for authentic champions. Their epic 2012 final round duel in Melbourne would live forever in the hearts and minds of all who saw it because the Serbian and the Spaniard represented themselves and their sport so commendably, because they demonstrated that great tennis players are athletes of rare class and character, because they handled the rigors of an excruciatingly long contest with ineffable grace and dignity. Djokovic and Nadal were the standard bearers of their sport and tennis could be very grateful for that.

452

CHAPTER THIRTY-TWO

Honorable Mention Matches

Included here are matches (listed chronologically) that narrowly missed inclusion among the top 30 of all time.

1. SUZANNE LENGLEN d. DOROTHEA LAMBERT CHAMBERS 10-8, 4-6, 9-7, final, Wimbledon, 1919

The Frenchwoman lost only one match in her entire amateur career and was never beaten at Wimbledon. This was her closest call. Lambert Chambers—a seven-time Wimbledon singles titlist—was nearly forty-one. She served for the match at 6-5 in the third set and had two match points in that game. Lenglen survived these tests and never looked back.

2. BILL TILDEN d. BILL JOHNSTON 6-1, 1-6, 7-5, 5-7, 6-3, final, U.S. Championships, Forest Hills, 1920

Tilden took the championship of his country for the first time over the rival who had beaten him in the final the previous year. "Big Bill" would overcome "Little Bill" in five of his victorious seven finals at the U.S. Championships. This was perhaps their highest-quality clash.

3. RENE LACOSTE d. JEAN BOROTRA 6-3, 2-6, 6-0, 2-6, 8-6, final, French Championships, 1929

In this collision between two of the famed "Four Musketeers," the cunning Lacoste, who had fashioned a five-set victory over Bill Tilden in the 1927 final, triumphed over his countryman. Lacoste narrowly escaped after Borotra staged a couple of spirited comebacks. Having been beaten by Henri Cochet in the title match of 1928, Lacoste regained his title in a superbly contested match.

4. FRED PERRY d. DON BUDGE 2-6, 6-2, 8-6, 1-6, 10-8, final,
U.S. Championships, Forest Hills, 1936

Budge served for the match three times in the fifth set, and had two match points, but the Englishman refused to concede. Perry had won his third consecutive Wimbledon earlier in the summer. This triumph gave him a third U.S. National Championship as he concluded his amateur career with one of his best wins.

5. ALICE MARBLE d. HELEN JACOBS 6-0, 8-10, 6-4, final,
U.S. Championships, Forest Hills, 1939

Collecting her third of four singles titles at Forest Hills, Marble was challenged persistently in the second and third sets by her country-woman. Competing on a windy afternoon, Jacobs led 3-1 in the third set. The final game of the match produced seven deuces. Jacobs had five game points for 5-5 and saved two match points before bowing gamely. Marble was the first female player to be described as "playing like a man." She attacked brilliantly behind her serve with searing approach shots. Her aggressive style was developed on the hard courts of California.

6. SARAH PALFREY COOKE d. PAULINE BETZ 3-6, 8-6, 6-4, final,
U.S. Championships, Forest Hills, 1945

These two American stalwarts had met four years earlier in the final of their nation's Grand Slam event, with Cooke claiming victory in straight sets. As they reprised that encounter, Betz was the top seed and favored to topple the No. 2 seed Cooke. Betz was up a break in the third set, serving at 4-3, two holds away from the title. But an enterprising Cooke collected three games in a row to record the most gratifying victory of her career.

7. PANCHO GONZALES d. TED SCHROEDER 16-18, 2-6, 6-1, 6-2, 6-4,
final, U.S. Championships, 1949

Allison Danzig of The New York Times wrote of Gonzales following this epic clash: "One can hardly give the champion too much praise for his moral fiber." Both Americans were aware of the stakes—the winner would inevitably move on to a career in professional tennis while the loser would be held back. Gonzales toppled Schroeder in another of his seemingly impossible comebacks. The outcome remained in doubt until 4-4 in the fifth set. Schroeder had won Wimbledon that year, coming through four times in five-set matches. On his way to this battle with Gonzales at Forest Hills, he had won two more five-set contests—over Frank Sedgman and Billy Talbert. On this day, Gonzales was stronger down the stretch.

8. ROBERT HAILLET d. BUDGE PATTY 5-7, 7-5, 10-8, 4-6, 7-5, fourth round, French Championships, 1958

In one of the most closely fought matches in the history of international tennis, Haillet upended the 1950 Roland Garros champion. Patty had a 5-0, 40-0 lead in the fifth set. Then, in one of the most improbable turnarounds ever recorded on a big stage, Haillet took seven straight games and climbed all the way back to victory.

9. ALTHEA GIBSON d. DARLENE HARD 3-6, 6-1, 6-2, final, Forest Hills, U.S. Championships, 1958

The determined Gibson had become the first African American ever to record a triumph in a major championship with her success at the French Championships in 1956. The following year, she was the victor at both Wimbledon and the U.S. Championships. Earlier in 1958, she had successfully defended her Wimbledon crown. She was at the absolute peak of her powers, but the tenacious Hard—who would eventually secure three majors in singles—moved out in front of Gibson in this clash and seemed on her way to an important victory before Gibson imposed her bigger game and turned the contest around emphatically in the end.

10. MARGARET SMITH d. LESLEY TURNER 6-3, 3-6, 7-5, final, French Championships, Paris, 1962

In this dramatic meeting of two Australian women, Smith struck back boldly from 3-5 down and match point down in the final set to beat Turner in a compelling final for her first of five French Championship titles. Turner—who took the tournament the following year—was better suited to the slow clay court surface, but was conquered in the end by a superior all-around player.

11. ROY EMERSON d. CHUCK McKINLEY 3-6, 6-2, 6-4, 6-4, Davis Cup Challenge Round, Cleveland, 1964

Emerson's win clinched the Davis Cup for Australia in a thrilling finish. After his teammate Fred Stolle had stopped Dennis Ralston to even the score between the two nations at 2-2, Emerson rallied from a set down against the formidable McKinley, who was the 1963 Wimbledon champion. At twenty-eight, Emerson was at his peak, performing with characteristic athleticism, displaying his patented rocking motion as he set up his powerful serve, volleying with increasing efficiency across the last two sets.

12. MARIA BUENO d. ROSIE CASALS 6-2, 10-12, 6-3, semifinal, U.S. Championships, Forest Hills, 1966

Bueno was on her way to claiming her fourth and last title on the grass courts at the West Side Tennis Club. Casals was seventeen, and a rising star who captivated fans everywhere she went with her exuberant game and court presence. Their clash was brilliantly played on both sides of the net. It was thought then that Casals would win her share of major championships, but she fell just short of that standard in singles while establishing herself as an outstanding doubles player.

13. NANCY RICHEY d. BILLIE JEAN KING 4-6, 7-5, 6-0, semifinal, Madison Square Garden International, New York, 1968

The two top women in the United States had not played each other in a singles match for the better part of four years. Their last meeting had been at Forest Hills in 1964, when Richey stopped her adversary in a straight-set quarterfinal. In this classic confrontation between the net charging King and the counter-attacking Richey, a dramatic reversal of fortunes took place. Richey lost the first set and trailed 5-1 in the second. In the ninth game of that set, she saved a match point. The Texan completed a run of twelve consecutive games to prevail against her greatest rival. Less than three months later, Richey ousted King in the semifinals and went on to win her second and last major—the French Open in Paris.

14. KEN ROSEWALL d. CLIFF RICHEY 6-8, 5-7, 6-4, 9-7, 7-5, quarterfinal, Wimbledon, 1971

Like his sister Nancy, Cliff Richey became the top-ranked player in American tennis. He had achieved the No. 1 U.S. ranking in 1970 by stopping Stan Smith in the semifinals of the Pacific Coast Championships in Berkeley, California. In that stunning encounter, Richey and Smith simultaneously reached match point at 4-4 in a fifth set tie-break. Richey made an almost miraculous diving forehand volley winner to win. But in this 1971 battle with Rosewall, he was less fortunate. He led two sets to love, went up a break in the third, but could not sustain his authority. He was twice up a break in the fourth, but was unable to press his advantage. In the fifth, he had the determined Australian at 15-40 in three different service games, but Rosewall prevailed. This was an all court gem of a tennis match.

15. JOHN NEWCOMBE d. BJORN BORG 4-6, 6-3, 6-3, 6-2, final round, WCT Dallas Finals, 1974

Newcombe was one of the finest fast court players of his era. He won seven major singles championships, including three at Wimbledon. Had he not been involved in the 1972 and 1973 boycotts of that event, he would surely have won at the All England Club at least one more time. In this meeting with the seventeen-year-old Borg, Newcombe was mesmerized at the beginning by the Swede's heavy and well-disguised topspin. The Australian fell swiftly behind 4-0. From that juncture, however, he put his highly observant mind to work and picked Borg apart meticulously. The score of this contest does not begin to do justice to the quality of the tennis.

16. MANUEL ORANTES d. GUILLERMO VILAS 4-6, 1-6, 6-2, 7-5, 6-4, semifinal, U.S. Open, Forest Hills, 1975

In this evening clash under the lights, Vilas was in command. He led two sets to love and later built a 5-0 fourth-set advantage. Then he saw five match points erased by the Spaniard in this battle of left-handers. Orantes managed to construct a victory from what appeared to be a certain defeat. His comeback ranks among the grittiest ever made at a major. The next day, exploiting his superior clay court skills, Orantes dismantled Connors 6-4, 6-3, 6-3 to claim his only major title.

17. CHRIS EVERT d. EVONNE GOOLAGONG 6-3, 4-6, 8-6, final, Wimbledon, 1976

Of all the delightful duels between the American and the Australian, this was their most memorable. Evert had never beaten her seemingly care-free rival on grass before. Their rivalry had begun on the same Centre Court four years earlier when Goolagong had recouped from a set and 3-0 down to win in three sets. In this confrontation, Evonne's instinctive grass court game lifted her to a 2-0 final-set lead. Evert rallied and served for the match at 5-4, only to drop two games in a row. But from 5-6 in that gripping final set, Evert demonstrated her mental toughness and came away with the second of her three Wimbledon singles titles.

18. JIMMY CONNORS d. ADRIANO PANATTA 4-6, 6-4, 6-1, 1-6, 7-5, fourth round, U.S. Open, 1978

In the first year of the Open on hard courts, Connors overcame an inspired and gifted rival on a day when he was often outplayed. Panatta—the Italian and French Open winner of 1976—attacked Connors diligently. He served for the match at 5-4 in the fifth set, reached 30-30, but was broken there by two scorching returns from the American. Panatta, serving at 5-6, recovered from 0-40 and saved four match points. In that high tension game, Connors provided one of the most astonishing shots of his career, curling a one-handed backhand passing shot around the net post for a winner. Panatta double faulted on the fifth match point to conclude an exhilarating contest. Buoyed by that triumph, Connors marched to the title without the loss of a set in his last three matches.

19. JOHN MCENROE d. JIMMY CONNORS 6-4, 4-6, 7-5, 4-6, 6-3, semifinal, U.S. Open, 1984

This match was played on a landmark historical day. Stan Smith had opened the program by defeating John Newcombe in a closely contested Men's 35 final. Ivan Lendl won his men's semifinal from match point down against Pat Cash. Martina Navratilova came from a set down to defeat Chrissie Evert in the women's final. McEnroe and Connors finished their business after 11 p.m. that evening, but not before waging perhaps their best-ever battle. Connors missed a large opening when he did not convert a 3-1 third-set lead. Despite connecting with seventy percent of his first serves, McEnroe was broken seven times across five sets by a highly charged Connors. Four years earlier—despite losing eleven straight games at one stage—McEnroe had beaten Connors in another epic five-set semifinal at the Open. It was a riveting encounter, but not the equal of the standard set by both men in this 1984 meeting.

20. HANA MANDLIKOVA d. MARTINA NAVRATILOVA 7-6 (3), 1-6, 7-6 (2), final, U.S. Open, 1985

Mandlikova was an immensely gifted shot maker who could produce winners from anywhere on the court. She possessed a rare combination of power and touch. Mandlikova would win four major singles championships in her sporadically brilliant career, taking all of the big titles save Wimbledon, where she was twice a finalist. Mandlikova's triumph in this match was her finest performance. She wasted a 5-0 first-set lead before holding back Navratilova to move out in front. Navratilova was in top form in the second set, but Mandlikova regrouped and served for the match in the third. Ultimately, she played a magnificent tie-break to conclude a scintillating battle of constant attacking tennis.

21. STEFAN EDBERG d. IVAN LENDL 6-7 (3), 7-5, 6-1, 4-6, 9-7, semifinal, Australian Open, 1985

Lendl was the world's best player as he approached this showdown with Edberg in the second to last Australian Open ever held on grass courts. In Edberg, Lendl confronted a first-rate grass court player, a placid Swede who was faster than anyone in his time at getting in behind his serve to make the first volley. This was the first meeting ever between Lendl and Edberg at the majors; eventually, these two accomplished men would garner fourteen singles majors between them. After trailing two sets to one, Lendl found his range convincingly off the ground, taking the fourth set, negotiating a service break in the opening game of the fifth. At 4-5 in that final set, Lendl fended off three match points, but in the end he could not contain the unrelenting Edberg, who followed up on this crucial victory by upending countryman Mats Wilander to capture his first major singles championship at the age of nineteen.

22. MONICA SELES d. JENNIFER CAPRIATI 6-3, 3-6, 7-6 (3), semifinal, U.S. Open, 1991

Seles, seventeen, was near the top of her game. Capriati, fifteen, was on her way to a long and ultimately successful career. The two teenagers produced a bruising backcourt battle, featuring corner to corner rallies of the highest caliber. Twice in the final set—at 5-4 and 6-5—Capriati served for the match. She was two points from victory at 30-15 and again at 30-30 in the twelfth game. Somehow—through a combination of immense willpower and ground stroke skill—Seles staved off defeat and achieved one of her gutsiest triumphs by taking the tie-break 7-3. Seles ousted Martina Navratilova in the final. At that time, she was the most daunting competitor in the women's game, fearless and indomitable, able to force her will on everyone she confronted.

23. PETE SAMPRAS d. ANDRE AGASSI 6-4, 6-3, 4-6, 7-5, final, U.S. Open, 1995

Of the thirty-four meetings these two American icons had between 1989 and 2002, this was in many ways their most consequential contest. Agassi was ranked No. 1 coming into the Open, while Sampras was stationed at No. 2. Each man had already secured one major title earlier in the year, with Agassi the victor at the Australian Open, and Sampras ruling at Wimbledon. This match would have lasting implications. Both men knew that a defeat in the last Grand Slam championship of 1995 would be devastating. The key to the outcome was the last point of the opening set. They produced their rally of the match, a riveting twenty-two-stroke exchange. Sampras won that spectacular point with a topspin backhand crosscourt winner to break Agassi's serve, and never really looked back. Agassi—who had won four tournaments and twenty-six matches in a row— was not the same player for a long while. Sampras maintained his mastery of the game.

24. MARTINA HINGIS d. MONICA SELES 3-6, 6-3, 7-6 (5), final, Hilton Head Island, S.C., 1997

At sixteen, Hingis was enjoying her finest year as a professional tennis player. She had already collected her first major crown at the Australian Open, establishing herself as the youngest ever to take that title. Hingis was unbeaten for the year as she headed into this final-round appointment with former No. 1 Seles. The clay court conditions seemed to suit her game more than Seles's, but there was little to separate two great players on a day when both were striking the ball commandingly. In the final set of a thoroughly absorbing clash, Seles trailed 2-5, but she saved three match points and astoundingly won four games in a row. The left-hander served for the match at 6-5, reaching 30-0. But Hingis tenaciously broke back. Once more, Seles took charge, moving to 4-2 in the tie-break. But, in the end, Hingis prevailed, taking five of the last six points for a hard fought triumph.

25. STEFFI GRAF d. VENUS WILLIAMS 6-2, 3-6, 6-4, quarterfinal, Wimbledon, 1999

In her fourteenth and final Wimbledon, Graf met a player who was destined to capture the title the next two years and five times overall. This match was delayed several times by rain. They started an hour late at 1 p.m., endured three more rain delays, and completed their skirmish in near darkness. Nevertheless, the thirty-year-old German and nineteen-year-old American played with striking power and admirable control under difficult conditions. Graf gave an inspired performance. It was a battle worthy of a final, with experience triumphing over youth. Graf has seldom seemed more effusive on a tennis court, and was proud to stop the overpowering American on a fast court. The German went on to the final before losing in her last Centre Court match to Lindsay Davenport.

26. SERENA WILLIAMS d. KIM CLIJSTERS 4-6, 6-3, 7-5, semifinal, Australian Open, 2003

The top-seeded American and the No. 4 seed from Belgium played their most memorable match against each other on this occasion. Clijsters was causing Williams a multitude of problems with her speed, anticipation, extraordinary defensive capabilities and fortitude. After taking the first set and then dropping the second, Clijsters moved with vigor to a 5-1 final-set lead. Clijsters had two match points when she was ahead 5-2. But Williams was unwavering and filled with inner conviction. She captured six games in a row to record one of the finest comebacks of her career. In the final, she defeated her sister Venus in three sets to collect a fourth consecutive Grand Slam title, an achievement dubbed a "Serena Slam" by many followers of the sport.

27. MARAT SAFIN d. ROGER FEDERER 5-7, 6-4 5-7, 7-6 (6), 9-7, semifinal, Australian Open, 2005

In September of 2000, Safin had turned the tennis world upside down, stunning Pete Sampras 6-4, 6-3, 6-3 to capture the U.S. Open, snapping the American's eight-match winning streak in Grand Slam tournament finals. Safin was twenty and seemed to have the world of tennis at his feet. But he could never quite replicate the spectacular display he put on against Sampras in the years that followed. In 2005, however, he recaptured much of his old zest and shot making sparkle at the Australian Open. The year before, Federer had stopped Safin in a straight-set final in Melbourne, but this time around the mercurial Russian lifted his game considerably, outperforming Federer in the backhand to backhand rallies with his greater weight of shot. And yet, he was down match point at 6-5 in the fourth-set tie-break. Federer seemed to have the match won when he came in behind his serve, but Safin lobbed over him and took the net away. Federer attempted a between the legs shot rather than a conventional lob, and it failed. Safin recovered to win the match in five magnificent sets, but not before Federer rallied from 5-2 down in the fifth and saved six match points. Safin defeated Lleyton Hewitt in the final for his second major title.

28. VENUS WILLIAMS d. LINDSAY DAVENPORT 4-6, 7-6 (4), 9-7, final, Wimbledon, 2005

The two big hitting Americans were meeting for the third time in a major final. Five years earlier, Williams had ousted Davenport in the finals of both Wimbledon and the U.S. Open. But Davenport was a much better conditioned athlete at this stage of her career, trimmer and sharper, covering the court with more alacrity. Davenport served for the match at 6-5 in the second set but did not have the confidence to hold at that critical juncture. In the tenth game of the third set, Davenport had a match point, but an audacious Williams went for broke characteristically and hit a backhand winner up the line. In the end, Williams was fortunate to win, but her steadfastness in the tight corners of the contest was the reason she prevailed. The two-hour-and-forty-five-minute battle was the longest ever Wimbledon women's singles final—and one of the highest quality skirmishes.

29. NOVAK DJOKOVIC d. ANDY MURRAY 6-1, 3-6, 7-6 (2), semifinal, Italian Open, Rome, 2011

The Serbian was in the midst of an astonishing campaign in 2011. He had won six consecutive tournaments and thirty-six matches in a row as he headed into this encounter with Murray. Djokovic had crushed Murray in straight sets at the start of the season to win his second Australian Open crown on hard courts, as Murray suffered a third loss in a major final. But this time around Murray pushed Djokovic to the hilt on clay. In the final set, Murray served for the match, leading 5-4, 30-15, only to double fault. Three times in that game, Murray stood two points away from taking the match, but Djokovic made some stupendous returns and eventually came through in a final set tie-break.

30. NOVAK DJOKOVIC d. ROGER FEDERER 6-7 (7), 4-6, 6-3, 6-2, 7-5, semifinal, U.S. Open, 2011

For the fifth consecutive year, Djokovic and Federer clashed in the latter stages of the Open. The Swiss had stopped the Serbian without losing a set in the 2007 final, and had then triumphed over his formidable rival in the 2008 and 2009 semifinals. Djokovic, however, had halted Federer in a stirring 2010 semifinal on Arthur Ashe Stadium, saving two match points at 4-5 (on his serve) in the fifth set with bold winners, winning three games in a row to complete a remarkable comeback. In 2011, Djokovic made an even more astounding recovery. Federer served for the match and stood at 5-3, 40-15 in the fifth set. Djokovic walloped a dazzling forehand return winner crosscourt to save the first match point and then saved a second. The Serbian collected seventeen of the last twenty-one points and four games in a row for this startling victory over a dazed Federer. He then beat Rafael Nadal in four sets for his first U.S. Open crown two days later.

CHAPTER THIRTY-THREE

Ranking the Greatest Matches of All Time

For the purposes of this book, I have listed the selected matches chronologically. Readers thus have an easier time tracking the different eras of tennis and placing these matches in historical context. But, as a writer and tennis historian, I have decided to rank the matches here. The ranking is based on a wide range of factors: the importance of the match; the significance of the occasion; the lasting implications of the results on the lives of both players; the level of play from both combatants.

Any ranking list is highly subjective. Mine is no exception. Be that as it may, I have tried to balance the best matches of the different eras, so as to produce a list that reflects the appearance of new champions in each and every era and not shortchange any particular period in the history of tennis.

1. **RAFAEL NADAL d. ROGER FEDERER 6-4, 6-4, 6-7 (4), 6-7 (9), 9-7, final, Wimbledon, grass, 2008**

2. **BJORN BORG d. JOHN MCENROE 1-6, 7-5, 6-3, 6-7 (16-18) 8-6, final, Wimbledon grass, 1980**

3. **SUZANNE LENGLEN d. HELEN WILLS 6-3, 8-6, final, Cannes, France, clay, 1926**

4. **DON BUDGE d. BARON GOTTFRIED VON CRAMM 6-8, 5-7, 6-4, 6-2, 8-6, Davis Cup, grass, Wimbledon, 1937**

5. **KEN ROSEWALL d. ROD LAVER 4-6, 6-0, 6-3, 6-7 (3), 7-6 (5), WCT Dallas Finals, indoor, 1972**

6. **CHRIS EVERT d. MARTINA NAVRATILOVA 6-3, 6-7 (4), 7-5, final, French Open, clay, Paris, 1985**

7. **NOVAK DJOKOVIC d. RAFAEL NADAL** 5-7, 6-4, 6-2, 6-7 (5), 7-5, final, Australian Open, hard courts, 2012

8. **PANCHO GONZALES d. CHARLIE PASARELL** 22-24, 1-6, 16-14, 6-3, 11-9, first round, grass, Wimbledon, 1969

9. **PETE SAMPRAS d. ANDRE AGASSI** 6-7 (7), 7-6 (2), 7-6 (2), 7-6 (5), quarterfinal, U.S. Open, hard courts, 2001

10. **HENRI COCHET d. BILL TILDEN** 2-6, 4-6, 7-5, 6-4, 6-3, semifinal, Wimbledon, grass, 1927

11. **MONICA SELES d. STEFFI GRAF** 6-2, 3-6, 10-8, final, French Open, Paris, clay, 1992

12. **MARGARET COURT d. BILLIE JEAN KING** 14-12, 11-9, final, Wimbledon, grass, 1970

13. **PETE SAMPRAS d. BORIS BECKER** 3-6, 7-6 (5), 7-6 (4), 6-7 (11), 6-4, final, ATP Tour World Championships, Hanover, Germany, indoor, 1996

14. **LEW HOAD d. TONY TRABERT** 13-11, 6-3, 2-6, 3-6,7-5, Davis Cup, Melbourne, Australia, grass, 1953

15. **MARTINA NAVRATILOVA d. CHRIS EVERT** 6-7 (4), 6-4, 7-5, final, Australian Open, Melbourne, grass, 1981

16. **ROD LAVER d. TONY ROCHE** 7-5, 22-20, 9-11, 1-6, 6-3, semifinal, Australian Open, Brisbane, grass, 1969

17. **JUSTINE HENIN d. JENNIFER CAPRIATI** 4-6, 7-5, 7-6 (4), semifinal, U.S. Open, hard courts, 2003

18. **HELEN WILLS MOODY d. HELEN JACOBS** 6-3, 3-6, 7-5, final, Wimbledon, grass, 1935

19. **JIMMY CONNORS d. BJORN BORG** 6-4, 3-6, 7-6 (9), 6-4, final, U.S. Open, 1976

20. **PANCHO GONZALES d. LEW HOAD** 3-6, 4-6, 14-12, 6-1, 6-4,final, U.S. Pro Championships, indoor, Cleveland, 1958

21. **BILLIE JEAN KING d. EVONNE GOOLAGONG** 3-6, 6-3, 7-5, final, U.S. Open, Forest Hills, grass, 1974

22. **JOHN MCENROE d. MATS WILANDER** 9-7, 6-2, 15-17, 3-6, 8-6, Davis Cup, St. Louis, indoor, 1982

23. **SERENA WILLIAMS d. MARIA SHARAPOVA** 2-6, 7-5, 8-6, semifinal, Australian Open, hard courts, 2005

24. **JACK KRAMER d. DON BUDGE** 6-4, 8-10, 3-6, 6-4, 6-0, semifinal, U.S. Pro Championships, grass, Forest Hills, 1948

25. **MARIA BUENO d. MARGARET SMITH** 6-4, 7-9, 6-3, final, Wimbledon, grass, 1964

26. **STEFFI GRAF d. MARTINA HINGIS** 4-6, 7-5, 6-2, final, French Open, clay, 1999

27. **STAN SMITH d. ILIE NASTASE** 4-6, 6-3, 6-3, 4-6, 7-5, final, Wimbledon, grass, 1972

28. **ROGER FEDERER d. ANDY RODDICK** 5-7, 7-6 (6), 7-6 (5), 3-6, 16-14, final, Wimbledon, grass, 2009

29. **MAUREEN CONNOLLY d. DORIS HART** 8-6, 7-5, final, Wimbledon, grass, 1953

T30. **ARTHUR ASHE d. JIMMY CONNORS** 6-1, 6-1, 5-7, 6-4, final, Wimbledon, grass, 1975

T30. **FRED PERRY d. ELLSWORTH VINES** 7-5, 3-6, 6-3, 6-4, Pro Tour Opening, Madison Square Garden, New York, indoor, 1937

CHAPTER THIRTY-FOUR

The Best Players of All Time

Men

1. ROGER FEDERER

He captured five Wimbledon crowns in a row from 2003-2007 and was victorious five consecutive times at the U.S. Open as well (2004-2008). He also has won a men's record sixteen major singles titles. Moreover, Federer advanced at least to an unimaginable twenty-three straight semifinals at the majors. He stands alone at the top of my list at the best ever because of his unfailingly high standards, unassailable record and the extraordinary versatility of his court craft.

2. PETE SAMPRAS

The best big-match player the game has ever seen, his dominance of the entire decade of the 1990's was a staggering feat. Not only did he win Wimbledon seven times, but he never lost a final on the sacred Centre Court. At his best, I believe Sampras was better than anyone else who has achieved eminence on a tennis court, but Federer finishes above him in my rankings because he won all four majors at least once while the American did not succeed at Roland Garros.

3. ROD LAVER

The only player, man or woman, to capture two Grand Slams, the Australian's 1969 sweep of the majors was majestic, the most substantial feat realized by any tennis player in history. Laver turned professional after his 1962 Grand Slam, missing all of the majors from 1963-67 while out in the wilderness of pro tennis. He inevitably would have piled up a cluster of majors during that stretch, but the fact remains that he took six of his eleven major tournament triumphs as an amateur when he was not forced to confront the top professionals. Be that as it may, Laver was a magnificent competitor and a dazzling shot maker with a multi-faceted game of surpassing excellence.

4. JACK KRAMER

Surely he is the most underrated of all great tennis champions. He did his finest work in professional tennis after capturing only three major singles titles as an amateur. Yet Kramer performed in a league of his own for five years as a pro. He introduced the "Big Game" to tennis, and during his time at the top no one could come close to touching him. He was overwhelmingly efficient, breaking down even his most formidable opponents systematically, a masterful percentage player. Kramer deserves a higher place in history than most critics have afforded him.

5. BILL TILDEN

Taking his ten major titles between 1920 and 1930, Tilden may have been the game's best-ever match player. Tilden took tennis to another level in his time with a wide range of strokes and an unparalleled strategic sense. As a young player, his backhand was vulnerable. Once he perfected that stroke, Tilden became the supreme player of his day. His performance on court was always dramatic because he liked to toy with opponents, risking defeat yet ultimately taking control.

6. BJORN BORG

Displaying surprising versatility for a confirmed baseliner, Borg not only won six French Open titles, but altered his game admirably to suit the lawns of Wimbledon and secured that title five years in a row. The implacable Swede failed in four U.S. Open finals and left the game too soon at twenty-five. Nevertheless, he won at least one Grand Slam tournament for eight years in a row, a record he shares with Sampras and Federer.

7. RAFAEL NADAL

Surely the most ferocious competitor I have ever seen, the indefatigable Spaniard must be acclaimed as the best-ever men's clay court player. But he is a great player on any surface. When he sinks his teeth into a match and finds his range, he can be unstoppable as he pounds his adversaries into submission with his relentless brand of heavy topspin. The left-hander has as much heart as anyone who has ever played the game.

8. DON BUDGE

The first player ever to record a Grand Slam (1938), he had a beautifully crafted, all-court playing style, featuring a backhand that was the
envy of all who faced him. He carried himself as only a champion
could. What Tilden did for tennis in the 1920's Budge was for the
thirties. Many authorities of that era in tennis—including the late Jack
Kramer—placed Budge at the top of the list of the all-time great players because he had such a well-proportioned game with no apparent
weaknesses.

9. PANCHO GONZALES

A singularly daunting competitor and one of the most durable of all
top players, he turned professional at twenty-one and could not compete again at the majors until he was forty. In the intervening years, he
would have undoubtedly collected a cluster of large prizes. His eight
triumphs at the prestigious U.S. Pro Championships demonstrate how
remarkable he was at the height of his powers.

10. JIMMY CONNORS AND ANDRE AGASSI

Both men won eight major championships and were in the forefront
of the sport for two decades. Connors was decidedly more consistent
than his younger compatriot, spending five years in a row as the No.
1 ranked man in tennis during the 1970's, celebrating twelve consecutive years among the world's top three. He is the only player ever
to capture the U.S. Open on three different surfaces—grass, clay and
concrete. Agassi, however, recorded a career Grand Slam, becoming
the fifth player ever to realize that feat. In the final analysis, I could
not leave either American out of this all-time top ten, but regretfully
I could not include either John McEnroe or Ivan Lendl on this list
despite their many towering accomplishments.

Women

1. STEFFI GRAF

The game's greatest female player for eight years, she recorded twenty-
two major championship victories beginning in 1987 and ending in
1999. She became only the third woman (in 1988) to win a Grand
Slam, and yet her presence was felt for more than a decade thereafter.
Although Margaret Court won more majors, Graf is the only player—

male or female—to win every Grand Slam event at least four times in singles. Her incomparable forehand, her extraordinary coordination and an unmatched zest for competition lifted Graf to her preeminent level.

2. MARTINA NAVRATILOVA

No woman player has had a more complete game. A magnificent athlete, she was virtually unbeatable for five years in her prime. From 1982-86, she lost only fourteen matches. She secured a record nine Wimbledon singles championships, accounting for half of her Grand Slam singles crowns on that celebrated ground. No woman packaged the serve with the first volley so unremittingly.

3. CHRIS EVERT

Her durability and determination set Chrissie apart from all rivals. In fifty-six career Grand Slam tournament appearances, she missed the semifinal cut only four times. In nineteen consecutive U.S. Open appearances, she never failed to advance to at least the quarterfinals. For thirteen consecutive seasons—1974 to 1986—she set a record that may never be broken by winning at least one major title every year. She collected a record seven French Open championships and won 125 straight matches on clay courts to establish herself as the premier player of them all on that surface. No woman in history has played the game better for longer than Evert.

4. HELEN WILLS MOODY

In a much honored career, she won nineteen Grand Slam tournaments, one more than both Navratilova and Evert. Her eight Wimbledon singles tournament triumphs have been eclipsed only by Navratilova. Although the majority of critics placed Suzanne Lenglen above her as the best female player of the first half of the Twentieth Century, she is the better player in my estimation because she sustained her talent in top-flight tennis for longer than Lenglen or any other woman of her time.

5. MARGARET SMITH COURT

The best Australian female tennis player of all time, she has collected more Grand Slam singles titles than anyone, securing twenty-four majors from 1960 to 1973. Eleven of those triumphs were at her native Australian Championships, however, where her opposition was frequently undistinguished. Nevertheless, the towering serve-and-volley-er managed to rule on the red clay courts of Roland Garros five times, demonstrating her versatility and resolve indisputably.

6. SERENA WILLIAMS

On ability alone, Williams would be much higher on this list. A prodigious athlete universally admired for her unshakable drive and immense willpower, she has won majors in three different decades. Heading into 2012, she had won thirteen majors, including a career Grand Slam. A good many experts believe that, at her best, Williams could defeat any woman player in history. She is an overpowering physical force, with an overwhelming serve and a sizzling ground game. All she has lacked is consistency, but who knows precisely what is in store for Serena in the years ahead?

7. SUZANNE LENGLEN

A fragile and emotional competitor, she never lost a match at Wimble-don or her native French Championships. But in her only appearance at Forest Hills in 1921, she retired after losing the first set to Molla Mallory and did not return to the U.S. Championships. A ballerina on a tennis court, she soared gracefully past one opponent after another through a glorious career. Most who watched her during her prime, including the esteemed tennis historian Ted Tinling, were convinced she was the greatest female tennis player of all-time.

8. MAUREEN CONNOLLY

The first woman to win a Grand Slam (1953), she seemed destined then to dominate the game for as long as she wanted. An accident when she was riding a horse the following year ended her career, but did not diminish her stature. A hard-hitting, unrelenting baseliner, she cut down her foes with powerful shots off both sides and an immense will to win.

9. BILLIE JEAN KING

Much like Gonzales in men's tennis, she was the competitor you would select to play for your life in a one-match situation. Devoid of fear on the big occasions, she won six Wimbledon singles champion-ships and twelve majors altogether, joining the career Grand Slam club. A brilliant volleyer, she controlled points with an intelligent attacking style and a powerful personality. Had she not been driven by a multitude of causes, she might have added even more luster to her record.

10. MONICA SELES

Before she was stabbed in the back at a German tournament in the spring of 1993, she seemed certain to take the women's game into another realm. Her two-fisted strokes off both sides were devastatingly potent and her intensity was unmatched. At nineteen, she had already won eight major titles. After the stabbing, she did not return for nearly twenty-eight months. Despite securing one more major singles title in 1996, she was never the same player. Yet she must be graded among the ten best of all time.

CHAPTER THIRTY-FIVE

The Greatest Strokes of All Time

Tennis is an ever evolving sport. Each generation of competitors advances the game and the technical and technological strides made from decade to decade have been remarkable. But, in my view, the great champions were destined to excel in any era. Put Bill Tilden or Don Budge or Rod Laver out there with today's equipment and training techniques, let them use the modern rackets and strings, allow them to find a way to win against the modern breed of competitors, and they would do very well indeed. The same can essentially be said for the best strokes. Imagine great shot makers of the past transferring their talent into the modern game, changing their grips and developing new methodology. The view here is that they would adjust accordingly. They were masterful then; they would be masterful now.
Tennis has been graced with a wide range of players who have inspired us with their skills at hitting certain strokes better than anyone else in their time. Here are my picks for the best shots of all time and for the players who have demonstrated the most mental toughness across history.

FIRST SERVE
Men
1. PETE SAMPRAS He made the serve the cornerstone of his game and no one in history has done it better or more elegantly. No one was harder to break or more difficult to read. He could do anything he wanted with his delivery, finding all four corners with ease and supreme deception. Sampras was unreadable at his best, explosive and deadly accurate, capable of serving clusters of aces. His first serve was very big, but he was not out to break the record for velocity, relying instead on incomparable precision and a masterful motion that never

let him down. It was an unstoppable weapon.

2. PANCHO GONZALES He may well have had the prettiest serve the game has yet seen. Gonzales demoralized his chief rivals with his craftiness. His service action was immaculate and entirely reliable. He always looked effortless. He moved his serve around the box skillfully, demoralized rivals with his immense power and exploited his opponents' weaknesses ruthlessly with his outstanding delivery. He could serve his share of aces but was particularly adept at finding the weakness in an opponent's return.

3. BORIS BECKER The burly German was a stupendous server. His weight transfer was remarkable, as was his grip. Becker—unlike most of history's other great servers—used essentially an eastern forehand grip for his delivery. That probably helped him with power, but he also could swing you wide with the slice serve and get plenty of kick when he needed that as well. Becker serving at his best was awfully intimidating.

4. GORAN IVANISEVIC The big left-hander could not match Sampras or Gonzales as a strategic server, but he was fearless in coming after opponents with brute force and surprisingly good placement. His magnificent first serve carried him into the Wimbledon final on three occasions in the 1990's before he finally claimed the crown in 2001 as a wildcard ranked No. 125 in the world. It was a nightmare for adversaries to deal with his ad court serve because Ivanisevic could go wide with a vicious slice or go flat down the T with blinding speed.

5. ROGER FEDERER and **JOHN ISNER.** Because he dazzled so many learned observers across the years with his propensity to hit virtually any shot in the book at any given moment, we tend to overlook Federer's incomparably smooth and purposeful first serve. At his best, Federer's serve is the most precise in the game. The 6'9" Isner has one of the biggest first serves ever, and an unfailingly pure motion. Isner's delivery is devastatingly potent and almost impossible to read.

FIRST SERVE
Women

1. SERENA WILLIAMS Watching Serena Williams serve when she is in peak form is astonishing. Her motion is the most natural of any woman player I have ever seen. Her toss is reliable, her velocity impressive, her ability to rack up free points ever apparent. It is a daunting first serve, delivered with power and panache. As the serve goes, so goes Serena Williams.

2. VENUS WILLIAMS Venus has some technical flaws in her serve that can surface. She can fall into the habit of dropping her head after the toss, but the fact remains that her first serve has been one of the biggest weapons ever showcased in women's tennis. She can be overwhelming when serving well and it has been a primary strength all through her career. Venus in full flight garners an extraordinary number of free points with the remarkable velocity of her first serve.

3. ALICE MARBLE During her heyday in the late 1930's, Marble became the first woman to impose an aggressive and unrelenting playing style. She could hit the kick serve, a more severe American Twist, or flatten it out. As a serve-and-volleyer, she followed her delivery into the net, but without possessing such an excellent first serve, she could never have played that way in her time.

4. MARTINA NAVRATILOVA More heralded for her acrobatic play at the net, Navratilova was intimidating with her willingness to keep coming forward behind her serve. She did not have a big first serve, but as a lefty she pulled her opponents out wide with her slice serve in the ad court and hurt them as well with a kicking first serve in the deuce court. She was a masterful percentage server, mixing speeds and spins, changing direction ably.

5. ALTHEA GIBSON When this tall African-American woman dominated the game in 1957 and 1958—winning Wimbledon and the U.S. Championships in both years—she brought with her to the arena an ultra-aggressive style of play, most notably a formidable first serve that was tailor made for fast courts. No woman before Gibson had produced such a potent serve.

SECOND SERVE
Men

1. PETE SAMPRAS For all practical purposes, it was as if Sampras did not really have a second serve. He had two first serves. For the first half of his career, Sampras seldom served-and-volleyed on his second delivery, but that changed from 1997 on. Once he started applying that extra pressure, the second serve—already immense and daunting—became that much tougher. Toward the end of his career, he was willing to risk more double faults while going for even bigger second serves and it was worth his while. His second serve stood in a class of its own.

2. JACK KRAMER The author of the first full-fledged "Big Game" among the men, Kramer was an incomparable attacking player. He prided himself on not having much of a disparity between his first and second serves—and there never really was that much of a difference. Kramer crushed his opposition with the depth of his second serve, the best of his time by far.

3. JOHN NEWCOMBE When Newcombe was performing at the top of his craft, he had an awfully good first serve that struck fear into the hearts of his rivals. But it was his second serve that essentially set him apart. He kept the second serve impeccably deep and then closed in to put away first volleys. In his era, Newcombe's highly-reliable second serve was decidedly better than anyone else's.

4. ANDY RODDICK The American owns one of the most powerful and celebrated first serves of his era. The extreme power of that delivery was largely responsible for his rise to No. 1 in the world in 2003. But Roddick's second serve is extraordinary as well. He gets so much kick and extreme bite on the second ball that his rivals are hard pressed to find a way to combat it. It is a magnificent second serve.

5. PATRICK RAFTER The Australian won two U.S. Opens and made it to two Wimbledon finals by virtue of his capacity to spring forward as swiftly as anyone behind his serve and into the forecourt. Rafter's first serve was a good one, yet his second impressed me more. The heavy kicker was particularly effective on hard courts, bounding high, allowing Rafter to take utter control of points.

SECOND SERVE
Women

1. SAMANTHA STOSUR The 2011 U.S. Open champion has a wickedly-kicking second serve that is not only the best in today's game, but in my book the best ever. Stosur's ad court second serve is almost unanswerable, bounding high and deep to the backhand, making life miserable for her adversaries, even those with extraordinary two-handed backhand returns.

2. SERENA WILLIAMS As extraordinary as her first serve surely has been, Serena's second serve is of the same high quality. She keeps her opponents at bay with her depth, spin, variety and control. Even on those days when her first serve is slightly off the mark, Williams often endures because her second serve is so difficult to attack.

3. MARTINA NAVRATILOVA There was never much of a disparity between Martina's top of the line first and second serves. She never set out to be a big server, but rather relied on location and depth to take charge. Most importantly, her second serve would kick up high and enable her to close in for the first volley. She could also go wide in the ad court with slice or into the body with heavy spin. Navratilova's second serve depth was a trademark.

4. BILLIE JEAN KING One of the finest strategic servers of her era, King was an astute match player who knew how to make opponents uncomfortable on their returns by changing speeds and spins to exploit their weaknesses. King's second serve was exceedingly well designed for her to get to the net quickly behind it. It was not overwhelming but she got in swiftly behind her serve and forced her opponents to keep their returns awfully low. She could swing her slice serve remarkably wide in the deuce court, hit the effective kicker to the ad court, and was always purposeful. In her prime, the bigger the situation, the better she served.

5. MARGARET COURT Because she was so tall and rangy, Court was highly intimidating as she worked her way forward on serve. There were times when her nerves would cause the stately Australian to double fault in the tense corners of tight contests, but, by and large, she got the most out of her second serve and directed it anywhere she wanted. A consummate attacking player, Court's second serve on her finest days of work was a true barometer of the state of her game and her level of confidence. Her depth and placement were the twin virtues of her second serve.

RETURN OF SERVE
Men

1. ANDRE AGASSI With his astonishing hand-eye coordination, the man from Las Vegas took the return of serve to another level. He could read the serve with uncanny regularity and would take the initiative away from the server in an instant with his crackling returns off both sides. His two-handed backhand return was probably more dazzling than his forehand return, but he could be vulnerable to well-placed wide slice serves. His two-handed backhand return was probably better than his forehand return, but off both flanks he imposed himself spectacularly and returned with ferocity.

2. JIMMY CONNORS The left-hander's posture on the return differed from Agassi's. He stood farther back to give himself more time. But Connors would drive his returns so flat off both sides that he could make the biggest and best servers look very vulnerable. His booming returns would jump off his Wilson T2000 racket with astounding pace, and the serve-and-volleyers of his generation were usually at his mercy.

3. NOVAK DJOKOVIC The Serbian's elastic reach on his two-handed backhand sets him apart from just about anyone in his field. He can be pulled wide to his backhand, yet still snap back the return with gusto. He may yet develop the finest return of all time, but already Djokovic has established himself near the top of the list with his unflinching manner, and his capacity to attack second serves and handle first serves with outstanding control and precision.

4. LLEYTON HEWITT The Australian was one of the grittiest competitors ever to set foot on a court, but he had to work inordinately hard to beat rivals with larger arsenals and considerably more power. Hewitt overcame that deficiency because his return of serve was unfailingly consistent. He could get more big serves back into play than just about anyone. He did not return with as much aggression as some of the others who shined in that department, but no one probed more convincingly.

5. ANDY MURRAY The best British player of the modern era, Murray always has a wide range of options at his disposal. He is crafty, versatile and imaginative. His game is multi-faceted. But perhaps his finest attribute is his propensity to strike his returns with conviction and unshakable authority. His feel on the forehand return is impeccable and his two-handed backhand return is brilliant because he is so flexible and accurate.

RETURN OF SERVE
Women

1. MONICA SELES When the left-hander was ruling the world of women's tennis with her relentlessly piercing two-handed shots off both sides, her return of serve was one of her largest virtues. She was ceaselessly looking to back her opponents up with her uncompromising returns. Off either the forehand or the backhand, she went all out, but controlled her aggression and played the percentages on her terms.

2. STEFFI GRAF Unlike Seles, Graf did not turn the return of serve into a weapon off both sides. Her forehand return was much more damaging, and adversaries served to that side at their own peril. Her backhand return was largely a chip, but it was effective as well. And there was always the danger that Steffi would run around her backhand to blast inside-out forehand returns that featured impeccable footwork.

3. CHRIS EVERT In her time, Evert faced some first-rate servers in Billie Jean King, Margaret Court, Virginia Wade, and, of course, Martina Navratilova. Her return had to be sharp and unerring. Against serve-and-volleyers, she made them volley up off her dipping returns; against baseliners, she got great depth with outstanding control. All in all, she was a terrific returner because she missed so few and set herself up to take control of points.

4. VICTORIA AZARENKA In establishing herself as the No. 1 ranked woman in the world early in 2012, Azarenka brought a bright array of strengths with her to the arena. But, above all else, her return of serve was the best feature of her big hitting game. She is ultra-aggressive without being reckless, and the pressure she applies on opponents with her returns is immense.

5. MARIA SHARAPOVA This feisty and unwavering competitor excels on the return of serve. Her returns are scorching off both sides. She drives through the ball relentlessly and has a knack for taking the initiative away from her rivals with the depth and extreme velocity of her returns. Sharapova is devastatingly potent when she is receiving and her second serve returns are of the highest caliber.

FOREHAND
Men

1. ROGER FEDERER Some hit the ball more mightily off the forehand side, and others were flashier, but Federer's forehand is the best I have ever seen. His capacity to station himself inside the baseline and shorten the court for his opponent has surpassed all others. Once he is inside the court, he can go either way—inside-in or inside-out—and hit winners at will. In top form, he clips more lines with his majestic forehand than anyone and yet he makes very few mistakes for someone so adventuresome.

2. RAFAEL NADAL The Spaniard's forehand has always been his trademark shot. Nadal tortures his rivals with his rhythmic precision off the forehand. The hop he gets on the forehand with the heaviest and most penetrating topspin of all time is almost mind boggling. He can go full tilt for hours on end and hardly miss a forehand, but it is not as if he is pushing his shots back into play; he is pulverizing the ball and weakening his opponent's will simultaneously. He sends his adversaries into submission with a barrage of heavy forehands, weakening their resolve in the process. His ball control off the forehand is amazing. I give Federer the edge over Nadal for the best forehand ever, but it is a very close call.

3. IVAN LENDL The former Czech who became an American citizen transformed the world of tennis with his playing style, most importantly with his signature inside-out forehand. There were an abundance of serve-and-volley competitors along with more conventional baseline practitioners during his era, but Lendl changed it all, serving with impressive power to set up his magnificent semi-western, inside-out forehand—the shot that carried him to eight major titles. Lendl's power and accuracy with that forehand had never been witnessed before.

4. BILL TILDEN Over the course of the 1920's, when Tilden ruled tennis and studied the technique of the sport with all-consuming interest, the American influenced the sport immensely. He had an estimable first serve and he improved his backhand markedly, but the forehand was Tilden's finest shot. He drove through the ball classically and confidently and it was a stroke that would not break down under pressure. The Tilden forehand was a shot made for the ages.

5. BJORN BORG, PETE SAMPRAS and **JUAN MARTIN DEL POTRO** Although many observers took more notice of the Swede's two-handed backhand because he joined Jimmy Connors and Chris Evert to popularize that shot in the 1970's, his forehand was in many ways superior. Borg ushered in a brand of heavy topspin that was unprecedented and the forehand took him to the top of the sport. He passed particularly well off the backhand and disguised his two-hander adeptly, but the Borg forehand defined his greatness more than anything else. Sampras had the most explosive running forehand of all time and he could do quite a bit of damage from the middle of the court off that side as well. His magnificent forehand was relatively flat and it was awesome when he was on. Del Potro is changing the face of the modern game with his explosive flat forehand, the biggest in the sport today. It is a prodigious weapon, released with blinding speed. More than anything else, his sizzling forehand was the reason he halted Federer in a five-set final at the 2009 U.S. Open.

FOREHAND
Women

1. STEFFI GRAF This was among the easiest selections to make among the best strokes ever produced. Considering how much pace she got on this explosive shot, it was made all the more remarkable by her grip—essentially a continental, on the border of an eastern. She would get into position early and with supreme racket head acceleration she would sweep through the ball and strike countless outright winners with her flat stroke. She had little margin for error, yet the forehand seldom let her down. In my view, it stands in a class by itself as the best ever.

2. MAUREEN CONNOLLY A natural left-hander who played tennis right-handed, Connolly had a beautifully produced one-handed backhand that was a shot which came more easily to her. The fact remains that Connolly's forehand paved the way for her to win the Grand Slam in 1953. She placed the same value on fast footwork as Graf. Her inexhaustible attention to detail and sound mechanics gave Connolly a magnificent forehand.

3. HELEN WILLS MOODY Brought up on the hard courts of California, taught to play the game from the baseline with steadfast conviction, realizing the importance of controlling the climate of her matches, Wills Moody was not called "Little Miss Poker Face" without good reason. She was relentlessly disciplined in her court craft, making the backcourt her home, refusing to make mistakes yet hitting her ground strokes hard. Her flat forehand—hit unfailingly deep and close to the lines—was far and away the best of her era and one of the finest ever.

4. MONICA SELES Authorities often debated whether Seles was better off the forehand or the backhand. Both were left-handed, two-fisted strokes. Each was taken early. She could explore the most acute crosscourt angles or direct her shots within inches of the baseline off either side. Unlike most of her peers, Seles's forehand was not one dimensional.

5. SERENA WILLIAMS On her finest afternoons, when her timing is on and her concentration is sharp, Williams can be uncontainable off the forehand. She covers the ball with just enough topspin and takes it early, often from an open stance. It is the shot she uses to open up the court, to either release winners or advance to the net. She can be breathtaking off that side at her best, but her ranking is not higher because her brilliance off that side can be sporadic.

BACKHAND
Men

1. DON BUDGE When he captured the Grand Slam in 1938—the first player ever to realize that feat—Budge had it all, but the single biggest strength in his game was his majestic backhand. Most of those players who preceded Budge at the top of tennis were better off the forehand, but his backhand was the first of its kind. His aggressiveness off that side was ground breaking in many ways. He drove the backhand essentially flat and all students of the game marveled at its magical simplicity.

2. KEN ROSEWALL The diminutive Australian's backhand was legendary. He prepared early, turned his shoulders unfailingly, kept his eyes glued to the ball, but, most significantly, Rosewall's backhand was a slice. Across the history of tennis, many slice backhands have been used primarily for defensive purposes, but not Rosewall's. His slice backhand worked in every way: as a rally shot, as a passing shot, for the lob, and on the return of serve. It was multi-faceted. It was incredibly versatile. And above all else, it was unmistakably elegant.

3. JIMMY CONNORS Watching Connors launch into one of his two-handed backhand drives was one of the great joys for all erudite observers from the early seventies until the outset of the 1990's. Connors retained the old fashioned flavor of a flat, one-handed backhand, producing flat and penetrating two-handers of unrelenting depth and immense power, yet gaining stability with his right hand. His backhand was the picture of purity. It was his signature shot.

4. NOVAK DJOKOVIC A mesmerizing athlete, Djokovic can be forced well off the court by wide balls to his two-handed backhand and still recover in time to play the shot with assertiveness and astounding control. He returns with unswerving authority off that side, and in long rallies from the baseline, his two-hander is rock solid. Djokovic finds just the right blend of flat and topspin shots with his two-handed backhand. This shot made him the great champion he became.

5. LEW HOAD and **GUSTAVO KUERTEN** One match away from winning the Grand Slam in 1956, Hoad at the height of his powers was impenetrable. The gifted Australian had every shot in the book, could perform brilliantly on any surface and was universally admired for his immense talent. Off the ground, his one-handed backhand was widely appreciated. He drove through the ball with an essentially flat stroke and was lethal off that side. To be sure, he was a streaky player, but when he was on, there was nothing he could not do on a tennis court, including cracking the backhand mightily. Kuerten's one-handed backhand was the cornerstone of his game—a majestic, sweepingly beautiful, fluid, one handed stroke that carried him to three French Open crowns. Kuerten sparkled off that side, hitting winners at will, driving the ball both crosscourt and down the line with extraordinary pace and minimal topspin. His backhand was singularly inspiring in its time.

BACKHAND
Women

1. CHRIS EVERT While both Connors and Borg made substantial contributions toward the cause of the two-handed backhand, it is safe to say that Evert's impact was larger. Her success charted a new course for women's tennis and the two-hander became a staple. But that did not mean it was easy to replicate the geometric precision of her backhand. The daughter of an outstanding teaching professional named Jimmy Evert, she worked diligently on her two-hander. It was the shot that never deserted her across the years. In rallies, her depth was unmatchable and she seldom missed. Her returns were crisp and solid and her passing shots were unimaginably precise and unerring. Meanwhile, the topspin lob was always at her disposal. In my book, the Evert backhand was the best in the history of women's tennis and the precursor for so many great two-handers to replicate.

2. MONICA SELES Just as Djokovic broke new ground by taming the Rafael Nadal forehand with his backhand, Seles did essentially the same thing with her lefty two-handed backhand against Graf. The German always was more comfortable running around her backhand to play the inside-out forehand, but if you could keep her pinned deep in her forehand corner, she was not able to control rallies in the same manner. Seles forced Graf to do that by virtue of the depth and speed of her two-handed backhand crosscourt, forcing Graf back on her heels. That was no mean feat. The Seles backhand was immaculately executed.

3. JUSTINE HENIN The Belgian brought an awful lot to the table of competition. She was a complete player with all of the tools to succeed in her trade. Yet her one-handed topspin backhand was her trademark. Henin's backhand was sweepingly beautiful, a spectator's dream, an opponent's nightmare. She was willing to miss off that side because her goal was to make things happen off the backhand, and, if that meant making some aggressive errors, so be it. But she more than balanced the scales by sprinkling the court with clusters of topspin backhand winners, going down the line or crosscourt, long or short.

4. LINDSAY DAVENPORT At nearly 6'3," Davenport was an imposing physical presence on a tennis court. Over the years, she became decidedly better as a tennis player and athlete by losing weight, gaining momentum in the process. Across time, her two-handed backhand was strikingly effective, particularly crosscourt. She kept it uncomplicated, going for one deep, penetrating and flat shot after another until she could break down the defenses of her adversaries.

5. EVONNE GOOLAGONG The Australian often looked like a ballerina on a tennis court, but never more so than on the backhand side. She was very flexible, using the slice backhand to keep herself in rallies, raising the tempo whenever she saw an opening to release her glorious topspin backhand. She did not have to think when she hit a backhand—it was all flowing and instinctive. The Goolagong backhand remains frozen in the minds of tennis fans everywhere.

FOREHAND VOLLEY
Men

1. JACK KRAMER The Californian believed fervently that a good offense would always overcome a tough defense. That is why he designed his game to go to the net whenever he had an opportunity. From close range, he was convinced that on a fast surface no one could stop him. Kramer volleyed phenomenally off both sides and had no weaknesses in the forecourt. But his forehand volley was the guiding light of his game, punched with not only control but power. He could handle the high forehand volley, dig out the low ones and close in tight to put away the sitters. Kramer did this better than anyone else.

2. JOHN NEWCOMBE The Australian's philosophy was not far away from Kramer's. He made his living at the net. He was comfortable and confident in that territory. He trusted his volley thoroughly. The seven-time Grand Slam singles titlist was quick to read the battle plan of his opponents whenever he was up at the net and was decisive in his execution, particularly on the forehand volley. Confronting great rivals like Laver and Rosewall, Newcombe knew he would have to make more than his share of difficult low forehand volleys. He was seldom found wanting in that department.

3. ROY EMERSON The reason this proud Australian captured no fewer than twenty-eight major titles in singles, doubles and mixed doubles was because of his renowned fitness and his uncompromising serve-and-volley style. Emerson was a terrific athlete and once he got his hands on a volley, he was not often going to make a mistake. Emerson volleyed with firmness and conviction and he had an awfully good forehand volley that was one of his primary attributes as a player.

4. PATRICK RAFTER In his two U.S. Open championship runs, and his two journeys to the finals of Wimbledon, Rafter exhilarated the galleries in New York and London with the spring he had in his step. He would propel himself forward swiftly behind his kick serve to play his first volley—no one could surpass him in that endeavor. I will never forget Rafter's forehand volley display in dissecting Michael Chang in the semifinals of the 1997 U.S. Open. Rafter cast aside Chang in straight sets and, in my mind's eye, I still see him punching away one forehand volley after another with absolute assurance.

5. JOHN McENROE The New Yorker did wondrous things on the volley, off either side. What I liked about his forehand volley was his incomparable feel. Not only would he make his signature drop volleys off that side, but his touch was so astounding that he could take the low forehand volley off his shoelaces and deposit it at impossible angles and improbable spots. He kept his volleys low, making it difficult for his rivals to pass him. McEnroe was inventive at the net, a master of finesse and a genius in many ways.

FOREHAND VOLLEY
Women

1. JANA NOVOTNA The 1998 Wimbledon champion became one of the most proficient players ever at the net. She was agile in the forecourt, her technique was excellent and she was decisive in her execution. I felt her forehand volley was the best ever among the women because she could punch it with speed, depth, and precision—and she did it all in textbook fashion.

2. LOUISE BROUGH The winner of six major singles titles, and another twenty-nine in doubles and mixed doubles, Brough was one of the great female players of the late 1940's and 1950's. The primary reason she was so successful was her prowess on the volley. She was solid off both sides. Her forehand volley was first rate. She could make the low forehand volley more regularly than just about anyone in her era.

3. MARTINA NAVRATILOVA Early in her career, the forehand volley could be a glaring weakness for Navratilova, but during the 1980's she improved that shot significantly. From that juncture forward, it became almost technically flawless.

4. MARGARET COURT. In her heyday, Court was always among the best on the volley. She had remarkable range at the net, and it was exceedingly difficult for opponents to find openings to drive the ball past her with more than sporadic success. They nicknamed her "The Arm" because of her capacity to cover the net so thoroughly. Her forehand volley was exemplary in every way.

5. BILLIE JEAN KING Like Navratilova, King could have off days when her forehand volley would let her down. But the fact remains that, at her best, King could get down to make the forehand volley better than anyone. She was never lazy in her approach to volleying, sticking assiduously to the fundamentals and producing those volleys as if she had been born to make them. No one understood good technique on the volley better than the ever inquisitive King.

BACKHAND VOLLEY
Men

1. STEFAN EDBERG The Swede was his era's best at the net, by a considerable margin. He was the quintessential serve-and-volleyer, with a heavy kick serve designed to allow Edberg to get exceedingly close to the net for his first volley. His forehand volley was awfully good, but his backhand volley was stupendous. Edberg was supremely confident on the backhand volley, which he could "stick" better than anyone. Either high or low on the backhand volley, Edberg always had all of the answers, displaying finesse, precision and the capacity to put it away whenever possible.

2. TONY ROCHE The formidable Australian's backhand volley was virtually on a par with Edberg's—some would say that Roche's was even better. His shoulder turn and soundness were his enduring virtues as a player. No one wanted to allow Roche to hit that backhand volley if they had a choice because he invariably would keep the low ones deep and put the high ones away emphatically. Roche played the backhand volley with clinical efficiency.

3. KEN ROSEWALL While the understated Australian was more revered in some circles for his backhand ground stroke, the fact remains that his backhand volley was every bit as impressive. Rosewall altered his game when he left the amateur ranks and turned pro, realizing he had to approach the net more frequently. Once that change occurred, Rosewall put his stellar backhand volley on display with growing assurance. It was ineffably good.

4. ROD LAVER The two-time winner of the Grand Slam was spectacularly versatile, capable of taking his place alongside any of the great shot makers of all time. But I believe no one gave him the plaudits he deserved for his backhand volley. This deeply humble left-hander had good feel and great control on that side and he never wavered when he was set up for a backhand volley.

5. PETE SAMPRAS Over the second half of his career, the American became more committed to following his second serve in at almost all times. Sampras made serious strides in his ability to volley with the best in his business. He had a very good forehand volley as well, but his backhand volley was outstanding. Even when he was stretched out or reaching down to his shoelaces, he would make even the toughest backhand volleys look remarkably easy.

BACKHAND VOLLEY
Women

1. MARTINA NAVRATILOVA This outstanding left hander's athleticism was displayed most convincingly when she was stationed up at the net. Her speed and anticipation was second to none and her long reach on the backhand volley was phenomenal. It seemed almost impossible to get a ball by her on that side. Navratilova could not only pound her volleys for winners at sharp angles but also could use her touch for some astounding drop volleys.

2. BILLIE JEAN KING Her technique and flair on the backhand volley was comparable to Navratilova's. King had a much better backhand than forehand off the ground. On the volley she was highly skilled off both sides, but her backhand volley was more of a weapon. She would knife it away with total conviction, go down the line as well as crosscourt and her footwork and forward movement was outstanding.

3. EVONNE GOOLAGONG Goolagong was very comfortable at the net, relishing the challenge to end points with her dazzling athleticism and staggering grace. Goolagong's backhand volley was awesome. Navratilova and King were more adept at making the low volley in many ways, but Goolagong was the best on high backhand volleys and backhand overheads. She would leave audiences gasping when she played that shot.

4. MARIA BUENO The Brazilian's elegance and grace were reminiscent of Goolagong. This fierce competitor hit a heavy ball off the ground, but her forte was the volley. Bueno had wonderful touch and vision at the net, which made her such an estimable grass court player. She knew exactly what to do with the backhand volley and had one of the best ever.

5. VIRGINIA WADE The winner of three singles majors on grass courts—including Wimbledon in 1977—Wade possessed a terrific first serve. It was among the most potent of her time and she followed it in persistently. Up at the net, she was comfortable and usually in command, exhibiting very good lateral movement. Her backhand volley was first rate. Wade could knife that shot crosscourt with extraordinary regularity.

OVERHEAD

Men

1. PETE SAMPRAS Tennis fans enjoyed the spectacle of the famous "Air Sampras" leaping overhead, as the American would jump far off the ground and put away acrobatic smashes that no one else would even attempt. But his conventional overhead should have been more fully appreciated. He could retreat behind the ball faster than anyone and put away the overhead in either direction. He was masterful and artful in that capacity, with his early racket head preparation one of the keys to his success. The Sampras overhead was the best the game has yet seen.

2. JOHN McENROE Against the likes of Jimmy Connors and Bjorn Borg among others, McEnroe had to guard against the lob with much frequency. He did so astoundingly, getting himself swiftly in position, hitting the smash with power and control, signaling to the opposition that they would only succeed by hitting perfect topspin lobs over his head and out of his reach.

3. PANCHO GONZALES Although his overhead may not have been as devastatingly potent as his serve, the great Gonzales was terrific with the smash as well. Gonzalez had the best of instincts when it came to anticipating the moves of his rivals. He could not be fooled easily by an opponent trying to lob. He reacted quickly and decisively and belted his overheads brilliantly into the clear. He was sound and assertive on the overhead.

4. ROGER FEDERER Most observers easily envision Federer releasing his sweepingly beautiful forehand or his effortless serve, but not enough has been made of his excellent overhead. The Swiss displays his athleticism and astounding coordination whenever he hits an overhead. His preparation is impeccable, his execution sound, his ability to put his smashes anywhere he wants unarguable. Federer's overhead is one of the most underrated shots in the modern world of tennis.

5. TONY TRABERT In capturing five major singles titles across the 1950's and later establishing himself as one of the leading professionals, this American treasure prided himself on the completeness of his game and his adaptability to different surfaces. Trabert could do it all, combining versatile backcourt craft with a top notch serve and a sound volley. His overhead was solid, dependable, well executed and structurally sound, a shot he could count on at any time to conclude a point on his terms.

OVERHEAD
Women

1. MARTINA NAVRATILOVA No woman ever got back for the overhead faster than Navratilova. She prepared impeccably, got behind the ball quickly and then never played it overly safe. She hit it awfully hard, angled her smashes away convincingly and hit the overhead with brutal efficiency.

2. MARGARET COURT Although she did not dispatch her overheads with the same velocity or authority as Navratilova, Court was very consistent with her overhead, exploiting her great height and reach, making it known to opponents that they would need to get extraordinary depth on their lobs, or they would simply lose the point.

3. MARGARET OSBORNE DUPONT Probably no woman player hit more overheads over a lifetime of competition than this estimable American. She collected thirty-seven majors altogether in singles, doubles and mixed doubles, taking six of those championships in singles, claiming three of the four Grand Slam events on her own. duPont was exceptionally able at the net and her overhead was first rate.

4. MARIA BUENO The Brazilian displayed both grace and power on her overhead, which was one of her many attributes on the court. Bueno's mobility was a chief reason why she was so successful at the net and she could deal with opponents who tried to loft the ball out of her reach and over her head. Bueno's smash was formidable.

5. PAM SHRIVER When a poll of the leading players was taken in 1982 by *World Tennis* magazine to determine the best in various stroke categories, Shriver was the player who stood at No. 1 for the women on the overhead. The tall native of Maryland was potent on the smash, putting away the short lobs decisively. But she knew how to play the percentages and did not miss many smashes because she would play it safer when the situation required a more conservative response.

LOB

Men

1. ILIE NASTASE The first man ever to master both the forehand and backhand topspin lob, Nastase was unassailable in this capacity.

2. BJORN BORG The Swede disguised his topspin lob off his two-handed backhand as well at it could be done. It was always impossible for opponents to read his intentions.

3. MANUEL SANTANA The Spaniard was a magician as a shot maker and his lob was one of his great attributes. Santana could confound his adversaries with his topspin lob off the forehand.

4. MATS WILANDER The Swede was nearly as adept with the topspin lob as his countryman Borg. He kept the likes of Boris Becker and Stefan Edberg off guard with his propensity to use the lob at all the right times.

5. JIMMY CONNORS and **ANDY MURRAY** The lob was an underrated aspect of the Connors arsenal. Known more for his ability to knock the cover off the ball, Connors concealed his lob brilliantly, especially off the backhand side. Murray is very cagey in his use of the lob, both offensively and defensively. He has great feel on the underspin lob and good disguise on his two-handed backhand topspin lob.

LOB
Women

1. CHRIS EVERT No woman has ever lobbed more skillfully off both sides. She could flick the topspin lob off her two-handed backhand at will and later in her career added the topspin lob off the forehand. But she also could slide underneath the ball off the forehand and lob magnificently down the line. Her lob was the most versatile of all female competitors.

2. MARTINA HINGIS The Swiss stylist had outstanding ball control and very good passing shots as well. She lobbed skillfully, most notably with her two-handed backhand.

3. STEFFI GRAF The German could be vulnerable on her backhand passing shots. But she could lob extremely well off that side to keep her net rushing opponents honest.

4. NANCY RICHEY The American's flat and impeccably produced ground strokes off both sides were the twin pillars of her success in many ways, but to topple the likes of Billie Jean King and Margaret Court, she needed an excellent lob, which she implemented intelligently at all of the right times.

5. ARANTXA SANCHEZ VICARIO The Spaniard was as tenacious as they come as a counter-attacker and her lob was superbly crafted.

PASSING SHOT
Men

1. RAFAEL NADAL The Spaniard's running forehand passing shot is a gem. With his two-handed backhand, he can pick apart his rivals either crosscourt or down the line.

2. BJORN BORG One of the sport's finest athletes, Borg was able to produce passing shots of the highest order time and again to thwart the likes of John McEnroe whenever they dared to come to the net. The imperturbable Swede passed stupendously.

3. ANDRE AGASSI. Against some of the finest attacking players of his era—men like Pete Sampras, Boris Becker and Patrick Rafter—Agassi had an uncanny knack for making one spectacular passing shot after another. He passed brilliantly and relentlessly off both sides, delighting the galleries with his counter-attacking skills, particularly off his impeccable two-handed backhand.

4. LLEYTON HEWITT The diminutive Aussie found himself frequently up against adversaries who could overpower him. But he was a remarkably precise ball striker who could pass brilliantly off both sides, and that—along with his return of serve—set him apart.

5. NOVAK DJOKOVIC Although the Serbian competes largely from the back of the court against other outstanding baseline practitioners, he is always up to the task of making excellent passing shots under pressure. He can angle his forehand pass at the sharpest of angles and go anywhere he wants with his two-hander, displaying equal confidence in his down the line and crosscourt shots.

PASSING SHOT
Women

1. CHRIS EVERT The Floridian's capacity to make the most arduous of passing shots look absolutely routine was one of her trademarks. She passed beautifully off the forehand (especially crosscourt) but her acutely angled two-handed backhand passing shot was both spectacular and nearly unstoppable and her down the line pass off that side impossible to anticipate.

2. TRACY AUSTIN The Californian was much like Evert with her propensity to thread the eye of a needle and find the smallest of openings to make passing shots.

3. MONICA SELES Her devastatingly potent and accurate two-fisted ground strokes were the chief reason why this woman became an all-time great. Her disguise off both wings on the passing shot was astounding.

4. LESLEY TURNER BOWERY This Australian stalwart drove the ball purposefully off both sides and always appeared unruffled when opponents charged the net against her, counter-attacking with coolness and precision.

5. NANCY RICHEY The Texan loved having a target. She kept her passing shots unfailingly low and confounded her net rushing opponents over and over again with her unerring accuracy.

MENTAL TOUGHNESS
Men

1. RAFAEL NADAL No one in the history of tennis has competed with such quiet fury and unbridled intensity. In my book, Nadal is the toughest player mentally the game has yet seen, the champion with the strongest disposition, a man with a limitless supply of willpower.

2. JIMMY CONNORS. Strikingly reminiscent of his fellow left-hander Nadal as a competitor in many ways, Connors roused himself to many exhilarating triumphs on days when he seemed nearly certain to lose. He was courageous, unswerving, and defiant. Connors was a warrior through and through, and as unwavering as any tennis player I have ever witnessed.

3. PANCHO GONZALES The most ferocious of all champions, Gonzales was fueled by anger, appealing questionable line calls vociferously before raising his game to another level.

4. PETE SAMPRAS He made the game look easy, carrying himself calmly through long afternoons and strenuous contests, but few have equaled or surpassed his mental durability or imposed themselves more when it counted. He willed himself to more than his share of victories.

5. ROD LAVER He dazzled the world of tennis with his multitude of gifts as a player and was a sportsman of the highest order. The fact remains that Laver's mentality was what defined him as one of the great champions ever. He knew how to survive even when he was off his game.

MENTAL TOUGHNESS
Women

1. CHRIS EVERT The most unflappable and unflagging of competitors, Evert's mindset was what separated her more than anything else from her rivals. She won more than her share of big matches with her temerity and was not afraid to lose. Her steely demeanor and unshakable desire to win made her the toughest female tennis competitor of all time.

2. HELEN WILLS MOODY She did not get the nickname "Little Miss Poker Face" without good reason. This Californian was inscrutable on the field of battle, giving nothing away, masking her emotions fully at all times.

3. SERENA WILLIAMS As fearless a player as the women's game has produced, Williams was the best of all at fighting her way out of the rough terrain of tight contests. She has had days when she has essentially beaten herself, but Williams is an astonishing match player and competitor.

4. MONICA SELES How could this dynamic player be left off of this list? She was as intimidating as any woman who has played the game, bearing down hard and unrelentingly, displaying grit and gumption every step of the way.

5. STEFFI GRAF and **BILLIE JEAN KING** The German probably detested losing more than just about any champion ever has. Her desire to succeed was almost tangible. Graf was a competitor of the highest order and a fighter through and through. King was a player of wide ranging emotions, but there was no one better at responding to a big match situation and bringing out her best to suit the occasion.

Acknowledgements

Many people, both directly and indirectly, have been enormously helpful to me throughout my career as a tennis journalist, which commenced in the early 1970's. I am grateful to *World Tennis* magazine founder Gladys M. Heldman and Ron Bookman, who hired me to work at the magazine in 1974, and gave me the opportunity to write for that publication until 1991. Gladys and Ron—who have both passed away—taught me incessantly about the craft. Former *Tennis Week* editor/publisher Gene Scott gave me the forum to write regularly for his magazine from 1992 until 2007. Bud Collins long ago allowed me to work behind the scenes with him on telecasts starting in 1972, and helped me to establish a foothold in the electronic world. John Barrett—the erudite commentator for the BBC—lent me his wisdom more than I probably deserved, and the late Herbert Warren Wind of the New Yorker believed in me almost more than I did in myself. The late Ted Tinling taught me more about the inner workings of tennis than anyone else, and his generosity of spirit enriched my life more than he ever knew. S.L. Price of *Sports Illustrated* has long been one of my most trusted and generous colleagues, and Joel Drucker has shared his considerable wit and insights with me through the years.

I have been a columnist for Tennis Channel since 2007, and am grateful for their unbending support. CEO Ken Solomon is not only gregarious but an uncommonly decent and collegial fellow. David Egdes is a man of quiet dignity and professionalism. My web site partners Josh Ross and Ari Brock have been a pleasure to work with. And Brad Falkner is an immensely loyal and capable individual who has gone well out of his way to champion my cause.

Everyone at the International Tennis Hall of Fame has been supportive. Tony Trabert has done an astonishing job as President, and

Stan Smith is stepping into that role ably. Chris Clouser and Mark Stenning are doing great things for the sport. Doug Stark, Christine Verhar and Nicole Markham are total professionals.

I am indebted to all of the people mentioned above, as I am to the remarkable players I have watched and interviewed. I must pay homage to the brilliant song writer Burt Bacharach, whose soaring melodies have enriched my entire life. No writer has influenced and inspired me more than the lyrical Pete Hamill. I have been reading his extraordinary body of work for more than forty years, and have learned abundantly from his craftsmanship. Last, but not least, I am deeply thankful to my wife, Frances, my son, Jonathan, and my daughter, Amanda. They have all understood and tolerated my tennis obsession, and their backing was crucial during the many days and nights that I put into researching and writing the manuscript.

Steve Flink
Katonah, New York
February, 2012

Also From New Chapter Press

The Education of a Tennis Player
—BY ROD LAVER AND BUD COLLINS

Rod Laver's first-hand account of his historic 1969 Grand Slam sweep of all four major tennis titles is documented in this memoir, written by Laver along with co-author and tennis personality Bud Collins. The book details his childhood, early career and his most important matches. The four-time Wimbledon champion and the only player in tennis history to win two Grand Slams also sprinkles in tips and lessons on how players of all levels can improve their games. Originally published in 1971, *The Education of a Tennis Player* was updated in 2009 on the 40th anniversary of his historic second Grand Slam with new content, including the story of his recovery from a near-fatal stroke in 1998.

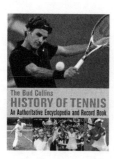

The Bud Collins History of Tennis
—BY BUD COLLINS

Compiled by the most famous tennis journalist and historian in the world, this book is the ultimate compilation of historical tennis information, including year-by-year recaps of every tennis season, biographical sketches of every major tennis personality, as well as stats, records, and championship rolls for all the major events. The author's personal relationships with major tennis stars offer insights into the world of professional tennis found nowhere else.

On This Day In Tennis History
—BY RANDY WALKER

Fun and fact-filled, this compilation offers anniversaries, summaries, and anecdotes of events from the world of tennis for every day in the calendar year. Presented in a day-by-day format, the entries into this mini-encyclopedia include major tournament victory dates, summaries of the greatest matches ever played, trivia, and statistics as well as little-known and quirky happenings. Easy to use and packed with fascinating details, this compendium is the perfect companion for tennis and general sports fans alike.

The Wimbledon Final That Never Was...
–BY SIDNEY WOOD

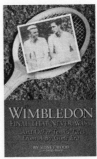

The curious and spectacular story of Wimbledon in 1931 is told in detail by the crowned champion in this illuminating tennis biography. Also included is a compilation of short stories that deliver fascinating anecdotes of the 1930s and a signature document of the play and styles of 20th-century tennis legends.

Roger Federer: Quest for Perfection
–BY RENE STAUFFER

Regarded by many as the greatest tennis player in the history of the sport, this authoritative biography charts the success of Roger Federer, drawing from exclusive interviews with Federer and his family as well as the author's extensive experience covering the international tennis circuit. Comprehensive and compelling, this account provides an informed overview of the Swiss tennis star, from his start as a temperamental player on the junior circuit to his triumphs at the U.S. Open and Wimbledon.

Acing Depression
–BY CLIFF RICHEY
WITH HILAIRE RICHEY KALLENDORF

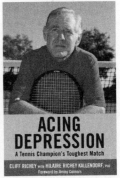

Chronicling the tumultuous life of the original bad boy of tennis, this engaging memoir describes one man's public battle with clinical depression. Cliff Richey was best known for the 1970 season in which he won the Grand Prix, the Davis Cup, and was rst in the American tennis ranking. Documenting his 10 year ght for control of his mind, aided by antidepressant medication, the determination and strength that afforded him the nickname of "The Bull" is highlighted.